NAVAL SCIENCE 3

NAVAL SCIENCE 3

SECOND EDITION

Naval Knowledge, Leadership,
and Nautical Skills
for the NJROTC Student

Cdr. Richard R. Hobbs, USNR (Ret.)

NAVAL INSTITUTE PRESS
Annapolis, Maryland

Naval Institute Press
291 Wood Road
Annapolis, MD 21402

Library of Congress Cataloging-in-Publication Data

Hobbs, Richard R.
  Naval science 3 : naval knowledge, leadership, and nautical skills for the NJROTC student / Richard R. Hobbs. — 2nd ed.
      p. cm.
  Includes bibliographical references and index.
  ISBN 978-1-59114-367-3 (alk. paper)
  1. Naval art and science—Textbooks. 2. Naval art and science—United States—Textbooks. 3. United States. Navy—Textbooks. 4. United States. Navy Junior Reserve Officers Training Corps—Textbooks. I. Title. II. Title: Naval science three.
  V103.H63 2009
  359—dc22
                                          2009041918

Printed in the United States of America on acid-free paper
21 20 19 18 17 16   9 8 7 6 5 4

To Rowe and Katherine

Contents

NAVAL SKILLS

ACKNOWLEDGMENTS
for the Second Edition

One of the most satisfying aspects of my professional career over the past three decades has been my association with the NJROTC program. I remain convinced that this program represents one of the finest and most worthwhile endeavors that exist to serve American youth.

Many thanks are due the various NJROTC staff and curriculum advisory members, NJROTC instructors, and various subject matter experts who made numerous suggestions for the first edition of this book and for needed changes and updates in this second edition.

The NJROTC unit at Annapolis High School in Annapolis, Maryland, graciously supplied many of the photos of cadets engaged in various activities that appear in the leadership section of this book. Except where otherwise identified, the other photographs and line art used in the book came from the photo archives of the U.S. Naval Institute, and from the photo files of the Chief of Naval Information.

Finally, thanks are due the editorial and production departments of the Naval Institute Press for their many contributions to the successful production of this volume.

NAVAL KNOWLEDGE

Sea Power and National Security

Sea power, as a former chief of naval operations defined it, is "the sum of a nation's capabilities to implement its interests by using the ocean areas for political, economic, and military activities in peace or war in order to attain national objectives." The main components of sea power, he stated, are naval power, ocean science, ocean industry, and ocean commerce. From this broad definition it is clear that sea power has a profound effect upon nearly every aspect of national security, commercial prosperity, and social welfare. It includes our merchant marine, oceanography, ocean engineering, marine research and technology, and our naval power.

Sea power is of fundamental importance to the United States. We are, first and foremost, a maritime nation. We have depended upon free use of the seas since before the Revolutionary War. Even today, how well we understand the significance of the oceans and how well we use them has much to do with the welfare of our nation.

1 The Importance of Sea Power

Throughout history the oceans have always been important to humankind, as they have been a major means whereby travel, commerce, cultural exchange, and military power projection have been accomplished. Since World War II, four major developments have emphasized the importance of the oceans even more. Two of these are political, and two are technological.

The first major political development has been the rapid increase in new nations since World War II. Only 51 nations formed the United Nations after the war; today there are over 190. Many of these are underdeveloped Third World countries, tempting targets for more aggressive nations.

The second political development is the steady increase in the interdependence of all nations of the world since World War II. The Internet and international commerce have linked all nations of the world together to a degree unprecedented in the history of the world. The United States today is committed by treaty or agreement to assist in the defense and development of well over half the world's nations. Through our participation in the United Nations, we render indirect assistance to even more. Many of these border on oceans or seas. These oceans and seas are often the means by which any needed assistance can be delivered.

The first of the major technological developments is the "inland reach" of sea power. The sea is no longer just a means of attack of coastal targets or shield against invasions. It has become a

The Navy's reach was always limited to the range of its guns until the advent of aircraft and missiles. Cruise missiles like this Tomahawk being fired by the guided missile cruiser USS *Shiloh* greatly extend the capabilities of modern warships.

vast arena from which awesome weapons of mass destruction such as nuclear-tipped ballistic and cruise missiles can be launched from nuclear-powered submarines beneath the surface, or cruise missiles and attack aircraft from surface ships. These weapons can reach not only coastal areas but also targets far inland. This has changed military strategy profoundly, for there is now no place on Earth beyond the range of direct attack from the sea.

The second major technical development is nuclear technology. Nuclear energy has both constructive and destructive uses. On the constructive side are fission reactors used for ship and submarine propulsion at sea, and large-scale electrical power generation ashore. On the destructive side is the thermonuclear warhead that can be launched from land, sea, or air to obliterate any target against which it is used.

Today our Navy's strength extends to the farthest corners of the globe. Mobile sea-based forces both extend the defensive perimeter around the United States, and make possible military power projection and deterrence against aggression wherever needed.

Strategic Ocean Areas

As was discussed in *Naval Science 2*, there are four main ocean areas that are of prime strategic importance to the United States.

The first is the Atlantic, which includes the Mediterranean Sea, the North Atlantic, and the western approaches to Europe. This area was the main site of confrontation between the Western allies and the Soviet bloc during the Cold War. The second area is the Pacific Ocean, extending from the Bering Strait off Alaska to the Strait of Malacca in Southeast Asia. This was the site of two wars and many other confrontations between the United States and its allies and Communist states such as North Vietnam, China, and North Korea.

The third prime strategic ocean area is the Arctic Ocean, which lies north of our North American continent and separates it from Asia. The advent of the nuclear submarine made this ice-encrusted ocean into an important area of naval operations when in the mid-1960s submarines of the Soviet Union, United States, and other NATO nations began routine cruises under the polar icecap. It has also been proposed as a route for submarine transport of crude oil shipments, and more recently with the increased melting of much of its surface ice, for surface shipping along the legendary Northwest Passage.

The fourth area is the vast Afro-Asian ocean, which includes the broad reaches of the South Atlantic and Indian Oceans, as well as the Middle-Eastern oil transportation routes through the Red Sea, Suez Canal, and Persian Gulf.

In these strategic ocean areas there are a number of geographic chokepoints (bottlenecks) through which the world's maritime traffic must pass in order to conduct international trade and deploy naval forces. Many of these chokepoints were identified in the Maritime Geography unit of *Naval Science 2*. Much of our worldwide maritime strategy is concerned with how best to protect their continued use by the United States and our allies, while denying their use to any prospective enemy.

The Mobility of Sea Power

In contrast to land forces, whose mobility and resupply capability is limited by the geographical features and political constraints of the terrain in which they operate, seaborne naval forces have several advantages. The open sea is a vast, level highway over which no nation can claim sovereignty. Thus naval forces can move much more quickly than land forces wherever they wish, and disperse whenever and however necessary. They can establish a line of defense far from their national shores, making it easier to prevent attack by enemy forces. And they can easily replenish fuel, stores, and ammunition at sea whenever required.

The presence of mobile sea forces near land areas where conflict threatens to break out can often act as a deterrent. Combat-ready seaborne forces can be quickly sent to any potential problem area. Their timely arrival in an area of tension may be sufficient to calm things down and prevent a conflict from escalating to war.

Merchant Marine

A strong merchant marine (commercial shipping) is a vital element of sea power. This belief was part of Alfred Thayer Mahan's doctrine of sea power. The merchant fleet must be kept competitive if it is to meet the growing needs of industry and provide logistic support to our forces overseas.

There was a time in American life when it seemed that we had an unlimited supply of raw materials. We were nearly self-sufficient in most commodities and did not need to purchase or sell materials abroad. However, our increasing population, growing rate of consumption of resources and energy, and technological needs have changed those circumstances. In fact, for some time now we have been dependent on many other nations for much of what we need to maintain a strong economy, keep our people at work, and manufacture our products.

In order to maintain our economy, there are about eighty strategic resources that the United States cannot do without. We rely on imports to satisfy our needs for many of these resources. For instance, we must import some 85 percent of the manganese required to produce steel. We import around 85 percent of the bauxite from which aluminum is refined. We import more than 99 percent of our nation's tin, and over 90 percent of the chromite used to toughen steel. Ninety percent of the columbite used to construct nuclear reactors, make stainless steel, and manufacture rockets and missiles is also imported. Since the late 1960s we have imported a large portion (some 70 percent in recent years) of our petroleum. Moreover, foreign markets for our farm products and manufactured goods have become increasingly important to the U.S. economy in recent years.

Most nations understand the doctrine of freedom of the seas under international law, though some have varying interpretations. In wartime, however, a belligerent nation will do all in its power to disrupt the passage of commercial shipping to its opponents. Throughout history, whenever powerful nations have lost control of the seas, they have fallen. There is no reason to believe that things will be different in the future.

For these reasons the United States needs a strong merchant marine. The flow of ocean-borne commerce must not be stopped by any enemy if we are to maintain our national security, as well as the health and stability of our domestic economy. Keeping the sea lanes open is a vital mission of the U.S. Navy, for these lanes are the lifelines of America.

Oceanography

The oceans contain a wealth of animal and plant life. Every known mineral can be found on the sea bottom or suspended in seawater. The sea is the last great storehouse of food and minerals on Earth. Oceanography, covered in *Naval Science 2,* is the science that will find ways to properly tap the resources of the sea for the benefit of the world. We must learn to use these resources fully, without depleting sea life or polluting the sea environment.

Many littoral nations (those with ready access to the seas) are engaged in oceanographic research. The United States is becoming more aware of the need for oceanographic research, and consequently has completed many major projects in recent years.

We know that we must increasingly turn to the sea for resources that we previously obtained on land: food, fresh water, minerals, and energy. Vast new resources have already been discovered in the continental shelf (a narrow belt around the continents). International agreements have given littoral nations exclusive rights to develop all the natural resources in the continental shelf adjacent to their own shores.

Minerals of all kinds can be extracted from seawater, but as yet this is cost effective for only a few chemicals and elements. Processing seawater to obtain fresh water for drinking and irrigation is being done in a few places around the world where natural fresh water is in short supply. Harnessing the tides for a boundless supply of energy is presently done only in a few locations, mainly in Holland, France, and Canada. However, it could be done on nearly every seacoast where the tidal range is sufficient.

The science of farming of the sea is called aquaculture. This practice may in time make possible the cultivation of plants and fish that can produce a large portion of the protein needed by the world's people.

Commercial fisheries have not begun to realize the potential of the ocean harvest. They have concentrated on only about 20 varieties of fish out of more than 20,000 known species. Almost all sea life is edible. Even tiny high-protein plankton and algae are being investigated as possible sources of food.

Humankind has barely begun its search for knowledge of the ocean's depths. U.S. efforts to increase basic and applied research in oceanography are quite recent. Our progress has been slow. There is no question that we have the capability and scientific knowledge for this effort. What we must develop is a national awareness of the importance of the seas and the will to move ahead boldly with its exploration.

The Continuing Importance of Sea Power

No one denies the growing importance of space exploration to the future of humankind. But even as we gaze toward the stars, dreaming of space ships and distant planets, we must still live on planet Earth. While expeditions to distant stars and colonies on the planets or the Moon may happen someday, it is far more practical to consider the proper use of the Earth for the sustenance of future generations. With nearly three-fourths of the globe covered by water, it is inevitable that the oceans will play a vital role in the future of the human race.

As humankind turns seaward for fresh water, food, oil, natural gas, and raw materials, it becomes very evident that no country can live in isolation from the rest of the world. The trade routes of the seas have become the arteries of life. Sea power has evolved into an essential ingredient for sustaining life, political independence, and economic prosperity.

Balanced sea power makes possible a flexible national strategy. With sea power we can use the seas for trade, energy resources, and economic development. We can project power from mobile bases at sea and bring pressure to bear with amphibious forces. We can prevent trouble from erupting, and suppress it when it does with the Navy–Marine Corps team. We can send our Sailors and Marines ashore as ambassadors of good will, making friends and allies confident of our ability to support them in times of trouble or natural disaster. Our reassuring presence promotes stability in

an otherwise troubled world. In short, sea power gives the United States the ability to carry out policy that supports our national interests and fosters peace in the world.

Sea power, however, depends on people—highly trained and dedicated people who believe in their mission. They must respond rapidly and decisively to changing world events. It is up to *all* Americans—service people, civilians, professional people, and students—to learn about the importance of sea power. There is one fact that we must never forget: the sea and the United States are inseparable.

STUDY GUIDE QUESTIONS

1. What two major political developments since World War II have increased the importance of the oceans?

2. What does "inland reach" mean as related to sea power?

3. What two aspects of nuclear technology have affected sea power?

4. What four ocean areas are of prime strategic importance to the United States?

5. What is unique about naval operations in the Arctic Ocean?

6. What three benefits do our fleets gain because of their ability to move freely on the high seas?

7. Why is it important for the United States to maintain a strong merchant marine?

8. What is the importance of oceanographic research?

CRITICAL THINKING

1. Research how much we could reduce our dependence on imported materials if we upgrade recycling programs of all kinds and seek alternatives to fossil fuels.

VOCABULARY

deterrence	oceanography
merchant marine	littoral nation
manganese	aquaculture

2 The U.S. Merchant Marine

Ships engaged in commerce that carry goods and liquids from one place to another over the world's oceans and waterways are called *merchant marine* ships. They range in size from huge oil tankers the size of aircraft carriers to small cargo and passenger vessels that ply inland waters and rivers. U.S. merchant marine ships are an important part of U.S. sea power. They convey American products to markets around the world, and bring foreign products and raw materials essential to our economy back to U.S. ports. During a war, merchant shipping delivers most of the equipment and supplies needed by our forces deployed overseas.

In this chapter we will briefly summarize the history of the U.S. merchant marine, discuss how it supports our nation in peace and war, and describe some of the main types of ships that make up our modern-day merchant marine.

Historical Background

The U.S. merchant marine has experienced several extremes between expansion and decline over the many years since the birth of our nation. It flourished during the early days of the American republic while Europe was at war, and reached a peak in the 1850s, due in large measure to the superiority of American-built clipper ships. Just prior to the Civil War, our merchant marine was second in size only to that of the British.

During and after the Civil War, however, our merchant marine suffered a dramatic decline. This happened for several reasons. Chief among these was the effect of the Southern commerce raiders during the war, which preyed upon Northern merchant shipping around the globe and virtually drove it from the seas by war's end. After the war the nation's focus turned to westward expansion. Our depleted merchant marine suffered from European competition, noncompetitive wage scales, soaring insurance costs, and steadily increasing domestic shipbuilding costs. The latter three factors have continued to plague the U.S. merchant marine to the present day. Not since the Civil War has the U.S. merchant marine been among the leaders in the world, except when spurred by the demands of war.

By the time of World War I, the volume of American imports and exports had grown a great deal, but only about 10 percent of this trade was carried in ships flying the U.S. flag. A large effort to remedy this situation was made during the war, which resulted in over two thousand ships being built. Unfortunately, a competitive edge could not be sustained after the war. In 1936 Congress passed the Merchant Marine Act, which provided for the payment of construction and operating subsidies so American ship owners would consider expansion. The Maritime Commission was established under the law to administer the act.

During World War II, the U.S. shipbuilding industry again went into high gear. Between 1939 and 1945, almost six thousand merchant ships were built. Close cooperation with the Navy resulted in Liberty and Victory ships designed to meet the auxiliary needs of the wartime Navy and capable of being mass-produced at a phenomenal rate. The U.S. merchant marine accumulated a magnificent record. Although its ships and crews were subject to every kind of enemy attack, with per capita casualties exceded only by the Marine Corps, it nevertheless succeeded in carrying millions of tons of varied cargo across every ocean. Strategic materials essential to industry were often brought back to the United States following delivery of wartime military cargoes overseas.

In 1951, the Maritime Commission was abolished and its function was taken over by a new agency called the Maritime Administration (MARAD). MARAD administers federal programs to develop, promote, and operate the U.S. merchant marine, including routing, research and development, and regulation of registration. It also maintains reserve fleets of government-owned ships essential for national defense, operates the U.S. Merchant Marine Academy at Kings Point, New York, and administers grants-in-aid for state operated maritime academies in California, Maine, Massachusetts, New York, and Texas.

After World War II, the U.S. merchant marine once again entered a long period of decline that has lasted to this day. This decline was caused by the combined effects of foreign subsidies and the high costs of both shipbuilding and ship operations in the United States as compared with most foreign maritime nations. For the past several years, only a limited number of new U.S. ships has been built in U.S. shipyards, and foreign ships now carry most American cargo on the high seas.

National Policy and the Merchant Marine Acts

There were three important acts passed in the years 1920, 1928, and 1936 that sought to promote the development of the U.S. merchant marine. Several additional acts have been passed since, the last in 1996, that modified some of the provisions of the earlier three. The Merchant Marine Act of 1936 was described above. Probably the most significant of all of them was the Jones Act of 1920. Its purpose as stated in the act is that it is necessary for the national defense and proper growth of foreign and domestic commerce that the United States shall have a merchant marine of the best equipped and most suitable types of vessels sufficient to carry the greater portion of its commerce and serve as a naval auxiliary in time of war or national emergency. It specified that all domestic waterborne commerce between two points in the United States must be carried by U.S.-owned and -operated vessels. Subsequent federal regulations also require that at least half of all U.S. government cargos be carried by American-flag shipping.

The Impact of Waterborne Commerce

Throughout the globe, the preferred method of transporting large quantities of raw materials and manufactured trade goods is by water, because this is the fastest, most efficient, and least costly way. Some 80 percent of all world trade goods travel by water. The other transport systems—rail, truck, aircraft, and pipeline—support, augment, and complement waterborne transport.

As mentioned in the previous chapter, the economies of all nations of the world have become interdependent to a degree never before seen in the history of the world. No nation has all the resources it needs to be completely independent, nor can any nation's economy thrive without marketing its goods beyond its borders. The United States, for example, must import over one hundred vital metals and minerals from more than sixty countries, including almost 70 percent of our petroleum, nearly 100 percent of ores such as aluminum and chromium, and a growing percentage of finished steel products. Grain from our farms is marketed worldwide, and income from our manufactured products sold

Unfortunately for the United States, few new American-flag vessels like this gas turbine–powered Prudential Lines freighter are being built and operated by U.S. companies.

overseas represents a vital and steadily growing part of our national economy. Some 90 percent of our domestic and foreign trade travels via the sea lanes. There can be no doubt about the importance of waterborne commerce to the prosperity and high standard of living of the American people now and in the future.

The primary commercial purpose for operating the merchant fleet is, of course, to make a reasonable profit. However, this is much easier said than done. U.S. shipping companies often have to compete with rebates given by foreign manufacturers to foreign shipping companies to carry their products at premium rates. A rebate is a nice term for a kickback or bribe, a practice that is illegal under U.S. law, but an accepted way of doing business in many foreign countries. Also, a poor record of labor stability in American maritime unions has periodically tied up U.S.-flagged ships. These factors, along with the perennial problems of rising taxes and insurance costs and higher shipbuilding and labor costs over the years, have caused the percentage of American cargo carried in American ships to drop to less than 3 percent of the current annual total. There are just over 400 commercial oceangoing ships of more than 1,000 gross tons in the U.S.–flag fleet—of an estimated total of some 29,000 in service worldwide.

In the United States there are some 350 ports that handle freight, passengers, or both. Over 2 billion tons of cargo and 150 million passengers pass through these ports each year. Currently, the ten leading U.S. marine ports, in the order of the value of shipments handled, are the ports of Los Angles, California; New York/New Jersey; Long Beach, California; Houston, Texas; Charleston, South Carolina; Norfolk, Virginia; Tacoma, Washington; Baltimore, Maryland; Oakland, California; and Seattle, Washington.

Because much of the world's oceangoing commercial fleet is aging at a fairly rapid pace, orders for new and larger merchant ships of all descriptions are increasing at building yards worldwide, especially in Asia, where Japan and South Korea together account for some 70 percent of the world shipbuilding market. Unfortunately the United States does not get much of this business, because of higher labor and construction costs here. Most of the large shipbuilding yards in the United States specialize in the construction of naval vessels, although most also build some high quality commercial vessels. The five largest U.S. shipyards in the United States are Northrop Grumman/Newport News, Newport News, Virginia; Northrop Grumman/Ingalls, Pascagoula, Mississippi; General Dynamics/Electric Boat, Groton, Connecticut; General Dynamics/Bath Iron Works, Bath, Maine; and Northrop Grumman/Avondale, in New Orleans and Tallulah, Louisiana, and Gulfport, Mississippi.

Modern Merchant Ships

Tankers, ships designed to carry liquid cargoes in bulk quantities, are the most numerous ships in the active U.S. merchant marine and are the most common type of ship plying the high seas. They vary greatly in size, with the largest modern jumbo tankers ranging up to over a half million tons. Large tankers are used mainly to carry crude oil from oil producing regions to refineries. Smaller ones can carry crude but generally carry refined products. Many tankers belong to the major oil companies, with their ships carrying their own brand name of refined products. The majority are owned by independent operators who charter their ships.

Tankers can and do carry other liquid cargoes besides POL (petroleum, oils, lubricants), including various chemicals and even wine. The most specialized types of tankers are the *liquefied natural gas (LNG)* and *liquefied petroleum gas (LPG) carriers*. These are sophisticated and expensive ships designed to carry natural gas and other forms of petroleum gases in a liquid state at extremely high pressures and low temperatures.

A highly sophisticated type of tanker is the liquefied natural gas (LNG) carrier, like the SS *El Paso Southern* shown here. They carry natural gas liquefied at −260° Fahrenheit.

Tankers comprise the largest segment of the active U.S. merchant marine and are the most numerous ships on the high seas.

Modern *intermodal ships* are designed to interface seamlessly with modes of inland transportation such as trucks, trains, or inland waterways. *Containerships* have revolutionized waterborne freight transport worldwide. They are the most productive intermodal ships in the U.S. maritime service. The larger ones can cruise at 33 knots and carry some 8,000 prepackaged 20-foot-equivalent-unit (TEU) containers. Even larger capacity 10,000 to 20,000 TEU containerships are now being designed. The standard size of the containers plus their inherent security greatly enhance both ease of handling and protection against pilferage. A large containership can be offloaded and reloaded in less than twenty-four hours by only about ten longshoremen (cargo handlers) using semiautomatic cargo-handling equipment, instead of the eighty-plus longshoremen required to load and unload conventional freighters in the past. Moreover, containership crew sizes have decreased from

forty or more to around twenty over the last decade, and may ultimately shrink to under half a dozen as more automated ship technology becomes available in the coming years.

Once offloaded, containers can be placed easily aboard semi-truck trailers or railroad flatcars for efficient transport overland to their destinations. This ability makes possible sea–land bridge freight transportation operations that have made international trade far less dependent on strategic waterways like the Panama Canal.

Roll-on roll-off (RoRo) ships have ramps and large hold openings designed to accommodate either containerized or unitized cargoes, or wheeled and tracked vehicles. In contrast to the containership, this type of ship requires few facilities ashore—merely a strong ramp from pier to ship, compatible with the mobile cargo.

The containership SS *Hawaiian Enterprise* of Matson Navigation Lines. One of the intermodal ship types, containerships are among the most efficient ships in the maritime service. Ships like this one can carry over a thousand preloaded containers that are loaded aboard by special cranes.

Royal Carribean's cruise ship *Brilliance of the Sea* at anchor at Mykonos, Greece. With a displacement of 90,000 tons and length of 293 meters, the ship is representative of many of the newer and larger cruise ships now being placed in service. Luxury accommodations can be provided for up to 2,500 passengers. (ShipParade photo by Richard Maidment)

Another type of ship that has become increasingly important in recent years is the *cruise ship*. These ships are built to accommodate anywhere from several hundred to several thousand passengers on pleasure cruises lasting from several days to several weeks or more. Newer cruise ships can be as long as three football fields, and they are outfitted to provide their guests with every amenity that would be expected in luxury hotels on land. Some 70 percent of these passengers come from North America, and 20 percent from Europe. It is estimated that the cruise shipping industry generates some $60 billion for their operators annually.

Merchant Marine and National Defense

An important auxiliary function for the U.S. merchant marine is to aid in the national defense. There are five important ways in which the merchant marine serves in this role: military sealift, transport of strategic material, direct support of military operations, use as auxiliary combatants, and support of foreign policy. Each of these will be discussed in the following sections.

Military Sealift

The merchant marine transports most of the supplies and equipment needed to support U.S. military forces in both peace and war. This support may be intended for either U.S. or allied forces, and can be carried by either U.S. or allied ships. Airlift can complement sealift to provide initial fast response requirements, but sealift has always carried the great bulk of the total heavy lift requirements. In all recent large-scale operations involving U.S. forces, including Operations Desert Storm, Enduring Freedom, and Iraqi Freedom, 95 percent of all the heavy equipment, fuel, and munitions was transported to the area of operations by sea.

In time of war, the entire U.S.-flag fleet is subject to requisitioning by the secretary of commerce to meet national defense needs. However, this might not be necessary in a small limited war. The situation determines the needs. At present, analysis indicates that the U.S. merchant marine would be inadequate to meet our military needs in a large-scale general war. Only with significant augmentation by foreign-flag shipping could the United States meet its national requirements in a large-scale war. Such augmentation might, however, be problematical if these foreign nations chose not to support our needs.

Shipping for U.S. national defense requirements can come from the following sources:

Military Sealift Command (MSC). MSC is an organization within the Navy that controls most of its replenishment and military transport shipping. It also is one of three service commands that report to the U.S. Transportation Command, responsible for coordinating the movement of DOD personnel and logistics worldwide. The mission of the Military Sealift Command is to provide ocean transportation of equipment, fuel, supplies, and ammunition to sustain U.S. forces worldwide both in peace and wartime for as long as operational needs require. In support of its mission MSC routinely operates more than 120 ships worldwide on a daily basis, and has access to more than one hundred other ships usually kept in reduced operating status in U.S. ports.

Except for hospital ships, which are painted white with large red crosses on their sides, MSC naval auxiliary ships are painted gray like U.S. Navy ships, but can be identified by blue and gold stripes on their stacks. They are designated U.S. Naval Ships (USNS rather than USS), and are crewed mostly by civilian mariners. They regularly engage in underway replenishment operations with the fleet. MSC's newer fast sealift (FSS) and large medium-speed roll-on/roll-off (LMSR) ships are among the largest and fastest cargo ships in the world, and can carry large quantities of wheeled and tracked vehicles at speeds up to 30 knots.

Maritime Administration (MARAD). The Maritime Administration maintains a fleet of more than fifty Ready Reserve Force (RRF) ships that can be activated in from four to twenty days and transferred to MSC to provide surge capability when required. They consist mainly of RoRo and crane ships, and are maintained at U.S. ports close to potential military load-out sites by small-cadre crews augmented by additional merchant seamen when needed. RRF ships can be readily identified by distinctive red, white, and blue markings on their stacks.

MARAD also maintains the National Defense Reserve Fleet (NDRF), old mothballed Navy and merchant ships kept at NDRF anchorages at Beaumont, Texas; Suisun Bay, California; and the James River, Virginia. They receive far less maintenance than RRF ships, and would require between thirty and sixty days to be activated.

Sealift Readiness and VISA Programs. Under the provisions of the Sealift Readiness Program (SRP), up to half of all U.S.-flag merchant ships may be voluntarily conscripted for military use in time of national emergency. Although in effect since 1978, the SPR has never been activated to date. The Voluntary Intermodal Sealift Agreement (VISA), enacted in 1997, creates a partnership between the U.S. Government and the U.S. maritime industry to provide commercial sealift and intermodal support services required to meet any future national mobilization needs. VISA participants get priority preference when bidding on DOD peacetime cargo.

Active Merchant Fleet Sealift Readiness Program. The Sealift Readiness Program is designed to improve the response of private operators to national defense needs. Half of U.S.-flag merchant ships are designated under the program as being liable for conscription for military sealift duties by the secretaries of defense and transportation in time of national need. Others are liable to be called on an incremental basis, if required.

Effective U.S.-controlled ships. These are ships owned by U.S. citizens or corporations that are licensed by and fly the flags of other nations such as Liberia, Panama, and Honduras in order to escape the high insurance and wage costs associated with U.S. registry. Ships in this category are said to be operating under "flags of convenience." There is some question as to the responsiveness of these ships in all but the most dire of national emergencies, and some doubt as to how valuable they would be in a military sealift capacity since most of the ships are bulk carriers such as tankers, ore carriers, and grain carriers. Also, most of their crews are foreigners who may not support American interests in wartime.

Foreign-flag ships. A final possible source of U.S. sealift assets is the charter of foreign-flag ships. There are obvious political drawbacks here, so the reliability of this source in time of national emergency is marginal at best.

Transport of Strategic Material

In addition to military cargoes, the merchant marine must carry the strategic materials and energy resources that support the national economy and defense establishment. Our allies also require such sealift. Britain, for instance, must continually import food to sustain its population, and Japan is totally dependent on imported oil. If the U.S. industrial complex is to support our forces and those of our allies in time of war, the movement of cargo across the oceans to and from the United States must continue.

However, an important concern has arisen in this area. From the commercial standpoint, in order to maximize efficiency increasingly larger ships are needed to satisfy the ever-growing industrial demand for bulk strategic materials, particularly crude oil and metallic ores. Consequently, fewer but larger and more productive ships are being built to meet the commercial requirements. In a wartime situation the United States and its allies could ill afford to lose many such big commercial ships, for such attrition would immediately have a serious impact on imports of strategic materials.

In time of a national emergency, defensive features would need to be incorporated into our merchant ships. Fortunately, a provision exists that mandates certain defensive characteristics in ships built with government construction subsidies. The additional cost of such features is funded by the Department of Commerce on the basis of Navy recommendations. Among the features that can be incorporated into ships for better defense are improved compartmentation, helicopter pads, foundations for self-sustaining container cranes, overhead and ramp adjustments for RoRo ships, and

An underway replenishment operation with the oiler USNS *Leroy Grumman* simultaneously refueling a Navy aircraft carrier and a destroyer. The replenishment ship USNS *Supply* is in the background.

more rugged materials than would be necessary for purely commercial use.

Direct Support of Military Operations

Ships of the merchant marine can be used in direct support of some military operations. This was done to a considerable extent in World War II, particularly with tankers that were fitted with underway refueling rigs. Some bulk freighters were also fitted for transfer of cargo at sea. More recently, there has been some design work and testing using containerships in this role, but more remains to be done.

Another example of direct fleet support is the sealift of follow-on supplies to support an amphibious operation. This was also done extensively during World War II. The follow-on support should arrive within five days of the initial amphibious assault. It consists mainly of troops, weapons, and supplies that cannot be put ashore during the initial landings but are necessary to keep the offensive going. Normal resupply thereafter would also most likely be delivered by merchant ships.

Auxiliary Combatant Role

Merchant ships can be easily converted to perform a variety of combatant roles. The history of this adaptation goes back to the privateer in the Revolutionary War and War of 1812. Later, merchant raiders, or Q ships (ships that looked like cargo vessels but that had camouflaged weapons), were used, principally by the Germans, in the two world wars. The United States converted tankers and freighters into escort carriers in World War II. Also, most World War II amphibious troop and cargo ships were converted merchant ships. There are many possible military applications for the fast, modern ships now entering the merchant marine. For example, they could be fitted with defensive weapon systems or sonar, and RoRo ships with their large clear main decks could support military aircraft such as helicopters and V/STOL (vertical takeoff) planes.

Support of Foreign Policy

A frequently overlooked contribution of the merchant marine to national defense is its role in support of foreign policy. Historically, the British and American merchant fleets were very instrumental in developing the nineteenth-century foreign policies of those nations, and the Soviets made much use of their merchant marine to support their foreign policy toward Third World nations during the Cold War years of the twentieth century.

The United States, however, has not actively pursued this option for a long time. The potential to promote U.S. foreign policy through the American merchant marine is great and should be more seriously considered. At present, however, most U.S. foreign aid and trade goods are shipped in foreign-flag ships. Moreover, the trend toward larger ships with cargoes in containers further diminishes the opportunity to "show the flag" in underdeveloped countries. Such countries may have only small ports that lack the expensive facilities to handle containerships, and the local market for goods may be too small to make calls by huge containerships profitable.

The Future

The hard fact is that the United States is an island nation that needs merchant ships at sea and trained Sailors in those ships. The ships must be able to serve the needs of the nation in both commercial and defensive capacities.

The U.S. shipbuilding industry must push technology to cut cost. The nation must intensify efforts to develop modern modular weapons installations for the defense of merchant ships and to facilitate the use of containerships in support of the naval fleet.

The American people must not lose sight of the fact that the nation's prosperity and survival depends on our ability to use the seas for international trade. The combination of strong naval forces and a strong merchant marine, together serving the commercial and strategic needs of the nation, is the beginning of true sea power.

STUDY GUIDE QUESTIONS

1. Why is the U.S. merchant marine an important part of U.S. sea power?

2. Why did our merchant marine decline during and after the Civil War?

3. What did the Merchant Marine Act of 1936 authorize in order to help American shipping companies compete against foreign companies?

4. What is the basic means for moving vast quantities of raw materials and manufactured goods throughout the world?

5. What are the key factors that have caused American cargo in American ships to drop to less than 3 percent of total?

6. A. What are the five leading ports in the United States?

   B. What are the five largest U.S. shipyards, and where are they located?

7. What is the most numerous type of ship in the U.S. merchant marine and the most commonly seen on the high seas?

8. A. How does the containership work?

   B. What are its most significant advantages?

9. What are the major advantages of RoRo ships?

10. What are five ways in which the U.S. merchant marine contributes to national defense?

11. What is the mission of the Military Sealift Command?

12. A. How can MSC ships be identified?

    B. What designator is used to identify them?

13. A. Why are increasingly larger ships being constructed for the world's merchant marine?

    B. How could this be a military disadvantage in the event of war?

14. How may merchant ships be used in direct support of military operations?

CRITICAL THINKING

1. Obtain economic data for the nations of Japan and Great Britain from the "CIA Factbook" Internet pages or any other economic reference. Compare and contrast these nations in regard to their imports/exports of food, fuel, other energy sources, and manufactured goods.

2. Trace the decline of the American merchant marine from Civil War days to the present, citing the major factors involved and effects on U.S. foreign trade.

VOCABULARY

subsidies	rebates
containership	U.S.-flag ships
auxiliary combatant	jumbo tanker
USNS/USS	LNG carrier
RRF ships	RoRo ships
heavy lift requirements	modular weapons installations

3 Grand Strategy

The use of national power and influence to attain national security objectives is known as *grand strategy*. It is the most important and least understood aspect of national defense. The lifeblood of a nation and trillions in national treasure relies on a dependable grand strategy. Since we are a government of and by the people, all Americans should be knowledgeable about U.S. grand strategy; this is our national plan for the future.

National, Grand, and Military Strategies

Strategy does not pertain only to the military or to armed combat. Both civilian and military leaders must consider strategic matters at the national level. *National strategy* combines all the capabilities of a nation, during peace as well as war, to attain national interests and objectives. Within national strategy there are political, economic, diplomatic, legal, and naval and military strategies, both international and domestic. All of the national strategies together constitute *grand strategy,* the art and science of employing national power to exert desired degrees and types of control over the opposition. This can be done through threats, force, rewards, diplomacy, subterfuge, and other means.

Military strategy involves physical violence or the threat of such violence. It seeks victory through force of arms. Grand strategy, if successful, will attain national objectives without violence. Perhaps more important, grand strategy looks beyond victory to a lasting peace. Military strategy must be controlled by the grand strategy of which it is an important part. The true aim of grand strategy, then, according to British strategist Liddell Hart, is to "seek a situation so advantageous that if it does not of itself produce the decision, its continuation by a battle is sure to achieve this." Even the first strategist, Sun Tzu, said that "to subdue the enemy without fighting is the acme of skill."

Evolution of Grand Strategies

A study of grand strategy is such a complex and fascinating task that it is impossible to cover the subject in a brief chapter such as this. One way to study strategy would be to try to digest the concepts and principles of strategy as written and carried out by the world's greatest acknowledged strategists. This would include *The Art of War,* written sometime between 400 and 320 B.C. by the first great mind to shape strategic thought, the Chinese general Sun Tzu. His concepts rank with the most profound of all time, and most of his ideas are just as applicable in our world today as they were in his.

Another great ancient strategist was Alexander the Great of Macedonia (356–323 B.C.), the first Western grand strategist. He dreamed of a world empire, an idea many since him tried to achieve without as much success. Alexander determined that war is always conducted on two levels: physical and psychological. His campaigns can be studied today as examples of how to apply every principle of war, both militarily and in other ways.

Hannibal of Carthage and Scipio Africanus of Rome, the major opponents in the Second Punic War (218–201 B.C.), were both exceptional military strategists. So was Julius Caesar (110–44 B.C.). Niccolo Machiavelli (1469–1519), the great Florentine politico-military theorist, broadened strategic thinking when he wrote on the sources, applications, and limitations of power. His unscrupulous concepts of diplomatic and military conduct later served to inspire the dictators of the twentieth century.

During the sixteenth century, knowledgeable thinkers of the day began to differentiate between strategy and the tactics to achieve it, linking military action with political policy at the international level. Frederick the Great of Prussia (1712–1786) became the next great grand strategist, developing from his central geographic position the concept of "interior lines" on the battlefield. However, he used statesmanship to even better advantage to secure the foundation of the German Empire.

Napoleon Bonaparte of France (1769–1821) applied existing strategic theories to perfection. Except for his 115 military maxims he did little writing, but he made many strategic contributions indirectly through subsequent writers who critically reviewed his campaigns. The two most important of these were Antoine Jomini (1779–1869) of France and Karl von Clausewitz (1780–1831), a Prussian. Jomini began the modern, systematic study of the subject of war, particularly the maneuvering of troops to occupy territory. The nineteenth-century French military leadership and many American Civil War field commanders used Jomini's strategic concepts.

Clausewitz concerned himself with the basic nature of war. His book, *Vom Kriege* (On War), is generally acclaimed as the most influential dissertation on strategy ever published. Much of it can be applied successfully to modern times, though some modifications have to be made for present-day circumstances. Clausewitz showed that war has both social and political aspects. Probably his most famous statement is that "war is not merely a political act, but also a real political instrument, a continuation of policy carried out by other means." He continually asserted that military and political strategy must go hand in hand.

Clausewitz recognized the concept of "limited aims for limited warfare," with the purpose of wearing down an opponent. In other words, he saw beyond the battlefield toward the enforcement of policy over an enemy. A later strategist, Hans Delbrück, a German, further clarified Clausewitz's meaning. He showed that Clausewitz had defined two methods of conducting war: annihilation of the enemy in decisive battle, and limited warfare or strategy of exhaustion. In the latter concept, the commander could move between battle and maneuver. The political object of war could be obtained by means other than all-out battle, such as by occupying territory, blockade, or destroying crops and commerce.

In the mid-nineteenth century, technology and social revolution made their imprint on strategic thinking. The Industrial Revolution resulted in an ever-increasing list of innovations that would facilitate warfare on a global scale: propulsion systems, communications, and means to project power overseas. Educational systems were developed to train professional officer corps, and the social concepts of the day were used to shape the attitudes and aptitudes of people. Foremost of the philosophers of the time who added a whole new dimension to modern strategy was Karl Marx, the writer of *Das Kapital,* the basis of modern communism.

Schools of Strategy

There are three traditional schools of strategic thought: maritime, continental, and aerospace. These theories will be briefly summarized below from the strategic standpoint. All have their merits, depending upon the nations that have embraced them, and all have had some details of their original theses altered to reflect current circumstances.

The Maritime School

In the late nineteenth century, the great American naval strategist Alfred Thayer Mahan, then president of the Naval War College in Newport, Rhode Island, developed a strategic theory that would revolutionize naval strategic thought. In 1890, after extensive studies of the strategies of Napoleon, Jomini, Clausewitz, and the English admiral Lord Nelson, he published a brilliant text on naval history and strategy, *The Influence of Sea Power upon History, 1660–1783.* This book, and subsequent writings by Mahan, had a profound influence on the theory of warfare and on naval policy and strategy in the United States and abroad from that time forward.

Mahan advocated a large navy, overseas bases, and national greatness through sea power. He emphasized the significance of commerce in war, and of economic warfare through the application of sea power. He was convinced that a coalition of nations in com-

Acclaimed as the greatest American naval strategist, Alfred Thayer Mahan published his famous text on naval history and strategy in 1890. It revolutionized naval thought, and had a profound influence on the theory of warfare and on the development of naval policy and strategy in the United States and abroad.

mand of the seas could best acquire the trade, wealth, and resources of the world and be more likely to win future wars. He applied Frederick the Great's concept of interior lines of communication to naval strategy, arguing that central position in the world's seas was even more important than central continental position. He viewed concentration of naval forces and command of the sea approaches as fundamental to the United States' attainment of insular safety, national greatness, and prosperity.

President Theodore Roosevelt and the U.S. Navy quickly adopted Mahan's theory of naval strategy and the use of the Navy as an instrument of national power. When the United States acquired overseas possessions as the result of the Spanish-American War in 1898, our strategic position was dramatically changed, and the nation emerged as a world power. This would permanently alter the strategic balance of power among the nations of the world.

The geography of the Earth has not changed since Mahan's writing, though politics and weapons have. There is no question that the United States is a maritime nation and always will be. Mahan's theory of maritime strategy remains completely applicable to America and its allies. Insular safety is no longer a valid concept, however, with the advent of land- and sea-launched intercontinental ballistic missiles.

The Continental School

Some thirty years after Mahan's writings, in 1919 British geographer Sir Halford J. MacKinder published an alternative thesis that emphasized the strategic importance of geographic landmasses. In his work, *Democratic Ideals and Reality,* he hypothesized that by controlling Asiatic Russia and most of Eastern Europe, an area he called the "Heartland," a central land power could eventually extend control to the rest of the world.

MacKinder believed that the nation in control of this strong, centralized land position could move powerful armies in any direction with little opposition. The first goal of such a nation would be to subjugate the rest of Europe and Asia; this geographic rimland of Eurasia he named the "Inner" or "Marginal Crescent." The next step would be to conquer Africa, which, along with Eurasia, he called the "World Island." Once consolidated, he believed that the nation in control of the World Island would control the bulk of the world's resources. Then it would be just a matter of time before the remainder of the world, called the "Outer" or "Insular Crescent," would fall under the domination of the central land power.

World Wars I and II were in many ways fought to prevent MacKinder's premises from becoming reality. Interestingly, his theories also foretold the nature of much of the conflict that would occur between the Soviet Union and the West during the Cold War years that followed. The Soviets played the role of the continental land power that sought to extend its domination of the Heartland to the World Island and beyond. However, it was ultimately blocked from gaining control of the "Inner Crescent" (the Middle East and Southeast Asia) by the dominant sea power, the United States, and the other Western European NATO nations.

Many contemporary strategists still support MacKinder's basic theories, although the continental school ideal of totally secure interior lines of communication in the heartland has been shattered by aircraft and intercontinental missiles. In addition, the development of an adequate system of roads and rail transportation sufficient to establish these interior lines has not occurred to date.

The Aerospace School

With the advent of modern aircraft and guided missiles after World War II, many proponents of modern air power declared both Mahan's and MacKinder's theories obsolete. One such critic who gained prominence was U.S. Air Force strategist Major Alexander de Seversky. Benefiting from earlier work by Italian army air officer Giulio Douhet and the experiences of World War II, de Seversky in his 1950 book, *Air Power: Key to Survival*, put forth a competing theory. It was based on the premise that complete air superiority, as opposed to just local or temporary air superiority, is possible. He criticized overseas bases as untenable, downgraded the importance of naval and land combat, and stated that "the manifest destiny of the United States is in the skies." In his view the main area of East-West confrontation would be across the Arctic Ocean, not the Atlantic or Pacific.

De Seversky drew a circle centered on the United States, showing the 5,000-mile strike radius of contemporary manned bombers. A similar circle was drawn centered on the Soviet Union. The southernmost extremities of these circles represented United States or Soviet air dominance areas. The central area where the circles overlapped he called the "Area of Decision"; it encompassed the bulk of the Eurasian and North American continents, and the entire Arctic region. Here is where he postulated the struggle for mastery of the air would be decided, and with that decision, domination of the globe.

Most strategists today believe the aerospace theory is entirely too restrictive. People and nations are located on the Earth's surface, and so are its resources. Resolution of conflict and exploitation of resources must be accomplished by forces on the land, regardless of the aerial outcome. This was demonstrated in the Vietnam War in the 1960s and 1970s, in Desert Storm against Iraq in the early 1990s, and again in the invasions of Afghanistan in 2001 and Iraq in 2003. Destruction of the surface by air attack leaves nothing for anyone.

Grand Strategy and Preparedness

World War II and its aftermath proved beyond any doubt that modern war had grown more total than ever. Military strategy now had to be considered, along with science, industry, diplomacy, and psychology, as an integral part of a national grand strategy. War has now become, more than anything, a contest of opposing political and economic ideas waged on all fronts in the international arena.

A key factor in such a competition is preparedness, both military and nonmilitary. Preparedness is a matter of maintaining the appropriate strength or power base from which to launch the ideas and take the actions essential to the implementation of the grand strategy.

Among Clausewitz's teachings is the following, which anyone who would reduce American preparedness should seriously consider:

> Woe to the Cabinet which, with a policy of half measures and a fettered military system, comes upon an adversary who . . . knows no other law than that of his intrinsic strength. Every deficiency in activity and effort then is a weight on the scales in favor of the enemy. If bloody slaughter is a horrible spectacle, then it should be a reason for treating war with more respect, but not for making the sword we bear blunter and blunter by degrees from feel-

ings of humanity, until once again someone steps in with a sword that is sharp, and hews away the arms from our body.

Clausewitz's statement points out that a government cannot deter an adversary from waging war with half measures and inadequate military strength. Every sign of deficiency will be used to advantage by the opponent. If we hope to avoid war, then the best strategy is to be fully prepared to fight one should our national survival require it.

Evolution of U.S. Grand Strategy

U.S. grand strategy has evolved through several phases from the earliest days of our republic to the present day, in response to the ever-changing dynamics of the world around us.

In the first phase, referred to as the period of *Western hemispheric defense (1783–1898),* entangling alliances were shunned. The United States tended toward isolationism while shrewdly recognizing the balance of power that existed in Europe, and the fact that the British Royal Navy's command of the seas ensured our national security. The Monroe Doctrine, for example, was allowed to stand almost unchallenged because of the balance of power existing in Europe after Napoleon's defeat in 1815.

The second phase of U.S. strategy, *limited interventionism,* emerged with the victory in the Spanish-American War of 1898 and lasted through the two world wars until 1948. The United States revised its long-standing policy and began to participate in world affairs. We acquired territories overseas, while retaining our traditional economic and political relationships with Europe. Our sea power, spurred by Mahan's writings, became our major military force, showing the flag, protecting our commerce, and extending our periphery of defense to the overseas territories. This reliance on the U.S. Navy as almost a "single weapons system" worked satisfactorily in the Pacific. In Europe, however, the absence of a strong U.S. Army presence to meet, in a timely manner, the challenges of Germany enabled that country to embroil the world in two global wars.

The third strategy phase, called the *containment of communism,* began with President Harry Truman's administration after World War II, when the wartime alliance with the Soviet Union ended and the Cold War started, with Communist nations showing worrisome expansionist tendencies and supporting revolutions in developing countries worldwide. It ended with the dissolution of the Soviet Union and the end of the Cold War in 1991. This strategy evolved through two stages: massive retaliation and flexible response.

Massive retaliation. After the demobilization of the U.S. military following the end of World War II, America had little left with which to counter Communist aggression except its monopoly in nuclear weapons. It was the time when Western nations signed the major mutual defense and collective security pacts such as NATO and OAS, many of which are still in effect today. The United States pro-

vided the nuclear umbrella integral to each of those treaties. Nuclear deterrence was the basis of national strategy, and the threat was massive retaliation for any major aggression. This strategy worked during these years, and deterred major war. However, massive retaliation failed to discourage the outbreak of limited wars along the eastern rim of Asia from Malaysia to Korea in the 1950s. The strategy of reliance on a single weapon system proved to be inadequate for the challenge of the times. Other options had to be developed.

Flexible response. During the presidency of John F. Kennedy in the early 1960s, the U.S. strategy was modified to cope with all levels of aggression. This made necessary the development of an ability to apply controlled force decisively against any kind of aggression, at times and places of our choosing. The armed forces were directed to be ready to suppress, simultaneously, a general war, a major conventional war in Europe or Asia, and minor insurgencies or revolutionary wars worldwide. Such an ambitious undertaking soon hit budgetary roadblocks. Flexible response was too expensive, and the American public was unwilling to pay the price to maintain such force capabilities.

The strategy, however, was valid. It was the manner of implementing it that needed revision. All of the aspects—credible deterrence, collective security, and appropriate response—had to be present. President Richard Nixon made good progress in refining the strategy to a viable doctrine before his resignation in 1974. All subsequent presidents have adjusted U.S. strategy according to the basic guidelines proposed by the Nixon Doctrine of the early 1970s.

There are seven major principles of current U.S. strategy, all descendent from the Nixon Doctrine. Each can be emphasized or

Following the terrorist attack of 11 September 2001, President George W. Bush formulated the *Bush Doctrine,* which asserted a right of preemptive attack against terrorists and any countries harboring them.

modified as conditions require. These principles are:

- A concept of strategic nuclear sufficiency, rather than an attempt to maintain nuclear superiority
- A strong conventional capability, assisted by increased participation and improved defense capabilities of allied nations
- Adequate peacetime general purpose forces for meeting a major attack against our allies in either Europe or Asia and helping with local contingencies such as terrorism as required
- Smaller U.S. active forces, with greater emphasis given to their readiness and modernization
- Emphasis on a strong research and development program to maintain our technological superiority
- Security assistance for the defense needs of friendly nations
- Meeting the U.S. military needs with an all-volunteer active force in all services and continued support of the reserves

In the years following the terrorist attacks on the United States in September 2001, President George W. Bush developed the so-called *Bush Doctrine*, which held among other things that the threat to the United States posed by terrorists who could be equipped with modern weapons of mass destruction is so severe that it justifies preemptive attacks upon them and any countries harboring them. Although controversial, the new doctrine was used in part to justify the invasions of Afghanistan in 2001, and Iraq in 2003.

However they may continue to evolve, all these principles are based on a fundamental truth that all persons concerned with grand strategy must recognize, regardless of their political persuasion: military power has become a major bargaining chip in international relationships. Inferiority in any area becomes a critical weakness, which can be exploited by any actual or potential adversary.

U.S. Military and Maritime Strategy

The national military strategy of the United Stated today includes three principal elements: deterrence, flexible response, and forward strategy.

Seabee personnel construct a six-room schoolhouse in Maroni, Camoros, in support of the humanitarian assistance element of U.S. maritime strategy as set forth by the chiefs of the maritime services in 2007. (Kenneth Fidler)

One of the major issues confronting new President Barak Obama as he took office in early 2009 was the U.S. strategy with respect to international terrorism. Here, he is shown delivering a major address to Marines at Camp Lejune, North Carolina, concerning the future conduct of the wars in Iraq and Afghanistan. (Michael Ayotte)

Deterrence of aggression requires the capability and resolve to prevail at any level of conflict, so that potential adversaries will consider their own risks to be unacceptable. This means that our military forces must be able to respond effectively to any contingency, from showing the flag and combating piracy to retaliating against nuclear attack. This *flexible response* may involve strategic or theater nuclear forces and general purpose forces. In order to respond in a timely manner and extend our defense perimeter as far as possible from our shores requires a *forward strategy* of maintaining a significant portion of our forces on deployment overseas, both at sea and in foreign ports and bases.

In 2007 the chief of naval operations and commandants of the Marine Corps and Coast Guard issued a joint document, *A Cooperative Strategy for 21st Century Seapower*, that set forth a new comprehensive U.S. maritime strategy for the rest of the twenty-first century. The first document of its kind to be issued jointly by all three maritime services, it reaffirms the importance of the traditional elements of forward presence, deterrence, sea control, and power projection to our naval strategy, and adds to them two more critical elements: maritime security and humanitarian assistance/disaster response. The *maritime security* element emphasizes the importance of international cooperation to maintain freedom of the seas, and the *humanitarian assistance/disaster response* element stresses the importance of participation in international and domestic relief efforts when natural disasters occur, such as the tsunami in Southeast Asia in 2004 and Hurricane Katrina in the Gulf region of the United States in 2005.

Future Strategic Trends

Much contemporary thought on the direction that our national grand strategy should take in the future focuses on the threat represented by worldwide violent extremism and terrorism. Some strategists see the major world conflicts of the past one hundred years as four distinct world wars. World Wars I and II were open conflicts for world domination resolved by force of arms and national mobilization of resources by allied nations to achieve victory. World War III was the Cold War, ultimately resolved not so much by open conflict involving force of arms as by the triumph of one ideology (Western democracy) over another (Soviet-style communism) by means of sustained political and economic pressure, while using military power for strategic deterrence and regional conflict resolution. World War IV is the global war against extremist violence and terrorism. In contrast to the other major conflicts that preceeded it, this war is being waged against adversaries having no firm allegiance to any country, about whom little is known, including who or where they are, and what tactics they might use and when. Their goal is to wage unending ideological warfare against us, our allies, and our way of life, as opposed to open military conflict. It is therefore difficult to bring modern high-tech military forces and weapons to bear against them, as there are few high value fixed targets or concentrations of forces to attack.

Against this enemy the national strategy has to be to defeat them by a kind of moral warfare, steadfastly emphasizing the humanitarian principles upon which our nation was founded, while continuing to challenge at every opportunity the extremist assertions used to justify their causes and gain credibility and support. The United States and its allies will need to take active leadership roles in issues of global concern that extremists can exploit to their advantage, such as global warming and development of alternative energy sources. We need to better utilize information warfare capabilities to gain timely intelligence on extremist tactics, operations, intentions, and capabilities. The United States needs to continue to upgrade its domestic defensive capabilities to counter any future overt or covert terrorist attacks, including our local, state, and regional civil defense capabilities. Finally, the United States must continue to take a proactive leadership role in world events, both for the welfare of our citizens and for the benefit of humankind.

STUDY GUIDE QUESTIONS

1. What name is used to designate the employment of national power and influence to attain national security objectives?

2. A. Who was the first great Western strategist?
   B. What did he postulate about the conduct of war?

3. What was Machiavelli's contribution to strategic thinking?

4. What did Karl von Clausewitz emphasize concerning strategy?

5. What are the three classic schools of global strategy?

6. What is meant by Clauswitz' statement concerning military preparedness ("Woe to the Cabinet...")?

7. What are the three principle phases through which U.S. grand strategy has evolved?

8. What are the seven key features of modern U.S. strategy developed from the Nixon Doctrine?

9. What are the three principal elements of U.S. national military strategy?

10. What two elements were added to the U.S. maritime strategy for the twenty-first century in 2007?

11. According to current strategic thought, what direction should our national grand strategy take in future years?

12. What differentiates "World War IV" against violent extremism from the world wars that preceded it?

CRITICAL THINKING

1. Sir Halford J. MacKinder wrote *Democratic Ideals and Reality*. How did Adolf Hitler use ideas from this book for his grand strategy in World War II?

2. Review the main themes in the writings of Captain Alfred Thayer Mahan and General Karl Von Clausewitz. Identify the ideas each had in common about global strategy.

3. Major Alexander de Seversky established the aerospace school of strategy in *Air Power: Key to Survival*. Review several major air campaigns of twentieth-century warfare, examine their outcomes, and show how each either supports or discredits de Seversky's theories.

4. If the United States is ever able to disengage completely from Iraq and Afghanistan, what do you think will then be the major threats to our security? What should be our strategy to counter them?

VOCABULARY

grand strategy
lines of communication
showing the flag
flexible response
ideological warfare

coalition
isolationism
massive retaliation
preemptive attack

4 U.S. Strategy and the Navy

The mission of the U.S. Navy is to be prepared to conduct prompt and sustained combat operations at sea in support of U.S. national interests. This basically means that maritime superiority for the United States must be ensured. The U.S. Navy must be able to defeat any potential threats to our continued free use of the high seas. In its simplest terms, defeating an enemy maritime threat means the neutralization of hostile spacecraft, aircraft, surface ships, and submarines that threaten the seaborne forces of the United States and its allies. The Navy carries out this mission within the framework of our national strategy in coordination with the other U.S. armed services and in combined planning with our allies.

U.S. national security is vital to the well-being of every American. Our military forces must be able to defeat aggressors if deterrence fails. New weapons technology, such as this Standard missile being launched from a Navy destroyer, helps defend our national forces against any potential enemy threat at sea. (Marcos Hernandez)

The Navy's two basic functions are sea control and power projection. These two functions are closely related. *Sea control* means mastery over the entire surface, subsurface, and air and near-Earth space above designated sea and littoral (shore) areas, or, in other words, over the *battlespace* within which naval operations are to be conducted. It also means preventing the approach of enemy forces within range of our forces or territory, and defense against enemy ballistic and cruise missiles. It does not imply complete control of all the world's ocean areas, but only where and when needed. Sea control is necessary so the Navy may have secure operating areas for the *projection of power*, such as carrier air strikes, amphibious assaults, and cruise missile attacks. The ultimate means of power projection is through fleet ballistic missile submarines, a principal element of the nation's strategic offensive force.

The U.S. Navy is responsible for three functional roles within the national military strategy: strategic nuclear deterrence, deployment of overseas forces, and security of the sea lines of communication.

Strategic nuclear deterrence. The effectiveness of the submarine-launched ballistic missile, combined with the near invulnerability of the ballistic missile submarine, constitutes the strongest and probably most survivable deterrent in our strategic nuclear forces. During much of the Cold War, this system was generally regarded as the principal stabilizing factor in the strategic nuclear balance between the United States and the Soviet Union.

Overseas-deployed forces. The Navy maintains operationally ready naval units overseas as part of other deployed American and allied forces. Well known in this capacity are the Sixth Fleet in the Mediterranean, the Fifth Fleet in the Indian Ocean, and the Seventh Fleet in the western Pacific. These ships are deployed where they can support forward-positioned U.S. and allied forces in peacetime and engage enemy forces should hostilities break out.

Security of the sea lines of communication. The success of the forward military strategy depends upon the Navy's ability to keep the sea lines of communication open, both to support deployed U.S. and allied forces, and to ensure a continued supply of vital imported raw materials for our industry. The protection of friendly ships close to enemy shores where they are most vulnerable to enemy air, surface, and submarine attack places a demanding burden upon the U.S. Navy.

UAVs such as the Predator shown here provide real-time infrared and color video to intelligence analysts and controllers both on ships at sea and on shore, and can be fitted with smart weapons for covert attacks.

Tactics versus Strategy

Tactics is defined as the art and science of fighting battles. Traditionally, it has been distinguished from strategy in a military sense. Strategy has always been concerned with the politics, economies, and planning that goes on in the prelude to battle. Strategy includes the large movements and disposition of forces among the theaters of operations and the direction of the overall campaigns. Tactics, according to Karl von Clausewitz, is the "formation and conduct of single combats in themselves."

Strategy gives tactics its direction, although strategy is often limited by the tactical capabilities of the forces employed. Tactics depend on the strategic considerations involved with the planning and conduct of campaigns; successful tactics meet the strategic requirements of the broad plan.

Modern Tactical Innovations

The tactical considerations of the atomic age permeated all aspects of warfare during the Cold War, and to a great extent since. The key to survival in atomic warfare is dispersal, and that is dependent on mobility. The first atomic weapons were mass destruction bombs designed to neutralize industrial cities or huge concentrations of forces. With the dispersal capability of modern infantry divisions and the mobility of naval forces, however, it became necessary to develop low-yield nuclear artillery and rockets to fit the changing tactical picture. Just as ships are intended to be mobile and largely self-sufficient, the modern army division includes both air and ground transport to aid in dispersing its forces.

Though atomic weapons are surely here to stay, several limited wars and numerous insurrections have been fought since 1945

without them being used. This does not mean that strategists and tacticians can eliminate these weapons from their planning. To do so would certainly be foolish if a potential adversary were known to possess them. But it is at least conceivable that humankind will take the necessary effort to prevent these and other weapons of mass destruction from being used in any future conflict.

Another technical innovation that was used for the first time to great tactical advantage in Operation Desert Storm in the Persian Gulf War in 1991, and later in the invasions of Afghanistan in 2001 and Iraq in 2003, is the "smart" weapon, such as laser-guided bombs, rockets, and programmable cruise missiles. These highly accurate precision weapons have greatly increased the probability of successful target destruction with just a single shot or attack, often from far greater ranges than were possible before. They are more "surgical" in nature, and greatly reduce the possibility of collateral damage to innocent civilians and private property.

More recently, much use has been made of various kinds of remotely controlled *unmanned aerial vehicles* (UAVs) to conduct all manner of surveillance of enemy installations and personnel, and on occasion to attack them using the various kinds of precision weapons described above. They range in size from drone aircraft launched from airstrips and ships, to model airplane–size ones that can be launched by troops in the field. More about them will be presented later in this textbook.

These and other innovations will undoubtedly continue to have far-reaching effects on all aspects of military and naval tactics in the future.

Naval Force Capabilities

The U.S. Navy must have certain capabilities if it is to be able to support our national strategy. The Navy's ballistic missile submarine (SSBN) fleet has long been a vital part of our nation's *strategic nuclear triad*, along with land-based intercontinental ballistic missiles (ICBMs) and long-range strategic bombers. Since the 1960s this triad has supported our national strategy of nuclear deterrence against attack by weapons of mass destruction by any nation having this capability. All other forces in our Navy are called *general purpose* forces. In order to support other aspects of our national strategy, they must have the tactical capabilities summarized below.

Offensive power. Naval forces must have sufficient power to be capable of projecting power through such means as carrier and amphibious battle forces, and destroying all hostile forces in the theater of operations by weapons such as guns and missiles. The Navy's offensive capabilities in the theater must be credible to allies for defense and to potential enemies for deterrence.

Defensive strength. Deployed naval forces must be able to quickly react to and defend against any enemy attack within a given theater. Such attacks might range from localized actions initiated by terrorists to large-scale attacks by forces equipped with both conventional weapons such as guns or antiship missiles, or weapons of mass destruction. Naval defensive capabilities must include long-range detection systems such as airborne early warning, quick-reacting command and control systems, and effective defensive weapons systems including those designed for defense against ballistic and cruise missiles.

Logistical independence. Naval forces must be capable of sustaining themselves for extended periods of time, and for much longer periods by underway replenishment by mobile logistic supply forces. Ships must be able to ride out heavy weather, and to steam long distances without refueling. Overseas bases may be helpful for sustaining deployed forces during peacetime, but they may become a liability in time of war.

Command and control. The naval commander must be able to communicate with and monitor assigned forces through a system for command and control. This system also connects forward-deployed naval forces with one another, the supporting shore establishment, forces of other services and nations, and government and nongovernment agencies.

Modern command and control systems have five subdivisions: command, control, communications, computers, and intelligence, or C4I for short. They include all information systems, equipment, software, and infrastructure that enable the commander to direct assigned forces.

The Navy is currently implementing a revolutionary new C4I network. When fully implemented, it will revolutionize the way in which naval operations are conducted. Based on cutting-edge information and communication technology, the network will use a common database instantly accessible from land, sea, and air to provide real-time access to all information required for the conduct of naval operations. It will link together not only all U.S. operational forces and support activities involved in these operations, but also any allied forces as well.

Tactical nuclear weapons capability. The Navy must be able to employ tactical nuclear weapons if confronted with them. Only with equivalent weapons capability can the U.S. Navy expect to fight and win at sea.

Naval Warfare

Naval warfare is conflict in which at least one of the opponents is operating from the sea with surface ships, submarines, or sea-based aircraft. The three corresponding naval warfare areas are surface, subsurface, and aerospace. The forces that are used in these warfare areas each have their own characteristics, strengths, and limitations. The art of naval warfare is to employ these forces in such a way as to exploit the strengths and minimize the weaknesses of each. This objective has led to the integrated use of all three types of forces in mutual support to gain advantage over an enemy. Moreover, naval forces now and in the future must be able to work together with those of other services and other nations

The ability to project power ashore is one of the Navy's main missions. This artist's rendition shows two land-attack Tomahawk missiles being launched from the USS *Ohio*, a former nuclear ballistic missile submarine now converted to a guided missile submarine.

in all tactical warfare areas in order to meet the multidimensional threat posed by our potential enemies.

The Navy is tasked with both sea control and power projection in all three warfare areas. Its tactical warfare tasks are classified as *fundamental* and *supporting* tasks. The fundamental warfare tasks are the following:

- **Air warfare (AW):** The destruction of enemy air platforms and airborne weapons, whether launched from air, surface, subsurface, or land platforms. AW includes all the measures used to achieve air superiority.

- **Undersea warfare (USW):** The destruction or neutralization of enemy submarines, mines, and other undersea forces.

- **Surface warfare (SUW):** The destruction or neutralization of enemy surface combatants and merchant ships. Its aim is to deny the enemy effective use of its surface warships, support ships, and cargo-carrying vessels.

- **Strike warfare:** The destruction or neutralization of enemy targets ashore through the use of conventional or nuclear weapons. This includes any enemy strategic nuclear forces, shipyards, and any operating bases from which the enemy might launch an attack against United States or allied forces.

- **Amphibious warfare:** Attacks launched from the sea by naval forces and landing forces embarked in ships and craft designed to make a landing on a hostile shore. It includes close air support or shore bombardment in support of troops in contact with enemy forces.

- **Mine warfare:** The use of mines and mine countermeasures. It consists of the control or denial of sea or harbor areas through the laying of minefields, and the countering of enemy mine warfare through the destruction or neutralization of hostile minefields.

- **Information warfare (IW)**: Actions taken against an adversary's information or information systems, while defending our own information and information systems.

The supporting warfare tasks are the following:

- **Special warfare**: Naval operations that are unconventional in nature, and often clandestine in character. Special warfare often accomplishes other fundamental warfare tasks, but does so in a unique manner. Examples of special warfare are underwater demolition, special mobile operations, coastal and river interdiction, beach and coastal reconnaissance, and certain tactical intelligence operations. In the Navy many of these tasks are carried out by SEAL teams, among the most highly trained and capable special warfare personnel in the U.S. armed services.

- **Ocean surveillance**: The observation of ocean areas to detect, locate, and classify potential aerospace, surface, and subsurface targets, and the reporting of this information to users in a timely manner. A target may be any hostile, neutral, or friendly platform of interest. Ocean surveillance provides the updated operational setting in which Navy commanders deploy forces to do battle. It supports and depends upon C4 (command, control, communications, and computer) and intelligence, and so must be integrated with both.

- **Intelligence**: The assessment and management of information obtained via surveillance, reconnaissance, and other means to produce timely warning of the location, composition, capabilities, and tactics of opposed forces. National leaders and military commanders who correctly use interpreted intelligence are able to make decisions based on accurate knowledge of the enemy's forces and capabilities.

- **Electronic warfare**: The electronic support for all warfare tasks. Its primary objective is to ensure effective use of the electromagnetic spectrum by friendly forces, while determining, exploiting, reducing, or denying its use by an enemy.

- **Logistics**: The resupply of combat consumables to combatant forces in the theater of operations. A principal goal of naval logistics is to make the operating forces as independent as possible of overseas bases. This is accomplished mainly by sealift, either from mobile logistic Navy ships or the U.S. merchant marine. Logistics are often the major factor in determining the success or failure of an operation.

Naval Tactical Forces

There are two categories of major naval ships: combatants and auxiliaries. The combatant category includes vessels classified as warships, such as aircraft carriers, surface combatants, submarines, and amphibious warfare ships. Auxiliaries include primarily mobile logistic and support ships, such as oilers and repair ships.

Of this total group of ships, the fleet ballistic missile submarines are part of the U.S. strategic forces. All other naval vessels are regarded as general purpose tactical forces.

SEAL teams are probably the best-known special-warfare personnel in the Navy. Their missions are rugged, and so must they be, as these SEAL trainees show.

Each type of ship has unique tactical capabilities and different primary and secondary missions in the conduct of naval warfare and support of U.S. national military strategy. Navy planners and tacticians attempt to structure our naval forces in such a way that there is always a proper balance of ship types to accomplish the expected warfare tasks.

The grouping of units to achieve a proper balance for a specific tactical requirement is called *tactical force organization*. Navy units are operationally deployed in task organizations designed for specific jobs, as, for example, an undersea warfare (USW) task group, carrier strike group, an amphibious task force, or an underway replenishment group.

Under normal conditions, about 30 percent of our active operating naval forces are deployed overseas in a fully operational status. Another 40 percent are operationally ready, but assigned to fleets working out of U.S. ports. These are ready for immediate deployment to reinforce forward-deployed forces if required. The remaining 30 percent are in a reduced operating status, undergoing planned maintenance or conducting basic training. In time of increased tension, the deployed forces can be increased to 50 percent or more for limited periods. Under extreme conditions of general mobilization, up to 85 percent of the fleet could be deployed, as it was during most of World War II.

Current naval planning foresees far greater emphasis on joint and combined operations in littoral (coastal) areas in the years to come. This means that in future conflicts our naval forces can expect to operate closely with elements of the Air Force, Army, Coast Guard, reserve forces, and available allied forces to accomplish the desired objective of force projection onto land. The exact composition of strike and support forces will be tailored to meet the specific requirements of each mission.

STUDY GUIDE QUESTIONS

1. What is the mission of the Navy?
2. What are the Navy's two basic functions?
3. What is the advantage of having naval forces deployed in peacetime overseas?
4. What is the tactical key to survival in atomic warfare?
5. What are the essential tactical capabilities of our general purpose forces?
6. What are the three naval warfare areas?
7. What are the fundamental tactical warfare tasks of the Navy?
8. What are the supporting tactical warfare tasks of the Navy?
9. How do Navy planners and tacticians attempt to structure Navy tactical forces?

CRITICAL THINKING

1. Research the factors that would contribute to a warship's survivability in the event of an attack by atomic weapons at sea. Why would dispersal of forces be an important tactic at sea in this type of attack?
2. Given the demise of the Soviet Union following the Cold War, is it still important for the United States to maintain its strategic nuclear triad? Why?
3. Why is it of ongoing importance today that the U.S. Navy and the other U.S. military services maintain a defensive missile shield capable of intercepting incoming enemy guided and ballistic missiles?

VOCABULARY

power projection	unmanned aerial vehicle (UAV)
battlespace	strategic forces
tactics	littoral area
smart weapons	C4I
nuclear triad	strategic deterrence
tactical nuclear weapons	joint and combined operations

5 National Security and Modern Conflict

As explained previously, *national strategy* combines all the capabilities of a nation to attain its national interests and objectives. One of the most important of these objectives is the maintenance of national security. While military power is the primary means by which national security is maintained, it is not the only thing. All aspects of a nation's power must be considered in the total strategy.

Political policy is of primary importance in all national security strategy. It is through politics, both at home and abroad, that the minds and actions of people can be influenced. There are other important considerations as well. A nation's economy, including its natural resources, industrial capacity, and finances, is a very important element of national power and can be used to attain national objectives. The strength and will of its citizens is also important, including their numbers, location, morale, and education. Geographic position, natural defenses, terrain, and the food supply are all significant factors. Finally, a good scientific and technological base is important both for national security and commerce.

Threat Evaluation

National security factors are meaningful, however, only when viewed in context with external and internal threats. The most obvious threat to any nation is military. But national security can be harmed just as badly by political, economic, and psychological warfare as by force of arms. A good example of this is the effect of instability in the Middle East on the supply and price of oil in the United States and Europe. The military threat is merely easier to identify, and perhaps the easiest to counter if a nation has the will to keep sufficient forces in readiness.

There are three basic considerations in evaluating possible external threats to a nation's national security:

- Capabilities—What *can* a potential adversary do?
- Intentions—What *will* the adversary do?
- Vulnerabilities—What are the adversary's weaknesses?

Although not the threat it once was, the Russian Kiev-class carrier *Novorossiysk* shown here is still a formidable warship. Note the missile launchers forward, and the VTOL fighter aircraft aft.

Capabilities means the ability of a state to satisfy its objectives or to stop others from threatening it—in peace as well as in war. They are the sum total of national power: political, military, economic, social, scientific, technological, psychological, moral, and geographic. Capabilities are only useful when combined with the means of applying that power effectively.

Intentions concern a state's determination to execute certain plans. Intentions are subjective and often easily concealed. They are shaped by interests, objectives, policies, principles, and commitments, many of which may be unknown to outsiders. Determining the intentions of a potential adversary is extremely difficult. An adversary's probable course of action, however, must always be considered in determining one's own best strategy. A rule of thumb is generally applied: the best indication of intentions is not what people say, but rather what they do.

Vulnerabilities are the weaknesses of a nation, which, if struck by any action or means, will reduce the war potential, combat effectiveness, or national will of that nation. Nations' vulnerabilities differ: they may include the ease of interdiction of key transportation routes, the vulnerability of major industrial centers, dependence on overseas imports of raw materials or fuels, weak or unpopular governments, and so forth. The list is extensive.

The *intelligence* process is used to gain the information necessary to make estimates of the situation or threat that might face a nation. Data concerning capabilities, intentions, and vulnerabilities must flow in a never-ending stream to intelligence specialists, who must process, analyze, and evaluate this information.

They arrive at *intelligence estimates* that are provided to the decision-making leaders. This evaluated, integrated, and interpreted information required for the development of national security objectives, policies, and plans is called *strategic intelligence*.

The purpose of estimates is to forecast intentions. The strategic intelligence specialist has a greater chance for success than does the combat intelligence officer, since the former has more time to study and reach conclusions concerning enemy capabilities, habits, and vulnerabilities. Estimating intentions, however, is a dangerous occupation. It is so because no one can positively determine what actually is in the minds of potential enemy leaders. Wide background knowledge, wisdom, experience, and judgment are necessary, and even then the strategist must recognize that the best intelligence estimators are subject to error because they are human. Threat evaluation is a difficult and vital process, but one on which every government and nation is dependent for survival.

The strategic planner must assess the *degree of risk* associated with various possible courses of action that could be taken to achieve national objectives. This means, simply, the probability of success of a course of action versus the stakes. The degree of risk is almost entirely a matter of judgment. Defeat and failure can result from miscalculations such as overrating one's own capabilities or underrating those of the opposition. Sometimes unavoidable *calculated risks* (actions having some degree of risk associated with

them) must be taken in order to make best use of the available resources, be they economic, military, or other. To do this intelligently, the planner must be well informed and alert to any possible negative effects on the overall grand strategy.

Principles of War

If all measures short of war fail, and war comes, there are certain principles that have evolved over the centuries that govern warfighting strategy and tactics. They have been used by all successful military commanders, both famous and infamous, since biblical times, including Hannibal, Julius Caesar, Napoleon, Lord Nelson, Grant, Eisenhower, Nimitz, and Schwarzkopf, to name just a few. Taken together, these are called the *principles of war*. They are as follows:

- **Define the objective.** Every military operation should be directed toward a clearly defined, decisive, and attainable objective. Whether the objective is destroying an enemy's armed forces or merely disrupting the ability to use forces effectively, the most significant preparation a commander can make is to express clearly the objective of the operation to subordinate commanders.

- **Mass forces.** Use strength against weakness. A force, even one smaller than its adversary, can achieve decisive results when it concentrates or focuses its assets on defeating an enemy's critical vulnerability.

- **Maneuver.** Place an enemy in a position of disadvantage through the use of speed and agility to gain an advantage in time and space relative to the enemy's vulnerabilities.

- **Take the offensive.** Seize, retain, and exploit the initiative. Offensive action allows the commander to set the terms and select the place of confrontation, exploit vulnerabilities, and seize opportunities from unexpected developments.

- **Economize force.** Employ all combat power available in the most effective way possible; minimize combat power spent on secondary targets. A successfully coordinated strike at an enemy's critical vulnerability can have far more significance than an attempt to attack all vulnerabilities at once.

- **Achieve unity of command.** Ensure coordinated effort for every objective under one responsible commander. Whether the responsibility involves a single independent unit or a complete battle force, unity of command is achieved by assigning a single commander at every level of command.

- **Maintain simplicity.** Avoid unnecessary complexity in preparing, planning, and conducting military operations. The implementing orders for some of the most influential naval battles ever fought have been little more than a paragraph. Broad guidance, rather than detailed and involved instructions, promotes flexibility and simplicity. Simple plans and clear direction promote understanding and minimize confusion. For example, the operation order for Operation Desert Storm summarized the allied objectives in a single sentence: "Attack Iraqi political-military leadership and command and control; sever Iraqi supply lines; destroy chemical, biological, and nuclear capability; destroy Republican Guard forces in the Kuwaiti theater; liberate Kuwait."

- **Achieve surprise.** Strike an enemy at a time or place or in a manner for which the enemy is unprepared. It is not essential that an enemy be taken completely unaware, only that the enemy becomes aware too late to react effectively. Concealing capabilities and intentions by using covert techniques and tactics provides the opportunity to achieve surprise.

- **Maintain security.** Never permit an enemy to acquire unexpected advantage. Alert watchstanders, scouting forces, and the use of electronic emission control all reduce vulnerability to hostile acts, influence, or surprise.

Interestingly, many of the foregoing principles are also applicable to activities other than warfare, such as various board games like chess and athletic contests like football and soccer. Most successful head coaches in these and other sports are well aware of these principles at either the conscious or intuitive level, and employ them to good effect to win their games.

Modern Forms of Armed Conflict

In modern times, there are three main forms that large-scale armed conflict might take. These are general war, limited war, and various kinds and degrees of revolutionary war. Each of these is discussed in the following sections.

General War

General war is defined by the U.S. Joint Chiefs of Staff as "armed conflict between major powers in which the total resources of the belligerents are employed, and the national survival of a major belligerent is in jeopardy."

At one time, victory in such a war was considered to be worth any privation. Speaking before the House of Commons in 1940 in the darkest days of World War II, Winston Churchill bravely said, "You ask what is our aim? I can answer in one word: victory—victory at all costs; victory in spite of all terror, victory however long and hard the road may be, for without victory, there is no survival."

Speaking of the Korean War in 1951, General Douglas MacArthur sagely advised, "There is no substitute for victory." This is an easily understood statement, but one that might not be so easily understood today.

Victory in the context of the term general war, as it is now defined, might be very hollow indeed. A global struggle with the unrestricted use of mass destruction nuclear weapons would endanger life everywhere on Earth. Victory in such an event would be hard to imagine for either side, or, for that matter, for any of the survivors on Earth.

General war on this scale, and with this potential, has no precedent in history. The risks are huge and probably overshadow any gains. There is almost no margin for strategic error. Therefore, for the first time in history we now devote more mental energy to the prevention of general war than to plans for fighting such a war. This, however, has not caused nations to give up ideas of becoming dominant powers in their regions, or in the world. Rather, the very fact that the risks of war have grown larger enables a clever antagonist to gain strategic advantage by exploitation of the opponent's fear of these risks. Nuclear stalemate has not invalidated the use of force or changed sound strategic concepts. Just as in the past, calculated escalation of force is often used to attain political objectives.

Possible Causes of General War

There are six potential actions that might cause a general war to occur:

- Deliberate initiation
- Accidental initiation
- Miscalculation
- Misunderstanding
- Entanglement
- Irrational acts

Probably no sane leader would ever deliberately start a general war, unless one of two preconditions existed: threat of destruction or assurance of victory. If a leader had positive evidence that his or her country was about to be destroyed by a nuclear attack, that leader might think there was nothing to lose by launching one first. Or if a country made a spectacular technological breakthrough that would make retaliation unlikely, the leader might consider that the risk would be far outweighed by potential gains. But because the long-term effects of a nuclear war are so unknown and far-reaching, deliberate initiation of such a war seems unlikely as long as the potential victim maintains a credible military deterrent.

The United States now has such preponderant military power that it is difficult to imagine how an opponent could envision overcoming it. However, proliferation of nuclear weapons or other weapons of mass destruction among unprincipled countries or terrorists could lead to general war through accident, miscalculation, or misunderstanding in the future.

Conflicts resulting in entanglement of major powers are always a danger. Wars can be touched off intentionally by a third country or coalition for a variety of motives. Collective security systems, pledges, and other involvements with nations constantly in conflict with neighbors in areas vital to the major powers (such as Israel and the Arab states in the Middle East, India and Pakistan, and the two Koreas) pose such dangers.

Irrational acts can never be discounted. The danger is not so much the possible mental breakdown of a leader as that leader's consideration of totally illogical, unwarranted, or unrealistic approaches to a problem. When considering this possibility, one must be aware of cultural differences between peoples. For instance, Americans generally place a high value on human life. This is not necessarily the case in other cultures or countries. As recent history has shown, there will probably always be individuals, groups, and even nations that are willing to sacrifice innocent lives for political or economic gains, or to advance extremist ideologies.

Limited War

This falls between the extremes of general war and the so-called cold war. The previous section discussed the totality of nuclear general war; cold war, in which all measures short of armed combat are used to attain national objectives, is the other extreme. *Limited war* is defined as "armed encounters, other than incidents, in which one or more major powers or their proxies voluntarily restrict their actions in order to prevent escalation to general war." A *proxy war* is a form of limited war in which a major power avoids direct military involvement by having satellite states engage another major power or its allies.

These limitations or restrictions are seldom affected by formal agreements. They usually result from understandings that are conveyed by means other than direct diplomatic meetings. The understandings may be made known through a speech of the chief of state, official releases to the media, or perhaps an exchange of notes through diplomatic channels in third countries. Interpretation of the rules that limit operations may be rather broad, but clearly the intent is to prevent escalation to nuclear warfare.

Wars may be limited in a number of ways, such as by limiting objectives, arms, targets, forces, or geographic operations. Limiting objectives is usually avoided, so restraints most often involve means, not ends. For example, the U.S. national security objective in Korea—the containment of communism—was successfully attained, but the secondary goal of unifying Korea was abandoned. The object in limited war is to select goals that avoid the appearance of directly endangering the enemy power's vital interests.

In any war, arms limitations, particularly limitations of nuclear weapons, are controversial. Most civilized people agree that strategic nuclear bombardment of population centers should be avoided, but what about the use of smaller tactical nuclear weapons designed specifically for battlefield use or the destruction of enemy missile silos? Argument against their use is centered on the probability that once introduced for any purpose, both the size and extent of their use could rapidly escalate. An opposite contention is that tactical nuclear weapons should be used in limited war situations "in the overall best interest of humanity and civilization." The argument here is that if they are used once or twice on the right targets at the right time, further aggression can be stopped and future limited wars can be deterred from ever starting. Each argument poses a strategic dilemma.

The use of chemical and biological agents poses the same kind of problems for strategists dealing with limited war.

Careful target selection also is an important factor in limiting the scope and intensity of war. All manner of limitations and understandings can be imposed. The Vietnam War was a classic example of target limitation imposed by political leaders. At one time, few targets other than enemy troops, armored vehicles, and logistics in transit could be struck by U.S. Navy and Air Force aircraft. Many important facilities essential to the North Vietnamese war effort, such as bridges, ports, rail yards, and industrial areas, were exempt. Haiphong Harbor was restricted both from aerial attack and the laying of mines until the very end, enabling massive quantities of war equipment to be delivered without hazard. Political, not military, prohibitions prevailed in the effort to limit the war. According to many analysts, the Vietnam War was lost largely because of these limitations. Would it have been won if these constraints had been removed, or would such actions have escalated the war, perhaps involving other nuclear powers? No one will ever know.

Limitations as to type, number, roles, and origins of military forces can also affect a war. Defensive, support, and advisory troops are less provocative than major combat elements. Proxy forces avoid major power confrontations. Forces from alliances or the United Nations are often less objectionable than those from individual states. Use of naval and air power is less risky than an invasion by ground forces, which immediately implies more than a temporary presence. All of these factors figured into the limited wars fought in Korea and Vietnam. Soviet troops never actually participated in either war. The Chinese insisted their forces in Korea were all volunteers, despite the obvious fiction of that claim. The fact that UN forces fought in Korea against the Chinese "volunteers" tended to reduce the impact of the cold fact that the United States was in reality at war with China.

Geographic limitations are inherent in limited war. The area of conflict is mostly restricted to a relatively small region, or a single country. Additionally, there often are safe havens that are left alone. In the Korean War, for instance, Chinese staging areas across the Yalu River were constantly under observation by U.S. reconnaissance planes but were completely immune from any United Nations attack. During the Vietnam War, the Communists had a safe haven in Cambodia for years in the Parrot's Beak, a portion of land projecting deep into South Vietnam near Saigon. Allied forces were prohibited from advancing toward Baghdad in the 1991 Gulf War, and al Qaeda and the surviving Afghan Taliban have found sanctuary for years in the mountainous terrain along the Pakistan-Afghanistan border following the U.S. invasion of Afghanistan in 2001.

Revolutionary War

Revolutionary war can take a number of different forms. Today, it often involves a conspiracy, culminating in a coup, that overturns an established government. Few people actually are involved, and little is changed but the leadership. In times past, it took the form seen in the United States in 1776, and in much of South America in the early nineteenth century: a colonial war for independence from a mother country, with opposing armed forces engaged in traditional warfare, ending with a formal treaty of peace and recognition of sovereignty. The French and Russian Revolutions, in contrast, were explosive upheavals of the masses. They turned out the old royalty and then consolidated the unexpected victories by means of infighting among various revolutionary groups until one dominant group emerged.

Revolutionary war basically involves efforts to seize political power by force of arms, destroying the existing government of a country and possibly its political, social, and economic structures in the process. Such warfare today is carried on in most cases by military insurrection or insurgency fostered by dissident elements among the population. These revolutions are often called wars of national liberation or people's wars, and they have been numerous in the emerging nations of Africa and Asia since World War II.

From the standpoint of its perpetrators, revolution is total war. The philosophy of such revolution, as expressed by Mao Tse-tung, is brutal: "Any and all means are justified to attain desired ends, without regard for stupid scruples about benevolence, righteousness, and morality."

Such revolutionary wars are primarily political and social processes rather than military operations. Insurgent actions steadily weaken popular support, the national economy, and the international status of that government. The military leadership is discredited, for it cannot suppress insurgent actions everywhere at once; morale in the government forces drops as the situation deteriorates. At every retreat, the insurgents advance; at every loss, the strength of the revolution increases. By the time the coup de grâce (mortal stroke) is administered, little resistance is left.

Prerequisites for Revolution

There are three prerequisites for a successful revolution: dissatisfaction with the status quo, a cause, and a carefully directed organization.

Insurgent revolutions most often occur in underdeveloped countries where slowly improving economies create expanding gaps between those in power and the majority of the people. Zealots often surface in such societies, where rising expectations breed impatience and dissatisfaction. Friction develops because of communication gaps between rich and poor, young and old, peasants and small businessmen, bureaucrats and the public, ethnic groups, and religious groups. The insurgents can exploit these

An Osama bin Laden propaganda poster recovered by Navy SEALs in an abandoned al Qaeda classroom in Afghanistan during the early days of Operation Enduring Freedom in 2001.

frictions. If, in addition to these circumstances, corruption in government or social and economic injustices are widespread, the situation is ripe for revolution.

The second prerequisite for any revolution is an emotional cause, one worth dying for. It must have broad appeal and be vague enough so it can be interpreted to each person's satisfaction. It does not have to be realistic or even attainable. Patriotic and nationalistic causes such as freedom from oppression, human rights, equal opportunity, and self-determination can stimulate the imagination of anyone, especially those who feel any change will better their own lot.

Finally, the insurgents must be organized and directed by a closely knit group of clever leaders skilled in mobilizing and manipulating people. One of the first steps is the establishment of a subversive shadow government. This group constantly vies with the legal government to undermine its control and continually purges weaker elements from its own membership.

A classic example of these prerequisites was the rise to power of the Taliban in Afghanistan following the defeat of Soviet forces there in the late 1980s. They took advantage of the disarray of the legitimate government following the Soviet withdrawal, arms and money supplied by the West and Osama bin Laden during the conflict, and religious zealotry among a small segment of the population to secure control of the country by 1998. Once in power, they imposed all manner of restrictions on the populace, especially women, which led to the country gaining a reputation as one of the most oppressive regimes in the world by the end of the 1990s. They remained in control of the country until their harboring of

The USS *New York*, LPD-21, christened in 2008, was built in part with scrap steel from the ruins of the World Trade Center buildings attacked by terrorists on 11 September 2001. It is the fifth of the newest *San Antonio*–class LPDs, designed for missions that include special operations against terrorists.

Al Qaeda terrorists caused the coalition led by the United States to oust them from power in 2001-2.

Revolutionary wars are difficult for established regimes to combat. To do so, it is vital that militant causes such as the following be eliminated: corruption and crime, unequal treatment and opportunity before the law, discrimination against minorities of any category, economic troubles and unemployment, and a breakdown in traditions because of lax educational, spiritual, and moral standards. Even when rebels or terrorists know their initial position is weak, they can be encouraged by future possibilities and can become determined to pursue their course.

Terrorism

In recent years another more sinister form of warfare has burst onto the world stage—terrorism. In this form of warfare, a small group of individuals outside the established government attempts to bring about political change by the creation and exploitation of fear. Actions taken always involve violence or the threat of violence. The aim, as in more traditional forms of revolutionary war, is to try to undermine confidence in the government and the legitimate political leadership. The terrorist groups generally have only a limited number of members, and often few resources and not much firepower. They tend to rely largely on spectacular hit-and-run actions to achieve their objectives. A prime example is, of course, the 11 September 2001 attack on New York and Washington, D.C., by bin Laden's al-Qaeda plane hijackers.

STUDY GUIDE QUESTIONS

1. What main factors affect a nation's national strategy?
2. A. What are the three basic considerations in evaluating an external threat?

   B. Which is most difficult to assess?
3. A. What are intelligence estimates intended to do?

   B. Why are they so important?
4. What are the nine principles of war?
5. What is general war?
6. What are the six potential actions that might cause a general war to occur?
7. What circumstances might cause entanglement of major powers in a war that could escalate to general war?
8. How are understandings concerning limitations in a limited war conveyed to the nations affected?
9. What are the two schools of thought concerning the introduction of tactical nuclear weapons to the battlefield?
10. How may selective use of force be used to limit wars or reduce danger of major power confrontations?
11. Why are naval and air operations less risky than ground force invasion?
12. What is the major difference between traditional revolutionary wars, as fought in the eighteenth and nineteenth centuries, and modern wars of national liberation?
13. What was Mao Tse-tung's concept of modern revolutionary war?
14. What are the three prerequisites for revolution?
15. What new form of warfare has emerged in recent years?

CRITICAL THINKING

1. As mentioned in the text, many of the classic principles of war are routinely though perhaps unconsciously used in many sports to achieve victory. Choose a sport, and describe how each principle of war is applied to it by winning coaches and teams.
2. With the rise of violent extremism worldwide, has the threat of nuclear war in fact increased or decreased in the modern world? Explain the rationale for your answer.

VOCABULARY

threat evaluation
intelligence estimate
general war
limited war

safe haven
coup de grâce
proxy war

Naval Operations and Support Functions

Broadly speaking, the term *naval operations* refers to the day-to-day conduct of all actions involving units of the U.S. fleet in the oceans of the world. It can also refer to the activities of the department on board a ship that is concerned with the planning and accomplishment of these actions. *Naval communications* is the transmission and reception of military instructions and information by sound, electronics, or visual means. It is the means by which naval operations are executed. *Naval intelligence* gives government and military leaders the information about potential or actual enemies needed to make good decisions. It is often an integral part of naval operations, and is transmitted through naval communications. *Naval logistics* provides the means of support for naval operations, while *naval research and development* ensures that the Navy operates with the latest technology. All five areas are interrelated insofar as the daily operations of naval units are concerned. The chapters to follow will describe these areas in sufficient detail to give some understanding of the activities that take place in each.

Naval Operations

The employment and movements of various types of naval ships and other naval forces in carrying out the Navy's mission is collectively called *naval operations*. These operations can range from missions carried out by individual combat units, ships, or aircraft, to large-scale evolutions done by an entire fleet.

In his blueprint for the U.S. Navy of the twenty-first century, *Sea Power 21*, Admiral Vernon Clark, chief of naval operations (CNO), stated that henceforth there will be three basic concepts underlying all future naval operations: sea strike, sea shield, and sea basing. *Sea strike* is the ability to project offensive power from the sea worldwide, whenever and wherever required. *Sea shield* concerns naval operations related to homeland defense, and defense of U.S. and allied sea and land forces and territory abroad. *Sea basing* concerns the maintenance of deployed fast response forces sufficient to carry out the Navy's mission worldwide, and their sustainment from the sea. These three operational concepts will be tied together and managed by means of an enhanced computer-based command and control system that will incorporate the latest Internet and information systems technology to provide unprecedented ability to coordinate all aspects of naval operations.

Naval Task Force Organization

The Navy's operating forces are divided into a number of fleets: Eastern Pacific, Third; Western Pacific, Seventh; Indian Ocean, Fifth; Western Atlantic, Second; and Mediterranean Sea, Sixth. The Navy's fleets are subdivided into task forces, groups, units, and elements. Warships are grouped to achieve the proper balance for specific tactical jobs; this is called the battle group organization. The battle groups, or strike forces, are made up of those ships designed for combat at sea. These are the warships: carriers, surface combatants, and submarines. Other groups comprise the amphibious force, mobile logistic force, and support force.

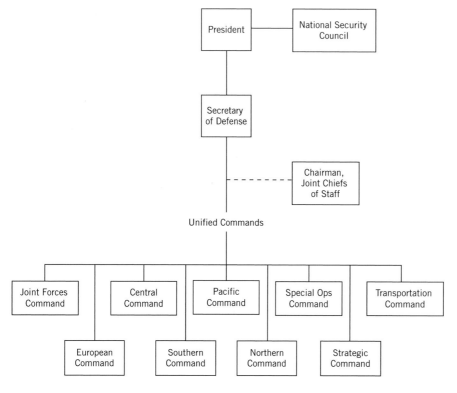

U.S. national defense command structure.

Command and Control Organization

Naval forces are organized for their roles as task-oriented, Navy–Marine Corps teams. Command authority for naval forces, as with all U.S. military forces, starts with the president and extends through the secretary of defense, with advice from the chairman of the Joint Chiefs of Staff, to the unified or specified commanders. A *unified* or *specified command* is a command with a broad, continuing mission under a single commander. A *unified command* has a geographical area of responsibility, referred to as a *theater*. A *specified command* has functional responsibilities, such as for special operations or space. Naval forces are assigned to these unified or specified commands for operations; currently there are no specified commands assigned.

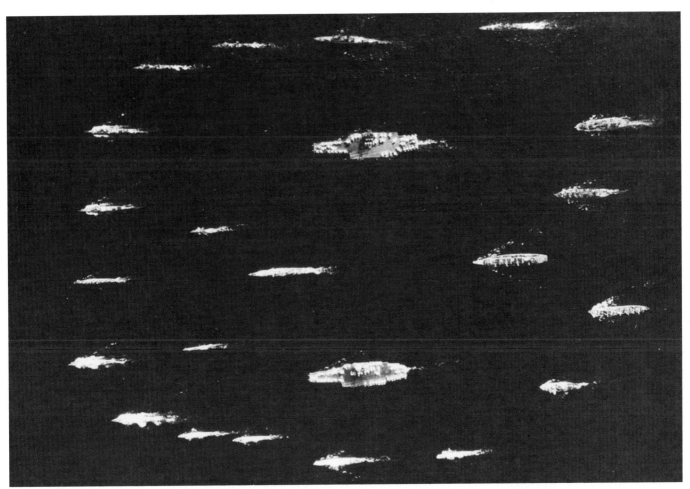

A naval battle group steaming in an old-style circular formation in the Mediterranean Sea. Destroyers and frigates are the bulk of the circular screen, with four fast ships of the mobile logistics support force in the rear. Two submarines, a cruiser, and two aircraft carriers steam in the protected circle. Today these ships would be much more spread out, with most not even in sight of one another.

Unified and specified commanders typically organize their forces for specific warfighting tasks by forming a joint task force. Joint task forces are composed of forces from two or more services. The services provide forces to the joint task force, whose commander organizes these forces into operational and support components as the mission demands. For most types of modern operations, naval forces are assigned as part of a joint task force.

A commander may establish various *support relationships* between subordinate commanders when one unit or organization can aid, protect, complement, or sustain another force. A commander normally establishes a support relationship by directing one force (the supporting force) to provide support to another (the supported force).

To help carry out command responsibilities, commanders are also normally assigned a *staff* appropriate to their level of command. The staff assists the commander in carrying out his or her duties by providing specialized expertise and allowing a division of labor. The staff is not part of the chain of command and thus has no authority of its own, although the commander may delegate authority to a staff officer if he or she so chooses. In such cases, the staff officer exercises that authority "by direction" of the commander.

Striking Forces

A *strike* is a form of power projection meant to damage, seize, or destroy an objective. Types of naval forces used to make strikes are carriers, cruisers, destroyers, and submarines. These ships may operate independently or together. If they operate together, they are called a *strike group*. Naval striking forces carry out national military policy, in peace or in war. Their presence near a trouble spot may serve as a stabilizing influence.

Mobility, one of the greatest assets of naval striking forces, and a constant state of readiness enable them to make surprise attacks from any point on navigable waters. A modern naval strike may range from coastal regions to great distances inland, depending on the weapons used. A naval striking force can be available immediately for prompt and decisive action if international disputes occur.

Modern Naval Striking Forces

Today's naval striking forces are built primarily around the carrier, just as in World War II. There are also some striking forces built around cruisers or destroyers and frigates.

The missions of carrier strike forces are still basically the same today. These are

- To seek out and destroy enemy air, surface, and subsurface forces
- To make preinvasion strikes against enemy airborne aircraft and airfields
- To provide close air support
- To strike against remote enemy installations
- To protect amphibious forces from enemy attack

While many of these missions are in support of amphibious assault forces, the primary purpose of the carrier strike groups, as they are called today, is to win command of the seas. To do this, they can make strikes, sweeps, and raids. A carrier strike is an operation planned to destroy an enemy base area or strong point. A series of strikes against several enemy targets in a general area is termed a *sweep*. A *raid* is a sudden destructive attack against a limited area or facility, with no intention of holding the territory attacked.

The modern carrier strike group (CSG) usually has one carrier along with the necessary escort and support ships. Unlike World War II formations, with concentric circles of protective escort ships surrounding the carriers, today's formations are spread over vast expanses of sea, often with the ships out of sight of one another. Dispersion makes it more difficult for an enemy to determine the defense plan, or to target multiple ships in a single attack. Guided missile ships, radar picket vessels, submarines, fast replenishment ships, and airborne early-warning (AEW) aircraft have been added. Some of these may remain close to the carrier, while others may range farther from the CSG to increase chances of spotting enemy activity by electronic means. The earlier the warning of impending attacks, the better are the chances for defense and launching counterattacks.

Protecting the carrier strike group from surprise air attack are the airborne early-warning aircraft and combat air patrol (CAP) fighters. Other airplanes may do tactical scouting. Still others will attack the enemy to damage, destroy, or demoralize enemy forces. Surface action groups (SAGs) may be formed from the surface warships of the CSG and detached for particular tasks, such as destruction of isolated enemy units, shore bombardment, or scouting missions.

Surface Action Groups

When surface action occurs, it is usually a series of rapid engagements, often overlapping. Surface warfare ships such as cruisers and destroyers are moved in and out of battle for attack, pursuit, or mopping-up operations. Maneuvers to change from an approach or cruising formation to a battle disposition, or formation, are called *deployment of forces*. This is a *tactical deployment* for battle and differs from a normal overseas deployment of ships to the Mediterranean on a cruise, for example. A battle formation is not a precise formation, for each ship must be able to meet its own opposition as it occurs. However they may be arranged, surface warships in a battle formation are usually close enough to each other that some mutual support is possible. Such ships are often referred to as a *surface action group* (SAG).

Fleet Aviation Organization

Naval air forces are broken down into *functional air wings*, each of which supports squadrons of one type of aircraft such as fighter, AEW, attack, control, and patrol. The functional wings are responsible for training and preparing their squadrons for deployment, either aboard ships or in the case of patrol squadrons to advance bases. A squadron may contain anywhere from four to fifteen aircraft, usually of the same type and model, and from 150 to in excess of 400 personnel, depending on the kind of aircraft, mission, and duty assignment.

When a squadron is deployed on an aircraft carrier, it becomes an operational unit of the air wing of that carrier, which is comprised of various types of squadrons. Typically a carrier air wing today consists of several F/A-18 strike fighter squadrons, plus airborne early-warning (AEW), electronic attack (EA), and helicopter squadrons, totaling altogether seventy to eighty aircraft. Upon completion of a deployment, usually of about six months in duration, the individual squadrons return to their respective functional wings to begin another training cycle.

Air Warfare

All air warfare may be roughly broken down into three main classifications: air-to-surface, air-to-air, and surface-to-air.

Air-to-surface strike warfare includes all measures used by aircraft to attack surface targets on land and sea, including guns, missiles, bombs, and other types of air-dropped ordnance. Although carried out primarily by attack aircraft, in recent years fighters, patrol aircraft, unmanned aerial vehicles, and especially helicopters have been increasingly used in this role. Major subcategories of air-to-surface warfare are undersea warfare (USW) and surface warfare (SUW).

Air-to-air warfare is that carried out by one or more aircraft against each other. The primary type of plane involved in this type of warfare has been the fighter, but attack planes and sometimes helicopters also get involved on occasion, as do surveillance and airborne early-warning (AEW) aircraft that detect incoming hostile aircraft. Although in modern times long-range missiles have largely replaced guns as the main air-to-air combat weapon, it may still be necessary to get in close and engage enemy aircraft with guns in the classic *dogfight*. Many modern tactical aircraft require a crew of two—one to fly the airplane, and the other to operate the complex fire-control and weapons systems of today's sophisticated aircraft.

An F/A-18E Super Hornet assigned to the "Fighting Redcocks" of Strike Fighter Squadron VFA-22 lands on the flight deck aboard the aircraft carrier USS *Ronald Reagan* (CVN 76). (Gary Prill)

Surface-to-air warfare, called simply *air warfare* (AW) in the fleet, includes all measures designed to counter attack by hostile aircraft or guided missiles. Active AW uses aircraft, antiaircraft guns, missiles, and electronic countermeasures. *Electronic countermeasures* are used to jam radars, confuse guidance systems, and present false targets. Passive AW uses such tactics as cover, concealment, and dispersion.

An AW ship formation is designed to provide *defense in depth* to the carrier or other high-value ships in the battle group. AW operations occur in three phases as attacking aircraft approach the formation. The first phase involves searching for, finding, evaluating, and reporting the enemy attack force. This is followed by initial AW defense measures. Taken while attacking aircraft are still distant from the force, these may include electronic deception, aircraft intercepts, and long-range surface-to-air guided missile fire. The third phase begins when the enemy aircraft or the missiles they launch have come within antiaircraft gun range of the main body of ships. This involves close-range defense by rapid-fire guns of both large and small caliber, short-range missiles, and evasive maneuvering.

Defense in depth against an air attack demands careful coordination between widely dispersed ships in the formation. The attackers can climb to very high altitudes or they can come in just over the waves. No matter what their altitude, their speed is likely to be supersonic. And they can fire missiles that can home in on target ships from miles away, which means that defenders must be able to react and compute defensive fire-control solutions instantaneously.

An AW coordinator is in charge of a team that directs air defense for the entire formation. Using computerized tactical data links, the coordinator guides with direct communications and elec-tronics the weapons systems of all ships involved with air defense. The most modern system of this type in the fleet today is called *Aegis*, which was described in *Naval Science 1*. Aegis cruisers and destroyers are able to effectively combat the most serious threat to surface ships, the low-altitude antiship missile. This virtually automatic system is regarded as the best defensive and offensive system for task groups ever developed.

Surface Warfare

Surface warfare at sea has been conducted ever since two enemies went to sea in boats and later in ships. Like carrier-based strike forces, surface attack forces are primarily intended to establish command of vital sea areas so that friendly forces may operate there and enemy forces cannot.

Until the advent of naval aviation and submarine warfare in the early part of the last century, virtually all naval warfare was conducted between opposing surface forces. Combat was sometimes between individual ships, like many of the famous actions in the American Revolution. Many major naval battles were fought between opposing battle fleets, such as the Greeks and Persians at the Battle of Salamis in 480 B.C., the defeat of the Spanish Armada by Britain in 1588, and the Battle of Jutland fought in World War I between the English and the Germans.

In World War II numerous surface actions were fought to establish control of vital shore areas, straits and other navigational chokepoints, and sea routes over which war supplies traveled. In the Korean and Vietnam Wars, surface actions involved mainly support of forces ashore and transportation of war materiel, and denial of these capabilities to enemy forces.

Subsequently, surface forces were used to convoy U.S. and allied oil tankers through the Strait of Hormuz and the Persian Gulf during the Iran-Iraq War, to enforce trade sanctions and launch cruise missiles against Iraq during Operations Desert Storm and Iraqi Freedom, and to launch cruise missiles against enemy forces in Afghanistan during Operation Enduring Freedom. More recently, they have been used to protect shipping against piracy in the waters off the Horn of Africa.

Long-range surface-to-surface missiles such as the Tomahawk add greatly to the capabilities of surface forces today. These missiles allow naval surface forces and attack submarines to strike land targets from positions far offshore, formerly a capability reserved for carrier air forces and ballistic missile submarines.

Surface ships used in surface warfare today include guided missile cruisers, frigates, destroyers, and a wide variety of patrol, littoral combat, and mine warfare craft. They have many capabilities and missions, ranging from peacekeeping in the troubled areas of the world to drug traffic interdiction in the waters of the Caribbean and the Straits of Florida.

The converted nuclear-powered guided missile submarine USS *Ohio* (SSGN 726). Formerly the lead ship of the *Ohio*-class SSBNs with the designation SSBN 726, the *Ohio* along with three of its sister ships was refitted as a guided missile submarine and relaunched in her new role in 2005. In its new configuration the ship can carry up to 150 Tomahawk cruise missiles and a contingent of sixty Navy SEALs for special warfare operations.

Submarine Warfare

Historically, the mission of a submarine has been to seek out and destroy enemy surface ships, both naval and merchant. After the advent of the nuclear attack submarine in the 1950s, the submarine's basic mission changed. While it still seeks to destroy surface ships, its primary objective is now to sink enemy submarines. The development of the nuclear-powered ballistic missile submarine introduced yet another mission: to attack enemy strategic targets such as missile sites, heavy industry, and rail and other transportation networks with ballistic missiles.

Fleet ballistic missile submarines carry twenty-four Trident 4,000-mile-range sea-launched ballistic missiles (SLBMs). They operate on 120-day rotational cycles. During their submerged patrols they operate completely independently. They are permitted to receive messages, but not to respond. They are manned by two complete crews—Blue and Gold—each with about 155 officers and enlisted men. In a typical cycle, a crew will take its ship on a two-month patrol, return home for a month's leave, have a month of refresher training ashore, and then be ready to start another deployment. While one crew is ashore, the other is on patrol with the boat.

Several former fleet ballistic missile submarines have been converted to guided missile submarines (SSGNs) to better use their capabilities to launch large numbers of cruise missiles against land targets in any future conflicts. Attack submarines can also launch cruise missiles, and they were used in this role in both Operations Desert Storm and Iraqi Freedom, as well as in Operation Enduring Freedom in Afghanistan.

Undersea Warfare

Until 1917 there was no adequate means of finding a submerged submarine. During World War I, however, three major developments established antisubmarine warfare (ASW), now referred to as *undersea warfare* (USW).

The first of these was the *convoy system*. This method of grouping ships together for mutual protection with destroyers as escort ships proved to be very effective. Proposed by Admiral William Sims, the convoy system enabled over 2 million American troops to cross the Atlantic to Europe without a single loss of life due to submarine action.

Second was the introduction of the directional hydrophone. This was the beginning of effective underwater sound detection equipment. Hydrophones could be lowered from two or three destroyers or submarine chasers at the same time. Using a mathe-

A depth charge explodes behind a patrol vessel along the U.S. Atlantic coast during World War II. Until the U-boat menace was brought under control, the Allies suffered heavy shipping losses in the Battle of the Atlantic.

matical process called *triangulation*, the submarine's location could then be pinpointed by the sounds of its engines and propellers.

Finally, the *depth charge* gave the destroyer a weapon that could destroy a submarine underwater. Essentially a large canister of high explosives, the depth charge could be rigged to detonate at a preset depth.

American scientists improved on the hydrophone system during World War II, calling it the sound navigation and ranging system (sonar), or underwater sound ranging system. By bouncing sound pulses off the hull of a submarine and measuring the time lapse until the return of their reflections, the range and bearing of the submarine could be determined almost exactly. The science of underwater sound has continued to advance. Using sonar ranges and bearings to contacts, computers can quickly figure their courses and speeds, and if necessary program weapons to attack them, taking into account such variables as water temperature, salinity, and pressure.

Since World War II significant advances in USW have been made. The helicopter has become a major USW platform. The highly maneuverable nuclear-powered attack submarine (SSN) has become the most effective USW vessel. The SSN can use sophisticated sensing devices to find and attack enemy submarines with homing torpedoes and a variety of long-range missiles (including subsurface-to-subsurface types).

Modern cruisers, frigates, destroyers, and USW aircraft, both shore-based and carrier-based, have a variety of sensors to locate and attack submarines. Some of these include the following:

- *Radio sonobuoys,* which contain a hydrophone and radio transmitter to help locate submarines by transmission of a submarine's noises to the aircraft
- *Magnetic anomaly detection* (MAD) gear, which detects variations in the Earth's magnetic lines of force created by a submarine
- *Dipping sonar,* a device lowered into the sea from a hovering helicopter to echo-range a submarine
- *Infrared detection,* a method involving electronic detection of heat emitted from submarines
- *Towed arrays* of sensors that can be streamed behind warships to detect low-level sound emitted from submarines at long range

Once detected, the submarine can be attacked with depth charges, antisubmarine missiles, and homing torpedoes.

Amphibious Warfare

Amphibious warfare, like surface warfare in general, goes back for centuries, to the ancient Greeks and their assault on Troy. Amphibious assaults and withdrawals have played key roles

An aviation ordnanceman loads disposable radio sonobuoys into a P-3 Orion patrol aircraft. The sonobuoys can be dropped on the water around a suspected submerged submarine, allowing an operator on the aircraft to track its movements. (John Collins)

throughout history, including the American Revolution and the Civil War. Undoubtedly the most famous amphibious operation of World War I was the ill-fated Allied invasion of the Gallipoli Peninsula in the Turkish Straits. There, logistics and communications were inadequate, heavy mining caused major ship losses, and strongly entrenched Turkish forces could not be driven from their fortifications. The lessons learned from the disastrous Gallipoli campaign assisted in the development of modern amphibious warfare doctrine.

In World War II amphibious operations were developed into a highly refined military science. Dozens upon dozens of landings took place in the Pacific against strongly held Japanese islands. Lessons were learned from mistakes made in the early assaults, and eventually a smoothly functioning Navy–Marine Corps team operation developed. In the European theater, landings were even larger in scale, involving hundreds of thousands of troops in the invasions of North Africa, Sicily, Italy, and France. The invasion of Normandy in France brought ashore l million men, 183,000 vehicles, and 650,000 tons of supplies from 3,000 vessels in the first twenty-eight days of the assault!

Amphibious warfare uses nearly all types of ships, aircraft, weapons, and landing forces to carry out a coordinated military attack against a hostile shore from the sea.

There are four principal objectives for amphibious operations:

- To capture territory from which a land campaign can be launched and supported (it may be to outflank and surprise, or to gain a base for forward movement of forces)

- To capture a land area from which air operations can be launched and supported

- To prevent enemy use of selected territory or facilities

- To destroy enemy facilities, interrupt their communications, and cause them to spread their forces to try to respond to amphibious raids

The amphibious operation is highly useful because of its mobility and flexibility. In other words, it has the ability to concentrate forces and to strike with great strength at selected points. It exploits the element of surprise. At the right time, it can strike where the enemy is known to be weak. In fact, the mere threat of an amphibious assault may be sufficient to cause the enemy to disperse his forces and make expensive and wasteful efforts to defend a long coastline. The amphibious striking forces of the United States normally consist primarily of Navy and Marine Corps forces but may include personnel and equipment from every service.

Marines practice a fast rope-out egress from a hovering V-22 Osprey aircraft. Such aircraft provide the Marine Corps with a quick-strike capability far inland during an amphibious operation. (Lana Waters)

Information Warfare

The gathering, transmission, storage, processing, and accessing of information has always been of concern to war fighters, and is critical to success in modern warfare. *Information warfare*, sometimes called *information operations*, is any action taken to negatively affect the information or information processing capabilities of an enemy, safeguard our own information, or exploit that information militarily. It includes such things as electronic warfare, psychological warfare operations, military deception, computer network defense, and operations security.

In order to provide timely processing of information at all levels, the Navy is currently implementing a revolutionary new command, control, communications, computers, and intelligence (C4I) network called ForceNet. When fully implemented, it will revolutionize the way in which naval operations are conducted. Based on cutting-edge information and communication technology, ForceNet will use a common database instantly accessible from land, sea, and air to provide real-time access to all information required for the conduct of naval operations. It will link together not only all U.S. forces involved in these operations, but also any allied forces as well.

Space Warfare

The use of space-based communications, intelligence, and navigation systems has become increasingly important to the Navy. Naval aviators were among the first selected for astronaut training, and they served as crew members on many of the early space exploration missions, as well as in the space shuttle program. Navy navigation satellites have been providing global all-weather positioning information to both military and civilian users since the 1960s, and communications satellites have been a mainstay of the Navy communications system for many years.

Space satellite systems play a key role in linking widely dispersed forward deployed naval forces with each other, the supporting shore establishment, forces of other services and other nations, and government and nongovernment agencies. They have become indispensable tools in the command and control of naval forces.

Today's naval forces are one of the DOD's largest users of space systems, relying on space support for most ship-to-shore communications, precision navigation, combat information and intelligence, and weather forecasting.

Space systems provide a unique capability to collect and disseminate large volumes of information. They can provide sustained, covert surveillance of the battlespace to allow timely indications and warning of hostile actions. They can detect, classify, and identify high-interest targets and can help in assessing battle damage. They can provide highly accurate positional data to aid navigation, weapons direction, mapping and charting, and search and rescue. Finally, they can tie together naval, joint, and multinational forces

Communications satellites like this one being launched by the space shuttle Discovery add a whole new dimension to naval capabilities and tactics. (NASA photo)

across large areas of the globe by means of high-capacity, secure communications.

Because of their extended line of sight, space systems have unique characteristics that make them especially valuable to naval forces. They provide global coverage of areas of interest. Depending on their orbits, satellites can provide either periodic short-duration coverage of specific points on the Earth's surface, or continuous, long-dwell coverage of larger areas. Communications satellites are now the primary means of providing immediate worldwide connectivity to all naval forces at sea, regardless of the location, weather, or type of operation.

The development of increasingly capable satellite systems is continuing and will undoubtedly result in the addition of many more capabilities in the future, including precise targeting and guidance for long-range cruise missiles, large-area electronic surveillance and warfare coordination, and completely passive detection and tracking of enemy ships, aircraft, and missiles. All these will have a great effect on future naval tactics and strategies.

STUDY GUIDE QUESTIONS

1. As set forth in *Sea Power 21*, what are the three concepts that will underlay all naval operations in the twenty-first century?

2. A. What is the striking force centered around an aircraft carrier called?

   B. What is its purpose?

3. A. What is the CAP?

   B. What is its purpose?

4. What are the three main classifications of air warfare?

5. What are the phases of AW operations for a ship formation?

6. What is Aegis designed to do?

7. A. Historically, what has always been the mission of the submarine?

   B. With the coming of the nuclear-powered attack submarine (SSN), what became its primary attack mission?

8. What were the three major developments that established undersea warfare during World War I?

9. A. What is the primary electronic detection device used in USW operations?

   B. What are some variations of it that can be used to locate and attach submarines?

10. What are the four possible objectives of amphibious operations?

11. What is information warfare?

12. What are the warfare capabilities of today's space satellite systems?

CRITICAL THINKING

1. Research the opening days of the invasion of Afghanistan in 2001 or Iraq in 2003 and describe the naval operations that took place.

2. Find pictures taken by satellites on the Internet. How high were the satellites when they took the pictures and what were the smallest things they could see on the Earth?

3. Locate a picture of a sonobuoy. Draw it and identify its major parts. Describe how it works and identify two major types.

VOCABULARY

naval operations	specified command
unified command	combat air patrol (CAP)
striking force	electronic countermeasures
raid	SAG
sweep	SUW
convoy	USW
information warfare	sonar
CSG	psychological warfare
air warfare (AW)	towed array

2 Naval Communications

Communication means transmitting a message so the receiver understands it accurately. The tools of communication are written and spoken words. In order to communicate well, ideas must be put in the form of words that accurately convey them. This is especially important when the messages are commands or orders.

Naval communications is the transmission and reception of military instructions and information by sound, electronics, or visual means. The Navy operates worldwide, so it needs a global communications network. A commander must be able to communicate orders to or from ships, shore stations, and aircraft.

Communications makes it possible for a commander to evaluate a situation and determine appropriate courses of action for his units from a central command post. Without the ability to communicate, there could be no coordinated action among ships, aircraft, and ground forces.

Naval communications must be reliable, secure, and rapid in both peace and war. Of the three, reliability is the most important; it must never be sacrificed for security or speed. If a choice must be made between security and speed, the originator must decide which of the two is more important.

Naval Telecommunications

The term *naval telecommunications* includes all of the communications effort within the Department of the Navy. These telecommunications are of three types: electrical/electronic, visual, and sound. The main function of naval telecommunications is to meet the communication needs of the operating forces. Its secondary function is to allow administration of the naval establishment. Telecommunications includes routing, reproducing, distributing, record keeping, and encrypting and decrypting naval messages.

Telecommunications and Command

The naval telecommunications system includes all communications facilities on shore. The largest of these facilities are called naval communications stations (NavComSta). They have both transmitting and receiving equipment to give support to the fleet in a specific geographic area. Fleet commanders control all tactical communications of ships and aircraft under their command.

For the operating forces, telecommunications is the voice of command in tactical situations. It is the way in which ships and

Satellite communications dishes at Wahiawa, Hawaii, for the satellite-based Mobile User Objective System (MUOS) that will eventually link together all U.S. and allied forces within a theater of operations. (John Ciccarelli)

aircraft talk to one another. The communications organization aboard ship is under the direct control of the commanding officer. The size of shipboard communications organizations depends on the size and type of the ship. A large ship, such as an aircraft carrier or amphibious command ship, has a separate communications department. In other ships, such as destroyers or auxiliaries, the communications division is part of the operations department. Shipboard communications facilities have ample communications equipment for their needs, plus expansion capabilities in the event of emergency.

Electrical/Electronic Communications

Today, we usually refer to electrical communications as electronics, which has to do with the movement of electrons in a conductor (wire), the dissemination of radio waves in or above our atmosphere, or the generation of sound pulses in water.

Radio is one of the Navy's main forms of communication. Radio circuits are potentially the least secure of all communications, however, so most radio messages are *encrypted*, that is, sent in code. Most Navy radio messages are now encrypted electronically, so *decryption* by unauthorized listeners is considered nearly impossible.

Radiotelephone (R/T). The radiotelephone (voice radio) is considered one of the most basic military communication devices. Because it is easy, direct, and convenient to operate, it is used routinely for tactical communications among surface ships, ground forces, and aircraft. There is almost no delay in transmission, and acknowledgments can be returned immediately. Most tactical R/T equipment has line-of-sight capability only; that is, the radio waves go in straight lines and do not follow the curvature of the Earth. Over-the-horizon (OTH) R/T communication can be done using low frequency radio or communications satellite links. Most R/T transmissions are sent in plain language, so there must be strict *circuit discipline*, that is, prescribed frequencies, language, and procedures must be used. Broadcast R/T is considered the least secure means of electronic communications, because anyone within range can copy the message. For voice communications requiring high security, automatic encryption devices are used that superim-

pose random noise patterns on the broadcast signal. Only properly equipped receivers can decipher such messages.

Those using R/T voice radio communications must pronounce words properly and have a thorough knowledge of the phonetic alphabet. Because the phonetic alphabet is used routinely in the Navy and other services and will often be used during the NJROTC course of study, all cadets should learn it.

Satellite communications. Most long distance and data communication in the Navy today is done via satellite. The Navy is very active in space satellite communications research and development. Essentially, satellite communications are an application of long distance radio relay, wherein ships, ground stations or aircraft can communicate with each other via satellite relay stations high above the Earth. There are several different groups or constellations of military communications satellites presently in orbit and more planned for the future. The services also make use of commercial communications satellites to provide extra capability when needed. These links enable instant communications with military units worldwide, and allow for live reception of televised sporting events and personal e-mail and video cam services wherever a service member may be deployed.

Tactical data links. The Navy and other armed services transmit tactical data among surveillance and weapons control system computers on ships, ground stations and aircraft via transmission of digital data over radio networks called *tactical digital information links (TADILs)*. Data transmitted over these links either directly or via communication satellites can enable geographically dispersed forces to receive a complete tactical picture of everything happening in a designated battlespace for hundreds of miles. Other links transmit tactical data between aircraft, or between air controllers on land or aboard ship and the tactical aircraft they are directing.

International Morse Code

International Morse code is used for naval communications transmitted by flashing light. The code is a system in which the characters (letters, numbers, and punctuation marks) are represented by various combinations of dots and dashes. A skilled signalman sends code in evenly timed dots and dashes in which the dash is three times as long as the dot.

Many NJROTC cadets may want to learn international Morse code well enough to send and receive their names or short messages.

Visual Communications

Visual communications may be done over short distances, weather conditions permitting. Visual means are often as reliable and convenient as radio, and usually more secure. Radio waves go out in all directions (omni-directional), whereas visual signals can only be received by observers relatively close by, and in the case of flashing

The phonetic alphabet and international Morse code.

Flaghoists are read from the top down, outboard to inboard. Flaghoist signals used for tactical communications and maneuvering are based on the standardized *Allied Naval Signal Book.*

A signalman mans his light aboard the aircraft USS George Washington (CVN 73). (Joseph Hendricks)

light, only those in the line of sight. Visual signals include flaghoist, semaphore, and flashing light (signal light).

Visual communication is versatile, reliable, silent, and economical. It can be used to talk with merchant ships or foreign mariners who cannot easily communicate in English, through the use of standardized international codebooks. Further, it has the advantage of using simple equipment that does not often break down. Visual signaling is efficient and economical because it shares the communications load with radio while not using the electronic frequencies.

The signal bridge can perform all the functions of radio except for long-distance communications. The signal force identifies other shipping and challenges unidentified vessels and sometimes aircraft.

Flaghoist. Flaghoist signaling is a rapid and accurate system of sending tactical signals or international code during daylight. A flaghoist signal system can send maneuver instructions more uniformly than any other system. Signals are repeated by those receiving them, thus ensuring that the message is received accurately. Meanings of signals that may be sent by flaghoist are contained

in classified signal books held by ships in the allied navies and in international codebooks carried by all naval and merchant vessels on the high seas.

There is a signal flag for each letter of the alphabet, one for each numeral from zero to nine, and others with special uses. A total of sixty-eight flags and pennants can be used to send thousands of signals. Decks of signal cards are available to use in learning the signal flags and pennants.

Flashing light. Signaling by flashing light can be done either by day or night either by using a signal light pointed at an addressee or by yardarm blinkers, which allow it to be seen omnidirectionally (360 degrees). The message is sent by means of international Morse code, with "dots" and "dashes" of light formed by opening and closing shutters across the face of the signal light. The transmitting signalman sends one word at a time with a slight pause

A signalman uses semaphore flags to send a message to a nearby ship. (Greg Messier)

between the letters. The receiving signalman flashes a dash after each word is received, meaning that it has been received and he or she is ready for another.

Flashing light signaling after dark can also be done with infrared lights or filters, which make the signal invisible unless it is viewed through a special optical receiver. Infrared light signaling is called Nancy. It is a very secure method of communication and can be used effectively up to about 7½ miles.

Semaphore. Semaphore uses hand flags for short-distance communications between ships. It is faster and more secure than flashing light. At night, semaphore can be done using lighted wands. Ships in close steaming formations or alongside for underway transfer and replenishment operations commonly use semaphore.

Because of its speed, semaphore is better than other visual means for long messages. Speed and security are the major advantages of semaphore. Its major limitation is its short range, limited to only a few hundred yards.

A signalman sends semaphore signals by moving his or her arms in various positions representing each letter of the alphabet. In order to increase the range and visibility of movements, he or she holds two hand flags attached to short staffs. A good signalman can send or receive about twenty-five letter groups a minute. Only thirty positions need to be learned.

As a point of interest, semaphore is often used as an effective way to communicate with one another by civilian lifeguards manning isolated lifeguard towers along lengthy public beaches.

Sound and Pyrotechnic Signaling

Sound communications include whistles, sirens, bells, and underwater acoustics. The first three are used by ships for sending a variety of emergency warning signals.

These include navigational signals prescribed by the rules of the road such as fog and maneuvering signals, air raid, breakdown,

Semaphore alphabet and special signals.

and collision warnings, and wartime communications between ships in convoy.

A waterborne sound communications method called *Gertrude* uses an underwater telephone system associated with submarine or destroyer sonar equipment. It can communicate either by continuous wave (CW) or voice. It is limited in range and not very secure.

Pyrotechnics are used for emergency signals. They are mainly of the "fireworks" variety: pistol flares; colored shell bursts, including parachute flares; aircraft parachute flares; Roman candles; and a number of colored float- and smoke-type flares. The color of the flare determines the meaning of the signal.

Distress signals indicating that a ship or person needs help are covered in the Rules of the Road and Maneuvering Board unit in this text. All ships at sea are required to maintain a listening watch on radio distress frequencies at all times. It is a fundamental law of the sea that any vessel that sees or hears a distress signal must render assistance if at all possible.

STUDY GUIDE QUESTIONS

1. A. What is "communications"?

   B. What is "naval communications"?

2. Why are effective communications in the Navy so important?

3. What three qualities must naval communications have?

4. What are the main and secondary functions of naval telecommunications?

5. What are the largest of the Navy's communications facilities called?

6. Which officer is in charge of a ship's communications organization?

7. A. What is a radiotelephone?

   B. What alphabet is used for voice communications by radio?

8. What are communications satellites?

9. How is tactical data sent between ships and aircraft in today's Navy?

10. How would your full name be sent in Morse code?

11. What are the main Navy visual communications methods?

12. What is the principal use of flaghoist?

13. A. What are three ways of communicating by flashing light?

    B. What is the advantage of the Nancy system?

14. A. What is semaphore?

    B. How can it be used at night?

15. A. What sound communications are used by ships, and under what conditions are they used?

    B. What is the Gertrude system?

CRITICAL THINKING

1. Research satellite communications, and describe how this communications system affects voice and Internet communications.

2. Do you think cell phone technology is good for transmitting important information on the battlefield? Support your answer.

VOCABULARY

encryption

tactical data link

international Morse code

circuit discipline

phonetic alphabet

pyrotechnics

semaphore

decryption

radiotelephone

telecommunications

flaghoist

Gertrude

Nancy

3 | Naval Intelligence

Intelligence, or information about an actual or potential enemy, can give government and military leaders the knowledge they need to make good decisions. Intelligence can reduce the possibility of surprise, evaluate enemy strength, and predict an enemy area of operation. It can mean the difference between peace and war. In the event of war, it can be the difference between victory and defeat.

General Definitions

In general terms, intelligence is knowledge upon which a political or military decision or course of action may be based. Intelligence information covers many subjects: geography, transportation, telecommunications, political and economic conditions, armed forces, technical developments, and biographical data on leaders. All these different areas fit together like parts of a puzzle. It is necessary to consider each part in relation to others.

The *Encyclopedia Britannica* defines military and political intelligence as "that information acquired on a national scale, usually about a rival, but sometimes about an ally or a neutral country." There is an important difference between information and intelligence. *Raw information* is the material collected from all sources about a given subject or country. This information becomes *intelligence* after it is gathered together and analyzed in order to be useful to a political or military leader in making decisions.

Intelligence is often considered to be a mysterious and dangerous activity undertaken by glamorous spies. The famous story of Mata Hari, the beautiful German spy of World War I, and the fictional adventures of James Bond, Agent 007 of the British Secret Service, have given intelligence gathering a "cloak-and-dagger" image. Intelligence collection has had its moments of intrigue, mystery, and danger, but most such work is like work in any other military staff job. The main difference is that governments do not disclose how their intelligence organizations work. The practice has been to protect intelligence activity by strict security regulations.

Espionage is the attempt to obtain information about a foreign government covertly (in secret), through the use of spies and other undercover operations. *Counterintelligence*, or *security*, is the protection of a nation's secrets. It is designed to prevent foreign countries from getting vital diplomatic, economic, and industrial information as well as military information of intelligence value. Counterintelligence, therefore, is a continuing need in peace and war.

The Intelligence Cycle

The *intelligence cycle* is the process by which information is acquired, gathered, transmitted, evaluated, analyzed, and made available as finished intelligence for policy makers and military commanders to use in decision making and action. There are five steps in the intelligence cycle:

- **Planning and direction.** This involves the management of the entire intelligence effort from identification of the need for data to the final delivery of an intelligence product to a consumer.

- **Collection.** This involves the gathering of raw information from which finished intelligence will be produced. There are many sources of this information. Open sources include such things as radio and TV broadcasts, newspapers, periodicals, and books. Covert sources are agents and spies and, on occasion, defectors who are willing to provide valuable information obtainable in no other way. Technical collection, such as by the use of surveillance electronics and satellite photography, has also come to play an indispensable part in modern intelligence collection.

- **Processing.** This step involves the conversion of the vast amount of information coming into the system from all sources to a form more suitable for producing finished intelligence, such as through decryption and language translations. Information that does not go directly to analysts is sorted and made available for rapid computer retrieval. Processing also refers to data reduction and interpretation of information gathered on film and tape through the use of highly refined photographic and electronic analysis processes.

- **Analysis and production.** This refers to the conversion of basic information into finished intelligence. It includes the assembly, evaluation, and analysis of all available data, and the preparation of a variety of intelligence products. Intelligence data is frequently incomplete and at times can be confusing. Various analysts who are subject-matter specialists in various areas weigh the information in terms of reliability, validity, and relevance. They integrate the various pieces of data into a meaningful whole, put the information in context, and produce finished intelligence that includes assessments of events or developments and judgments about the implications of the information to the end user.

- **Dissemination.** The last step in the cycle, which logically feeds into the first, is the distribution of the finished intelligence to the consumers whose needs initiated the process. Typically, dissemination is accomplished by means of various distribution lists, each made up on a "need to know" basis. Intelligence may be disseminated by oral briefings, messages or written reports, published studies, and photographs and other media. The continuous flow of accurate, timely naval intelligence is essential to planning successful naval operations. Good intelligence, properly used by commanders, has saved thousands of lives and won many battles.

Types of Intelligence

Intelligence may be classified according to source, such as signals (SIGINT), communications (COMINT), electronics (ELINT), photo (PHOTINT), and human intelligence (HUMINT). It may also be described by the area to which it pertains:

- *Naval intelligence* is concerned mainly with collecting information of interest to the Navy. It includes information about foreign (both friendly and unfriendly) ships, weapon systems, naval strategies and tactics, harbor and port facilities, and any other data that might help the Navy carry out its mission. Intelligence collected at sea or during battles is tactical in nature. By using such intelligence, a commander can try to decide what the intentions of the enemy are, and modify the battle plan accordingly.

- *Air intelligence* is information about the offensive and defensive capabilities of actual or potential enemies and their vulnerability to air attack. Such intelligence may be both strategic and tactical. Air intelligence officers work with specially trained photo interpreters. They study photographs made by satellites and aircraft to try to learn as much as possible about an area of interest.

Spy planes like the SR-71 Blackbird were used extensively during the Cold War era to gather intelligence. The SR-71 could fly at altitudes above 80,000 feet at speeds in excess of Mach 3, above and beyond the effective limits of most contemporary antiair missile systems. (Air Force photo)

During the 1960s and 1970s, special secret high-speed jet aircraft such as the U-2 and SR-71 Blackbird were developed that could fly above the ceilings of most defensive weapons and photograph wide bands of the surface with special high-resolution cameras. When these "spy planes" returned from their missions, air intelligence officers could examine the resulting film and learn a great deal about such things as enemy fortifications, bombing damage to enemy facilities, troop dispositions, and the like. This type of intelligence was extensively used during the Vietnam War and many of the other conflicts involving U.S. forces since then.

The Global Hawk UAV is a large Air Force endurance drone, able to cruise at 400 miles per hour for thirty-five hours. It can scan an area the size of the state of Illinois in just twenty-four hours. (Air Force photo)

During these same years the Navy used stand-off reconnaissance aircraft such as the EA-3, RA3, and EP-3 to gather intelligence by flying near the enemy's borders and coastlines. Supersonic aircraft such as the RF-8, RF-4, and RA-5C were used over land areas to gather photo intelligence and bomb damage assessment (BDA) immediately following air strikes on enemy targets.

In the 1980s and 1990s continuing advances in photographic and space technology made possible the use of Earth satellites to obtain much of the kind of photo intelligence previously available only from reconnaissance aircraft and spy planes. Today's spy satellites can spot objects as small as a grapefruit from their orbits. Some are steerable, meaning that their orbits can be changed at will to observe any area on Earth of particular interest to our intelligence agencies. Some are equipped with infrared detectors that can "see" and instantly report such things as the heat of a missile launch, bomb blast, or a ship or even a submarine operating at shallow depths at sea.

Much use is being made of remote-controlled unmanned aerial vehicles (UAVs) for reconnaissance and intelligence-gathering purposes, as well as clandestine launch platforms for missile attacks on enemy personnel and other high-value targets. They range in size from small drone aircraft to large model airplanes, and can be launched by ships or from impromptu airstrips adjacent to areas of operations. In 2008 U.S. military services had some six thousand UAVs, and they flew a total of some 400,000 hours of missions over Iraq and Afghanistan. Even smaller UAVs fitted with miniature cameras for battlefield intelligence are available for use by ground troops.

The U.S. Intelligence Community

The U.S. *intelligence community* consists of all the agencies and individuals who produce intelligence in the United States. The modern community began to take shape with the passage of the National Security Act of 1947, which, in addition to reorganizing the U.S. armed services, created the National Security Council (NSC) and the Central Intelligence Agency (CIA). The intelligence community as we know it today was established by an executive order of President Ronald Reagan in 1981. As a result of analysis of the failures and shortcomings of the community following the terrorist attacks of 11 September 2001, relationships within the community were greatly modified by the Intelligence Reform and Terrorism Prevention Act of 2004 (IRTPA). One of the major provisions of the act was the establishment of a Director of National Intelligence (DNI), who would henceforth set priorities and manage the budget of the national intelligence community. He is also the intelligence adviser to the NSC. The NSC sets domestic, foreign, and military policy related to national security. It is chaired by the president, and its regular attendees include the vice president, secretaries of state, defense, and treasury, and the DNI. The chairman of the Joint Chiefs of Staff is its military adviser, and other heads of departments and senior officials are invited to attend when appropriate.

There are many federal agencies that play major roles in the U.S. intelligence community. In addition to the CIA, these include the Federal Bureau of Investigation, the Department of Homeland Security, and Department of Defense (DOD) agencies such as the National Security Agency, the Defense Intelligence Agency, and the individual military service intelligence agencies.

The Central Intelligence Agency

The mission of the Central Intelligence Agency (CIA) is to provide the president, National Security Council, and other policy-making government and military officials with comprehensive foreign intelligence on matters related to national security. It also conducts counterintelligence activities and other missions related to foreign intelligence and national security, as directed by the president. Because it is a separate agency, it serves as an independent source of analysis on topics of concern to intelligence consumers at all levels of government and in the military services.

The Federal Bureau of Investigation

The Federal Bureau of Investigation (FBI) is the primary agency of the U.S. Department of Justice. It serves as the chief federal criminal investigative service, as well as the main domestic intelligence

Color-coded terrorism risk advisory scale established by the Department of Homeland Security in 2002.

agency. Its major priorities are protection against domestic terrorism, espionage and other foreign intelligence operations carried out in the United States, and cyber warfare; protection of civil rights; and combating organized, white-collar, and significant violent crime. Headquartered in Washington, D.C. with fifty-six field offices in major cities throughout the U.S., it employs some 30,000 agents, supervisors, lab technicians, and support personnel.

Department of Homeland Security

The Department of Homeland Security (DHS) was established in 2002 to better coordinate all civilian activities related to both defense of the American homeland against terrorist attacks and emergency disaster response, following the September 2001 terrorist attacks on the Pentagon and World Trade Centers. It includes more than twenty formerly separate government agencies, including the U.S. Coast Guard, Customs Service, Secret Service, Immigration and Naturalization Service, and the Federal Emergency Management Agency (FEMA). At the time of its creation it represented the largest reorganization of the federal government in American history, and the most extensive reorganization of government agencies since the National Security Act of 1947. The act creating it also established the Homeland Security Council, consisting of the president, vice president, the head of DHS, and several other cabinet members. With over 200,000 employees, DHS ranks as the third largest cabinet department, after the Department of Defense and Department of Veterans Affairs.

The DHS has oversight responsibility for many aspects of national security and intelligence functions previously scattered among many different federal departments, including domestic terrorist threat assessment, immigration and customs enforcement,

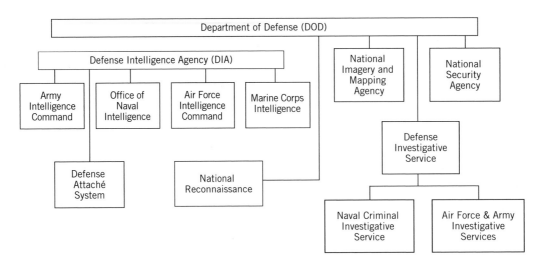

Key intelligence organizations within the Department of Defense.

border and port security, and response to natural disasters and incidents involving nuclear materials or biological or chemical agents.

As a means of keeping the American public advised as to the current level of terrorist threat activity, in late 2002 the DHS instituted a five-level color-coded risk advisory scale ranging from low to severe, that can be widely disseminated via TV and warning signs posted throughout the United States. As the threat level increases, so do security measures at all U.S. government facilities and military bases, including at higher levels searches of all entering vehicles and personnel.

DOD Intelligence Agencies

Eight of the agencies comprising the U.S. intelligence community are within the Department of Defense (DOD). These are the Defense Intelligence Agency (DIA), the National Security Agency (NSA), the National Reconnaissance Office (NRO), the National Imagery and Mapping Agency (NIMA), and the various military service intelligence organizations. Also serving important intelligence roles within DOD are the Defense Attaché System, the Defense Investigative Service (DIS), and the investigative services of each of the military services, including the Naval Criminal Investigative Service (NCIS).

The Defense Intelligence Agency

The Defense Intelligence Agency (DIA) is a designated combat support agency and the senior military intelligence component of the intelligence community. Established in 1961, its primary mission is to provide all-source intelligence to the U.S. armed services, and coordinate all military intelligence resources. Key areas of emphasis include targeting and battle-damage assessment, weap-

ons proliferation, warning of impending crises, support to peacekeeping operations, maintenance of databases on foreign military organizations and their equipment, and, as necessary, support to UN operations and U.S. allies.

The chain of command for the DIA runs from the secretary of defense through the Joint Chiefs of Staff to the director of the DIA. Headed by a three-star military officer, its staff of both military and civilian personnel is mainly located at the Defense Intelligence Analysis Center at Bolling Air Force Base in Washington, D.C.

The National Security Agency

The National Security Agency (NSA) was founded in 1952 by President Harry Truman. As a separately organized combat support agency within DOD, NSA plans, coordinates, directs, and performs signals intelligence and information security functions in support of both defense and nondefense U.S. government activities.

The National Reconnaissance Office

The mission of the National Reconnaissance Office (NRO) is to coordinate the spaceborne reconnaissance needs of the U.S. government. Its mission is accomplished through research, development, acquisition, and operation of the nation's intelligence satellites. Throughout the Cold War years the work of the NRO was so secret that even its existence was classified until 1992.

The director of the NRO is appointed by the president and confirmed by Congress as the assistant secretary of the air force for space. The secretary of defense has the responsibility, together with the director of central intelligence, for the management and operation of NRO. It is staffed by personnel from the CIA, the military services, and DOD.

The National Imagery and Mapping Agency

The National Imagery and Mapping Agency (NIMA) was established in late 1996. The mission of NIMA is to centralize responsibility for the imagery and mapping needs of the U.S. government, a function that before its creation was spread among a dozen different government agencies. With headquarters in Fairfax, Virginia, NIMA operates major facilities in northern Virginia; Washington, D.C.; Bethesda, Maryland; and St. Louis, Missouri. Its work force of some nine thousand people is staffed by mostly civilian professionals in fields such as cartography, imagery analysis, the physical sciences, and computer and telecommunications engineering.

Military Service Organizations

Each military service within DOD, including the U.S. Marine Corps, has its own intelligence organization that concentrates on tactical intelligence unique to its specialized needs. The Navy's organization is called the Office of Naval Intelligence; it will be described in more detail below. However, though military intelligence personnel may train for a wide variety of contingencies, they cannot devote sufficient resources to develop expertise for all possible operations. Military commanders, therefore, have long recognized the value of independently produced national intelligence. When the expertise of their own intelligence organizations falls short, U.S. military commanders will often look to the broader U.S. intelligence community to provide the required expertise.

The U.S. Defense Attaché System (DAS) operates under the DIA. All military personnel assigned to attaché posts are members of the ambassador's staff and have diplomatic passports and status. The mission of a military attaché in a foreign country is to collect military and political information and report it to the DIA and the parent service of the attaché. This is done legally and overtly (openly), not as espionage. The senior armed forces attaché on a diplomatic post is the defense attaché. Other officers are the U.S. Navy attaché, U.S. Army attaché, and U.S. Air Force attaché. The defense attaché may be of any service and is responsible for the supervision and coordination of all attachés assigned. In addition to collecting and reporting information of intelligence interest, attachés represent the DOD to the host government and its armed forces.

Naval Intelligence

The director of the Office of Naval Intelligence (ONI) is responsible for carrying out the intelligence mission of the Navy. When capitalized, the term *Naval Intelligence* refers to this organization. When referring to the information gathered and processed, the term *naval intelligence* is not capitalized.

Located primarily in the National Maritime Intelligence Center in Suitland, Maryland, ONI is the national production center for global maritime intelligence. It is the center of the Navy's expertise for all maritime surface, subsurface, and air-related intelligence issues.

The Naval Criminal Investigative Service (NCIS) is the counterintelligence and investigative arm of the Navy. Its purpose is to investigate personnel and situations when requested by higher authority. NCIS concentrates its efforts solely on criminal and security investigations. Matters investigated must be directly related to the Navy and Marine Corps and must be serious enough to be felony offenses punishable under military law. Typical investigations involve arson, black marketing, espionage, sabotage, narcotics violations, and losses of classified information.

Foreign Intelligence Organizations

The general organization of intelligence agencies in most foreign countries is quite similar to the United States. A central directing organization in the home capital deals with political, economic, and industrial intelligence, security, and military intelligence. Since the main job of the security organization is to safeguard the country's intelligence system and operating methods, details about these organizations in foreign countries are usually scarce. Intelligence organizations are represented abroad by attachés at embassies and other diplomatic posts. Military intelligence is managed by the service intelligence chiefs.

While these aspects of intelligence are similar in most countries, security methods are usually considerably different. In the democracies, security measures are limited by laws that apply to all citizens. In authoritarian countries such as Cuba, China, and Iran, however, various kinds of *secret police* organizations such as the old Soviet KGB are responsible for internal security. Secret police agents are placed in all levels of society in order to get information about their own citizens and to try to stifle any opposition to the government. They may swoop down on unsuspecting citizens and spirit them away for questioning and torture in prisons from which few ever return.

External intelligence and counterintelligence in such countries are handled by highly secretive agencies that are bound by few if any laws and which typically report only to the national leadership. Activities known to fall within the scope of these agencies include sabotage, political and military assassination, and sponsorship of terrorists, spy groups, intelligence groups, and propaganda and agitation groups.

Espionage Operations

Almost all nations have espionage organizations. Many of their operations are carried out by secret agents called spies. They are usually well-trained specialists in either political or military affairs, the two main categories of espionage. They must have a great deal of self-discipline, courage, patience, and ability to see and accurately report important matters. A person who becomes a spy usually does so for one of these reasons: love of own country, hatred of a country or its form of government, or need for money. In addition, fear is often used as a motivator. This is either fear for the spy's own safety or, more commonly, fear that his or her family or relatives will suffer if the individual does not perform satisfactorily.

There is no question about the effectiveness of foreign espionage around the world. Spy rings have been uncovered in the highest levels of government and in the military services of most Western nations. Information about the latest computers, nuclear weapons, submarine quieting systems, and missiles has been stolen by both foreign and domestic spies in America and Western Europe. Radio bugging devices have been found in our embassies in many foreign capitals throughout the world.

Political espionage attempts to get important information about politics, industry, commerce, agriculture, labor, transportation, and other such matters. More recently, industrial espionage has become a major threat to companies developing new technologies in electronics, weapons systems, computers, and various high-value consumer products.

In peacetime diplomats from all countries are expected to observe and report what goes on in the places they are stationed. They must report current events in the host country to their home governments, simply because this information helps maintain relationships between the two countries.

So long as these diplomats conduct themselves in an open (overt) manner and do not attempt to bribe officials, steal documents, or sneak photos of forbidden areas, the host country welcomes them and gives them special privileges. If they are caught violating this trust, however, the host country may demand that they be *recalled* (sent home). Overt collection activities are considered the legitimate duties of diplomats, so they are not considered to be spies under international law.

Espionage, however, does not involve just a few spies and diplomats trying to gather military information. Rather, it is a mass effort, carried out in all fields, by thousands of people. Many of these are one-time informants. The intelligence organizations gather up bits and pieces of information from all over the globe and slowly piece together a story. A single fact dropped unintentionally may prove to be the missing piece of an important puzzle.

The Navy has much valuable information, so it can be expected that attempts are always being made to get answers from naval personnel. New electronic equipment, training exercises, readiness, amount and types of supplies and ammunition aboard, sailing dates and operational schedules, among many other things, are common topics of conversation among Sailors. The person in uniform must always be alert. In the past, agents have been found at naval installations taking pictures and stealing documents, bugging telephones, and talking to personnel when they are off duty.

Counterintelligence and Security

Espionage is combated by counterintelligence. Counterintelligence can be defined as the identification and neutralization of the threat posed by foreign intelligence services, and the manipulation of those services for the manipulator's benefit. The main job of counterintelligence personnel is to prevent espionage and treacherous acts and to seek out and arrest spies.

The chief of naval operations (CNO) controls all policies relating to the security of classified matter in the Navy. Instructions on the security system are issued by the CNO in a publication called the *Security Manual*.

But security rules, by themselves, do not guarantee protection. Many precautions must be taken to reduce the possibility of losses. If classified information or equipment is acquired, viewed, or analyzed by the enemy it is said to have been *compromised* (lost its secrecy). Classified material may be compromised by one of the following means:

- Capture or salvage
- Theft, espionage, observation, or photography
- Interception of communications traffic
- Electronic tracking devices
- Communications traffic analysis
- Cryptanalysis (breaking of codes)
- Carelessness of personnel

Despite the Cold War having ended, the United States remains a primary intelligence target for many countries and terrorist organizations, including some traditional allies who have increased their attempts to acquire economic and corporate secrets. What has changed in the post–Cold War world is the ease with which intelligence gatherers can operate in the United States. The relaxation of tension, plus continual advances in spying technology, have made it increasingly difficult for the United States to implement successful counterintelligence measures.

Security Classifications

In the United States, official material that must be protected in the interest of national defense may be classified in one of three ways, in descending order of importance: top secret, secret, and confidential. These classifications indicate the degree of protection to be given the material, equipment, or information. The appropriate classification is determined by the originator of the material, based on its content. *Top secret* is used for material that could result in great damage to the nation if revealed. *Secret* is for material that could cause serious damage. *Confidential* is for material that could be harmful to national security.

Some classified publications have very limited distribution. These are called *registered publications*. Each one is assigned an account number and is delivered either by an officer in the Armed

Forces Courier Service or from special registered publications vaults. At regular intervals, each of these publications must be accounted for by the command's registered publications custodian, and a report made to higher headquarters. Matter that usually falls into this category includes code and cipher books, communications books, tactical publications, and intelligence manuals.

Each ship, large aircraft, and naval facility has an *emergency destruction bill* for classified materials in the event of imminent capture by an enemy. Aboard ship, if there is no time for burning or shredding them, documents may be placed in weighted bags with holes and dropped into deep water. Coding devices and other classified equipment may be smashed and parts scattered in deep water, or melted by chemical bombs that are ignited by electric batteries.

Security Clearance

Before anyone is allowed to receive, see, or use classified information, he or she must have a *security clearance.* This is a document indicating that the person's background has been properly investigated by the government and stating for which classification level the person is cleared.

Persons who have authorized access to classified information must be of unquestionable loyalty, integrity, trustworthiness, and character. They must have personal conduct and associations that will cast no doubt upon their ability to safeguard classified information. The handling of classified material is a matter requiring the utmost trust and confidence, for the welfare of the whole nation could be at stake.

The existence, nature, content, or whereabouts of classified matter must not be divulged to anyone other than those who are authorized to use it in their official duties. No person is entitled access to classified matter solely because of his or her rank, office, position, or because he or she has a certificate of clearance. The latter only establishes eligibility for access. To whom information can be disclosed is determined not only by the classification of the material and the security clearance of the person, but also, above all, by whether the person has a *need to know* the information to do a job.

Consequences of Security Breaches

There have been several highly publicized incidents of serious security breaches (losses of classified materials or information) in the Navy and other government agencies over the years. One of the worst of these involved the compromise of secret ballistic missile submarine communications systems and other highly classified technology by a ring of individuals led by a Navy warrant officer named John Walker during the 1970s and early 1980s. It was widely concluded that much of the Soviet Navy's rapid advancements in submarine quietness technology in the 1980s could be directly related to the disclosures of Walker and the other members of his group.

Another serious case that surfaced in 1994 was that of a former CIA employee Aldrich Ames and his wife, who were charged in that year with obtaining more than $2.5 million from the Soviet and later the Russian governments for espionage activities they carried out for over nine years. Among other things, they passed to the Soviets the identities of hundreds of U.S. agents in Soviet-controlled countries, some of who were without doubt killed as a result during these years.

All of these individuals were convicted of security violations and are presently serving lengthy sentences in federal prisons.

Why would any loyal American, let alone uniformed naval personnel, engage in activities so harmful to our country? The answers are many, but in the final analysis, they break down into the same kinds of human flaws that have plagued humanity since the beginning of time: lust for power and sex, greed for money and other material benefits, and the inability to withstand blackmail or other kinds of personal threats. Since these human frailties will always be with us, it follows that every Navy person should be continually aware of the damage that a security breach can do to our Navy and our nation, and take all precautions possible to safeguard any classified material or knowledge that may be entrusted to him or her.

Should any Navy person be contacted for potential espionage purposes, or should they wish to report any possible espionage activities or incidents, there is a toll-free phone number that they can call anytime to report such suspicions.

STUDY GUIDE QUESTIONS

1. What is the definition of military and political intelligence?

2. What is the difference between information and intelligence?

3. What are the five steps in the intelligence process?

4. What kind of intelligence is naval intelligence primarily interested in collecting?

5. A. What is air intelligence?

   B. How is it gathered?

6. What is the U.S. intelligence community?

7. What is the CIA?

8. What new department was created in 2002 to coordinate national strategy against domestic terrorism?

9. What is the mission of the Defense Intelligence Agency?

10. What is the mission of U.S. naval and military attachés?

11. What is the organization responsible for carrying out the intelligence mission of the Navy?

12. If persons in a diplomatic status are caught violating their trust, what is likely to happen?

13. What is the loss of classified material or information called?

14. What are some of the ways in which classified material might be compromised?

15. A. What are the three levels of security classification given to official material?

    B. To what degree would national security be damaged by the compromise of each?

CRITICAL THINKING

1. John Walker was a Navy warrant officer who spied for the Soviet government. Research his crimes and list the things he sold to the Soviets and the impact this had on our national security.

2. During World War II the German military used a code machine called ENIGMA. Research this machine, and describe how the Allies broke the ENIGMA code.

3. Devise a secret code using the juxtaposition of letters and numbers. Describe how you would maintain the security of this code. Send a friend a message using your code. How hard do you think it would be to break your code?

VOCABULARY

intelligence	counterintelligence
espionage	DHS
intelligence community	CIA
secret police	overt, covert
classified material	security breach
bugging device	security clearance
compromised	DIA
registered publications	NSA
security classification	NCIS

4 Naval Logistics

World Wars I and II approached in scope what has since been defined as total war, in which the entire resources of the participant countries are called upon for victory. Such emphasis on logistics made these wars unique in the history of the world. Modern logistics may be said to have begun in World War I, when the United States was required to support a large American expeditionary force in Europe.

World War II was fought thousands of miles from the United States, with the exception of antisubmarine warfare along the Atlantic seaboard; logistics became the key to victory. In fact, it took 12 tons of food and equipment to supply each soldier sent overseas, and another ton every month to keep him going.

Today, just as it has since World War II, military planning must consider logistics along with strategy and tactics. Strategy, as discussed earlier in this book, is concerned with the general plan for the employment of the fighting forces. Tactics involves the specific maneuvers and techniques of fighting—the operational execution of the strategic plan. *Logistics* refers to the total process by which the resources of a nation, both material and human, are mobilized and directed toward achieving military goals. Thus, while strategy provides the scheme for the conduct of military operations, logistics provides the means.

Logistics as it applies to the support of naval ships and the shore establishment is referred to as naval logistics. In the follow-ing sections we will take a brief look at some of the areas of concern in modern naval logistics.

Logistics Planning

Were total war to come, the whole national economy would have to be mobilized efficiently. The U.S. national economy is complex. The experience of the last century has indicated that logistic problems of the future probably cannot be solved by plans made hurriedly under stress of war.

Believing that any future war would require total effort and place great strain on our economy, Congress incorporated the lessons of World War II into the national security organization. The National Security Act of 1947 recognizes clearly that responsibility for national security is a matter of concern for the entire nation and is not confined to the military forces alone. This act provides for a comprehensive U.S. security program integrating policies, procedures, and functions of all elements of the government related to national security.

The secretary of defense advises the president concerning the coordination of military, industrial, and civilian mobilization. This includes manpower, effective use of natural and industrial resources for military needs, and the organization of the national economy for war. Similar to the principles of war (discussed in

A C-2A Greyhound launches from the flight deck of the USS *John C. Stennis* (CVN 74) for a logistics mission during Operation Iraqi Freedom. (Josue Escobosa)

unit 1) that apply to all types of combat, there are certain *principles of logistics* that come into play in logistics planning at all levels. These are

- Responsiveness—providing the right support at the right time, at the right place

- Simplicity—avoiding unnecessary complexity in preparing, planning, and conducting logistic operations

- Flexibility—adapting logistic support to changing conditions

- Economy—employing logistic support assets effectively

- Attainability—acquiring the minimum essential logistics support to begin combat operations

- Sustainability—providing logistics support for the duration of the operation

- Survivability—ensuring that the logistic infrastructure survives in spite of degradation and battle damage

Within the Department of the Navy, logistics planning is the responsibility of the operational commander, who must ensure that his or her logistics experts coordinate all operational and logistical plans.

When given a mission, the commander's planning staff analyzes the situation, developing and proposing several possible alternative courses of action. The commander then selects from these the one he or she judges most likely to succeed. In many cases, logistics limitations and plans will become the deciding factor.

Functional Areas of Logistics

All logistics plans take into account six functional areas:

- Supply—includes design, procurement, contracting, receipt, storage, inventory control, and issuance of end items (ships, planes, tanks, etc.), spare parts, and consumables

- Maintenance—actions necessary to preserve, repair, and ensure continued operation and effectiveness of equipment, both afloat and ashore

- Transportation—the movement of units, personnel, equipment, and supplies from the point of origin to the final destination

- Engineering—the construction, damage repair, combat engineering, and maintenance of facilities

- Health services—the provision of medical and dental supplies, blood and blood products, and facilities and services in both combat and noncombat environments

- Other services—the provision of administrative and personnel support to operational forces, including record keeping, disbursing, food services, and legal services

Navy construction battalion rapid response vehicles provide support for an overland logistics mission near Ramadi during Operation Iraqi Freedom. (Michael Lavender)

The products of these six functional areas, when properly taken into account in the commander's operational planning, provide effective logistics support to the operating forces.

Elements of Logistics

Within each of the functional areas described above, there are four elements of logistics that come into play. These are as follows:

- **Acquisition.** This element pertains to procurement of *commodities*, such as food, petroleum, oils, and lubricants (POL), and repair parts; *facilities*, such as buildings and piers; *ordnance*, like missiles, ammunition, and mines; and major weapons and *end items*, such as ships, aircraft, and electronic systems. For the Navy the principal acquisition organizations are the various systems commands, the Defense Logistics Agency (DLA), the General Services Administration (GSA), and the Naval Facilities Engineering Command (NAVFACENGCOM).

- **Distribution.** This element concerns the methods used to get logistics support to the operating forces, taking into account what is being moved, its origin and destination, the lift assets available, and the urgency assigned. A single unified command, the U.S. Transportation Command, is in overall charge of strategic transportation for all U.S. armed services. For deployed forces, some 90 percent of all strategic lift is done by civilian-crewed ships of the Navy's Military Sealift Command. High-priority cargo, mail, and passengers are transported by strategic airlift provided by the Air Force's Air Mobility Command. Once in theater, further transportation is provided by combat logistic force ships that operate with the operating forces, and by boats, vehicles, and aircraft belonging to the deployed forces.

- **Sustainment.** This element pertains to the provision of adequate logistic support to permit continuous operations without interruption, as long as required. Forward-deployed naval forces carry with them sufficient initial stocks to support operations, but these must be replenished as they are consumed. Establishing and maintaining a reliable flow of war matériel, resources, and support services to operating forces is accomplished through the operation and management of supply systems, naval maintenance assets, and bases. In the Navy this element is a primary responsibility of the Naval Supply Systems Command, and for the Marine Corps, the Marine Corps Logistic Command.

- **Disposition.** This element concerns the handling, storage, retrograde (removal from the theater of operations), and disposal of matériel and resources. A major aspect of disposition is the avoidance of any damage to the environment, especially by oil pollution or other hazardous materials. The Navy oil spill response team is one of the largest in existence and has deployed to every major U.S. oil spill in the last three decades, along with personnel of the Coast Guard, the primary service responsible for oil pollution response. The process of disposition begins with the first piece of equipment or major item that must be removed from the operating theater for repair, replacement, or as excess for further distribution, and ends when the last forces depart, which are often the naval forces assigned to most operations.

The foregoing principles, functional areas, and elements of logistics are the building blocks upon which all effective logistics planning is done. All of these must be taken into account in order for any naval operation of any size to be successful.

A Seahawk helicopter conducts vertical replenishment operations from an oiler. (Jessica Bidwell)

Logistics in Modern Warfare

Each of the major U.S. commands in the Atlantic and Pacific regions have formalized contingency plans for what their forces would do and how they would be supported logistically in the event of a future general war. In recognition of the long surface-transportation time required to reach various locations in the interior of Western Europe and the Western Pacific, large stocks of war supplies and ammunition have been prepositioned at key locations such as certain U.S. bases in northern Europe and moored MSC cargo ships (called maritime prepositioned ships, or MPS) at bases in the Atlantic, Pacific, and Indian oceans. Other potential sites for prepositioned stocks are under continuous review as world conditions change. Though there is some risk of capture of these supplies by potential enemies in the regions should war break out, the necessity of timely resupply of U.S. and allied forces already in theater overrides this concern. Such prepositioned stocks would, it

is hoped, be sufficient to sustain military operations until further resupply could be accomplished, most likely by seaborne transport from the United States.

The methods and timing of resupply in any future general war are of growing concern to U.S. planners today because fuel and ammunition and other key consumables would be rapidly expended in the first days of modern warfare. In addition, the continued availability of cargo ships and tankers for wartime needs is questionable, given the steady decline of the U.S. merchant marine in recent years. Almost certainly, one major consequence of the shortage of available merchant ships in any large-scale future war would be a severe reduction of civil air transportation, since most large U.S. airliners would be needed to carry military supplies and personnel. Continuous analysis and planning are required to ensure adequate logistics support of all U.S. and allied armed forces in any future war scenario.

STUDY GUIDE QUESTIONS

1. When did modern logistics begin?

2. What is the relationship between strategy, tactics, and logistics?

3. What will probably have to be done from the logistics standpoint if the United States becomes involved in total war?

4. What are the seven principles of logistics that must be reflected in logistics planning at all levels?

5. What are the six functional areas of logistics?

6. What are the four elements of logistics that come into play in each functional area?

7. What are prepositioned stocks of war matériel intended to do?

CRITICAL THINKING

1. List the advantages and disadvantages of prepositioned war matériel in various locations throughout the world. Based on your list, are such stocks a good or bad idea?

2. There are logistics billets on the staffs of most major commands both afloat and ashore. Should these billets be filled by individuals whose entire careers are spent in logistics, or by individuals who have more generalized backgrounds in operations and other warfare specialties? Give the rationale for your choice.

VOCABULARY

logistics	war matériel
mobilization	acquisition
prepositioned stocks	commodities
POL	NAVFACENGCOM
MPS	

5 Naval Research and Development

The scientific and military strength of the United States depends to a large extent on a successful and comprehensive research program. Research and development (R&D) in the Department of Defense and its military branches is a major effort in terms of personnel, money, and materials.

All military services conduct various R&D programs in their areas of responsibility. In recent years, increasing numbers of these programs have been conducted jointly by the services, as, for example, the development of the next-generation joint strike fighter. The U.S. Coast Guard is also an active participant in the research and development program.

Navy R&D Management

Under the secretary of defense, the secretary of the Navy has policy control over the Navy R&D organization. Ultimate responsibility rests with that person. The assistant secretary of the Navy for research, development, and acquisition is responsible for management and control of R&D matters. The top adviser to these two civilian leaders is the chief of naval research. The chief of naval research is in charge of the basic research program of the Navy, coordinating all Navy efforts with the systems commands.

The agencies that ultimately develop and procure the equipments and weapons required by the Navy are the various systems commands (air, surface, and space), the Office of Naval Research, and the Marine Corps.

Office of Naval Research

Following World War II, naval leaders realized that technological and engineering R&D alone were not sufficient to ensure the long-range technical progress necessary to develop new weapons, equipment, and materials. The Navy, therefore, embarked on a program in the basic sciences that was to form the technical foundation for its research and development effort ever since.

In 1946 Congress authorized the formation of the Office of Naval Research (ONR) in compliance with an earlier recommendation by Navy secretary James Forrestal. The office was charged with planning and conducting a coordinated research effort in every field of basic science, in conjunction with the applied research and engineering development programs of the Navy.

One of the most technologically advanced ships in the U.S. Navy is the trimaran design of littoral combat ship such as the LCS 2 shown here, being built by the General Dynamics Corporation. When complete it will have a top speed of over 45 knots, a crew of fifty, and armament consisting of a SAM launcher, 57-mm gun, two minehunting helicopters, and UAVs.

The principal source of fundamental scientific knowledge in the United States traditionally had been the university research laboratory. Wartime experience showed that there was a need for a mechanism whereby university scientists could help find answers to the Navy's most pressing operational problems. The ONR thus started what was for a time the largest peacetime research program ever supported by a federal agency at educational and nonprofit institutions. This Navy program was an outstanding example of effective and beneficial government-sponsored research, and it continues to this day.

Known as the contract research program, this ONR-sponsored activity advances the search for new knowledge in those fields of science and engineering vital to naval needs and national security.

Under auspices of the program, the nation's finest scientists conduct research for the Navy at nearly every well-known scientific laboratory in the country.

The Office of Naval Research coordinates, executes, and promotes the science and technology programs of the Navy and Marine Corps through schools, universities, government laboratories, and nonprofit and for-profit research organizations. It provides technical advice to the chief of naval operations (CNO) and the secretary of the Navy and works with industry to improve technological manufacturing processes.

Departments within the ONR conduct research and development in information, electronics, and surveillance technologies; ocean, atmosphere, and space technology; engineering, materials, and physical science; human systems; expeditionary warfare; industrial and corporate programs; and industrial programs. It also oversees several special technical programs, among which are ongoing research into future naval capabilities, special science and technology programs, and grand challenges in science and technology for the future.

Under the auspices of ONR, areas of focus within the naval science and technology program in recent years include power generation and energy; maritime domain studies; information, analysis, and communication; naval warrior performance and protection; survivability and self-defense, including missile and torpedo defense; defense against improved explosive devices (IEDs); and many other cutting-edge technologies pertinent to naval warfare.

Naval Research Laboratory

The Naval Research Laboratory (NRL) in Washington, D.C., is the corporate research and development laboratory of the Office of Naval Research. It conducts a broadly based multidisciplinary program of scientific research and advanced technological develop-

An artist's rendering of a new drone for the Marine Corps that would operate from the flight deck of an aircraft carrier or amphibious assault ship, and fly at 300 miles per hour with a 500-pound payload of precision weapons or guns. (American Dynamics Flight Systems)

A demonstration model of a future stealthy robot strike aircraft. They would operate from an aircraft carrier, and be the first wave in a strike to take out enemy air defenses prior to sending in manned aircraft. Such aircraft might someday engage in air-to-air warfare with their enemy robotic counterparts.

ment directed toward maritime applications of new and improved materials, techniques, equipment, systems, and ocean, atmospheric, and space sciences and related technologies.

The NRL engages in research for the physical, engineering, space, and environmental sciences. It conducts exploratory and advanced development programs in response to the Navy's present and future needs and furnishes broad, multidisciplinary support to the Naval Air Warfare Center, the Naval Command, Control and Ocean Surveillance Center, the Naval Surface Warfare Center, and the Naval Undersea Warfare Center.

Naval Oceanographic Research Program

The primary military objective of the Navy's oceanographic program is to advance the knowledge of ocean, coastal, and seabed areas for the purpose of increasing the effectiveness of naval as well as other military weapons systems. This objective includes the design of ships and other equipment to satisfy oceanographic data collection requirements.

A secondary, nonmilitary objective is to advance the knowledge of all aspects of the ocean, coastal, and seabed areas to enable successful exploitation of those areas for economic, scientific, social, political, and prestige gains. This includes cooperation in formulating proposed international law applying to the high seas, territorial seas, continental shelves, and seabed areas.

National defense takes priority over other goals of the oceanographic effort. The Navy, however, is obligated to support the nonmilitary objectives of the national oceanographic program, so it manages ships and facilities to meet both requirements. The largest portion of knowledge gained from Navy oceanographic activities is not classified and is made available to national, international, and private organizations. Consistent with its own effort, the Navy also cooperates with national and private organizations devoted to the study of the marine environment.

Some of the Navy's work is carried out by private oceanographic organizations such as the Scripps Oceanographic Institute in California and Woods Hole Oceanographic Institute in Massachusetts. Other work is done by universities and various technical agencies. Much of the basic and applied research supported by ONR relates closely to the programs of a number of other federal agencies.

Advanced Research

Projects in advanced research are conducted by the Defense Advanced Research Projects Agency (DARPA), a special agency of the Defense Department. The purpose of this agency is to prevent technological surprise from harming U.S. security by sponsoring research in areas of high risk in terms of commercial applicability and profit potential. Private enterprises are reluctant to take on such projects. DARPA's program is structured in three major areas: national-level problems involving threats to U.S. national security;

A new Navy sea control ship such as that shown here will handle surface and undersea surveillance, antisurface and antisubmarine warfare, antiair warfare, and mine warfare, with V/STOL aircraft and helicopters.

operational dominance, wherein advanced systems and technologies are developed that will give U.S. military forces a decisive edge over prospective enemies; and high-risk high-payoff technologies that will enable quantum leaps in U.S. military capabilities.

Under the national-level problem areas are programs that provide support for the global war on terrorism and protection against biological warfare, among other things. Current operational dominance projects include development of advanced manned and unmanned combat systems, advanced C4 (command, control, communications, and computer) systems, and sensors. Areas being addressed under high-risk high-payoff technologies include advanced networking, brain-machine interface technology, biochemistry and biomagnetics, and microelectromechanical systems.

STUDY GUIDE QUESTIONS

1. Who manages the Navy's R&D program?
2. What is the mission of the Office of Naval Research?
3. What kinds of research does the Naval Research Laboratory do?
4. A. What is DARPA?

    B. What are the three main DARPA program areas?

CRITICAL THINKING

1. Should research and development efforts for the military be done exclusively by government laboratories, by private laboratories under contract to the government, or by both? Give the rationale for your answer.

VOCABULARY

ONR	NRL
R&D	DARPA

Military Law

In any organization of people, whether a business, school, community, athletic team, or military unit, there has to be an understanding of what can and cannot be done. There must be a code of law, rules, and established regulations by which all group members conduct themselves. Accordingly, civilized human beings have developed a number of law codes, each designed to fit a particular society.

Some of these law codes, or lists of laws, often studied in high school civics, government, or political science classes, are civil law, constitutional law, criminal law, and international law (discussed in unit 4). This unit will be primarily concerned with another code of laws: military law.

The force of government behind customs and codes of law transforms them into practical laws regulating the daily lives of people. These laws are further defined by court decisions and rulings by judges. To introduce the study of military law, the following sections will briefly cover the development of our various law codes and how they relate to each other in our society.

History of Law Codes

Civil law has a history going back to the first known code compiled by King Hammurabi of Babylon in about 1700 B.C. Roman law, drawn up by Emperor Justinian I (A.D. 527-565), developed into the basic civil law of most European countries. After twelve centuries of legal refinement, it was finally codified by Emperor Napoleon I of France in 1804. It is probably the greatest legacy passed on to modern society by that great leader. Napoleon's Civil Code, as it was called, has become the basic civil law of much of the world. Under the Civil Code, the accused must, to a large extent, prove himself or herself innocent of any charges filed against him or her by the state.

The development of law in English-speaking countries was different. England's King John I was obliged to sign the Magna Carta in 1215. From this beginning, a body of *common law* developed from decisions in the king's courts. Later, the burden of both criminal and civil cases became too great for a single court system, so civil cases were referred to the Court of Chancery. This developed into the body of *civil* or *equity law* in England, most of the British Commonwealth, and the United States. It is used to restore rights, compensate damages, and correct injuries in civil cases.

Criminal law, retained by the King's Court, was derived from that part of English common law designed to punish or deter wrongdoers by bringing them to court for justice. Trial by a jury of peers—citizens of equal status under the law—is a specific right under English common law and guaranteed to each American citizen in the Sixth Amendment to the U.S. Constitution. A fundamental feature of English and U.S. law is that the accused is presumed innocent until the evidence brought before the jury proves guilt beyond any reasonable doubt. This codified system of law is both revolutionary and evolutionary as compared to the Napoleonic Code.

The U.S. Constitution and Military Law

In the United States, all law is based on the Constitution, or, as it is called, *constitutional law*. The Constitution guarantees the rights of all citizens to equitable treatment under the law. It gives the Congress the power to provide and maintain a Navy and to establish rules and regulations for its operation, which collectively are referred to as *military law*.

In civilian life, criminal law seeks to protect society from the acts of its irresponsible members, without infringing upon their individual rights under the Constitution. Military law similarly restrains individuals for protection of the whole military society, but also establishes the prescribed conduct that all members must observe to preserve order and discipline.

Some acts considered rights in a civilian society might be offenses in a military society. For instance, "telling off the boss" is not unlawful for an American civilian, but in the military services it could be an offense punishable by court-martial. Civilians can quit their jobs if they do not like them; in the military, that constitutes a major offense called *desertion*. In civilian life, if people decide to jointly protest their working conditions or pay, they may strike; in the naval service, that action constitutes the offense of *mutiny*.

The defense of the nation is not the kind of business in which citizens can do their own thing when, or if, it pleases them. The demands of military service are such that positive control and an established code of conduct are required always. Readiness for emergencies, as well as coping with the emergency itself, demands a code of law differing in some degree from the normal civil code.

Military law is the law regulating the military establishment, including the military justice system. It is designed to preserve good order and discipline within the military service, in the same way that state and federal laws are designed to preserve good order in the civilian community. U.S. military law, like U.S. civil law, requires that the rights of each individual be protected and seeks to assure every person in uniform equal justice under the law.

The laws that govern the United States Navy had their origin in 1775, when the "Rules for the Regulation of the Navy of the United Colonies" were first established. These first laws were based largely on British common and Royal Navy admiralty law. Over the years since their formulation, the U.S. Navy laws have undergone constant modification and improvement to meet changing requirements up to the present day.

Navy Regulations

This is the set of basic laws governing the Navy today. *Navy Regulations* provides the broad guidelines for the organization and administration of the Navy, and specifies particular actions that can and cannot be done, and how the chain of command should handle these actions.

Important Navy Regulations

On all ships and stations, the most important articles of *Navy Regulations* are posted on bulletin boards or included in the *Ship's Organization and Regulations Manual*. Often, selected articles are quoted in the *Plan of the Day*, which is a chronology of planned events and important notes published daily and posted throughout the command. Some Navy regulations often posted and quoted are excerpted below:

1110. Standards of Conduct

All Department of the Navy personnel are expected to conduct themselves in accordance with the highest standards of personal and professional integrity and ethics.

1145. Service Examinations

Persons in the Department of the Navy, without proper authority, shall not have in their possession, obtain, sell, publish, give, purchase, receive or reproduce any examination paper, or any copy thereof, or answer sheet thereto, for any examination whatsoever which has been, is, or is to be, administered within the Department of the Navy.

1151. Direct Communication with the Commanding Officer

The right of any person in the naval service to communicate with the commanding officer in a proper manner, and at a proper time and place, shall not be denied or restricted.

1162. Alcoholic Beverages

Except as may be authorized by the secretary of the Navy, the introduction, possession or use of alcoholic beverages on board any ship, craft, aircraft, or in any vehicle of the Department of the Navy is prohibited.

1164. Equal Opportunity and Treatment

Equal opportunity shall be afforded to all on the basis of individual effort, performance, conduct, diligence, potential, capabilities and talents without discrimination as to race, color, religion, creed, sex or national origin.

1165. Fraternization Prohibited

Personal relationships between officers and enlisted members that are unduly familiar and that do not respect differences in grade or rank are prohibited.

1167. Supremacist Activities

No person in the naval service shall participate in any organization that espouses supremacist causes; attempts to create illegal discrimination based on race, creed, color, sex, religion, or national origin; advocates the use of force or violence against the government of the United States or the government of any state, territory, district, or possession thereof . . . or otherwise engages in efforts to deprive individuals of their civil rights.

Cruel and unusual punishments are forbidden under the UCMJ, in contrast to the days of sail, when flogging with a cat-o'-nine-tails was common.

The Uniform Code of Military Justice (UCMJ)

The trial and punishment of offenders in the U.S. armed forces are covered by a set of laws named the Uniform Code of Military Justice (UCMJ). The word *uniform* here means that the code is the same for all the services. The *Manual for Courts-Martial, United States* (MCM) and the *Manual of the Judge Advocate General* supplement the UCMJ and deal particularly with the administration of the law as decreed in *Navy Regulations* and the UCMJ.

All military leaders, especially officers, are responsible for ensuring that their knowledge of the code is adequate. They must know the fundamentals of military law. Officers must know the basics of court procedures, for they may be called upon at any time to participate in the conduct of a military court, or to investigate matters that have some bearing in such a court.

Since Navy personnel agree to abide by the Navy's law and regulations in their oath of enlistment, it stands to reason that each Navy person must learn what these laws are. Congress and the Navy have taken steps to ensure that all persons entering the Navy will know the laws and regulations most likely to affect them at their ship or station. Article 137 of the UCMJ directs that particular articles of the code be carefully explained to every enlistee at the time of entry on active duty, after six months of active duty, and at the time of reenlistment. It also requires that a complete copy of the UCMJ be made available to every enlisted person.

Overview of UCMJ Articles

The 146 articles making up the UCMJ are divided into twelve groupings. The first nine deal with general provisions, rules for apprehension and restraint, and the conduct of nonjudicial punishment (NJP) and courts-martial. Group 10, comprised of articles 77–134 and dealing with specific infractions of military law, is known as the *punitive articles*. These articles address acts that are in direct violation of acceptable military and, in many cases, civil law, and that would constitute a court-martial offense. They include offenses such as murder, assault, and larceny, and infractions against military behavior such as disobedience of lawful orders, absence without leave, and insubordination.

Under Article 55 of the UCMJ, cruel and unusual punishments are prohibited. In the days of sail, punishments by flogging, branding, or tattooing on the body were not uncommon. Today they are strictly forbidden. Public punishments that might tend to ridicule—such as shaving the head, placing offenders in the stocks, tying them up by the thumbs, and forcing them to carry about placards or heavy loads—are also prohibited by the UCMJ. Placing a prisoner "in irons," except for handcuffs when traveling in custody, is likewise not allowed.

More detailed study of the articles of the UCMJ may be done by referring to the MCM or to the text *Naval Law*, published by the Naval Institute Press.

STUDY GUIDE QUESTIONS

1. Why have societies developed codes of laws?

2. How do laws come into force?

3. What is the basic difference between the European Civil Code and English common law?

4. What is the basis of all U.S. law?

5. What is meant by a trial by a jury of peers?

6. Why is there a separate body of military law?

7. What is the relationship between discipline and military law?

8. What is the basic requirement of both military and civil law pertaining to individual rights?

9. What is the purpose of *Navy Regulations*?

10. Under *Navy Regulations*, what is the rule concerning the following subjects?

    A. Communications with the commanding officer

    B. Examinations

    C. Equal opportunity

    D. Alcoholic beverages

11. Which three publications explain all matters concerning U.S. military law?

12. Why must naval personnel be familiar with the UCMJ?

13. What kinds of cruel and unusual punishments are prohibited by Article 55 of the UCMJ?

CRITICAL THINKING

1. Research the fundamental difference between the presumed guilt or innocence of the accused under the English and U.S. system of law as opposed to the French system based on the Napoleonic code. Which do you think is better? Why?

VOCABULARY

regulations	nonjudicial punishment
common law	larceny
criminal law	court-martial
civil law	UCMJ articles

2 Discipline and Punishment

Military leaders must be alert to all actions by subordinates, praising when a good job is done, but correcting, and even punishing, if poor work or breaches in military discipline occur. The senior's approach must be one of continuing alertness, with consistent and fair actions taken in all cases.

A breach of discipline cannot be disregarded one day and rebuked the next. Under such conditions, personnel do not know where they stand and cannot establish a pattern of conduct that is consistent. If rules are ignored or regulations disobeyed and no one in authority seems to care, there is bound to be confusion. If regulations cannot or will not be enforced, it is better not to issue them in the first place.

Discipline can be strict without being stiff and formal. For a first offense, a light punishment that is prompt and just may serve far better than a severe one; a private reprimand at the start of a potential problem may prevent a later appearance at captain's mast or court-martial. Timely action is essential, since it leaves no doubt in the mind of the offender about the reason for the punishment. Delay fosters resentment toward the system.

Punishment must be just. In order to accomplish its purposes, it must be recognized as just and fair by the offender and shipmates. Penalties imposed must not be out of proportion to the seriousness of the offense. If the leader is exacting but fair, subordinates will not only live up to the leader's demands, but also respect and admire his or her attitude.

The *Bluejacket's Manual* states that when offenses against good order and discipline are punished by proper naval authority, punishment is imposed for three reasons: to deter offenders from breaking the rules again, to encourage them to do their duty, and to set an example. Note that these are positive reasons, not negative ones.

The desired goal of the Navy is positive discipline based on respect for leaders, confidence in their justice and fairness, and the compulsion of moral force. Discipline based on force alone cannot endure. Long-term discipline must be stimulated or induced from within the individual. True discipline develops loyalty and intelligent initiative.

Punishment is not personal, and it is not vindictive. It is not inflicted as revenge for misconduct, nor can it serve to right any wrong that might have resulted from any dereliction of duty. When seniors find it necessary to reprimand or place a person on report, they are officially doing their duty. All personnel in the Navy are obliged to obey and strictly follow the regulations, and to do so promptly. Therefore, lawful punishments imposed because of derelictions of duty should be expected. When fair punishment is meted out, it should be accepted and regarded constructively; that is, a lesson should be learned from the experience.

George Washington, like all great leaders, was a sound disciplinarian. He counseled his officers in 1776, "The best general advice I can give is to be strict in your discipline; that is, to require nothing unreasonable of your officers and men, but to see that whatever is required be punctually complied with. Reward and punish every man according to his merit, without partiality or prejudice."

Apprehension, Arrest, Restriction, and Confinement

Apprehension is the taking of a person into custody. *Arrest* is the restraint of a person by an order directing that person to remain within certain specified limits. Arrest is not imposed as punishment for an offense; the restraint is binding upon the arrested person by virtue of a moral and legal obligation to obey the arrest order, not by physical force. If under arrest, a person cannot be required to perform full military duty.

Instead of arrest, an accused person may be *restricted* to specified areas. The person may be required to perform all usual military duties while under such restriction. This is the usual form of restraint for persons awaiting captain's mast, or for persons awaiting court-martial on other than the most serious charges.

Confinement in brig or jail is physical restraint depriving a person of freedom. Confinement is not imposed pending trial unless deemed necessary to ensure the presence of the accused or because of the seriousness of the offense charged. Confinement must be imposed legally by oral or written orders.

Persons under arrest or confinement must be advised that they have the right to consult with a lawyer, that the lawyer may be present at any investigations, and that the lawyer may be either retained at the individual's own expense or appointed by the military authority without cost. No self-incriminating statement made in violation of Article 31 of the Uniform Code of Military Justice (UCMJ) is admissible in a trial by court-martial.

Initiating and Preferring Charges

In the Navy the usual procedure for initiating and preferring charges against enlisted personnel consists of submitting a written report detailing the alleged offense to the executive officer, or other officer designated by the commanding officer. The form utilized is called a *Report and Disposition of Offenses Slip*. It contains all the necessary information to process the case, including names of witnesses. Any commissioned officer or petty officer who sees a breach of discipline afloat or ashore may place naval personnel on report. For example, in the case of lateness in returning to the ship from liberty, the officer of the deck would place the offender on report as that person came aboard.

The formal written report consists of two parts: the technical charge and the specification(s). The charge tells what article of the UCMJ the accused is alleged to have violated. The specifications set forth the specific facts and circumstances involved with the violation. The executive officer (XO) must check the charges and specifications to ensure they are legally correct. The XO advises the accused of all particulars in the case, including the charges, witnesses, accuser, constitutional rights under the UCMJ, and rights concerning possible nonjudicial punishment (NJP) or court-martial proceedings.

After the executive officer reviews the charges, a preliminary investigation of the charges is begun, either by the executive officer or by an investigating officer he or she appoints. If the facts in the case are found to warrant disciplinary action, the investigating officer will fill out a charge sheet. If the investigating officer feels that a court-martial is not warranted, as is the case for most reported offenses, the facts are reported to the executive officer, and the accused is brought to nonjudicial punishment (captain's mast) for the alleged offense.

Preliminary Inquiry

Before taking any kind of disciplinary action, it is always necessary and wise to review all the facts. A step somewhat beyond the preliminary investigation leading to a captain's mast is the *preliminary inquiry*. Essentially, the inquiry is an informal investigation conducted for the purpose of determining whether or not an offense chargeable under the UCMJ has been committed, and whether reasonable grounds exist to support the allegation that the accused committed the offense. The officer making the preliminary inquiry collects and examines all evidence that could bear on the guilt or innocence of the accused. The officer also looks for facts in *mitigation* or *extenuation*, that is, circumstances that might tend to provide some plausible reason for the offense or lessen the punishment imposed.

If naval personnel are found to have violated either *Navy Regulations* or the UCMJ, they may then be subject to appropriate disciplinary procedures. Such procedures can range from informal oral or written rebukes to military trials called courts-martial in the more serious cases. The following sections will go into the conduct of these disciplinary procedures, including the makeup and conduct of military trials, the punishments that can be awarded by them, and the infractions of the UCMJ that may lead to such awards.

Disciplinary Actions

There are two basic classes of official naval disciplinary action: nonjudicial punishment, better known as *captain's mast*, and courts-martial. Captain's mast, often simply referred to as "mast," is a name that has come down from early sailing days. At that time, the usual setting for naval justice was on the weather deck, at the foot of the ship's mainmast. Often the whole crew was assembled to hear the proceedings and to observe the punishment, sometimes flogging with a cat-o'-nine-tails. In the Marine Corps, captain's mast proceedings are referred to as "office hours."

Commanding officers (COs) may impose nonjudicial punishment for minor offenses upon subordinate officers and enlisted personnel. This authority cannot be delegated unless COs are generals or flag officers or have unique senior responsibility in which they exercise general court-martial jurisdiction. Captain's mast is the cornerstone of the whole structure of naval justice and discipline.

Military offenses, as distinguished from common misdemeanors or minor crimes, may be divided into two classes: those involving neglect of duty, and those involving deliberate violations of instructions, orders, or regulations. Offenses classified as neglect of duty may result in punishment ranging from loss of liberty to that awarded by a court-martial. Deliberate violations of instructions, orders, or regulations are usually tried by court-martial. Such an offense is often of concern more for the defiance of authority it displays than for the consequences of the act itself. Offenses involving moral turpitude, such as theft, forgery, or serious acts against others, invariably result in adjudication by court-martial.

Military courts are conducted with the same care and formality as civilian courts. Great responsibility rests upon the officers or petty officers assigned court duties. The court must be conducted with dignity and ensure swift, efficient administration of justice. Being dealt with fairly and forthrightly in all matters brought before a court is the right of each person accused under the Constitution, the Uniform Code of Military Justice, and the *Manual for Courts-Martial*.

Nonjudicial Punishment

Prior to a captain's mast, the executive officer (XO) will normally hold a preliminary mast. Often called the *screening mast*, it is usually conducted almost exactly like captain's mast, except that the executive officer's purpose is to determine the gravity of the case and to ascertain the facts so that action may be recommended to the commanding officer. XOs may not assign punishment, but if conditions justify, they may dismiss the charges, since they have the responsibility for the routine, efficiency, and discipline of their units under their commanding officers.

Following the screening mast, the XO will furnish the CO with a list of any personnel upon whom charges have been preferred, whom the XO believes should appear at mast. The captain will hold captain's mast at a time and place most convenient for all concerned. All arrangements, including notification of the accused and witnesses and the accused person's division officer and leading petty officer, will be made by the executive officer and staff, including the master-at-arms force, the legal yeoman, and the personnel officer.

At the start of captain's mast, the captain will first warn the accused and any witnesses about the possible effect of their answers and explain their rights. These rights are similar to those recited by an investigating officer in a preliminary inquiry.

As each individual case is called before the CO, the accused and his or her division officer step forward. The charges and specifications (details of the infraction) are read, and the accused is asked if these charges are understood. The captain then hears the accused person's statement and that of any witnesses. The captain may ask the person's division officer and leading petty officer for comments concerning performance of duty. The personnel officer will provide the person's official record to the captain so that careful review can be made before any decision in the matter is reached. At all times during the procedure, the dignity, formality, and seriousness of a higher court are strictly maintained.

In passing judgment, the commanding officer may dismiss the case, officially warn the accused, administer an oral or written admonition or reprimand, administer punishment, or order the accused to be tried by court-martial. Punishments that may be awarded at captain's mast to enlisted personnel include an official admonition or reprimand, confinement on bread and water for a period not exceeding three days (rating of E-3 and below), correctional custody not exceeding thirty days, forfeiture of one-half pay not exceeding two months, restriction not exceeding sixty days, and reduction in pay grade to the next inferior level. The commanding officer may apportion the punishment among two or more of the above options.

Officers may be awarded nonjudicial punishment by senior officers in command, but they may not be confined, put in correctional custody, given extra duty, or reduced in rank. They may be placed under arrest in quarters, often referred to as "being in hack," or restricted from going ashore on liberty. One-half of their pay may be forfeited for not more than two months. In any event, an official letter to the chief of naval personnel by the commanding officer is required, and notation on the officer's next fitness report will be made.

Any person who considers the punishment to be unjust may make a written appeal to the commanding officer's superior authority. If the senior feels there has been a miscarriage of justice, the punishment may be modified or set aside, but it may not be increased, and a different punishment may not be awarded.

The Military Courts-Martial

When nonjudicial punishment is considered to be inadequate for an offense charged, the commanding officer may refer the case to one of three types of court-martial. In increasing order of severity, these are the summary, special, and general courts-martial. Severity, in this case, means the maximum punishments that may be awarded by the court.

A *summary court-martial* is convened by a commanding officer to administer prompt justice for relatively minor offenses through a simple court procedure. Only enlisted personnel may be tried by a summary court-martial. A summary court consists of one commissioned officer appointed by the commanding officer, preferably in naval courts a lieutenant or senior. This officer should be neither the accuser nor the investigator in the case, and should not be associated closely with the accused.

During the trial the summary court represents both the government and the accused; in other words, that person is both prosecuting attorney and defense counsel. Although the accused is not entitled to a military defense council, he or she may hire a civilian lawyer at his or her own expense. The summary court investigates both sides of the matter and ensures that the interests of both the government and the accused are safeguarded. Investigation beyond fair inquiry and ensuring that the person understands the charges is not required if the accused pleads guilty. If found guilty, the accused is advised of the right to present matters in extenuation or mitigation, to be considered by the summary court when awarding punishment.

Punishments authorized by the summary court are similar to those that may be awarded by the commanding officer at mast: confinement for not more than thirty days, forfeiture of two-thirds pay for one month, and reduction in pay grade. At the end of the trial, the verdict is announced, and if the accused has been convicted, the sentence of the court is pronounced. A record of the conviction and any punishment awarded is made in the individual's service record. Following the proceedings, the person is restored to duty within the limitations imposed by the summary court's punishment.

A *special court-martial* can be convened by a commanding officer to try cases involving offenses that warrant greater punishment than a summary court can award. The special court-martial has jurisdiction to try anyone subject to the UCMJ for any noncapital offense made punishable by the code, and some capital offenses if authorized by the president. The commanding officer, as convening authority for the court, draws up a convening order that specifies the time and place of meeting of the special court and appoints not less than three members to it.

The convening authority may also have a military judge—a law officer certified by the judge advocate general—appointed to the court, if available. After consultation with the defense counsel, the accused may request to have only this military judge serve

A Navy legalman acting as trial counsel makes an opening statement during a mock court-martial staged for a group of NJROTC cadets. (Scott Thornbloom)

as the special court. If the judge approves, he or she will serve as a one-person special court, with sole responsibility for conduct of the trial. An accused enlisted person may also request that one-third of the special court be made up of enlisted personnel. The convening authority may grant this if enlisted people with suitable qualifications are available from another unit to sit on the court. All members of any court should be senior to the accused.

The convening authority appoints an officer as trial counsel to conduct the case for the government; this person acts as prosecuting attorney. Another officer is appointed to act as defense counsel for the accused. The accused is afforded the right to have their own counsel for the defense. The accused can choose a civilian counsel paid at his or her own expense, military counsel of his or her own selection if such is reasonably available, or the appointed defense counsel.

The senior member of the special court-martial is the president, unless a military judge is detailed. Then that person will be the president of the court, even if the judge is not the senior member assigned. The grade of the president should be lieutenant or above. The president rules on legal procedures during the trial and instructs the court on the elements of each offense charged prior to closure of the court for vote, as well as what constitutes the presumption of innocence, reasonable doubt, and burden of proof. Before closure of the court for the vote on the sentence, the president advises it regarding the maximum authorized punishment for each offense. If president, the military judge is not considered a member of the court and does not vote on the guilt or innocence

of the accused, so there must be at least three other individuals serving as members.

The accused, on advice of counsel, may exercise what is known as a *peremptory challenge* of any member of the court. If exercised, the challenged member is dismissed from court duties by the president. No reason for the peremptory challenge need be given. If such challenge reduces the court membership below three, the convening authority must appoint another member.

Members of the special court-martial hear the evidence, determine the guilt or innocence of the accused, and, if guilty, render a proper sentence. In most cases, convictions and sentences require a two-thirds majority. Voting is by secret ballot, and all members must vote.

A special court-martial may adjudge punishment including a bad conduct discharge (BCD), confinement not exceeding twelve months, forfeiture of pay not exceeding two-thirds pay per month for up to twelve months, or (for enlisted) reduction to the lowest pay grade. Apportionment of punishments may be made as by a summary court-martial.

A *general court-martial* is the highest military tribunal. It may be convened only by the president, the secretaries of the various services, a flag officer in command of a unit or activity of the Navy or Marine Corps, a general officer in command, the commanding officer of a naval station or larger shore activity beyond the continental limits of the United States, and other commanding officers specifically designated by the president or service secretary. A general court-martial consists of a military judge and at least five members. Enlisted members may serve on the court if the accused requests. As with a special court-martial, the accused may request in writing, subject to the approval of the military judge, that the case be heard by the military judge alone.

A general court-martial has jurisdiction to try persons subject to the UCMJ for any offense punishable by the code. A general court-martial may also try any person who might be subject to trial by military tribunal, including civilians in situations in which martial law has been officially declared because of a breakdown of normal civilian authority.

Court procedures and responsibilities of the judge and members of the court and counsel are the same as in a special court-martial. The principal difference between the two is the greater severity of punishment possible in the general court-martial. These include all those punishments authorized in the UCMJ for the offenses the accused is found to have committed. These include death (for desertion in time of war, mutiny, sedition, or spying), confinement for life, dishonorable discharge, bad conduct discharge, dismissal of an officer, and total forfeiture of pay during the remaining period of a person's obligated service.

Review of Courts-Martial

After a court-martial has been completed, the convening authority performs an automatic review of each court-martial they convene to see that the trial court acted correctly, the accused person was not denied any rights to which they were entitled, and any sentence adjudged was not illegal or too severe. Recommendations from a staff judge advocate or legal officer will be given as necessary. After this careful review the convening authority may approve or disapprove the findings and sentence, and change either or both of them. He or she may reduce or suspend the sentence, or change it to a different one providing the severity of the punishment is not increased. When a trial results in an acquittal (finding of not guilty), the convening authority may not change it, or send the case back for retrial.

This review process is similar to the appeal in a civilian court conviction, except that in the military the review is done by higher authority in the chain of command, and is automatic. An appeal of a civilian court conviction is made to a higher court in the system, and will only be granted if reasonable grounds for one can be shown.

In the case of a summary or special court-martial, the convening authority forwards the trial record, along with recommendations, to the next superior with general court-martial jurisdiction for that officer's review. There, the staff legal officer furnishes a second legal opinion on the case. The senior may override the convening authority's recommendation if an error is found, call for a retrial, set aside in whole or in part findings of guilt and the sentence, or mitigate or suspend any part of an unexecuted portion of the sentence. Again, an acquittal may not be changed, nor any punishment increased.

A finding of any court-martial that awards severe punishment such as a bad conduct discharge must be sent beyond the officer exercising general court-martial jurisdiction to the Office of the Judge Advocate General (JAG) of the Navy. There, a Court of Military Review consisting of a three-judge appellate review panel carefully reviews every case in which an approved sentence affects a flag officer, or in which a sentence imposing the death penalty, dismissal of an officer, a dishonorable or bad conduct discharge, or confinement for one year or more has been imposed.

Above the Court of Military Review is a "supreme court" of military justice, the Court of Military Appeals. This court is composed of three civilian judges appointed by the president and confirmed by the U.S. Senate. An offender whose conviction has been upheld by the Court of Military Review has the right to petition the Court of Military Appeals to review the case. Such appeals are not automatic. If the petition is granted, the convicted person is entitled to a lawyer who will prepare a brief and argue the case before the court. Civilian counsel may be employed if desired.

Civil Jurisdiction

Military service does not free a person from the obligation to obey laws governing the civilian population when he or she is among them. Military personnel are subject also to civil courts when they are within civil jurisdiction. In general, offenses committed by a service person off base in civilian clothes against a civilian, or against some element of the civil government, lack the necessary service connection to make them military offenses punishable under the UCMJ. Since there are many possible sets of circumstances, it is often necessary for a court to make the determination as to whether or not the offense was service connected.

Examples of civil cases of this type that have occurred include not paying personal debts, wrecking a borrowed car, damaging furniture in a hotel, speeding on city streets, assault, and disorderly conduct out of uniform in a public place. While these cases may initially fall strictly within civilian jurisdiction, they may also become involved with military law. For instance, suppose a speeding, drunken, and disorderly charge is filed by the local police, and the service person is held in jail pending disposition of the case. If that imprisonment extends beyond the time of authorized leave or liberty, the service person is then chargeable under the UCMJ for unauthorized absence. Additionally, the person could be charged under Article 111 for drunken or reckless driving and under the General Article for bringing discredit upon the Navy.

If a service member is held by civil authorities, immediate steps should be taken to notify the commanding officer. If the person is acquitted of the charges, military charges normally will not be filed for the period of enforced absence. If the accused is found guilty and detained, the entire period of absence is considered as lost time for pay purposes, and that period is charged as unexcused absence.

Separations from the Service

As mentioned earlier, separation from the military service by award of court-martial is considered an extremely severe punishment. A bad conduct discharge may be awarded by either a special court-martial or general court-martial; a dishonorable discharge may be awarded only by a general court-martial.

Less severe separations from the service, however, may be administered in special cases under the UCMJ and other legislation and statutes established by Congress. Officers may have their commissions revoked prior to the time they complete three continuous successful years of commissioned service. This may be for disciplinary reasons or for other overriding needs of the service. Regular Navy officers holding permanent commissions may be discharged if their performance is adjudged unsatisfactory at any time prior to completion of twenty years of service. Lieutenants (junior grade) and lieutenants are subject to discharge if they twice fail selection for promotion. An officer facing disciplinary action may submit a resignation from the service; separation will be effected if the resignation is accepted by the secretary of the Navy.

The "character" of the discharge from the naval service is very important. The separation may be "under honorable conditions" or "under conditions other than honorable." The character of the discharge represents the opinion of the Navy concerning the circumstances of the separation. This character is very important in connection with veterans' benefits such as G.I. Bill education, reemployment rights, and pensions. Further, many employers are inclined to refuse employment to persons who have an inferior type of separation from the armed forces. Most large employers and professional schools inquire searchingly into armed forces experience and the character of the separation received. They often prevent entry into their company or school if the conditions are other than honorable.

Administrative separations with either character of discharge are also legally permissible under certain conditions. Broadly grouped under a heading of "undesirable," such conditions include incompatibility with service life, educational level and potential below-minimum standards (which precludes advancement to higher pay grade), persistent irresponsibility in financial management (which tends to bring discredit upon the Navy), and immoral standards of conduct evidenced by drug use or alcohol abuse, failure to pay just debts, repetitive sexually transmitted disease infections, or other abnormal social behavior.

STUDY GUIDE QUESTIONS

1. Why must discipline be handled in a consistent manner?
2. What is the basic difference between arrest and restriction?
3. Who may place offenders on report, and under what circumstances?
4. What is the purpose of the executive officer's screening mast?
5. What five judgment possibilities exist for the commanding officer after hearing a mast case?
6. What are the three types of courts-martial, in ascending order of seriousness?
7. What is unique about the tasks of a summary court officer?
8. What are the duties of the convening authority concerning a court-martial?
9. What are the tasks of a military judge if assigned to a four-person special court?
10. What are the court duties of the trial and defense counsels?
11. What is a peremptory challenge?
12. When may a general court-martial try civilians?
13. What punishments may be awarded by a general court-martial?
14. What is the purpose of a court-martial review?
15. How does the military review of a court-martial compare with a civilian appeal?
16. What are the functions of the Court of Military Review and the Court of Military Appeals?
17. When are service personnel subject to civil law?
18. What two kinds of adverse discharges may be awarded by courts-martial?

CRITICAL THINKING

1. Compare and contrast the rights of the accused under U.S. civil law as opposed to military law. Under which system if either do you think the rights of the accused are better protected?

2. What are the fundamental differences between lawful conduct of corporate officers in civilian life as opposed to leaders in the military services?

VOCABULARY

arrest	custody
restriction	reprimand
breach of discipline	peremptory challenge
infraction	appellate
allegation	convening authority
self-incrimination	dishonorable discharge
mitigation	administrative separation
extenuation	court-martial
jurisdiction	captain's mast
nonjudicial punishment	bad conduct discharge

International Law and the Sea

Just as there are dealings, arrangements, and contracts between people and companies, so there are international relations among the different countries of the world. These relations have evolved over many centuries, during which time the countries have developed their own culture, language, traditions, and codes of law. Each nation has always considered its most important objective the protection of its people and its boundaries against outside threat. Various countries have devised many concepts and policies to assist in this endeavor, such as isolationism, alliances, diplomacy, and powerful armed forces. They have worked out commercial and trade agreements to benefit their economies. They have cooperated to exchange culture and science. They have established the International Court of Justice and the United Nations as means of settling disputes. And they have gone to war with each other for good reasons and bad, both to survive and to conquer.

During the course of these events, the nations of the world have developed a body of rules under which they deal with each other. These rules, and their application, are called *international law*. Some of this law is formal, set forth in treaties and agreements, and some is informal, unwritten yet legally binding because of tradition and custom. The need for such a body of law has become increasingly great as the world has become increasingly more complex. Near-instantaneous communication, rapid travel, and the increasingly interdependent nature of the world economy all give rise to the need for an effective body of international law.

This unit will provide an overview of international law and the collective security arrangements that govern much of the present-day relationships among the sovereign states of the world. It will also discuss the fundamental precepts of the international law of the sea and the laws of war at sea.

Fundamentals of International Law

In order for nations to be able to conduct relations with each other on matters such as trade, exchange of money, tourists, boundary questions, communications, mail, and a host of other subjects, each of the contracting parties must be an independent and sovereign state. This means that the nation is free of foreign control and is able to conduct its own business in a legal manner.

In the United States, the Department of State handles most of our government's relations with other nations. Often, the business between our nation and others is conducted by our *ambassadors*—accredited persons who represent our government in the capitals of the foreign country. These ambassadors, on direction of our government, often engage in talks called *negotiations* with representatives of the host government. From these negotiations come treaties of friendship, military alliances, and commercial agreements that are mutually beneficial.

International Law and Diplomacy

In order to reach an understanding of what international law is, it might be helpful to consider the two component words individually. *International* means between nations, or between citizens of different nations. *Law* may be defined as "all the rules and principles of human conduct established and enforced by the authority, legislation, or custom of a recognized governing power." In combination, the words *international law* have been defined as "the system of rules and principles, founded on treaty, custom, precedent, and consensus, which civilized sovereign nations recognize as binding on the mutual relations between them." Some of this law is formal as prescribed in treaties and agreements, and some is informal, unwritten but legally functional because of tradition and custom. International law is divided into public and private bodies of law. The former deals with relations between sovereign states, and the latter with relations between individuals in different countries. Public international law will be the main focus of this text.

The United States has always regarded international law as an important part of our national laws. In fact, the Constitution itself directs that treaties form part of the supreme law of the land. Likewise, the Supreme Court has ruled that "international law is part of our law, and must be administered by the courts of justice" whenever legal questions arise in litigation.

Former secretary of state Dean Rusk emphasized the importance of international law to Americans in this way:

Law is the guardian of the presumption of good faith, which is the cement that holds our society together. In international affairs the steady consolidation of the rule of law is the alternative to the law of the jungle, and is an essential condition, in this nuclear age, for the survival of man. The law plays a vastly more important role in world affairs than occurs to most people. It provides international goals to which we must bend our national efforts . . . forms the basis for collective action by which nations guard the peace . . . knits together countries in an everstronger fabric of agreements about common policies and goals . . . [and] provides the tools with which mankind can deal with the utterly new problems we encounter on the Earth and in space around it.

Diplomacy is defined in the *Oxford English Dictionary* as "the management of international relations by negotiation, and the method by which these relations are adjusted and managed by ambassadors and envoys." The main point to emphasize is the method of negotiation. Diplomacy is a substitute for force. It is the means of obtaining the maximum benefit to the nation without resort to force.

Diplomacy always depends in some degree on the power—military, economic, moral, or allied—of the state for which the diplomat is acting. There may or may not be a threat of force, but without any power behind it, there is no likelihood of much success in any diplomatic negotiations over important issues between nations.

History of Diplomacy

The development of the art of diplomacy began well before the birth of Christ. The pharaohs of Egypt and other early rulers had agreements with rulers of other states concerning sovereignty, military assistance, refugees, and immigrants. The Greek city-states of Athens and Sparta built on this early experience, and by the time of Plato, about 400 B.C., they had developed and defined treaty law and methods of negotiation, principles of international arbitration, the rights and duties of aliens, the immunity of ambassadors, and the right of asylum.

During the Middle Ages, relationships based on diplomacy began between the kingdoms on the Italian peninsula. Venice, Florence, Genoa, Rome, and Naples, among others, were essentially independent city-states that were either at war or in alliances with each other much of the time. Agents called ambassadors were sent from one city-state to another to conduct the relations between them. The dwellings in which they lived on the foreign soil became known as *embassies.*

In the beginning, many of these ambassadors were merely spies, for many used bribes, lies, and other disreputable means to steal political documents or gain information of potential value to their rulers. Undoubtedly the most famous of these early diplomats was Niccolo Machiavelli of Florence. In 1513 he wrote a book called *The Prince,* which described his experiences and the diplomatic practices of the time, many of which were unscrupulous. Not all European ambassadors went to such extremes, but there is little doubt that the term *machiavellian,* which to this day is used to describe unethical political activities, applied to many of the royal courts of that time. Being an ambassador in these early days was not always conducive to long life, since bearers of bad news were sometimes executed.

In the late fifteenth century the Republic of Venice became the first government to establish permanent resident embassies in other countries. During the sixteenth century many of the Italian states developed two specialized government services: the diplomatic service, which looked after political matters, and the consular service, which concerned itself with trade and commerce. These two services together brought about closer relations between the states and formed the basis for modern international law.

Sources of International Law

International law is not compiled into a handy text that one can draw from the library. It is, rather, a body of law that has developed from a number of sources, a portion of which is unwritten. The International Court of Justice in The Hague, Netherlands, which rules in cases on the basis of "internationally accepted law," has provided that international law may be based on the following:

- International conventions, treaties, and executive agreements recognized by contesting states
- International custom (customary law) and general practice long established
- Judicial or court decisions in international tribunals and arbitration courts agreed upon by the countries having conflicting claims
- The commonly accepted teachings of highly qualified publicists (writers) and scholars in the field of international law such as Hugo Grotius, who in 1625 published a treatise, *The Law of War and Peace,* which earned for him the title "Father of International Law"
- The decisions of various national courts, including admiralty, prize, and consular courts, which contribute to the body of law and are referred to as the general principles of law recognized by all civilized nations of the world

Additionally, certain diplomatic correspondence contributes to the body of international law, in that these papers are a source of information regarding the attitude of states toward particular problems. Over a period of time, this correspondence can gain international acceptance as definitions of what the law is concerning particular issues.

Treaties, conventions, and agreements are sources of law that bind countries together just as a contract binds the parties to it under national law. A *treaty* is a contract between independent nations and depends for its enforcement on the interests and honor of the governments that are parties to it. Breaking a treaty will normally result in international repercussions at the least, and, in extreme cases, may lead to war. Treaties mostly cover the more vital areas of international relations, such as political commitments, military alliances, and settlement of territorial claims. They are considered primary sources of international law. *Navy Regulations* indicates the importance of treaties to naval commanders: "On occasions where injury to the United States or to citizens thereof is committed or threatened, in violation of the principles of international law or treaty rights, the senior officer present shall consult with the diplomatic or consular representatives of the United States, if possible, and shall take such action as the gravity of the situation demands. The responsibility for any action taken by a naval force, however, rests wholly upon the senior officer present."

The Sovereign State

In any discussion of international law, there is much terminology peculiar to that field. Much of this is commonly used without attention to subtle differences, while some is unique to the field. Before proceeding further, it is necessary to become familiar with some of this terminology.

The terms *state, nation,* and *country* are commonly thought of as synonymous, but there are subtle differences in precise meanings. The term *country* generally refers to the territorial limits or geographic boundaries on a map. *Nation* pertains to people and their common blood ties, language, customs, and, perhaps, religion. The word *state* stresses the governmental authority of the political entity.

In discussing international law, we normally are talking about the relationships between sovereign states—that is, legal entities that are considered capable of speaking for themselves. Under international law a sovereign state has three specific characteristics:

- It is a permanently organized legal society or government.
- It is a fixed territory, free from control of any other state.
- It has the ability to enter into associations with other states.

It is important to note that the geographic size of the state does not affect its sovereignty; the prime consideration is whether or not the state is independent of any outside jurisdiction (control). The tiny states of Luxembourg and Monaco are examples of this. The traditional doctrine of sovereignty also includes the right of a state to decide how to conduct its international affairs, and to resort to war when judged necessary to defend its national interests.

Sovereign states send diplomats to other sovereign states and conclude treaties with one another without interference. They are expected to live up to their treaty commitments, though an absolute definition of the term *sovereignty* would imply complete freedom to break treaties as well as make them if it is in the national interest of the state to do so.

While most of the world today is composed of sovereign states, there are some political entities that have a status that differs somewhat from the strict definition of the word. Switzerland, for instance, has been officially regarded as a *neutralized state* since the Congress of Vienna in 1815. It has been successful in maintaining its neutrality, and consequently, any invasion of its territory or involvement in any war, since that time. Formal permanent status of neutrality or neutralization by a treaty guaranteed by other states differs from self-proclaimed *neutrality*, which is the voluntary nonparticipation in a particular war. There are no guarantees in such neutrality other than the rights normally granted to neutrals in time of war by international law.

The Commonwealth of Nations (formerly known as the British Commonwealth) is a unique group in international law. Composed mainly of nations that were at one time under British colonial rule, Great Britain and its Dominions of Australia, Canada, New Zealand, and some fifty other countries enjoy complete sovereignty and independence in their internal and external affairs, but acknowledge an ideological allegiance to the British Crown based on common tradition and economic interest. India, for example, remains a member of the Commonwealth, even though it is a republic with no ties to the Crown.

Rights and Duties of Sovereign States

All sovereign states have rights, and with those rights are associated duties. Some rights are regarded as fundamental—the right of freedom from interference or intervention, the right of continued existence, and the right of self-defense. These rights are so fundamental that they have always been reserved for interpretation by each state in accordance with its own national policy. To that extent, each state is free to determine its own conduct. This implies that a sovereign state can do no wrong when acting on these matters in its own behalf—a situation that makes the quest for peace in a warlike world difficult.

Each state has the right of equal access to international courts. Also, each one can control its diplomatic relations with other countries. While all do not maintain embassies in every country, most have accredited (formally appointed) ambassadors who visit regularly, even though they are not resident. States have the right to enter into treaties with other states on matters of common interest.

The rights of existence and self-defense are of particular interest to the armed forces of a nation. Of unique importance in this regard is the legal right of a state to respond with military action in self-defense, even before an attack is clearly imminent. Consequently, if a neighboring state builds up its forces, it is considered sufficient grounds for a state to respond with a similar buildup in its own defense. In other words, no state is expected to wait passively until attacked, since the right of self-defense includes the right to prevent attack. The right to wage war in self-defense is recognized by

A cargo ship docked at Malaka Island in the Pacific takes on a load of dried meat of coconuts, the principal export of the island. Now independent, Malaka Island was a member of the Trust Territories of the Pacific Islands administered by the United States for many years following World War II.

the United Nations. However, preventive war is considered illegal, since such a war is based on the presumption that there might be an attack, not on the basis of proof of imminent attack.

For each right there is a corresponding duty in international law. For instance, duties of *belligerents* (states at war with each other) to observe treaties, care for prisoners of war, follow rules of warfare, protect aliens, protect human rights, and so forth are considered duties of states under the law. The fact that some nations have varying interpretations of the law does not exempt them from their responsibilities.

Independence in foreign affairs carries with it the right to diplomatic representation. The right of a state to have representatives in other states for carrying on diplomatic negotiations, and to receive similar representatives from others for the same purposes, is known as the *right of legation*. This does not mean that a state must send or receive envoys; the exercise of this right depends on the mutual consent of the nations involved. As mentioned earlier, however, most states presently exercise the right of permanent legation. It is general practice for the receiving state to accredit the chief of mission as the sending nation's representative, upon official presentation of the appropriate credentials to the chief of state and the foreign office.

The Vienna Convention on Diplomatic Relations of 1961 established the three classes of heads of diplomatic missions that currently are accepted by the United States and most other nations. These three classes are *ambassadors* accredited to heads of state, *envoys and ministers* accredited to heads of state, and *chargés d'affairés* accredited to ministers for foreign affairs. These are considered equals when serving as heads of missions, except in the areas of precedence and etiquette observed at official functions. An ambassador is the personal representative of the head of state of his or her country. A charge d'affairés is the lowest rank of a head of mission.

Recognition

Sovereign status can be attained in a number of ways. A treaty signed by several agreeing states may establish sovereignty. Former colonies may be granted sovereignty by their mother country. The acceptance of the new state into the world community of nations by other sovereign states, however, is largely a matter of their foreign policy.

The United States considers three factors to be necessary in order for our government to grant diplomatic recognition, which is the formal acknowledgment of national status:

- Control of the territory claimed
- The will of the people reflected in the government
- The preparedness of the new state to honor international obligations

When a state meets the above criteria, the U.S. government considers the government of the state to be a legal entity existing *de jure* (by law) under international law. It will then grant diplomatic recognition and exchange ambassadors.

There are other criteria that are also used to establish sovereign status and eligibility for diplomatic recognition. Essentially, these criteria include the existence of a government that is capable of exercising control over its people, a degree of stability, an established political existence, and in some cases admission as an independent state into an international organization such as the United Nations. The United States' view is that membership in the United Nations does not, in itself, constitute sufficient grounds for recognition by our government. Our relationships with the Communist governments of North Korea, Cuba, Laos, and Cambodia, for example, are only *de facto* (understood to exist in fact), but not *de jure* (by law). There may be some cultural or commercial understandings, or low-level exchanges of consular missions (as with Cuba), but no formal diplomatic recognition and exchange of accredited ambassadors.

Withdrawal of recognition of one state or government in a geographic area must be accompanied by recognition of another, according to most authorities on international law. Therein lay the legal problem concerning the United States' longtime recognition of the Nationalist Republic of China, with its seat of government in Taipei, Taiwan, as the *de jure* government of China. In 1972 the United States opened an American affairs mission in Peking, seat of the government of the Communist People's Republic of China, acknowledging its *de facto* presence. The United States considered it contrary to U.S. interests in Asia to officially recognize and exchange ambassadors for thirty years. But on 1 January 1979, the United States withdrew formal diplomatic recognition of the Taipei government, while retaining cultural and commercial relations with it, and formally recognized the People's Republic as the *de jure* Chinese government.

There is, however, a step short of formal withdrawal of recognition that nations more often exercise when some disagreement arises. This is called a *breach in diplomatic relations*. In this procedure, ambassadors are recalled, consular stations are closed or drastically reduced in size and number, and treaties either remain in force or are suspended for the duration of the breach, depending on the circumstances. In essence, this is the relationship that has long been in effect between the United States and Cuba. A breach of formal diplomatic relations has existed since 1961, when Fidel Castro announced to the world his Communist affiliations and alliance with the Soviet Union. When diplomatic relations were severed, the United States made it clear that the treaty granting us rights to the naval base at Guantanamo Bay remained in full force. To date, both nations have honored that treaty.

Military and Naval Attachés

According to international law, military and naval attachés are regarded as high-ranking members of the ambassador's official staff. They enjoy the same diplomatic immunities and protection as the ambassador. These include freedom to communicate with the home government; safety and security of self, staff, and family; inviolability of home and embassy; and certain jurisdictional immunities such as freedom from criminal and civil laws. However, the ambassador and each person on the staff must act in a manner befitting their rank and position, conforming to high standards of behavior. If a diplomat repeatedly breaks local laws, the host government may declare him or her *persona non grata* (not acceptable) and demand his or her removal.

Naval and military attachés of the United States are selected by their services and assigned by the Department of Defense to American legations or embassies overseas. The senior attaché, regardless of service, is called the defense attaché, and others are called assistant defense attachés. The naval attaché has traditionally been termed the ALUSNA, an acronym meaning American Legation, United States Naval Attaché. Prior to their appointment, their names may be submitted to the foreign state for approval if that state so requires. This is because military and naval attachés carry out important intelligence functions, and the receiving state has a right to guard its own security interests. In practice few states insist on advance notification unless it is a matter of *reciprocity* (similar actions by both parties). The United States, for example, does not require advance approval of military attachés sent to Washington unless the other state requires prior approval.

International Problems and International Law

International law is the set of rules that nations use to maintain and conduct their relations with other countries in the world. The U.S. government looks to international law for the solution of many of the basic problems that face the world.

It has been through the collective action of many countries that the world has avoided a third major world war thus far. A long period of vigilance and effort by international groups such as the North Atlantic Treaty Organization (NATO) was required before East-West tensions finally subsided. Collective efforts such as the Organization of American States (OAS) and various UN agencies will likely have to play a major role if tensions between the developed and underdeveloped nations are to continue to be resolved in the future. Only if the nations of the world have diplomatic and commercial relationships is there a chance for world peace, and international law provides the rules for such dialogue.

With modern technology affecting the entire environment on planet Earth, there must be international organizations and associations to work together to solve the complex problems that

A U.S. Navy attaché with the staff of the U.S. embassy in Rangoon, Burma (now Yangon, Myanmar), observes representatives of the crew of a visiting destroyer as they ring the giant bell of the Shwedagon Pagoda, a gesture of respect to the host nation.

will inevitably continue to arise. The effectiveness of the United Nations must be improved to assist in this effort. Nuclear test ban and nuclear weapons nonproliferation treaties must continue in effect to prevent the spread of radioactive byproducts throughout the world, affecting the air we breathe and the food we eat.

Cooperation among nations must also play a role in modern scientific endeavors beyond the Earth, in the area of space exploration. A space treaty was signed in 1967 providing for the exploration of outer space for the benefit of all countries and agreeing that no nations would claim sovereignty over celestial bodies. An Astronaut Rescue and Return Agreement has been signed that provides for assistance to astronauts in distress and safe return when rescued.

Another frontier that we are beginning to explore and use is the deep ocean floor. Several law of the sea conventions have been held to try to reach agreement on territorial limits, exploitation of the sea bottom, research and exploration of the continental shelves, ocean fishing, and nautical rules of the road. The worldwide exchange of meteorological information has helped make us better prepared to cope with the violence of storms that care nothing about international boundaries. Many world leaders have declared that international agreements on the law of the sea continue to be an important task before us at the present time, for it is there that we will probably go before we make widespread explorations into space.

Much on the international scene has happened in the area of satellite communications and television. Within the lifetimes of cadets reading this book, global communications have become commonplace. On worldwide TV networks like ESPN and CNN we can view major sporting events, the installation of a new pope, the marriage of a crown prince, or a summit conference between heads of state, no matter where, "live" and in color on our living room TV screen. It is now a simple matter to direct-dial a landline or cellular telephone call almost anywhere in the world. Interactive computer networks such as the Internet have ushered in an information revolution of instantaneous electronic communication worldwide. International law is only beginning to grapple with some of the legal questions regarding its use for illicit purposes, such as drug trafficking and pornography.

The economic development of the world is certain to bring with it an increasing division of the rich and poor Third World nations, until or unless viable solutions to this inequity can be found. Humanitarianism apparently is not sufficient reason for industrialized states to help improve the lives of the underdeveloped, hungry, and poverty-stricken ones today. But one day, the terrible dangers of overpopulation, shortages of food, global warming, and the restlessness caused by huge numbers of people in misery will be inescapable. Cooperation in this effort among all nations is essential for the survival of all mankind. We in the West are trying to build a world based on law; as we do so, we enter into a new phase of world history in which all nations must recognize shared interests and accept shared responsibilities. International law is recognized by the world community as the fundamental requirement for orderly relations.

Collective Security

The idea of forming an international organization for the purpose of peacefully settling disagreements between nations was proposed after every major war, beginning with the Congress of Vienna following the abdication of Napoleon Bonaparte in 1814. After World War I, substantial progress was made toward this goal with the formation of the League of Nations. Although the league failed to preserve peace and was ultimately disbanded, it provided the world with valuable experience in the association of states to settle political, economic, and social problems by peaceful means. Following World War II, on 24 October 1945, the United Nations organization officially came into being with the ratification of its charter by the majority of the original fifty member states. There are currently 192 sovereign states as members of the United Nations.

The United Nations

The basic purpose of the United Nations is to maintain international peace and security, to take effective collective action to prevent and remove threats to world peace, and to cooperate in solving international economic, social, cultural, and humanitarian problems. To accomplish these goals, the principle of the sovereign equality of all members is recognized. All members have agreed to fulfill the obligations of the charter, to settle their international disputes by peaceful means, and to give the United Nations every assistance in any action it takes in accordance with the charter.

Action in the United Nations is centered mainly in the Security Council. It comprises fifteen members. The five major powers—the United States, Great Britain, France, Russia, and the People's Republic of China—are permanent members, and ten other nonpermanent member nations are elected for two-year terms.

The headquarters of the United Nations, New York. The tall rectangular building to the left is the UN Secretariat, and the low building in the center with a partial domed roof is the General Assembly.

Procedural matters acted on by the council require at least nine affirmative votes for passage. In all substantive measures, however, the nine affirmative votes must include those of the five permanent major powers for passage. If any one of the so-called Big Five casts a negative vote, called a veto, the measure is defeated. Known as the Yalta formula, this voting arrangement was based on the assumption that if the Security Council was to carry out its responsibility effectively in the United Nations, agreement of the five major world powers was essential for any real action.

The Security Council can make recommendations and pass measures to maintain or restore international peace and security whenever it determines the existence of any threat to the peace, breach of the peace, or act of aggression. These measures may be actions not involving the use of armed forces, such as interruption of economic relations or severance of diplomatic relations. Or the action may be military operations by air, sea, or land forces to maintain or restore peace. The charter obligates member nations to place armed forces under United Nations command to carry out whatever actions are decided upon by the council. United Nations forces took part in the Korean War, and in more recent years, they participated in Operations Desert Shield and Desert Storm in 1991, in the Bosnian conflict, and in several humanitarian interventions in Africa.

International, Regional, and Collective Arrangements

In addition to the power of the Security Council to take action in cases of aggression, the UN charter specifically recognizes the right of members to act in self-defense, individually or collectively. The charter suggests possibilities of such arrangements, including regional associations, and allows such treaties as long as their activities are consistent with the purposes and principles of the United Nations. On this legal basis, the United States and most other nations have concluded many such treaties with states having common concerns. Membership in such regional organizations and collective defense pacts has given the United States military and economic commitments with some forty nations throughout the world. In addition, the United States has concluded defense pledges or agreements with about thirty other countries. Operation Enduring Freedom in Afghanistan in 2001–2002 was an example of a military coalition organized by the United States outside the purview of the United Nations. Our present worldwide collective security system has bound us to defend Latin America, Western Europe, and almost every non-Communist state in the western Pacific.

Regional organizations are arrangements between member states designed to address many of the political, technical, cultural, and educational problems that are of concern to the United Nations and its functional organizations. Regional does not necessarily imply a common geographic region, but rather that the countries in the pact have common interests in a given region.

Collective defense pacts are designed, as their name implies, for mutual and collective self-defense. Their legality comes from the fundamental right to self-defense recognized by the charter. Since this is a right of all sovereign states, a nation need not hold membership in the United Nations to be a party to such a treaty.

A key provision of all these pacts is that if one member state is attacked, the other member states will come to its assistance. The knowledge that an attack on any member will result in collective and individual action by all parties to such a pact makes aggression much less probable, and consequently such treaties are a strong deterrent to any potential aggressor nation.

The United States has been closely involved with the security of all the countries in the Western Hemisphere ever since the Monroe Doctrine in 1823. It stated that the United States would henceforth regard as an unfriendly act any attempt by a European nation to interfere in the affairs of the American countries or increase its possessions on the American continents. Regional solidarity between the American states has set an example for the world and has become the model of several other regional treaties and declarations placed in effect since World War II.

In 1948 an organization that comprised almost all of the independent states of the Western Hemisphere was formed (Cuba dropped out in 1962). Called the Organization of American States (OAS), its aims are to promote peaceful settlement of disputes among member states, to provide for collective security, and to encourage cooperation in economic, social, and cultural matters. Largely anti-Communist in its philosophy, the OAS is based on the general principles of the Monroe Doctrine, especially the provision that an attack on one American state would be considered an attack on all.

Important decisions on regional security taken by the OAS include support of President John F. Kennedy's quarantine of Cuba in 1962, the support of American intervention in the Dominican Republic in 1965, and in 1982, disagreement with the U.S. invasion of Grenada (despite the support of Grenada's neighboring island republics).

Another very important regional defense pact in which the United States is a key member is the North Atlantic Treaty Organization (NATO), formed in 1949. It is somewhat similar to the OAS, except that its primary purpose is collective defense. Like the OAS treaty, the NATO agreement states that an armed attack against one member shall be considered an armed attack against all members, and it provides for measures to meet such an attack. The North Atlantic treaty also endorses the doctrine of mutual aid, the principle that has been the basis of our foreign policy in Western Europe since the treaty became effective. Under this principle, the United States has provided friendly foreign nations with arms and equipment in order to develop their "individual and collective capacity to resist armed attack."

The membership of the North Atlantic Treaty Organization consists of the United States, Canada, Iceland, most of the nations of northern and western Europe, Greece and Turkey, and more recently, many of the former satellite states of the old Soviet Union. Additional countries may be invited to join in the future, including some of the member states of the Russian Federation.

Collective Security Trends

There has been much soul-searching in Congress and by prominent commentators of many political persuasions concerning U.S. involvement in collective security arrangements. The questions usually raised revolve around two fundamental issues:

- Do U.S. defense treaties contribute to the nation's security, or do they unavoidably involve the United States in costly wars where American interests are not at stake?

- Under what circumstances and for the benefit of which nations or governments should Americans be prepared to honor a pledge of defense by going to war?

Other questions involve the need for overseas bases and large standing military and naval forces, the rising costs of the defense budget, the priority of funds for social and economic problems at home, the moral aspects of arms sales to foreign countries, and concern over the extent to which Congress has been removed from the decision-making process on issues of war and peace.

All U.S. presidents since World War II, however, have been able to maintain a policy of continued commitment to the democratic cause worldwide, but with hope of movement toward greater sharing of the responsibility among the allied nations. Essentially, this evolving policy has three main aspects:

- The United States will honor all of its treaty commitments, both because of their merit and the need to maintain world stability, for to do otherwise would invite aggression.

- The United States will provide a shield if an aggressor nuclear power threatens the freedom of an ally or if the survival of the nation threatened is considered vital to U.S. security.

- In cases involving other types of aggression, the United States will furnish military and economic assistance when requested in accordance with treaty commitments. However, the United States will look to that nation directly threatened to assume the primary responsibility of providing the manpower for its own defense.

This policy is dynamic—stable but changing as conditions change, just as the degree of threat to the United States changes.

It is likely that collective security will continue to play a significant role in U.S. foreign policy. An attempt to retreat to isolationism would be a flight from reality. It is not likely that the United States will relinquish its claim to world leadership, for that would probably invite aggression worldwide.

STUDY GUIDE QUESTIONS

1. What are the official representatives of our government in foreign capitals called?

2. What is the body of rules that has evolved to regulate many of the relations between nations called?

3. What aspect of international law pertains to relations between independent nations?

4. How does the U.S. Constitution regard international treaties?

5. What is diplomacy?

6. Where did the principles of early international law originate?

7. Which official world body rules in cases involving application of international law?

8. Under international law, what three characteristics are necessary for a state to be regarded as sovereign?

9. What unique relationships still apply between Britain and its former colonies?

10. What are the fundamental rights of a sovereign nation?

11. What are the legal rights of a nation if it obtains evidence of imminent attack by another country?

12. What legal term is applied to countries engaged in a lawful war?

13. What is the step short of formal withdrawal of diplomatic recognition that countries may take when cooperation between them becomes very difficult?

14. A. What is meant by diplomatic immunity for ambassadors, attachés, and others of the embassy staff and their families?

    B. What may a host country do if an embassy staff member violates established standards of behavior?

15. A. What is the title of the senior U.S. service attaché assigned to an embassy?

    B. What does the acronym ALUSNA mean?

16. What recent technical innovation is international law beginning to address today?

17. What is the basic purpose of the United Nations?

18. Who are the five permanent members of the United Nations Security Council?

19. What actions can the Security Council take to maintain or restore peace and security in a given world situation?

20. What are the two main collective defense arrangements in which the United States is an active participant?

21. What is the keystone provision of each of the various collective defense treaties?

22. Which countries currently belong to NATO?

CRITICAL THINKING

1. Research the legal rights of foreign diplomats accused of a crime in the United States. Under what conditions do diplomats receive full diplomatic immunity?

2. Select one of the collective defense arrangements of which the United States is a participant, and research the legal obligations of the United States with regard to it.

VOCABULARY

ambassadors
diplomacy
negotiations
arbitration
aliens (international)
asylum
belligerent
machiavellian
diplomatic service
consular service
international conventions
envoy
treaty

sovereign state
jurisdiction
neutralized state
neutrality
right of legation
diplomatic recognition
chargé d'affairés
de jure
de facto
breach of diplomatic relations
reciprocity
persona non grata
ALUSNA

2   International Law of the Sea

The international law of the sea has evolved over centuries, from both custom and treaty. The most basic tenet of sea law is the principle stated by Hugo Grotius, a Dutch publicist considered to be the Father of International Law, in 1604: "No part of the sea may be regarded as pertaining to the domain of any given nation." This precept grew to become the basis of the "freedom of the seas" advocated by Britain and the United States and is now widely accepted by all maritime nations in the world.

Grotius's reasoning concerning freedom of the seas has been proven correct by the subsequent history of the world. Western civilization has become increasingly dependent upon the use of the sea for trade, transportation, and communication of ideas. It is not right for any nation to claim or reserve any part of the sea for exclusive use; the sea does not lend itself to possession or occupation, so any attempt to establish ownership would be difficult to defend with logic in court or with military force. Ownership and the ability to use or control are two entirely different things, however.

Since under international law a state has the right to defend itself and its citizens, it has become generally accepted that a coastal state should have the right of sovereignty over a narrow band of the sea adjacent to its coast for national security reasons. For centuries this territorial sea was considered to extend out 3 miles, the approximate range of a cannon shot from a shore battery in the seventeenth century. It was not until the early twentieth century, when Imperial Russia claimed a 12-mile exclusive fishing zone, that the 3-mile limit was challenged. When the Bolsheviks took over Russia, it was not long before they declared that this fisheries zone was in reality a territorial sea in which the Soviet Union had exclusive sovereign rights. As the twentieth century progressed, this breach in the formerly solid support for the 3-mile limit continued to widen further as the result of modern technology, population growth, and political change. The United States joined the majority of other maritime powers in accepting the principle of a 12-mile territorial sea in a Law of the Sea Conference in 1978, conditional upon a law of the sea convention that provides for unimpeded passage through, over, and under international straits overlapped by the 12-mile limit.

Precepts of the Law of the Sea

The main ideas that had formed the body of customary international law of the sea met little serious opposition until the middle of the twentieth century. Even then, it was only the extent of the territorial sea and fisheries limits that was disputed, not the fundamental concepts of sea law itself. The main precepts of the international law of the sea that have evolved over the centuries are

- The concept of freedom of the high seas, in which no nation may restrict any areas or resources to its exclusive use or sovereignty

- The concept of the territorial sea, which contends that coastal states have near-absolute sovereignty over a narrow band of waters adjacent to their coasts

- The concept of special contiguous zones, where special limited jurisdiction prevails, such as in the straits and channels, and where neither the rules of the high seas nor territorial seas pertain

United Nations Law of the Sea Conferences have met a number of times during the last decades. The stated purpose of these conferences has been "to develop rules for peaceful use of the seabed beyond the continental shelf to the entire spectrum of ocean uses." The UN General Assembly recognized that there was minimal chance for agreement, so it made provision for the conference to be postponed or adjourned until recalled whenever significant roadblocks arose. This proved wise indeed, for there was wide disagreement, mainly between the industrialized states and the underdeveloped nations. The principal issues that the conferences have had to deal with are

- The breadth of the territorial sea
- Passage through straits
- Fisheries
- The seabed
- Marine pollution
- Scientific research

Over the years some conventions have been agreed upon, but no global agreement covering the many items on the agenda has yet been reached.

The Impact of the Law on Navy Missions

International legal rules affecting the deployment and navigation of naval vessels have four possible adverse impacts. First, the rules may limit mobility. For example, restrictions on pas-

According to international law, innocent passage of a territorial sea requires that a submarine be surfaced and that an aircraft request overflight permission in advance of the transit, unless a specific bilateral treaty between the countries involved is in effect.

sage through international straits may prevent the passage of warships, thus increasing the reaction time in which such naval units could be deployed to specific troubled areas. Timely movement of naval forces may be necessary for self-defense, to defend allies, or to maintain political stability. It is clear that these requirements would best be served by international agreement on the narrowest possible territorial sea.

Second, legal developments might increase the vulnerability of naval vessels to surveillance. For example, by requiring warships to use only designated sea lanes, surveillance by enemy forces could be made much easier. Aerial reconnaissance, coast watchers, and electronic sensors all could be concentrated on the narrowed sea lanes defined by such law. In the case of many straits with sea lanes wide enough to allow submerged submarine transit, future submerged passage might be prohibited, since "innocent passage" in a territorial sea may not be made while submerged.

Third, naval vessels may suffer increased vulnerability to interdiction. If the narrow sea lane were in a strait, mining of that area or attack by enemy naval and air forces would be much simpler than if a broad sea area were involved.

Fourth, legal developments might impose limitations on oceanographic and intelligence-gathering activities within the 200-mile offshore zones. For example, if authorization is given to regulate scientific research vessels within the 200-mile economic resource zones, naval oceanographic research might be severely restricted or prohibited therein.

Territorial Seas

The increase of sovereign territorial sea jurisdiction to 12 miles in 1978 placed over a hundred straits previously navigable as high

seas in the category of territorial seas. The United States has maintained that transit of such straits, which include Gibraltar and Malacca, "should be regarded in law for what it is in fact: an inherent and inseparable adjunct of the freedoms of navigation and overflight on the high seas themselves."

Innocent passage is the right of vessels of one nation to navigate peacefully through the territorial waters of another nation. The prevailing interpretation of the law of the sea is that warships have the right of innocent passage through international straits that fall within the 12-mile territorial sea of a littoral country. Although no advance notification or authorization is normally required under international law, some states do require such notification unless a bilateral treaty has provided otherwise. The passage, to be innocent, must be merely transit without entrance to inland waters, and it must not be prejudicial to the peace, good order, or security of the coastal state. A ship may stop and anchor, if these actions are necessary for safe navigation.

The littoral (coastal) state must not hinder innocent passage. It must observe the principle of freedom of communication and prevent acts in its territorial sea that are prejudicial to the rights of other countries. It also must give adequate publicity to known dangers to navigation in its territorial sea. It can, however, protect itself from acts harmful to its security and may require that customs and health inspectors board the ship prior to its entry into internal waters, if that is the ship's intention.

Foreign ships in passage through territorial seas must comply with the laws and regulations of the coastal state, as well as the rules of international law. In particular, such ships must observe rules concerning

- The safety of traffic and protection of channels and buoys
- Pollution of the waters

- Conservation of the living resources of the sea
- The rights of fishing and hunting
- Hydrographic surveys
- Display of the ship's national colors and salutes as prescribed by the coastal state

Rules that apply specifically to submarines require that a submarine must transit a territorial sea surfaced, unless a specific bilateral treaty provision exists to the contrary. Under international law, the littoral state may conclude that an unauthorized submarine submerged in its territorial sea constitutes intent to infringe upon its security. It may take whatever defensive actions it deems necessary, including sinking the submarine. Aircraft, including naval aircraft, must request overflight permission over a territorial sea.

Straits and Archipelagoes

We have indicated the potential problems for the U.S. Navy that can arise with any extension of the territorial sea. The United States has stood staunchly for unimpeded navigation of warships and aircraft under rules of innocent passage throughout the conversion of many straits to territorial waters. Until the enactment of a multilateral or bilateral treaty that ensures such transit to U.S. ships, however, there is always the possibility that states adjacent to straits may attempt to impose unilateral restrictions on passage through them. Advance notice of transit or the banning of nuclear-powered vessels are possible examples of such restrictions.

If restrictions on passage through straits were imposed, access to and from the Baltic, the Mediterranean, the Persian Gulf, and the Red Sea could be severely impaired. Entry to semi-enclosed sea areas such as the Caribbean and the Sea of Japan could also be affected adversely. Constraints on aircraft overflights, particularly those intended to bring rapid logistic support to allies, could also occur.

Similar constraints could also apply to the passage of vessels and aircraft through archipelagic nations (nations composed of islands), such as Indonesia and the Philippines, and many smaller groups of islands that have attained sovereign status, such as Tonga, the Maldives, Solomon Islands, and Fiji. The United States backs the right of "archipelagic sea lanes passage," either on routes designated by the nation or on routes normally used for safe international navigation.

Bays and Gulfs

There has been much controversy over the question of where internal waters of bays and gulfs end and where territorial seas begin. A gulf is larger than a bay and extends deeper into the land. By established convention, if the entrance to a bay or gulf is 24 miles or less in width, a line can be drawn seaward of the narrows at the entrance. A number of states persist in claiming that certain bays and gulfs are internal waters. Rarely are these claims upheld by international law. The United Nations lists three basic elements that must exist before any such claim can be deemed valid: an effective claim to sovereignty by a national government, a continuous exercise of the authority claimed, and acquiescence by other nations. Libya has claimed the Gulf of Sidra unsuccessfully. Canada has long claimed Hudson Bay, with an entrance 50 miles wide, but many countries, including the United States, do not recognize this claim. The Bay of Fundy, with a 65-mile entrance, was claimed as Canadian waters by the British in 1852, but a subsequent international commission declared the claim to be invalid.

Denial of, or restrictions on, access to semi-enclosed bays, gulfs, and seas could pose a severe hardship on the U.S. Navy in carrying out its mission. For example, there have been proposals by some emerging Third World states located on the Indian Ocean to declare that entire ocean a "zone of peace and security," from which all warships would be barred. Such curtailments would severely limit the Navy's capability to carry out strategic deterrence, projection of power, and naval presence missions.

Rivers, Lakes, and Canals

Rivers that lie entirely within one country, such as the Potomac, Mississippi, Thames, or Rhone, are considered part of that country's internal waters. They are called *national rivers*. Rivers that form a boundary between two or more countries are called *international rivers*. If such a river is not navigable, as for example the Rio Grande between the United States and Mexico, the territorial boundary lies in the geographic center of the river. If it is navigable, as with the St. Lawrence, the center of the deepest channel is used to mark the boundary; technically this channel boundary line is known as a *thalweg*. Because the navigable channel often varies from the geographical center, the thalweg is used to determine the boundary so both nations' ships can navigate in the river.

International rivers are open to navigation by all ships, just as on the high seas. The same rule applies to rivers that pass through the territory of one state and serve as lines of communication for an interior state. The first state may not impede free flow of traffic to and from the interior state. The Paraná, leading to Paraguay through Argentina, is one example of this; the Rhine in Western Europe, the Danube in Eastern Europe, the Congo of Central Africa, and the Amazon system through Brazil also carry much international traffic. The use of these rivers is controlled by international treaties and agreements between the riparian (on the river banks) countries.

Lakes entirely within the boundaries of one country are the exclusive property of that country. Treaties usually set international boundaries in those that lie in more than one country. The Great Lakes are subject to agreements between the United States and Canada. Treaties between the two countries define the territorial limits of each country and address jurisdictional questions such as admiralty law, navigation, and limitations of warships.

Passage through manmade canals is controlled by agreement of the countries most concerned. In peacetime they are open to the use of all nations' ships, subject to a toll for the transit service. If nations not holding title or interest in the canal are at war, belligerent warships from either side may use it. The canal is closed to belligerents at war with the controlling state; for example, the Suez and Panama Canals were not open to Axis powers during World War II.

Law of the High Seas

As defined by the United Nations Convention on the High Seas, the term *high seas* means "all parts of the sea that are not included in the territorial sea or in the internal waters of a state." Over 70 percent of the world's surface is high seas, free for all the world to use in its commerce.

Freedom of the high seas includes freedom to conduct maritime commerce, to navigate, to fish, to lay submarine cables and pipelines, to fly over, and to undertake scientific research. In exercising these freedoms, reasonable regard must be given to the rights of others to use the high seas. For instance, it has been ruled that in the interest of general safety countries conducting weapon tests at sea should stay clear of traveled sea lanes. If a ship does enter the area, however, the test, not the ship, is stopped. The fact that the sea is common to all does not prevent international agreements concerning it. In fact, the world community of states has seen fit to establish a body of maritime law to ensure that freedom of the seas will apply equally to all. Consequently, conventions and treaties have been concluded on safety of life and traffic at sea, salvage, international signals, fisheries, the laying of cables and pipelines, oil pollution, and the suppression of piracy and the slave trade.

Every state has the right to grant its nationality to ships and has the right to sail them under its flag on the high seas. Such ships, whether military or civil, are subject to the exclusive jurisdiction of the nationality of the flag flown. In return for these rights, among others, the state must take all measures necessary to ensure the safety of the ship, crew, and passengers.

The following sections address in more detail the current problem areas concerning the law of the sea. These include problems related to economic zones, self-defense rules, exploitation of the continental shelf and seabeds, and fisheries.

Economic Zone Problems

Most coastal states now claim exclusive jurisdiction over living and nonliving resources within 200 miles of their coasts. In 1976 the United States extended its jurisdiction over fishery resources to 200 miles from its coasts. This jurisdiction is limited to fisheries and differs from sovereignty. Some countries have tried to claim absolute sovereignty that far from their coasts—and even beyond. In general, these countries assert that each coastal state has the right and duty to extend its jurisdiction into the high seas to whatever extent it deems necessary for its economic needs. The region extending beyond the 12-mile territorial sea to about 200 miles out is often referred to as the *economic zone.*

Many underdeveloped countries view the development of coastal fisheries as an answer to their economic problems, since fishing does not require the technology or tremendous capital needed for offshore mining or petroleum exploitation. Other developing countries hope to persuade foreign interests having capital, equipment, and know-how to explore and exploit their seabed for a share of the profits. Still others have no desire to harvest certain ocean resources for themselves but want to claim jurisdiction over them and permit others to exploit them in return for large license fees. They consider annexation of open space to be a legitimate means of compensating for the uneven distribution of the world's wealth.

When discussed in law of the sea negotiations, this issue has been called the question of the "residuum of authority." That is, with whom does the jurisdiction in the 12-to-200-mile economic zone rest—the coastal state or the international community as a whole? If the former, then the coastal state could arbitrarily impose restrictions on navigation within the zone. If the latter, only by consent of all the world's nations, either through treaty or by evolution of a new rule by custom, could restrictions on nonresource uses of the economic zone be imposed by the coastal state.

The U.S. Coast Guard is responsible for patrolling fishing grounds within the U.S. 200-mile fisheries zone. The Coast Guard cutter *Mellon*, guarding against violations, passes close by a Russian factory ship and several of its trawlers.

Aside from navigational constraints on naval and merchant shipping, strict control of the economic zone could hinder naval scientific and oceanographic research. Further, pollution jurisdiction could be used to harass merchant shipping or naval vessels transiting the area.

Self-Defense and Fisheries

In the legal sense, a territorial sea is not a part of the high seas, even though it is in a physical and geographic sense. The coastal state exercises exclusive jurisdiction—sovereignty—in its territorial seas. In contrast, it has only limited preventive or protective jurisdiction over any economic zone beyond. This may include exploration and exploitation rights on the continental shelf and seabed, fisheries, and self-defense measures.

Self-defense measures are easily understood from the standpoint of international law. It is a fundamental right of a sovereign state under the law to take all the defensive measures required to safeguard its existence, not only in its territorial sea, but also on the high seas. The fact that a nation takes action against threats to its security on the sea beyond its territorial jurisdiction does not mean it is extending its sovereignty to that point. The use of force in this area, however, requires that the situation definitely be a threat to the acting nation's security, and that the measures taken to repel the threat be reasonable. Before World War II, for instance, President Franklin Roosevelt declared a Defensive Sea Area beyond the 3-mile limit and gave orders to sink any German submarines found in that area. This order was a reasonable measure in view of the war in Europe and the fact that neutral ships had already been sunk by German submarines in these waters.

There have been more disputes over the protection of rights concerning fisheries than over any other international maritime issue since World War II. Fish have been harvested from the seas since the dawn of history, providing humans with food, income, and adventure. Freedom to fish on the high seas has been a part of customary international law. Since World War II there has been a steady increase in fishing activity in all the oceans of the world. New fishing fleets with factory ships serving as mother ships for dozens of smaller trawlers comb the principal fishing areas of the world. In a number of cases these fleets have depleted fish stocks to the point where important fisheries have been lost to the world, perhaps forever. Conservation has become a fundamental concern.

Though the concept of exclusive fishing zones for coastal states has become fairly well established, this is not an answer to the present and future needs of the growing world population. The demand for protein is so great that fish resources cannot be allowed to go unused in national preserves. Countries engaged in distant-water fishing, including both developed and developing countries, look upon fisheries as a primary means of obtaining food and foreign exchange. It appears logical and necessary to allow nations to exploit the fisheries of all the seas within prescribed limits.

The fisheries problem, then, is real and vital to many countries. Fair and intelligent agreements, both bilateral and multilateral, are necessary to satisfy the coastal states and the distant-water fishing nations. Along with these, there will have to be a strict application of conservation measures, and it is likely that these will have to be enforced by coastal states under international law designed to benefit everyone.

The Continental Shelf and Seabeds

Recent technological advances permitting the exploitation of the resources of the seabed and its subsoil have become matters of vital importance to many coastal states. With the discovery of oil and minerals in the seabed, nations have tended to assert their exclusive rights for exploration and exploitation of them. In general, this activity has concentrated on the continental shelf, but technology has advanced to the point where exploitation of deep ocean seabeds is well within the grasp of states with the means to pursue it.

The Geneva Convention on the Continental Shelf, made effective in 1964, defines *continental shelf* as "the seabed and subsoil of the submarine areas adjacent to the coast, but beyond the territorial sea, to a depth of 200 meters [656 feet], or beyond to where the depth of the superjacent waters [allows] exploitation of the natural resources."

In the past, the bed of the sea could not be occupied by any state, so the rule was that it was as free as the seas above it. In 1945, however, President Harry Truman proclaimed that the United States regarded the natural resources of the seabed and subsoil beneath the high seas contiguous to its shores to be subject to its jurisdiction and control. Since then, the law pertaining to the continental shelf and seabeds has evolved.

Science has determined that in excess of 100 billion barrels of oil lie under the U.S. continental shelf, compared with 21 billion in U.S. proven land reserves. To get the oil out, American companies have constructed drilling rigs or derricks in the high seas above the seabed. Geologists also claim that the continental shelf, which in some places extends 120 miles out, contains vast quantities of ores.

Today, all countries with continental shelves are in various stages of exploration and exploitation, and many have been successful. Foremost among these are Mexico and the United States in the Gulf of Mexico; Norway, Scotland, and Britain in the North Sea; and the United States off the California coast. The oil rig is considered an impediment to navigation on the high seas, so the Continental Shelf Convention specifies that a safety zone must be established around such installations up to a distance of 500 meters (1,640 feet), for the mutual protection of shipping and the installation itself.

Developing international law of the sea now recognizes that a coastal state exercises sovereign rights over its continental shelf for the purpose of exploring and exploiting its natural resources. The

The permanent Seabed Committee of the United Nations in general session in New York. The purpose of this committee is to work on the peaceful uses of the seabed and the ocean floor beyond the limits of the territorial sea.

exercise of such sovereign rights over the continental shelf does not alter the legal status of the waters above or that of the airspace over the water. This right of exploration and exploitation is limited, in that there can be no unjustifiable interference with the freedom of navigation, fishing, or scientific research.

Though exploitation of the continental shelf is still in its infancy, technology has now progressed to the point where the deep seabeds and the ocean floor may also become sources of raw materials. Scientific research has determined that extensive deposits of many strategic minerals lie on or close to the surface of the sea floor, in addition to inestimable amounts of oil in the subsoil. The mining of manganese nodules from the seabeds commenced in the early 1970s. The United States has proposed that the deep seabeds not be subject to any kind of claim by any state, but rather that all activities in the area be governed by international law in accordance with United Nations principles.

Rules of the Road

The nautical rules of the road were devised for the purpose of standardizing ship movements on the seas in various situations in such a manner as to avoid collisions at sea. The fundamental rules of meeting, crossing, and passing have evolved in response to the need for safety of waterborne vessels, their passengers, and cargoes. Without such rules, chaos would surely exist.

The international law currently in effect is called Regulations for the Prevention of Collisions at Sea, commonly known as the *international rules of the road* or also the *COLREGS*. The current law was revised in 1972 and came into effect in 1977. It was only the third revision since 1895, when British and French sailing rules gained international acceptance. These rules are worldwide

in application and cover all aspects of safe conduct of a vessel at sea, including lights, whistle signals, day shapes, and ship maneuvers under different circumstances. International rules of the road are now developed by a specialized agency of the United Nations called the International Maritime Organization (IMO). It comprises all the major shipping nations of the world.

The rules of the road are positive international law. They are specific and have proven to be completely enforceable. The rules are applicable to all vessels, large and small, warship and merchant. In the event of a collision, the case is heard in the admiralty court of the maritime nation having jurisdiction, and international law is uniformly applied to ships of all nationalities.

The international rules of the road generally apply in territorial seas and national waters, unless special internal rules have been adopted by a nation. In the case of the United States, inland rules, differing somewhat from international rules, prevail in specified inland waters. Sailors must acquaint themselves with all rules that apply to any nation they are about to visit.

Conclusion

The law of the sea is today in a state of flux and development. The United States must seek to ensure that future legal developments concerning the use of the seas do not adversely affect our ability to carry out naval missions. In this effort, the United States must take the lead in defending existing international legal rights and argue against any attempts to impose restrictions or bans in the following areas:

- Navigation through or overflight of an economic zone
- Innocent passage of warships through territorial waters, or advance notice for same

- Submerged transit or overflight of straits
- Entrance of naval vessels into semi-enclosed areas

The growing pressures for more exploitation of the resources from the seas make it exceedingly important for the maritime nations to come to agreement in many areas. Our capacity to exploit the seabeds, engage in advanced scientific research, fish, conduct ocean commerce, regulate pollution, conserve natural resources, and conduct peaceful naval operations are all interrelated issues, each dependent in some respect on international accords on the law of the sea.

STUDY GUIDE QUESTIONS

1. What is the basis of modern sea law as accepted by all maritime nations?

2. A. What is meant by the term *territorial sea*?

   B. What territorial sea width does the United States recognize?

3. What are the three main precepts of the international law of the sea?

4. What has been the purpose of the United Nations Law of the Sea Conferences?

5. What is meant by the term *innocent passage*?

6. How are submarines affected by rules applying to innocent passage?

7. A. What is an archipelagic nation?

   B. What are some problems that might arise regarding them from the standpoint of ship transits?

8. What has been the basic controversy concerning gulfs and bays as regards the territorial sea of a littoral nation?

9. A. What are rivers that lie entirely within one country called?

   B. If they form a boundary between two or more countries, what are they called?

10. What factor determines the boundary line between nations on an international river?

11. What rules govern the use of major canals by belligerent nations?

12. What does *freedom of the high seas* include within the meaning of the phrase?

13. What is meant by the term *residuum of authority* in the economic zone?

14. What is the key legal difference between the territorial sea and the economic zone beyond the 12-mile limit?

15. What self-defense measures may a nation take in the economic zone?

16. What particular resources are now becoming available from the seabed and subsoil of the continental shelf?

17. How does the Geneva Convention on the Continental Shelf define the term *continental shelf*?

18. Where is there now special activity in continental shelf oil exploration and exploitation?

19. What are the nautical rules of the road designed to do?

20. What type of court hears cases involving ship collisions on the high seas?

CRITICAL THINKING

1. Given the greatly increased ranges of modern artillery and missiles, do you think the current 12-mile limit for territorial seas is still valid, or should it be extended? Why or why not?

2. Research the kinds of minerals being extracted from the continental shelves around the United States. Where are there significant efforts being undertaken?

VOCABULARY

territorial sea	thalweg
innocent passage	high seas
contiguous zones	economic zone
continental shelf	residuum of authority
littoral state	exploitation rights
internal waters	archipelagic nation
inland waters	admiralty court

3 | The Law of War at Sea

The high seas in time of peace are free for the lawful use of the ships and people of all countries. The previous chapter mentioned many of these uses: maritime commerce, fishing, oceanographic research, and training exercises of naval surface and air units, among others. Because the high seas are not under the sovereignty of any state, the preservation of law and order thereon falls within the scope of international law. Until the technological advances of this century opened the seabeds of the ocean, sailors and ships were the only users. Consequently, a large portion of international law is concerned with ships—their rights and privileges, their traffic rules, admiralty law, and laws of conduct in peace and war.

Warships and the Law

Two specific requirements must be met in order for a ship to be termed a *warship*. First, the vessel must be commissioned as a part of the naval forces of a state and authorized to display an appropriate flag or pennant that identifies it as such. Second, the vessel must be commanded by a member of the military forces of that state and must have crew subject to military discipline.

Warships represent the sovereignty and independence of the state to which they belong. The jurisdiction of this state over them is exclusive under all circumstances, and any act of interference with them by a foreign state is an act of war.

This does not mean that a warship on the high seas is free of all restrictions. Rather, as always, responsibility accompanies privilege. The aspect of leadership, ever present in naval matters, appears here with vivid importance. In representing their countries, commanding officers of warships head their officers and crew in the same manner as ambassadors head their legations. The U.S. federal court has stated it this way: "The immunity granted to diplomatic representatives of a sovereign and to its vessels of war . . . can be safely accorded, because the limited numbers and the ordinarily responsible character of the diplomats or agents in charge of the property in question and the dignity and honor of the sovereignty in whose services they are, make abuse of such immunity rare."

Just as interference with a warship on the high seas is an offense against the sovereign in whose service the warship is employed, the abuse of privilege by a warship is a direct reflection upon the honor of that same sovereign. For this reason, every nation with a navy of its own has, by tradition and regulation, attempted to ensure that its warships conduct themselves at all times in a manner that brings credit to the nation they represent.

With privileges, of course, come duties. Commanding officers of U.S. Navy ships, in conformance with the Geneva Convention of the High Seas and U.S. *Navy Regulations*, must

- Render assistance to any person found at sea in danger of being lost

- Proceed with all possible speed to the rescue of persons in distress if informed of their need of assistance, insofar as such action may reasonably be expected of officers

- After collision, render assistance to the other ship, its crew, and passengers

Warships of all nations have a duty to suppress piracy on the high seas. In order that they might accomplish their duty in this respect, international law has recognized that warships have the right to approach, which can be exercised in either peace or war. Warships as a matter of practice, therefore, request the name and nationality of all merchant ships met at sea, usually by flashing light. This activity can keep a signal bridge busy indeed when a naval vessel approaches chokepoints in navigation. The commanding officer must justify any action beyond this standard inquiry. Any such action is done at the commanding officer's own risk, for if a foreign ship is hindered in violation of the freedom of the seas, this could cause embarrassment to the officer's government.

It is clearly the right of any country to forbid foreign warships to enter any of its ports. However, it is customary for nations to grant access to warships of nations with which they are at peace. Sometimes such visits are based on reciprocal rights by the other nation to return such a port call within a reasonable period. In the case of the Western allies, particularly in the Mediterranean, special agreements for visits have been concluded with certain countries in which U.S. Navy ships call regularly. In the absence of such agreements, however, the usual procedure to secure permission for a ship visit is through diplomatic channels, usually via the Department of State and the naval attaché in the nation to be visited.

When in a foreign port, a warship is considered an extension of the territory of its sovereign state and is not subject to any interference by local authorities. Police or port authorities are never entitled to board the ship without first obtaining the permission of the commanding officer, who is never required to submit to a search of the ship.

Such immunities do not mean the ship can act in a lawless manner. Responsibility and leadership are again the key to such privileges. By accepting the hospitality of the port, the warship consents to comply with harbor regulations concerning speed and traffic control, sewage disposal, health and quarantine restrictions, and so forth. If the ship does not meet such standards, valid grounds exist for complaint through diplomatic channels.

The officers and crew of a warship are completely immune from local jurisdiction (authority) while on board the ship in a foreign port. Similarly, it is customary for local authorities to waive all jurisdiction over officers or crew members ashore on official business. However, the situation is different when officers and enlisted personnel go ashore unofficially for leave or liberty. In most countries, local law and jurisdiction will apply to the visitors. In the case of U.S. Navy visits to allied nations, there often exists an arrangement, the Status of Forces Agreement, which specifies in detail how any problems are to be handled. All personnel on leave or liberty in a foreign country should be well advised on the local law and what to do should they get in trouble there.

There is a difference in the case of merchant ships visiting a foreign port. International law states that a merchant ship is subject to the jurisdiction of the nation being visited. This illustrates the fact that a merchant ship is not considered an extension of the "territory" of the nation of registry, as is a warship. This difference is probably best exemplified in the matter of asylum (zone of absolute safety). In the case of a warship, local authorities may not come aboard to arrest or remove an individual seeking asylum for political or personal safety reasons. In the case of a merchant ship, however, local police may come aboard, arrest, and remove an accused offender. The doctrine of asylum, then, is not applicable to merchant ships.

General Rules of War on Land and Sea

Navy Regulations states, "In the event of war between nations with which the United States is at peace, a commander shall observe, and require his command to observe, the principles of international law." This statement makes it clear that naval officers must be thoroughly knowledgeable of the rules of warfare.

Many definitions of "war" exist, but for this particular discussion the simple definition of war as "a legal condition of armed hostility between states" is applicable. It generally implies armed, physical conflict between nations, but in the legal sense, a state of war may exist before or after the use of force. The violence of war existed from 7 December 1941 until the Congress legally declared war on Japan the next day. The treaty of peace with Japan did not come into force until 1952, even though all fighting had ceased on 15 August 1945 and the surrender document was signed on 2 September. It would seem that such legal details would be unimportant, but such is not the case. War clauses in insurance policies, certain provisions of the Uniform Code of Military Justice, and certain presidential powers, among others, are hinged on the legal state of war, not necessarily the violence of conflict.

Because of the events of the Cold War, it is now generally recognized that the rules of war apply in all armed conflicts of an international nature, regardless of whether or not war is formally declared. In other words, military and naval actions between warring nations should follow the rules of war, whether the details of legality are present or not. It should be pointed out that the 1907 Hague Peace Conventions, in their attempts to broadly codify the laws of war, first recognized that the avoidance of war should be attempted as an ultimate goal in all cases. Second, they recognized that war is sometimes unavoidable and has to be accepted as a regrettable but legitimate means of settling disputes between nations. Because of this, it was agreed that the best that could be

The amphibious command ship *Blue Ridge* (LCC 19) en route to a port visit at Shimizu, Japan. In a foreign port, a warship is not subject to any interference by local authorities, but the ship must abide by normal harbor regulations and laws of the country being visited. (Heidi McCormick)

When on liberty in a foreign port, like these Sailors in Ho Chi Minh City in Vietnam, crew members from a Navy ship are subject to local law and jurisdiction. (John Beeman)

fore, may not adopt any means to inflict injury on the enemy. Rules exist so belligerents do not escalate a conflict to total war, with all of its devastating implications.

The limitation on land and naval warfare are, in general, similar. The first group of restrictions concerns the conduct of the war itself—for example, prohibitions on the use of certain weapons such as poisons, poison gases, and "dumdum" bullets. The second group protects persons who are not involved in the actual conduct of the war: civilians, sick and wounded members of the armed forces, and prisoners of war.

The three basic principles underlying the rules of civilized warfare have historically been humanity, chivalry, and military necessity. Of these, humanity is unquestionably the most important. It is the basis for all prohibitions imposed by international law on belligerents for the purpose of limiting excessive violence. Chivalry involves the qualities of bravery, honor, courtesy, respect for women, protection of the weak, generosity, and fairness to enemies. The principle of military necessity permits a belligerent to apply only the degree and kind of regulated force not otherwise prohibited by the laws of war. The rules of international law come above military necessity, because the latter does not constitute an acceptable defense for lawlessness in the conduct of war.

War at Sea

The major distinction between land warfare and war at sea lies in the fact that land warfare takes place primarily on the territory of one or several of the belligerents, while sea warfare is mostly fought on the high seas. These high seas are not within the sovereignty of either belligerent but are open to lawful use by all nations of the world. In such circumstances, there are bound to be conflicts between the interests of the belligerents, whose purpose is to destroy the naval power and maritime commerce of the enemy, and the legitimate interests of neutrals who seek to carry on their ordinary commerce with all nations, including the belligerents. While humanity, chivalry, and military necessity apply equally to war on land and at sea, in the latter, private enemy property, and in some instances, neutral property, is subject to confiscation by belligerent warships. In land warfare, such private property is generally required to be left undisturbed by the opposing forces.

Certain weapons that are generally prohibited by international law were mentioned in the last section. In addition, there are prohibitions against the use of certain types of mines and torpedoes unique to naval warfare. The Hague Conventions forbid the laying of unanchored, automatic contact mines, unless they will become harmless within one hour after the person laying them ceases to control them. Automatic minefields are not supposed to be laid solely for the purpose of intercepting commercial shipping, and precautions are supposed to be taken for the security of peaceful neutral shipping. Communist forces consistently violated the rules concerning mines in both the Korean and Vietnam Wars. They indiscriminately

hoped for was a general acceptance of humanitarian rules of warfare. Therefore, the Convention on Laws and Customs of War states that if any laws concerning certain aspects of war are absent from the code, "then the inhabitants and belligerents remain under the protection and the rule of the principles of the law of nations, as they [have been] established among civilized peoples, from the laws of humanity, and the dictates of the public conscience."

The Hague Conventions state that the rules of war do not apply except between contracting powers, and then only if all the belligerents are parties to the conventions. Even in World War II, some of the belligerents had not ratified the conventions. After the war, when defendants in war crimes trials from these countries claimed immunity because their nations had not ratified the Laws of War, the judges rejected this defense. Today the rules of war are considered customary rules of international law and are binding on all nations, whether or not they have signed specific agreements.

Rules of warfare are restrictive; they are designed to restrain the belligerents from the excessive use of force. Belligerents, there-

dropped mines of all types in rivers, floated them down rivers into the open seas, and laid them throughout harbors and bays without regard for commercial ships and peaceful fishermen. The rules were again violated during the Iran-Iraq War in the 1980s, when drifting mines were released into the Persian Gulf, causing damage to ships of several nations, including the United States.

Chemical, biological, and radiological (CBR) warfare may be used by United States forces only if and when authorized by the president. In general, the use of such weapons has been condemned by the United States, and President Richard Nixon halted the production of chemical and biological agents in 1969. It is known, however, that Soviet forces remained at a high state of training in the use of these weapons, and several of their former client states in the Middle East and many suspected terrorist organizations still are. CBR weapons, however, in the absence of international laws to the contrary, must still be regarded as lawful, subject to the general rules of humanity that govern the use of all weapons in wartime. The United States proposed that nuclear weapons be prohibited from use in the deep seabed and ocean floor, and a treaty to this effect was negotiated and approved by the United Nations in 1970.

Aerial or naval bombardment intended to inflict wanton destruction of populated places or other devastation not justified by military necessity is absolutely forbidden by the rules. The bombardment of undefended cities open for immediate occupation and bombardment for the sole purpose of terrorizing a civilian population are also forbidden. In World War II, it can be said without pride that both sides committed horrifying violations of this rule, the Allies in retaliation for Axis raids on cities in England. Medical establishments, hospital zones, museums, churches, and buildings housing religious organizations are entitled to special protection. Hospital ships and aircraft, when marked and operating as required by the Geneva Convention, may not legally be made the object of attack in naval warfare.

In general, a submarine must follow the rules of warfare applicable to surface ships. Under international law, before a merchant vessel can be sunk, the belligerent warship must give warning and enable the victim's crew and ship's papers to be debarked to a place of relative safety. During World Wars I and II, this rule was abrogated by both sides, each of which claimed that they adopted unrestricted submarine warfare in retaliation for illegal acts by the other. The matter was further complicated when merchant ships were armed, convoyed by warships, and ordered to fire upon or ram submarines on sight. Additionally, many merchant ships have now been integrated into the naval intelligence network. While the legality of attack without warning on such vessels is no longer clear, submariners maintain that their actions are legal because of their vulnerability when surfaced or otherwise located.

One permissible method that a belligerent may use to shut off an enemy's trade is the *blockade*. To make a blockade legal, it must be *effective*; that is, if a ship attempts to enter or leave a blockaded port, its capture must be attempted. Today, because of modern radar, aircraft, and submarines, a "distant blockading force" is more probable than a close-in force of warships, as in earlier times. The penalties for trying to breach a blockade are liability to capture and condemnation by a prize court. A limited and selective form of naval blockade directed against specific prohibited cargo (*contraband*) is called a *quarantine*. The classic example of a quarantine was carried out by the U.S. Navy in 1962 during the Cuban Missile Crisis for the purpose of stopping more Soviet missiles from being delivered to Cuba.

Belligerent warships may also cause a merchant ship to pause on the high seas and submit to visit and search for possible contraband. Contraband consists of all goods useful for making war that are destined for an enemy. Today, since governments of belligerent nations often take over control of all distribution of food, fuel, and raw materials, few items indeed would not be found on a published contraband list.

In the process of visit and search, the suspected vessel is directed by international flag hoist or other visual signals and radio to halt so qualified naval officers may board and examine the ship's papers, registry, ports of departure and destination, and nature of the cargo and other facts. If no contraband is found, an entry is written into the ship's logbook, and the vessel is allowed to proceed. If contraband is discovered, the ship may either be further searched on the spot or, more commonly, directed to accompany the warship into port so a search may be conducted thoroughly and in safety. Liability of the ship or cargo to capture is determined by a prize court, not the boarding officer on the high seas. If a vessel resists or attempts to flee, the warship may use force to restrain it and, if absolutely necessary, may sink it.

Enforcement of the Law

The most effective way of enforcing the laws of war is the official publication of the facts by the wronged nation, with intent to influence world opinion against the offending belligerent. This has proven effective in the world forum of nations. If the laws of war are breached, protests and demands for the punishment of offending individuals, as well as compensation, are probable. Reprisal for illegal acts may also be attempted, but may not be done for revenge alone. Neither can this measure be taken against civilian detainees or military prisoners of war. Acts of reprisal must cease as soon as they have achieved their specific objective. The final method of enforcement of the laws of war is by the punishment of war crimes. War crimes trials and the publicity that accompanies them can be an effective deterrent against future violations of the laws of war.

STUDY GUIDE QUESTIONS

1. Why does the preservation of law and order on the high seas fall within the scope of international law?

2. What specific requirements must be met in order for a ship to be termed a warship?

3. Who has exclusive jurisdiction over a warship?

4. How does the diplomatic status of embassy officials and their staffs compare with the status of warship commanding officers and crews visiting a foreign port?

5. A. Why do warships have the right to approach other ships at sea?

   B. How is this usually accomplished?

6. What is the status of the officers and crew on leave or liberty in a foreign port?

7. What is the fundamental jurisdictional difference between naval vessels and merchant ships when visiting foreign ports?

8. Why are the legal details as to a state of war important?

9. When do the rules of war apply to military and naval actions between states?

10. What is the basic purpose of rules of warfare?

11. What are the three basic principles underlying the rules of warfare?

12. What is a significant difference between land and sea warfare as regards private and neutral property?

13. What are the Hague Conventions rules concerning mines?

14. What is the U.S. policy concerning CBR warfare?

15. Under the rules of warfare, what institutions and ships are supposed to be exempt from attack?

16. Why was unrestricted submarine warfare generally practiced by both sides in World Wars I and II?

17. A. What are the legal requirements of a blockade?

    B. How does a quarantine differ from a blockade?

18. What action may belligerent warships take toward merchant ships on the high seas suspected of transporting contraband?

19. What is the most effective way to enforce laws of war?

CRITICAL THINKING

1. Research the rights of a foreign national seeking asylum aboard U.S. Navy vessels. Under what conditions if any are the commanding officers of such vessels obligated to return such individuals to local authority?

2. Research the Status of Forces Agreement concerning conduct of military service members in a foreign country that is party to the agreement. What are the rights of such service members concerning travel within and between the countries of western Europe?

3. Research at least two recent conflicts in which U.S. Navy vessels have exercised the right to board and search foreign merchant ships. Under what circumstances may this be legally done under international law of the sea?

VOCABULARY

jurisdiction	retaliation
right to approach	unrestricted submarine warfare
rules of warfare	blockade
principles of humanity	quarantine (by warships)
chivalry	contraband
CBR weapons	reprisal

Glossary of Naval Knowledge Terms

administrative discharge—a discharge of a person from naval service initiated by the government for reasons of unsuitability or inaptitude for service life.

air-to-air warfare—offensive and defensive measures carried out by one or more aircraft against each other.

air-to-surface warfare—measures used by aircraft to attack surface targets on land or sea.

air warfare (AW)—warfare directed against airborne vehicles; formerly called antiair warfare (AAW).

ALUSNA—acronym for a U.S. naval attaché, meaning American Legation, U.S. Naval Attaché.

asylum—protection and sanctuary granted by a sovereign state, within its territorial jurisdiction or in international waters, to a foreign national who seeks such protection because of persecution based on race, religion, nationality, or political affiliation.

battlespace—the total space within which a battle is conducted, including undersea, surface, air, littoral (coastal) areas, and near-Earth space.

belligerent—an opponent or nation engaged in warfare against another.

blockade—a naval operation wherein ships are prevented from entering or leaving certain ports or areas.

boycott—to abstain from using, buying, or dealing with, as a form of protest.

breach of discipline—a disciplinary infraction or violation of a rule of conduct.

compromise (security breach)—loss of security resulting from the revelation of classified information.

containership—a merchant ship equipped to load, transport, and discharge van-type boxes containing general cargo; the boxes then can be transported on land via trucks or trains.

convening authority—the command legally empowered to initiate a court-martial, court of inquiry, or board of investigation.

convention (law)—an agreement or pact, especially an international agreement dealing with a specific subject, such as the treatment of prisoners of war.

correctional custody—confinement to a specific area or place ordered as part of a punishment for a disciplinary offense.

counterintelligence—the act of keeping valuable information from an enemy, preventing subversion and sabotage, and gathering political and military information.

court-martial—a military or naval court appointed by a convening authority to try persons accused of offenses under military law.

deterrence—measures taken by a state or an alliance of states to prevent hostile action by another state.

diplomatic recognition—an acknowledgment or acceptance of the national status of a new government by another nation.

dishonorable discharge—a discharge resulting from a service member's misconduct, disobedience of Navy Regulations, or a serious violation of the UCMJ.

embargo—a government-ordered stoppage of foreign trade in a particular type of goods or commodity.

espionage—the act of spying on others, or the use of spies by a government to obtain secret military or political information about another government.

flag of convenience—a ship owned and controlled by a shipping company of one nation but registered and sailed under the flag of another, to take advantage of more favorable labor and insurance rates, taxes, or government policies and regulations.

forward presence—maintaining forward-deployed forces overseas to demonstrate national resolve, strengthen alliances, provide deterrence, and enhance ability to respond quickly to crisis situations.

general purpose forces—forces able to carry out a variety of offensive or defensive missions against an enemy.

grand strategy—an overall long-term plan of action to accomplish a desired national or military goal.

innocent passage—under international law, the right to make a transit of a nation's territorial waters in order to enter into or make a passage to international waters. The ship may not linger in the restricted waters except if in distress and may not engage in any act prejudicial to the peace, good order, or security of the coastal nation.

intelligence—any information of possible military value about an enemy.

intermodal ship—a ship that carries cargo that is then loaded directly onto other forms of transport, such as railroad cars or vehicles.

internal (inland) waters—waters located within the established boundaries of a nation.

international waters—waters external to any nation's territorial seas or internal waters, open to free use by the ships of all nations.

littoral—coastal regions along a shore, vulnerable to attack by naval forces.

littoral nation—a country having at least one shoreline bordering on international waters.

LNG carrier—a merchant ship specially designed to carry liquefied natural gas.

Maritime Administration—the department of the U.S. government charged with the control and oversight of the U.S. maritime industry.

military law—regulations and rules pertaining to the discipline and administration of the armed forces.

naval attaché—a naval officer on duty at an embassy, whose major duties are advising and representing the ambassador on naval matters and collecting intelligence. See also ALUSNA.

naval operations—significant activities conducted by naval forces at sea; day-to-day activities within the operations department of a ship.

neutrality—the state of nonparticipation in a war.

nonjudicial punishment—punishment by a commanding officer imposed on a service member without trial by court-martial.

NRL—Naval Research Laboratory.

OAS—Organization of American States; an organization composed of almost all non-Communist states of the Western Hemisphere.

ONR—Office of Naval Research.

peremptory challenge—the automatic removal of a prospective member of a military court-martial on demand from the accused, with no reason necessarily given.

preventive war—a war initiated by making a strike against an enemy to prevent the enemy from taking a presumed aggressive action.

psychological operations (PSYOPS)—operations intended to influence the emotions, motives, objective reasoning, and/or the behavior of target organizations, groups, and individuals.

quarantine—a limited form of naval blockade directed against specific prohibited cargo.

raid—a sudden attack against a limited area or facility.

R&D—research and development.

regulations—a body of written rules for conduct and procedures in a military organization.

reprisal—retaliatory action for an injury or attack.

restriction (punishment)—to keep on board a ship or shore station for some prescribed length of time as a punishment for a discipline offense.

sea power—the ability of a country to use and control the sea, and to prevent its use by an enemy.

sovereign—a self-governing independent country.

specified command—a broad command within a functional area.

strategic forces—forces capable of delivering offensive nuclear weapons against an enemy.

strike forces—forces intended to carry out an offensive attack against an enemy.

surface action group (SAG)—surface warfare ships comprising a battle formation.

sweep—a series of strikes against several enemy targets in a general area.

telecommunications—communication by electronic transmission of impulses, as by telegraphy, radio, or microwave.

territorial sea—the ocean waters within 12 miles of the shoreline, controlled by the coastal sovereign state.

thalweg—a boundary line between two nations consisting of the center of a navigable channel in a waterway separating them.

UCMJ—Uniform Code of Military Justice.

unauthorized absence—absence from a military unit without proper authorization.

unified command—a command with a broad continuing mission within a geographical area of responsibility.

unmanned aerial vehicle (UAV)—any of a number of small remotely piloted aircraft used for reconnaissance, fire control, and other military purposes.

U.S. flag ships—merchant ships registered in the United States and operating under the American flag on the high seas.

USNS—United States Naval Ship; a ship owned by the U.S. Navy but not commissioned as part of the Navy. Normally crewed by civilians and operated by the Military Sealift Command.

LEADERSHIP

The Challenge of Leadership

In *Naval Science 2* you were introduced to basic principles of leadership that will help you rise to higher levels of responsibility in your NJROTC unit and in other life activities in which you may be involved. This section will expand on the principles you learned earlier, and provide information on more advanced topics you will need as you proceed to higher levels of leadership within your unit and elsewhere. Many of the practices and qualities that are common to successful leaders both in the military and in civilian life will be discussed. In addition, some insight into the evaluation of performance of subordinates will be provided, along with information about effective techniques of how to give instruction, both of which will be very useful to you as you assume greater leadership roles within your unit.

Basis for Effective Leadership

Good leadership stresses the qualities that enable a person to inspire and manage a group of people successfully. Effective leadership, therefore, is based on personal example, good organization and administration, and personal moral responsibility. The second of these, organization and administration, deals with a leader's personal attention to and supervision of subordinates. Because the Navy is made up of people, naval leaders must learn to understand and value the many individuals with whom they must work.

The naval leader must have a philosophy of leadership based on firmly held moral values and integrity of character. Leaders must understand how to act toward seniors, peers, and juniors. A naval leader will be ineffective if he or she does not understand good leadership and administration and is not able to get the teamwork necessary for the unit to carry out its mission.

Leadership involves human relations—specifically those between a leader and a group. A leader must be able to impose, either through command or persuasion, his or her will upon that group. Also required is a willingness on the part of the leader to sacrifice personal time and material gain to achieve this personal "power." Still, a person who is to become a truly successful leader must first of all have learned the principles of good "followership," as set forth in *Naval Science 1*.

Philosophies of Leadership

Philosophies of leadership differ widely. One extreme view holds that leaders are born, not made. The opposite extreme contends that anyone who can master various leadership principles can

Leadership is an art, gift, or science by which a person can direct the thoughts, plans, and actions of others in order to obtain their obedience, respect, confidence, and loyal cooperation. This NJROTC class is fortunate to receive guidance from two very proficient naval leaders. (Kenneth Hendrix)

lead effectively. Other viewpoints stress leadership as a managerial process, or as a matter of character and moral development. Still another holds that leadership can best be learned by studying the lives of great men and women. Each of these philosophies has merit, but none, by itself, answers the question of how effective leadership can be developed.

There is no denying that some people are born with physical and mental qualities that make them natural leaders. However, history is full of examples of people who reached great heights of leadership as the result of study, discipline, and hard work, in spite of handicaps such as small size, physical disabilities, or a lowly family background.

Leadership is an art, gift, or science by which a person can direct the thoughts, plans, and actions of others in order to obtain their obedience, respect, confidence, and loyal cooperation. Each of these objectives is essential. Lack of any one probably would cause failure in any situation where leadership is needed.

Obedience

Obedience is the most important of the qualities that good leaders should strive to instill in their personnel. Obedience is necessarily the first lesson that must be learned by any military person.

The first lessons learned by children from their parents involve obedience: come here, go there, sit down, eat, don't touch, be careful, pick it up, etc. Obedience is necessary to teach the child to do basic activities and to protect him or her from dangers. In adult life, however, obedience is of greater concern in military life than in most civilian environments.

While disobeying the law will result in punishment of one sort or another in either environment, the loss of their jobs is probably the most significant result when civilians disobey their boss. The military "product," however, is defense of our country and our way of life. Military service people, therefore, must be more idealistic than the average civilian, since they are serving, protecting, and defending the United States and its allies—even to the extent of giving up their lives in peace or war. Thus there is a greater need for obedience from service members in uniform.

Obedience in the Military Services

In the military, an *order* is a directive to action of some kind, generally given by a senior to a junior. In the oath of service taken by all enlisted personnel upon enlistment, they promise to faithfully obey and carry out the lawful orders of those appointed over them. Obedience to orders has two forms in the military, each with its own time and place. *Blind obedience* is automatic response to orders such as commands issued during close order drill, or steering commands to a helmsman. There is no time for questioning or determining the reason for this type of order. *Reasoned obedience*, on the other hand, allows for some personal initiative in carrying out an order.

Reasoned obedience is the type most often desired in the Navy and NJROTC. Navy work involves constant learning, and it is known that people work and learn best when allowed to use their own ideas. Most day-to-day routine orders give the receiver some freedom in deciding exactly how to carry them out in a responsible manner.

Orders may be given in various ways. Polite phrases such as "please" or "would you" and other common courtesies may be used by a senior when giving orders, but even if the order has the sound of a request, it is still an order. When time permits, the leader may explain the reasons for an order. The juniors may be encouraged to ask reasonable questions, or even suggest possible alternatives, but this does not imply that subordinates may decide whether or not they will obey. Often, however, a more specific form of order called a *command* may be appropriate.

A command calls for immediate blind obedience. Courteous terms normally are not used in commands. There is usually no time for hesitation or questions regarding such orders. Examples might be commands to commence fire on an enemy, or to abort a dangerous landing approach to an aircraft carrier.

People obey the orders of lawful authorities because of either the hope of reward or the fear of punishment. Reasoned obedience to an order often involves hope of some kind of reward. This may take the form of a simple verbal compliment (such as "Well done!"), public recognition and praise, the privilege of greater responsibility, or improvement of status in the organization. Blind obedience to a command seldom lends itself to particular reward at the moment, and is more often associated with the threat of punishment should it be disobeyed.

The good leader should strive to have the respect, confidence, and loyal cooperation of subordinates, but it is impossible for him or her to lead without first obtaining their obedience.

The Military Leader: A Legal and Moral Obligation

Civilian executives hold their positions by virtue of superior knowledge and experience and strong character or personality. The executive probably is not legally responsible for the persons employed, and any concern for the well-being of subordinates is primarily a moral one.

Military leaders, on the other hand, have both a legal and a moral obligation to do all in their power to lead their subordinates effectively and to be concerned about their welfare. The president, as representative of the people of the United States, has granted each military leader extensive authority to do so based on a legal contract.

The military leader must depend upon subordinates to accomplish assigned missions. Consequently, leaders must be aware of their subordinates' capabilities and their limitations. The leader must personally be concerned with subordinates' health, welfare, and any problems that may affect their peace of mind and effi-

These NJROTC cadets are learning firsthand that it takes everyone pulling together with all their individual strengths and weaknesses to accomplish a mission. (Annapolis HS NJROTC)

ciency on the job, such as family illness, debts, and other difficulties. The leader must gain the confidence of his or her personnel so that they will feel free to consult the leader about any problems.

The Challenge of Leadership

The leader has an especially difficult task in trying to motivate disinterested persons or troublemakers who always seem to be present in most groups of people. Ideally, the leader will be able to guide and assist most such individuals to gain a sense of moral responsibility so they too can become assets to the organization. After all, everyone must live by rules and regulations, whether in the Navy or in civilian life. These rules, if followed, make life more pleasant and easier for all.

Personnel must be taught that the more they discipline themselves, the less they will have to be disciplined by others. They must be fully aware of their importance to the team. Their shipmates must be able to depend on them in day-to-day routine matters, as well as in battle. All should be led to understand that learning, advancing in rate, and assuming more responsibilities are duties of every Sailor and citizen, not just the choice of a select few.

In the Navy, as in the other military services, officers and petty officers have the responsibilities of leadership. Although each leadership position may be different, the challenge of leadership remains the same: to get people to do the job.

Leadership and discipline are vital in any military organization. The same qualities that make a good leader in the military services are equally helpful to the civilian leader.

STUDY GUIDE QUESTIONS

1. What is the challenge of leadership?
2. Upon what is effective leadership based?
3. What are the two extremes in philosophy of leadership?
4. What is the first lesson that military personnel must learn?
5. Why must military personnel have a more idealistic outlook on the importance of obedience?
6. A. What are the two forms of military obedience?

   B. Why is there a need for each?
7. What is the difference between a senior's request or order and a command?
8. What makes the military leader different from the civilian executive?

CRITICAL THINKING

1. In which ways is it harder to be a leader in the military than in civilian life? In which ways is it easier?
2. What are some ways of getting the cooperation of a disinterested or uncommitted subordinate?

VOCABULARY

moral responsibility	order
reasoned obedience	command
blind obedience	

2 Qualities of a Leader

No two leaders are exactly alike. They do not possess the same traits; neither do they accomplish their goals in the same ways. All great leaders, however, have certain characteristics and abilities. Not every leader will possess every quality discussed here, but all will have many of them. It stands to reason that it is important for a leader with less natural ability to work on those qualities needed to become more effective.

Moral Responsibility

A high sense of moral responsibility is one of the most important leadership characteristics. All truly great leaders have had personal codes of conduct that would not permit them to use their abilities and positions to take unfair advantage of their fellow citizens or subordinates.

Most of us understand the written and unwritten laws that guide our actions and know that appropriate punishments will likely result if we break them. It is more difficult, however, to define moral laws, since most of these cannot be legally enforced. Each person must establish these laws for himself or herself. Depending upon the person's character, the sense of moral responsibility may be extensive or almost nonexistent. The only enforcer is the individual's own conscience.

Loyalty

Loyalty means faithful and enthusiastic devotion to one's country, organization, and associates. In the military this must be broadened to include one's superiors and subordinates. Everyone must earn the right to loyalty.

Loyalty is a two-way street. Subordinates are particularly sensitive about loyalty extending downward to them and are quick to notice when it is absent. The loyalty of a senior toward his or her personnel has a great effect on the morale within the organization, and this may translate into that extra effort that is so often necessary to accomplish a mission.

Devotion to Duty

Devotion to duty may be defined as loyalty to the position or job one holds. In general, devotion to duty is shown by someone who not only exerts maximum effort on the present job, but also takes initiative to learn about tasks and billets demanding increased levels of responsibility. Positive recommendations, advancements, and promotions are likely to result from such performance of duty.

A young person showing ambition on the job in a civilian firm is considered a valuable asset; such a person might eventually be considered for a management role. Mere ambition is not enough in the military service, however. All in the military are expected to place duty above self. All must do their duty to the best of their ability at all times—not because of the personal gain that might occur, but because that is the best way to accomplish the mission. The unit might fail in its mission if some individuals fail to do their part.

Master Chief Petty Officer of the fleet West has demonstrated the best qualities of naval leadership throughout his service career. Note the new Navy working uniform he is wearing. (Jennifer Villalovos)

Professional Knowledge

The person who knows the job thoroughly is far better qualified to lead than one who does not. Mere schoolbook knowledge is not sufficient; experience is also essential. The new leader, therefore, must not hesitate to call upon more experienced individuals to assist when appropriate.

The person being relieved by a new leader normally provides information concerning the duties and difficulties of the job and the abilities and personalities of the assigned personnel. Subordinates will be eager to help, if their new leader shows interest in gaining from their experiences. It pays to be willing to listen to advice and suggestions, for most people will lose the desire to help if their leader shows lack of interest or caring.

Self-Confidence

Self-confidence is one of the most important qualities of leadership. As a leader's knowledge grows, self-confidence should also grow. In fact, knowledge is meaningless without confidence and ability. Past accomplishments and educational degrees by themselves will not suffice; proven ability on the job is the most basic requirement. Arrogance on the part of an untried, inexperienced junior officer or new leading petty officer will result in the loss of subordinates' respect, which will make the leader's job much more difficult.

Initiative and Ingenuity

The military services have so many regulations, instructions, and policies that a new leader might believe there is little room for personal initiative and ingenuity in the service today—but this simply is not so. Actually, with new ships, new equipment, new weapons systems, and new concepts of warfare, the demand for officers and petty officers with these qualities is greater now than ever before. All of these new developments require leaders with the imagination, skills, and daring to find the best ways to use new systems and new ideas.

In the NJROTC as in the Navy, few days will pass without some opportunity to exercise initiative and ingenuity. The new leader must take advantage of small, everyday opportunities in order to gain the self-confidence necessary to handle bigger challenges when they arise.

Before tackling any problem, though, it is necessary to have solid background knowledge of that problem. You can be sure that problems that exist today did not suddenly materialize out of thin air; problems grow over a period of time, as do new ideas and new equipment. Consequently, when problems need to be solved, it is wise to be aware of what has been tried before. To try again with a flawed method that has failed before is often a waste of time and effort.

Courage

It would be difficult to imagine a true leader who did not possess courage. Courage is the quality that enables us to accept our responsibilities and to carry them out regardless of the consequences. A courageous person can meet dangers and difficulties with firmness. A courageous person is not necessarily fearless, but has learned to conquer inner fears in order to concentrate on the tasks at hand. Courage is a quality of the mind and may be developed and strengthened with use. Each time a person overcomes an obstacle—whether it is a tough examination, or a sports opponent, or peer pressure—the courage of that individual will be strengthened.

We should be careful to add, however, that continuous success with every problem, while encouraging and satisfying at the time, may not necessarily prepare an individual for the disappointment of failure. Courage grows when a person learns to strive again for success after an initial setback.

Moral Courage

Moral courage means a show of firmness in difficult situations where the danger of death or injury is not an immediate concern. It is a form of courage less glamorous than physical courage—risking one's life to save another, being fearless in the face of enemy fire, or braving the unknown dangers of the deep seas or outer space. Situations requiring moral courage, however, occur far more often than the more glamorous ones.

The pressures of our daily lives can be great at times, and this is where moral courage comes in. It may be easier to allow the wrong thing to be done and to say nothing, or to observe incorrect procedures or damaged equipment and let it go unreported. Sometimes it is hard to disagree with a senior—or worse, to agree with a senior when you are certain that he or she is wrong. Fear of anger from seniors, fear of ridicule by peers, and lack of confidence due to immaturity or ignorance are some of the pressures that make the exercise of moral courage difficult.

Moral courage is necessary to ensure that seniors get the information they need to make good decisions—even if such information upsets them. A person needs moral courage to bring forth new ideas for improvement, especially if those ideas go against precedent or well-laid plans. The person who says nothing, or agrees with seniors and then criticizes them behind their backs, loses both the respect of juniors and the trust of the seniors. On the other hand, the leader who shows respect for the opinions of others, especially subordinates, is admired and respected for having moral courage.

It takes moral courage to admit one's mistakes. It takes moral courage to be honest, just, and truthful at all times. It takes moral courage to insist on abiding by regulations and laws when they are being disregarded by many others. It takes a very special moral courage to stick to one's high principles in the face of ridicule by peers and friends, because everyone wants to feel like "one of the gang."

All young people have a need for good examples of how to be the best they can be. This sharp NJROTC cadet demonstrates pride in himself and in his unit as he goes aboard a Navy training ship. (Annapolis HS NJROTC)

Ability to Organize and Make Decisions

A military leader's primary job is to coordinate the efforts of their personnel to achieve a common purpose. Leaders must be able to organize their subordinates so that their labors and training can be used to achieve the best results. A first requirement for effective organization therefore is a full awareness of the skills and capabilities of assigned personnel.

While it is entirely proper to call upon the expertise and experience of seniors to assist in the accomplishment of a mission, young leaders must eventually make most of the final decisions themselves. Without the ability to make good decisions, a leader is useless.

Subordinates expect clear-cut decisions from their leaders when they bring personal problems to them for discussion or when professional problems require solutions. If complicated problems arise, especially those clearly beyond a junior's authority, he or she will want to discuss them with a superior. Honest mistakes will occasionally occur, but from mistakes comes experience, and from experience comes wisdom.

Personal Example

All young people have a strong need for examples to live by. By following the good example of someone admired—father, mother, sibling, teacher, sports hero, or celebrity—the young person can acquire the qualities he or she needs for success. When leaders' conduct is outstanding, those around them are often inspired to pattern their own actions after them, to the good of the whole organization. No leader, then, can live by the rule of "Do as I say, not as I do." It will not work. As many recent events have shown, many bad things can happen to elected, appointed, and commissioned and noncommissioned military and civilian leaders if what they do in their private lives is not as exemplary as their public and professional lives.

No leader can ignore rules and regulations and still expect subordinates to follow them. Such a leader will not be trusted and will lose control of subordinates. Regaining respect and control once they are lost is exceptionally difficult.

Rank has its privileges, but that does not excuse improper conduct. Rather, when it comes to conduct, it should be stressed that rank also has its responsibilities. "Conduct" in the military means conduct ashore, as well as aboard ship or station. No good citizen and certainly no service member would do anything to dishonor the uniform, for such conduct can bring dishonor upon the United States and its armed forces.

Mutual Trust and Confidence

Officers and petty officers must set a proper example by letting subordinates know that they are trusted. If leaders fail to show trust in their subordinates, they will soon find themselves constantly checking up on their people, distrusting the records and reports prepared by them, and consequently performing their own duties less efficiently.

These two members of a NJROTC relay race team know that it takes mutual trust and confidence in each other's ability to make a good exchange of the baton in the stress of competition. (Annapolis HS NJROTC)

It would be naïve, however, to suggest that all leaders in the Navy, the government, business, or anywhere else are continuously efficient, invariably honest, and always perform their duties responsibly and with honor. We know that our leaders should do things that way, of course, and we have a right to expect that they do. When leaders fail to fulfill their responsibilities, society has the right to demand corrective action, and in serious cases, punishment under the law.

In any event, when a leader fails to back subordinates, shows favoritism, condones dishonesty, allows sloppy work, or evades legitimate regulations, the reputation of not just the leader involved but of all leaders in the organization is jeopardized. Mutual respect, trust, and understanding can prompt all hands to exercise a greater degree of personal responsibility. Then morale will be higher, efficiency will be improved, and burdens will be lighter.

The word of a leader should be dependable. Consequently, if leaders cannot make good on their word or their promises, they should not make commitments. *Never promise what cannot be delivered.* Keeping your word is important evidence of personal honor. If you do not make a special effort to uphold your word, you will lose the respect of subordinates and associates, and the attitudes of all around you will be adversely affected. A sense of honesty and mutual trust must be present if a military unit is to operate efficiently.

Conduct in Uniform

The naval leader must do all in his or her power to prevent improper actions by naval personnel. Often the cause for such actions is dissatisfaction with conditions in their unit, ship, or station. If a person does not like the work assignment or living conditions, feels that command policies are unfair, or has troubles at home, weaker subordinates may resort to unauthorized absence, to alcohol or substance abuse, or to other forms of escape. Such individuals may make it impossible for the unit to accomplish its mission.

A military leader has the responsibility to know the needs of subordinates and to know their anxieties. It is his or her duty to remind them of their responsibility to conduct themselves properly at all times, to reflect credit on their families, their service, and their nation, and to be ready to perform their duties whenever required to do so.

The big difference between civilian and military leadership, however, comes in the corrective actions expected of the leadership. In civilian institutions a certain degree of concern is generally exercised, often reflected in things like insurance coverage and some concern for health and safety conditions on the job, mostly to increase productivity, satisfy laws, or abide by union agreements. But there is little concern for, or involvement in, the employee's home life, recreation, financial well-being, ethics, or living conditions. The worker punches in, does the job, punches out, and leaves. A worker who doesn't do the job satisfactorily may be warned, but the supreme threat is the loss of the job by firing. On the other hand, a worker who is dissatisfied with a job may quit.

In the military, corrective actions are a primary responsibility of leadership. The leaders must know their personnel and take care of their needs, and must insist on the acceptance and exercise of personal moral responsibility. The naval leader must accept this responsibility by regulation, but must also do so for the practical reason that it is necessary if the crew is to be a working team that can respond properly to emergency situations and carry out the unit's mission.

Discipline

Discipline is the basis of true democracy. It requires rules of conduct that humans, through experience, have found desirable for governing relations among members of civilized society. Such rules of conduct do not deprive an individual of fundamental rights; in fact, they protect everyone's equal rights.

Formal rules that are put into effect by duly constituted authority, such as a city council or state legislature, are called *laws*. Other informal rules that have become a part of our culture by custom and usage are called *conventions*.

Discipline is the training that develops self-control, character, or efficiency. It is important both in civilian and military life. Discipline does not imply severity, unreasonable restraint of freedom, or unnecessary restrictions. Discipline means control of conduct so there can be a coordination of effort for the good of all.

A dictionary defines discipline as "control gained by enforcing obedience," or "that state of orderliness gained through self-control and orderly conduct." A description of discipline in military terms would be "that degree of control which moves an organized group to appropriate action upon receipt of an order, or in anticipation of that order when circumstances prevent its being given."

A military organization could not function properly without orderliness and orderly conduct. Admiral Arleigh Burke, USN, a former chief of naval operations, stated: "A well-disciplined organization is one whose members work with enthusiasm, willingness, and zest, as individuals and as a group, to fulfill the mission of the organization with expectation of success." The signs of discipline in a military organization can be seen in smart salutes, proper wearing of the uniform, and prompt and correct action in any emergency.

The purpose of discipline in the military services is to develop an efficient organization of personnel trained to achieve a common goal. Each person should know where he or she fits into the organization. Each should understand that all in the group have a common purpose and that all are to follow and obey their leader. Such a group is so well organized and trained that it can handle any emergency, as well as normal routine tasks. A well-disciplined military unit responds automatically to an emergency and will not panic.

A good leader knows that everyone responds to recognition for a job well done. Here, these NJROTC cadets receiving the winner's trophy after a drill competition know that their discipline and hard work has been acknowledged and rewarded. (Central HS NJROTC, David Poe)

Self-Discipline

True discipline demands loyal but reasoned obedience to authority. Such obedience allows for initiative and is present even in the absence of the leader. Self-discipline, therefore, is essential before true discipline can be developed. The self-disciplined person will always be dependable and will carry out responsibilities under all circumstances without need of direct supervision.

Self-discipline lessens the need for specific rules and regulations. Traffic laws, the Uniform Code of Military Justice, civil rights laws, alcohol and drug laws, and even things like school dress codes would be unnecessary if we were all perfectly self-disciplined individuals. Self-disciplined people need little or no supervision.

Self-discipline begins with the realization that there is a need for self-control. Development of self-discipline comes only through repeated practice of self-control. The person who has developed self-control in day-to-day life is also the one who can hold up in the face of hardship and danger.

Consistency In Disciplinary Action

In the military, disobedience of regulations must be handled immediately, justly, and consistently. Wrong-doing that is dealt with severely one day cannot be treated as insignificant the next. Such an approach can only result in confusion, poor morale, and distrust of the leader.

If service members are allowed to defy a regulation openly, they will develop an indifferent attitude toward other regulations as well. Two fundamental rules apply: (1) never make a regulation that you cannot or will not enforce, and (2) take immediate, fair action that leaves no doubt in the mind of the offender about the reason for the reprimand or punishment.

Delay in taking appropriate disciplinary action brings resentment toward the entire system—especially if the offender "gets off" because of a time lapse that dulls memories or makes it seem as though the offense has been overlooked. Wrong acts and poor performance require immediate guidance and correction in order to bring about the necessary changes.

New leaders may have a tendency to be too lenient with minor infractions, thereby penalizing good people while favoring bad ones. When this error is pointed out to some junior leaders, they may become uncertain of themselves, and in trying to compensate for the fault, they overreact, becoming too arbitrary. In either case the leader will lose the confidence of subordinates because of such inconsistency. It is best to chart a steady course when dealing with disciplinary matters.

Loss of Temper = Loss of Control

A leader cannot afford to lose his or her temper. Losing one's temper is usually considered to be a personal weakness and usually does not improve the effectiveness of the leader and his or her status within the organization. To be sure, it is not always easy to refrain from anger, but a conscious effort to do so must be made.

A person who loses control of himself or herself usually loses control of the situation. Rare is the case when proper action or desired results come from an expression of anger. In admonishing error or administering punishment, the leader must remain calm, impersonal, and dignified. A leader who is extremely incensed might want to pace the deck for a few minutes rather than take unwise, precipitous action. The calmer the leader is in the usual performance of duty, the more action he or she can get when the occasion demands. The leader who is inconsistent, quick-tempered, or constantly shouting only creates confusion and soon stops being effective, since those actions eventually will get little or no response from subordinates.

Knowing Personnel

It is vital that leaders get to know the people working for them. As part of this, it is important for the young leader to develop a style of communication with personnel that will create mutual respect. The key to this is learning the personality and character of every one of those juniors—understanding what makes them tick.

It is the duty of the leader to study their people, watch them, learn their approach to problems, work with them, and guide them. To maintain discipline, the leader must always be genuinely concerned about his or her people, and should not wait until they get into difficulties to help them. This means ensuring that they are comfortable and as well cared for as circumstances permit; seeing that they receive their fair share of earned privileges; and showing that their personal and family lives are of real interest. The good leader will always make sure people are fully aware of what is being done on their behalf.

A leader should bear in mind that everyone wants, needs, and responds to recognition. If the best in people is to be brought out, they must be made to feel important. They must feel respect from their associates, and they must feel that their superiors think they are competent.

A good leader continually strives to apply all that he or she can learn about human nature through experience and study. This knowledge can be obtained only by working at the job of human relations. The better his or her insight into human nature, and the better he or she understands the intelligence, education, and backgrounds of personnel, the more effective the leader will be in handling people.

Friendship versus Familiarity

In recent years personal relationships between leaders and subordinates, especially between those of the opposite sex, have become an area of great concern, both in the military and civilian life. The relationship between leaders and their subordinates influences discipline. There is a great difference between familiarity and friendship. The leader who talks to subordinates in a friendly manner, taking a personal interest in them and being concerned with their problems, quickly gains their confidence and respect. Young men and women want to be able to look to their seniors for guidance; they want to be proud of their leaders. Such leaders, because they are friendly and approachable, will be the first ones turned to for advice.

On the other hand, leaders who become *too* familiar with their subordinates will often have difficulty in leading them. The old adage "familiarity breeds contempt" is applicable to these situations, because subordinates who perceive themselves as favored may feel the leader will not require them to obey and perform well. Those who do not feel so favored may perceive unfair or unequal treatment, whether or not it actually exists.

The Navy and the other services all have strict regulations against seniors becoming overly familiar (developing close personal relationships) with personnel of lower rank, especially those in their immediate chain of command. Such relationships are called *fraternization*. Unsolicited or otherwise undesirable or inappropriate advances of one service member toward another based on sexual attraction, especially involving promises of reward or threats of punishment or other forms of intimidation, is called *sexual harassment*.

Fraternization and sexual harassment can be extremely destructive to the morale of both those directly affected and their fellow crew members or coworkers on the job. Such actions can-not be tolerated in the Navy or other military services, and those found guilty of this type of behavior are subject to severe discipline or separation from the service. Most civilian institutions are very concerned about these issues as well, both because of potential legal issues and also because of their impact on the productivity and morale of the organization.

STUDY GUIDE QUESTIONS

1. What are the qualities of a good leader that are discussed in this chapter?

2. Why must loyalty be a two-way street?

3. A. What is devotion to duty?

   B. How does it relate to healthy personal ambition?

   C. How does it relate to the ability to take orders?

4. What two main qualifications are necessary for a leader to be regarded as knowledgeable?

5. How can courage be strengthened?

6. A. What is moral courage?

   B. What are the principal factors that make moral courage difficult?

   C. How can a lack of moral courage lead to the loss of both the respect of juniors and the trust of seniors?

7. Why could it be especially dangerous to neglect reporting a disagreeable fact to a commander?

8. A. Why is decision making important for a leader?

   B. How can the young leader obtain help when confronted with problems beyond his or her experience to solve?

9. Why is the leader's personal example so important in leading subordinates?

10. Why are mutual trust and confidence so important in dealing with people?

11. What is Admiral Burke's definition of a well-disciplined organization?

12. What is the purpose of military discipline?

13. How does a person acquire self-discipline?

14. Why is consistency in disciplinary action essential?

15. Why is it important not to make rules that are unenforceable?

16. What is the usual result if leaders lose their temper?

17. Why is an understanding of human nature important in dealing with people?

18. A. Why is fraternization or familiarity between officers and enlisted personnel prohibited in the military services?

B. What is the difference between friendship and familiarity?

19. A. What is sexual harassment?

B. Why can it not be tolerated in the military services?

CRITICAL THINKING

1. Why is the issue of friendship and familiarity between leaders and subordinates within the same military unit of greater concern than between individuals working within a civilian firm?

2. What are some ways in which two individuals of different rank within a military unit can maintain a friendship while not violating military rules against fraternization?

VOCABULARY

character	fraternization
loyalty	sexual harassment
self-confidence	leniency
arrogance	infraction
initiative	familiarity

3 Evaluation of Performance

All people are involved in evaluation from an early age. Babies respond to some types of personalities better than others. Youngsters select friends based on performance and satisfying their needs for companionship. The process becomes more sophisticated and important as years go by. In the Navy and in NJROTC, officers are concerned with the selection of personnel for instructors, for school nominations, for advancement in rate, for filling billets in the unit, and for carrying out specific assignments. The overall performance rating of a naval leader is greatly affected by ability to select appropriate people for various roles, and to judge their capability to take on future assignments of greater responsibility.

Performance, Ability, Aptitude, Achievement

Performance refers to what a person does—actual behavior or actual output. *Ability* is often confused with performance. Ability often applies to performance over a considerable period of time; it also applies to what a person could do at a given moment, if the sit-

These NJROTC cadets are going though an important phase in personal development called progress assessment. Upon completion of this quiz, the individuals taking it can use it to judge for themselves how well they learned the material presented to them, and can take personal corrective action to improve future performance if necessary. (Annapolis HS NJROTC)

uation were right. Further out in time, it might sometimes refer to potential performance. For example, a long-distance runner may be hampered in a particular race by illness, but basic ability is not questioned. One often hears comments on potential performance such as, "He could do it if he really tried," or "She just doesn't seem to care." In the final analysis, true ability cannot be judged except by observing performance. It is the results that count!

Both performance and ability refer to the present—what the person is doing, or can do, now. *Aptitude,* on the other hand, refers to potential skills and abilities in the future. Aptitude tests of many varieties, such as the SAT (Scholastic Aptitude Test) and ASVAB (an armed services aptitude test), as well as evaluation of background experiences, can be used with good reliability to select individuals for training in certain areas. For example, high school musicians proved to be very adept radiomen in World War II, when an individual's ability to read international Morse code was crucial to the rating. Likewise, the farmhand who has driven and repaired tractors, cars, and machinery since age ten is a good prospect to become a successful engineman or machinist's mate. A long list of such examples could be made.

Achievement generally refers to performance in the past, often that which has already been evaluated. Achievement applies to work that has been done. When properly evaluated, past achievements of individuals in the same field can be quickly compared for selection for promotion or future job assignments. Properly evaluating the achievements of their subordinates is one of the most important responsibilities of a leader.

Evaluation in the NJROTC

Developing leadership ability is one of the main objectives of NJROTC. Students enrolled in this course should strive to become leaders in their school, unit, and community, and prepare for higher leadership roles later in life.

Already, the cadet officers of an NJROTC unit have been through a selection process to attain their ranks and their positions. Their predecessors undoubtedly helped their naval science instructors to make the current appointments. Perhaps more important to the cadet is the fact that their current officers and instructors must evaluate and nominate their successors at some time during the school year.

To advance in the NJROTC, as in the Navy, an individual needs to grow steadily both personally and professionally. The experience these cadets are getting as they learn how to handle the helm and engine order telegraph aboard a Navy training ship will serve them well. (Annapolis HS NJROTC)

Evaluations of prospective NJROTC cadet officers are based on character, honesty, motivation, academic effort and success, cooperation in unit ventures, record of loyalty to school and unit, appearance in uniform, and many other attributes. These evaluations will be reflected in their leaders' recommendations and result in awards, advancements, and promotions. Such is the way of the Navy as well, and it really is no different in civilian life. The system works; sound evaluation grounded in sound personal leadership is the key.

Self-Evaluation

It is not necessary for a person to wait until a formal evaluation time or period to evaluate his or her own performance. Everyone in the NJROTC, or anyone who aspires to get ahead either in the military or in civilian life, should go through a periodic *self-evaluation* process. Such a process is roughly like guiding a ship from one place to another. As navigator, you have to know your present location and where the ship is going, or you cannot possibly determine whether or not you are on the correct course to get there.

Goal Setting

Most people who have been successful in life did not achieve their success by luck or by proceeding in a random manner. Rather, a common thread in almost every success story is the setting of realistic and attainable *goals*. Such goals may be as simple as saving to buy a new piece of athletic gear, or as complex as getting an A in a tough high school course, or getting a job in a desired profession. Depending on how difficult the goal is to attain, one or more subgoals may also have to be identified—like waypoints along the route to the final destination.

Progress Assessment

Once realistic goals have been decided upon, the next step is to assess progress toward them. In the school setting, such progress assessment is facilitated by the assignment of periodic progress grades by the teacher. Broader progress can be assessed by such standardized tests as the preliminary and regular Scholastic Aptitude Tests (PSAT and SAT) and various achievement tests. In the military, progress is measured by periodic formal and informal performance ratings, advancement exams, and aptitude tests such as the ASVAB. Similar methods are used to assess progress in civilian occupations.

However, in all roles of life, truly successful people do not sit back and wait until they are formally evaluated to judge their progress toward the goals they have set for themselves. Rather, they go through an almost continuous process of self-evaluation to determine for themselves how they are progressing and whether corrective action is necessary to get back on track. After all, it is much easier to stay on course toward a goal by making periodic small corrections than it is to make large corrections only once or twice along the way.

The Self-Evaluation Process

The main tasks in any self-evaluation process are to set *realistic criteria* by which one may measure progress, and to make *realistic assessments* of performance against those criteria. In school, such judgments might involve performance on daily or weekly quizzes. In athletics, such criteria as times to run various distances in track, percentage of foul shots made that day in basketball, or percentage of first serves good in tennis might be useful. In personal relations, how well one handled tensions between oneself and, say, a teacher or friend could be assessed. The important thing is to be truly honest with yourself so that a realistic evaluation can be made.

If the self-evaluation indicates that some corrections are necessary, the next step is to decide on the most effective course of action to make the desired adjustment, such as by study or improving technique in the academic or sports areas, or personal behavior in the case of interpersonal relations. It is here that more successful individuals are often separated from those less successful, because such adjustments and changes in behavior are often accomplished only by hard and continuous effort.

To advance in the NJROTC, the Navy, or another armed service—and indeed in almost any organization—an individual needs to grow steadily both personally and professionally. One of the best ways to do so is to set both short-term and long-range goals for yourself in each area of concern, and then to take appropriate corrective action whenever trends develop that, if left uncorrected, would hinder your progress. The process may not always be fun, but it is exciting, and it provides you with a real feeling of accomplishment as you meet each short-term goal. Ultimately, you can get the most out of life as you achieve your major long-term personal and professional objectives.

STUDY GUIDE QUESTIONS

1. Explain why evaluation of performance of subordinates is important to officers in the Navy and the NJROTC.

2. What is the difference between a person's ability and his or her performance?

3. Why should NJROTC cadets know about performance evaluation?

4. Why is self-evaluation important?

5. What is a common factor in most personal success stories?

6. How can a person assess his or her progress toward a personal goal?

7. What are the main tasks in self-evaluation?

8. What must a person do to advance in the Navy or in any other large organization?

CRITICAL THINKING

1. Why is it important to seek input from a cadet's peers and their cadet leaders when evaluating them for possible cadet leadership positions?

2. How can the ability to go through a periodic self-evaluation process be of great benefit to those desiring to be better students or athletes in addition to those trying for leadership positions in the NJROTC?

VOCABULARY

performance
evaluation
aptitude

progress assessment
self-evaluation

4 How to Give Instruction

As you become an upperclassman in your school and achieve higher ranks within your NJROTC units, you will often be called upon to give either formal or informal instruction to schoolmates or to junior NJROTC cadets. In this chapter we will discuss many things that will be helpful when you find yourself in this situation. These include leaning theory, preparation for instruction, and techniques for delivery.

Learning Theory

The good instructor is master of many skills. Successful instruction demands competence in the subject matter and knowledge of teaching skills. But the methods of instruction depend largely on an understanding of how people learn and the ability to apply that understanding.

What Learning Is

One of humankind's outstanding characteristics is the ability to learn. People learn continuously from the time they are born until they die. As a result of a learning experience, people may change ways of perceiving, thinking, feeling, and doing. Thus, learning can be defined as a change in behavior as a result of experience. The behavior can be physical and apparent, or it can be intellectual or attitudinal, not easily seen.

Each student sees the classroom situation differently because he or she is a unique individual whose past experiences affect readiness to learn and understanding of the requirements involved. The responses differ because each person acts in accordance with how he or she sees the situation.

Most people have fairly definite ideas about what they want to do and achieve. The student brings these purposes and goals into the classroom. Some of these purposes may be personal, and others may be shared with classmates. Individual needs may determine what the student learns as much as what the instructor is trying to get him or her to learn. So the effective instructor seeks ways to relate new learning to the student's personal goals.

Learning is an individual process. The instructor cannot do it for the student; he or she cannot pour knowledge into the latter's head. The student can learn only from that which is experienced. Psychologists sometimes classify learning by types: verbal, conceptual, perceptual, motor, problem solving, and emotional. The

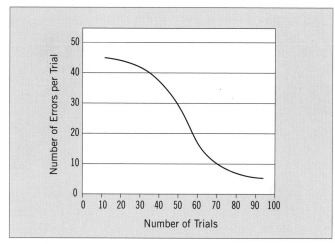

A typical learning curve for acquiring a skill. As the number of trials increases, the number of errors decreases rapidly until a learning "plateau" is reached, after which further improvement comes slowly.

learning process may include many types of learning, all taking place at once.

Research has shown that some of these types of learning appear to take place mainly on one side of the brain, while others occur mainly on the other side. Activities involving numbers, logic, word puzzles, and analysis appear to stimulate the left side of the brain, while activities involving music, imagination, colors, motion, and creative expression stimulate the right side. For many people, how they think, behave, and learn appears to be dominated by one side or the other, although much interaction takes place between the two sides. Traditionally, academic instruction has focused more on left-side activities, while somewhat neglecting the right side. Not surprisingly, much recent educational research has shown that the rate of learning can be greatly increased when instructors involve both sides of the brain in their teaching strategies.

The process of learning a skill appears to be much the same, regardless of whether it is a right- or left-brain activity. Graphs of the progress of skill learning usually follow the same pattern (see the figure). There is rapid improvement in the early trials. But the curve may tend to level off thereafter for significant periods of time. Such a development is a *learning plateau* and may signify any of a number of conditions. The student may have reached the limits of his or her capability; the student may be consolidating the level of

Navy divers give instruction in water survival skills to a group of NJROTC cadets during a Leadership Academy. The effective instructor is careful and thoughtful in the way he or she interacts with students. They should be challenged to learn, not intimidated. (James Foehl)

skill; interest may have waned; or the student may need a different method for increasing progress. One should keep in mind that the apparent lack of progress does not necessarily mean that further learning is impossible. The point is that a leveling process is normal, especially when learning motor skills, and should be expected after an initial period of rapid improvement. The instructor should prepare the student for this situation to ward off discouragement. If the student knows this may occur, frustration may be lessened.

Getting a student ready to learn is important. A student with a strong purpose, a clear objective, and a well-defined reason for learning something makes more progress than one who lacks motivation. A student who is ready to learn meets the instructor at least halfway, and this simplifies the instructor's job.

Several factors in the learning situation are known to speed, strengthen, or otherwise enhance learning:

- Learning occurs best when it progresses from *known to unknown* and *concrete to abstract.* The new learning can be attached to areas of existing knowledge.

- Learning is strengthened when accompanied by a pleasant or satisfying feeling, and learning is weakened when it is associated with an unpleasant feeling. An experience that produces feelings of defeat, frustration, anger, confusion, or futility in the student is unpleasant.

An instructor should be cautious about using *negative motivation* in the classroom. Impressing students with the seeming impossibility of a problem can make the teaching task difficult. Usually it is better to show that a problem is not impossible at all, but is within the student's capability to understand and solve. Regardless of the learning situation, it should contain at least some things that affect the student positively and give him or her a feeling of satisfaction. Every learning experience does not have to be entirely successful, nor does the student have to master each lesson completely. But a student's chance of success is increased if the learning experience is pleasant.

Certain states of mind of the learner are known to affect learning. *Motivation* is the drive or desire to do a particular thing. No one will learn something very well that he or she doesn't want to learn. The factor that has perhaps the greatest influence on learning is motivation, the force that causes a person to move toward a goal. This force can be rooted in any or all of the needs of the student—for example, the need for security, for new experience, for recognition, for self-esteem, for belonging, or for helping others. Such needs cause people to act, to move, to start working toward an objective, or to achieve a purpose. The instructor's responsibility is first to recognize and identify these needs in students, and then to seek ways of satisfying them through teaching.

Major Factors that Influence Learning

Much research has been done in recent years about the critical factors that influence how learning takes place. Some of these have already been discussed above. The results of this research are summarized below, in the form of nine major factors that influence learning:

- *New learning takes place in the context of past personal experience.* Students need to understand how new information relates to that which they already know.

- *Learning is dependent upon motivation.* A student must want to learn the new material.

- *Learning is reinforced through personal experience.* If a student has hands-on experience with a subject, he or she will put it into context better.

- *Learning is facilitated by linking with prior knowledge.* It is much easier to learn new material that is linked to something already known. One of the main goals of teaching is to help students make these links.

- *Learning is more efficient when new information is logically related.* By grouping new information in logical ways, the brain forms a *schema*, or concept, and gives it meaning.

- *Learning is enhanced by providing time for reflection.* Reflection, or extended thinking, helps put new information in long-term memory. Activities such as group discussion and writing in journals assist in this process.

- *Learning is enhanced by sensual and emotional involvement.* The more senses and emotional stimuli that are involved in learning new material, the better it will be retained in long-term memory.

- *Learning occurs best in an environment that enables more than one kind of learning.* Students have many different kinds or styles of intelligence (motion, visual/spatial, verbal/linguistic, musical, etc.) that need to come into play during learning.

- *Learning requires repetition.* It has been found that without repetition, new learning begins to fade in about thirty seconds. Instructors need to cover important new information several times in several different ways.

Interpersonal Interactions

Learning requires much of students. They must pay attention. They have to involve themselves actively, responding and manipulating. They are supposed to participate responsibly. To do all these things, students must feel secure, accepted, and capable of success. But even the most perfect lesson plan cannot develop such positive attitudes and feelings. The creation of such an environment is the instructor's responsibility, and the type and manner of instructor-student interactions can either improve or hinder learning. Therefore, the instructor must be aware of and work to avoid any of the conditions that inhibit learning.

The conditions that tend to hinder learning include the following:

Destructive sarcasm. Sarcasm (a mocking or cutting remark) can be funny—when watching a comedian dishing it out. It is not so funny to be on the receiving end in front of peers. It can hurt and embarrass students, and it effectively stifles learning. Instructors do best to forget sarcasm.

Intimidation. Some people have faced physical intimidation, and that is pretty scary. But intellectual intimidation may be even worse, especially when it comes to learning. It is the message that says the student is a stupid person whose opinions have no value, whose knowledge has no depth, and whose insights miss the mark. The intimidator picks out the student's errors and makes sure that everyone else knows about them. If the intimidator is the instructor, the student will dread the class, and learning will suffer.

Boredom. Boredom comes with monotony, with too much of the same. It comes with irrelevance and blandness. When bored, students no longer pay attention. They daydream. This failure to pay attention greatly hinders learning. No one likes to be bored; the result can be a poor attitude toward learning.

Frustration. Frustration occurs when students keep trying to do tasks beyond their abilities, or when tasks take too long to complete. The result is increased tension and a desire to get away from the task. It is cured through shortening tasks, making them easier to complete, and eliminating barriers to their completion.

Fatigue. Tiredness, whether physical or mental, inhibits learning. It reduces attention and motivation, and it decreases active involvement. Fatigue comes as a result of tasks that are too long or too difficult. Breaks, movement, and changes of pace revitalize learners.

Lack of purpose. If the student does not see any point in what he or she is doing, it is going to be all the harder to learn. Sense of purpose provides direction, helps focus attention, increases motivation, and thus assists learning and retention. Without it, students drift; they resist learning.

Sense of failure. A sense of failure depresses learning. It reduces motivation. It makes things seem not worthwhile. *Errors* can help students learn, but *failure* cannot. The key point is that there is a world of difference between making errors and feeling oneself a failure. The difference depends on the instructor's ability to help his or her students learn.

At first it may seem unnecessary to spend time telling prospective instructors about these conditions. They seem like common sense. However, new instructors are often overwhelmed by the role and feel safest when focusing their attention and energies on preparing and delivering a "good" lesson. It takes more than just good mechanics to produce learning. Instructors must understand and appreciate the fact that every classroom interaction is a potential teachable moment.

Preparation for Instruction

Every instructor, no matter how competent and experienced, needs to prepare before trying to present instruction. How well a lesson was prepared has a direct bearing on the amount of learning that can take place. Adequate preparation is a must for efficient and effective instruction.

The Lesson Plan

The first step in preparing to instruct is to prepare a lesson plan. Sometimes a lesson plan will already be prepared for you, in the case of lessons presented in conjunction with a formal course of instruction. Most Navy educational programs fall into this category. The instructor need only become familiar with the plan, and perhaps personalize it with a few notes. In other cases, however, no plan exists, and so you must make one up.

Format of a lesson plan. A lesson plan, as a minimum, should contain the following items:

- The *objective* or *outcome* of the lesson, including some specific criteria that should be achieved by the trainees.
- The *intended audience* for the lesson.
- Identification of any *training aids/equipment* needed for the lesson.
- The *technique(s) of instruction* you will use.
- An *outline of the material to be presented*, with enough detail to meet the needs of the instructor.
- The *means the instuctor will use to assess the effectiveness* of the instruction.
- A *closing* or *summary* of the lesson.

The length of the lesson plan can run from a page or less to several pages or more, depending on the material to be presented and your experience.

Site Preparation

Before instruction begins, you should ensure that the site of the instruction is adequately prepared. If the instruction is to take place in a classroom, for example, you might check the following:

- Is there an adequate number of seats/desks/tables for the expected number of students?
- If lighting, ventilation, heating, cooling, electric power, or other services will be required, are they sufficient and in good working order?
- Is adequate demonstration/board space and markers/chalk/erasers available?

- If audiovisual equipment will be required, is it available, hooked up, tested, and ready to run?
- Are sufficient numbers of any instructional materials such as books, handouts, paper, pencils, and the like present?
- Is any necessary equipment/hardware/computers on hand in adequate numbers and properly set up?

Similar checklists can be made up for exterior sites such as the drill hall or field, basketball court, or other places of instruction.

Personal Preparation

Along with readying the lesson plan, you should have decided on the best method of instruction to use for the occasion, based on the students and their level of knowledge or prior exposure to the subject matter. Depending on the method used, you may want to rehearse your delivery, techniques for chalkboard work, equipment handling, and the like. You may want to review the names of the students, in order to be able to ask questions and respond to students by name. Just before entering the area where the students are, you may want to check the personal appearance of hair, clothing or uniform, and shoes.

Techniques for Instruction

No one technique of instruction is ideal for all occasions on which instruction will be given. The technique you choose should fit the type of material to be presented, the objective of the instruction, the nature of the students who will receive the instruction, and your experience and personality.

There are several main methods of instruction that have been widely used by those involved in education both in the military and in civilian life, over the years. These are the lecture method, the lecture with audiovisual support, the demonstration, role playing, case study, the discussion method, and cooperative learning. Each of these will be described in the following sections, along with the particular advantages, disadvantages, and procedures for the more commonly used methods.

Lecture

A lecture is a presentation of information, concepts, or principles by a single individual to a group of listeners. It is one-way communication. The lecture assumes the instructor knows all and the student is ignorant of the subject matter. In this form of instruction, the students have little opportunity to ask questions or offer comments during the lecture.

Advantages. The lecture is the most efficient instructional method for presenting many facts or ideas in a relatively short time. Material that has been logically organized can be presented rapidly and concisely. The lecture is particularly suitable for introducing a subject. To ensure that all students have the necessary background

A lecture, as in this presentation about a ship's vertical launch system to a group of NJROTC students, is a fast and efficient way to impart a maximum amount of information in a minimum amount of time, but students often have little opportunity to ask questions or offer comments. (Joseph Caballero)

to learn a subject, the instructor can present basic information in a lecture. A brief introductory lecture can give direction and purpose to a demonstration or prepare students for a discussion. The lecture is a convenient method for instructing large groups. If necessary, a public address system can be used to ensure that everyone can hear. The lecture is sometimes the only efficient technique to use if the student-to-instructor ratio is high.

The lecture is often useful to supplement, summarize, or emphasize material from other sources, or for information difficult to obtain in other ways. If students do not have time for research, or if they do not have access to reference material, the lecture can fill the bill.

Disadvantages. Lengthy or overly frequent lectures without questioning of students can easily lead to boredom. The lecture tends to promote student passiveness. There is always the danger that the instructor may only be restating or repeating what a student could easily understand by quickly reading a few paragraphs in a textbook.

The lecture does not lead to maximum achievement in certain types of learning. Speech skills, cooperative group thinking, and motor skills, for example, are difficult to instruct through the lecture. Because it allows for little or no student participation, the lecture may also be inefficient for lessons in which complicated concepts and principles are developed.

It is hard for the instructor to judge how well the audience is reacting and whether student needs and interests are being met. The lecture assumes active listening and adequate note-taking skills on the part of the student. All students may not possess these skills.

Lecture Procedure

The first task for the instructor is the gathering of the required information for presenting the topic. He or she must determine the point of view from which the subject is to be presented and tailor the lecture to the student. After this preliminary preparation, the delivery technique for a lecture includes three main steps:

Step one: introduction. The instructor establishes contact with the class by introducing himself and stating the objectives of the topic. He or she gets the student ready to learn the material by developing interest through explanations of how the student will use the lesson material, why the student needs to know the material, and how the material will apply to future topics or the student's work. He or she then gives an overview of the lesson as a whole.

Step two: presentation. The instructional material breaks down the general concepts into their simplest component parts, which are presented one by one. The instructor provides examples, illustrations, explanations, and the like.

Step three: summary. The instructor provides recapitulation (a summary), which emphasizes and ties together the principal points of the lesson, including the objectives. This helps the students to select and take note of the most important parts of the information presented.

Guidelines for effective use of the lecture. Know the specific objectives of the topic. Ensure the lecture is well organized. Avoid monotonous instructing by varying voice stress and intensity. Watch the class actions (attentiveness) to determine the effectiveness of the instruction.

Lecture with Audiovisuals

The addition of audiovisual aids, such as the chalkboard, the movie and slide projector, and the overhead projector or presenter, is the most common variation of the lecture instructional technique. This strategy encourages comments and questions from students. Although audiovisual aids are both appropriate and useful with all instructional techniques, they are especially important with the lecture. A multiple approach through several senses makes for more complete understanding and greater retention.

Instructors who rely only on oral presentation find that their students frequently are unable to relate the new learning to any previous experience. The background of the group may be so varied that the new learning does not result in a clear concept common to all, but rather emerges in as many shades of meaning as there are students. Frequent use of visual materials by the instructor should help students grasp whole concepts where word explanations are often inadequate.

The student's imagination, while necessary to learning, cannot be expected to form completely accurate mental pictures of the concept about which he or she has been hearing. Thus it is important that the instructor use some kind of audiovisual material to relate concepts being discussed to reality. As soon as the object or picture is presented, the word descriptions come into focus with new meaning and lasting effect. The drill instructor, for example, would find it very difficult to communicate drill procedures without the use of charts, drawings, and diagrams. This, in turn, permits the student to translate the content into logical and meaningful knowledge. Many students are visual learners, and cannot absorb material well if it is just presented orally with no visual links.

Advantages. The lecture with audiovisuals is an efficient instructional method for presenting many facts or ideas in a relatively short time. Material that has been logically organized can be presented concisely in rapid sequence.

The lecture with audiovisuals is particularly suitable for introducing a subject, to ensure that all students have the necessary background.

The lecture with audiovisuals is often useful to supplement, summarize, or emphasize material from other sources or to provide information difficult to obtain in other ways. This is especially true when complex material is being presented. The audiovisuals will help to focus the student's attention on the specific concept being presented.

Disadvantages. The lecture with audiovisuals is not good for development of motor skills. Although the use of audiovisuals will help to hold the attention of the student, it still requires considerable skill in speaking on the instructor's part. This strategy also assumes active listening and adequate note-taking skills on the part of the student.

Procedure for Lecture with Audiovisuals

The first task for the instructor is the gathering of the required audiovisual aids for presenting the desired topic. The instructor should determine the point of view from which the subject is to be presented. After this preliminary preparation, the delivery technique for a lecture using audiovisuals is similar to the basic lecture method discussed earlier.

Demonstration

Demonstration is the process wherein one person does something in the presence of others to show them how to do it or to illustrate a principle. The demonstration is the most commonly used small-group teaching technique done in a classroom or laboratory to develop students' ability to operate equipment or acquire physical skills. It involves the presentation or portrayal of a sequence of events to show a procedure, a technique, or an operation, fre-

A lecture with audiovisuals, as this senior chief damage controlman is giving to a group from the Royal Thai Navy, helps students grasp whole concepts in situations where word explanations alone are inadequate. (Matthew White)

A group of NJROTC cadets takes part in a demonstration of how to handle a fire hose. Participation in a demonstration like this one is an excellent way for students to learn new skills. (Everett HS NJROTC, Casey Jones)

quently combining explanation with the operation or handling of systems, equipment, or material. Thus demonstration utilizes both hearing and sight to communicate the information.

Advantages. Demonstrations are especially beneficial in skill areas. They add to learning by giving students the opportunity to see and hear what is actually happening. They can be used to illustrate ideas, principles, and concepts for which words are inadequate, thus holding the student's attention.

Demonstrations can save money, since only the instructor needs materials. Demonstrations can reduce hazards before students begin experimentation or handling of materials involved. This is especially true in labs or workshops. Demonstrations lead to a reduction in the length of trial-and-error time.

Disadvantages. The demonstration cannot be properly used in large classrooms or with extremely small objects because all students cannot see. Demonstrations can be ineffective if the instructor only "shows and tells" without obtaining feedback from students.

Demonstrations may lead to imitation without understanding. Unless given proper direction and guidance, students may concentrate on the aids used and ignore the lesson itself.

Demonstrations can become time consuming.

Demonstration Procedure

The actual steps in a demonstration will vary as the situation changes. There are three basic steps, with several variations of step two.

Step one: show and tell. Related to every skill, mental or physical, there is a body of background knowledge that the student must know to perform the skill properly. Some kinds of background knowledge can best be taught in a standard classroom.

Others should normally be presented in the actual environment or laboratories, in conjunction with demonstrations.

Position the students and training aids properly. If the instructor directs the students to gather around a worktable or a training aid, he should recheck their positioning to make sure that everyone has an unobstructed view.

Show and explain the operations. Perform the operations in step-by-step order. Wherever possible, simultaneously tell and do. Do not hurry; speed in performing operations, or in moving from one operation to another, should normally not be emphasized in the demonstration step. The instructor should make certain that the students understand the first step before he or she proceeds to the second, and so on. Repeat difficult operations. Pause briefly after each operation to observe reactions and to check for understanding.

Special mention should be made of skills in which a distinction between right and left is important—for example, the manual of arms, or knot-tying. For teaching the manual of arms, or skills of a similar nature, the use of an assistant instructor or a well-coached student is advisable. The assistant stands so that the class may see what he or she is doing and performs the activity at the direction of the instructor. Meanwhile, the instructor can observe the reaction of the students.

Observe safety precautions. It takes a few more seconds to rig a safety line, put on gloves, or tag an electrical cable, but the time is not wasted. The students are being shown the importance of exercising extreme care in dealing with potentially dangerous equipment.

Give proper attention to terminology. The instructor must call each part of a training aid by its proper name each time he or she calls attention to it. But something more than just mentioning the names of parts is necessary if the students are to retain the correct nomenclature. The following suggestions will prove helpful:

- List the names of parts on a chalkboard or chart.
- Refer students to a previously made chart that shows the parts and their terminology.
- Conduct a terminology drill on the parts of the training aid while the aid is in its assembled or disassembled condition, as appropriate.
- Check student comprehension carefully. Ask questions during the demonstration that require the students to recall nomenclature, procedural steps, underlying principles, safety precautions, and the like. Watch the class for reactions indicating lack of attention, confusion, or doubt, but do not depend solely upon visual observations.

Step two: repetition. Keeping in mind the definition of the demonstration strategy, the lesson plan will always call for a demonstration step and usually a performance step. But generally there is a need for the inclusion of one or more repetition steps between the demonstration step and the performance step.

Step three: performance. The performance step is the step in which the students practice under supervision until they have attained the required proficiency. During this step, they apply what they have previously learned as a result of the demonstrations.

Guidelines for effective use of the demonstration. Practice or rehearse the demonstration in its entirety with an eye on time limitations. When it is time to put on the demonstration, make sure that all materials are at hand. Make sure that the students are situated such that all can see and hear. Use questions during the demonstration to obtain feedback. At the end of the demonstration, conduct a brief review of the steps involved or a short summary of what has happened.

Role Playing

Role playing is an instructional technique involving a spontaneous portrayal (acting out) of a situation, condition, or circumstance by selected members of the class. It is a form of improvisation in which the participants assume the identity of other persons and then react as they believe those persons would in a particular situation. Role playing is especially useful in helping students understand perspectives and different ethnic and cultural backgrounds, and in problem-solving situations where different roles are in opposition to each other. Role playing is often effective in counseling or tutoring.

Advantages. Role playing can be fun, interesting, motivating, and meaningful, and helps to break the routine of other classroom experiences.

Role playing provides insight into common individual and group problems, reveals different attitudes, and tests various ideas in a practical situation. Students learn to organize thoughts and responses instantly while reacting to a situation or question.

Disadvantages. Students sometimes emphasize performance (showing off) over the intended objectives of the topic. Role playing is time-consuming. Some students are unable to identify with the roles or situation. Hot topics and controversial issues sometimes get out of hand in role playing. Role playing may benefit only the actual participants unless the objectives for the class have been clearly specified.

Case Study

The case study is an instructional approach that requires the student to analyze problem situations that may be hypothetical or real. The student receives a "case"—a report containing all pertinent data. The student then must analyze the data, evaluate the nature of the problem, decide upon applicable principles, and finally recommend a solution or course of action. The case may be handled by the class as a whole, by subgroups of the class, or by an individual. Also, the case may be designed to be handled in varied time periods, ranging from a single class period to the entire course.

Analysis of the data involves such things as the use of reference materials prepared for the study, or knowledge and theory already possessed by others and listed in manuals and books. Evaluating and determining applicable principles calls upon the students to

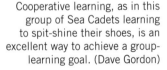

Cooperative learning, as in this group of Sea Cadets learning to spit-shine their shoes, is an excellent way to achieve a group-learning goal. (Dave Gordon)

make some kind of "reasons-why-this-has-happened" statement. Recommended solutions should be a natural outgrowth of the analysis and evaluation.

Discussion

The discussion technique of instruction is basically a supervised conversation during which the students take an active role by stating their views on a certain topic, at the same time that the instructor guides the group to discover certain principles.

The discussion may be implemented in a number of ways. The types of discussion include whole-class discussions, debates, panels, buzz sessions, and forums. Each type has its own slightly different characteristics. The whole-class discussion is the type generally referred to when instructors use this technique and is the type often found in the NJROTC classroom. The instructor simply leads an informal discussion involving the class as a whole. The instructor asks questions, clarifies comments, and makes tentative summaries to help students achieve understanding of the topic and stay on task. The emphasis is on student-centered rather than instructor-centered learning.

Discussion techniques get at attitude development. By taking part in meaningful discussion with fellow students, the participant finds his or her own values and beliefs both reinforced and challenged.

Discussion provides students with the opportunity to develop questioning skills and responses. It gives them the chance to develop organization and formulate answers.

Discussion is motivational. Since the role of the student is not as passive as with some other strategies, the student maintains a high degree of mental alertness.

Cooperative Learning

In cooperative learning, a class of students is subdivided into groups or teams within which the members work with and depend upon each other to accomplish a learning goal. Each team member is responsible for accomplishing some portion of the assigned objective as an individual goal. They then instruct other team members about what they have learned or accomplished, and receive similar information from the other members. Team members are encouraged to assist others to achieve their individual goals when needed, and to work together to achieve the overall group objective. The instructor monitors the individual group activities and may be used as a resource for the group, but does not actively take part in the group work effort.

A cooperative learning strategy is best used when sufficient time is available for the group to gather, discuss, digest, and disseminate information. It is an excellent strategy to use when the material to be learned is complex or important, and requires both mastery and retention in long-term memory.

Conclusion

No one can teach something to someone without doing it in some particular way, and that way of instruction has significant effects on the learning outcomes. In deciding which technique is best for a particular lesson or series of lessons, the instructor must consider the following aspects: the number, ability, maturity level, and previous experience of the students; the nature of the subject matter; and what needs to be emphasized—skills, knowledge, or values/attitudes.

The instructor must also consider the time requirements, the demands the technique will make on the instructor and students, the materials required, and the results expected. There is no single correct way to instruct a class; there are many good ways. Some things can be learned more thoroughly by observation or group involvement than through lectures or drill. Some materials need experimental and demonstration treatment. Controversial topics lend themselves best to discussion or role playing. The instructor must learn how to use the different techniques.

STUDY GUIDE QUESTIONS

1. What is the definition of learning?

2. What mental characteristics does the student bring into the classroom?

3. What are the types of learning as classified by psychologists?

4. Describe the shape of the typical learning curve.

5. When do people learn best?

6. What are the factors that speed and strengthen learning?

7. A. What is motivation?

   B. What is negative motivation?

8. What are the conditions that tend to hinder learning?

9. What should a lesson plan include?

10. What are the main techniques for delivery of instruction?

11. What are the advantages and disadvantages of the lecture with audiovisuals?

12. What are the steps for the demonstration type of instruction?

13. When is the use of the role-playing type of instruction appropriate?

14. What is the case study approach to instruction?

15. When is the use of the discussion method of instruction appropriate?

16. Under what conditions can cooperative learning strategies be employed?

CRITICAL THINKING

1. Learning requires much from the person receiving instruction as well as the instructor. What are some things a student can do to maximize their ability to learn during all types of instruction?

2. Make up a complete lesson plan for delivering instruction on some aspect of the NJROTC to fellow NJROTC cadets.

VOCABULARY

learning theory

psychologists

learning plateau

abstract

negative motivation

sarcasm

right-brain, left-brain

intimidation

audiovisual aids

role playing

case study

demonstration

lesson plan

cooperative learning

NAVAL SKILLS

Ship Construction and Damage Control

Navy ships are complicated. They have propulsion plants, weapons, storerooms, repair shops, offices, and operating spaces. They provide for their crew's living, sleeping, and eating needs. They are almost like cities with their lighting, sanitary, communications, mail delivery, water, and power systems. Large ships have libraries, dental and medical offices, legal services, newspapers, TV stations, chapels, and recreation spaces. All must be able to operate on their own for long periods of time.

Unlike commercial ships, naval ships must be capable of continuing their missions even if they are damaged either in battle or as a result of operations. Because of this, Navy ships have a damage control organization to deal with whatever damage may occur while keeping the ship in optimum operating condition. The following chapters will discuss the principles and nomenclature of naval ship construction and the damage control capabilities of naval ships.

1 Ship Construction

Ship designers try to build as many good features as possible into their ships while keeping in mind their intended missions. All ships are the result of compromise; not every desired feature can be built into every ship. Nevertheless, all ships have certain essential qualities. This chapter will highlight these characteristics and will discuss the fundamentals of ship construction and the nautical terms used to describe ships.

Principles of Ship Construction

The major factors considered in the construction of any naval ship are mission, armament, protection, seaworthiness, maneuverability, speed, endurance, and habitability.

The *mission*, or main purpose, of a ship is the biggest consideration in its design. The weapons systems, speed, crew size, and almost everything else are dependent on the ship's intended mission.

The *armament* consists of all the offensive weapons used to fight an enemy on or under the sea and in the air. Generally, we think of armament as being guns, torpedoes, missiles, and so forth. However the term also includes aircraft used for offensive purposes (an extension of the ship's attacking capability) and landing craft used for amphibious operations.

Protection means defensive features that help a ship survive enemy attack. In addition to its weapons, a ship's sturdy construction, armor, and compartmentation to limit the spread of flooding make up its protective features.

Seaworthiness describes the ship's ability to operate in all kinds of weather, high winds, and heavy seas. Stability, size, and freeboard (the hull space between the waterline and the main deck) determine a ship's seaworthiness. *Stability* refers to the way a ship returns to an upright position after a roll in heavy seas. Stability also affects the value of a ship as a weapons or aircraft platform.

Maneuverability means the way a ship handles in turns, in backing down, in going alongside another ship, or in evading enemy weapons. Combatants such as carriers and destroyers must be able to change course and speed rapidly.

Speed is affected by the weight (displacement) of the ship, its underwater shape, and the power of its propulsion plant. Speed gets a ship to the scene of action quickly and enables it to outmaneuver an enemy.

Endurance is the maximum time a ship can steam at a given speed. It depends on fuel capacity, freshwater capacity, fuel consumption, and storage space and refrigeration for food provisions. Most oil-powered ships can steam for one to two weeks without refueling, while nuclear-powered ships can steam for years. Fresh provisions need to be replenished about every thirty days, but dry stores (including canned foods) may be kept much longer. Another term sometimes used for endurance is *cruising range.*

Habitability refers to the features designed to provide comfortable living conditions for the crew. Adequate heads (lavatories) and washrooms; laundries; air conditioning; and comfortable, safe, and clean berthing and messing spaces are important habitability features.

Nautical Terms

In civilian life you become accustomed to using terms like upstairs, downstairs, windows, floors, ceilings, walls, hallways, and so forth. In the Navy, you must learn to describe objects and places aboard a ship using nautical language. To use civilian terms aboard a ship marks you as a *landlubber*, one who knows nothing of the sea.

In some ways, a ship is like a building. Its outer walls form the *hull*, the supporting body of a ship. Floors are called *decks*, inner walls are called *bulkheads* or partitions, ceilings are termed *overheads*, and hallways are *passageways*. Stairs are called *ladders*; an *accommodation ladder* is the stairs from the ship to a pier, and a *Jacob's ladder* is a portable ladder made of rope or metal used to climb up the side of a ship. The *quarterdeck* might be compared to an entrance hall or foyer in a building.

The lengthwise direction on a ship is *fore* and *aft*; crosswise is *athwartships*. The front of a ship is the *bow*; to go in that direction is to go *forward*. The back of the ship is the *stern*; to go in that direction is to go *aft*. The maximum width of the ship is the *beam*; locations off to the side are *abeam*. Locations behind the beam are *abaft*. Behind the ship, in the water, is *astern*. The forward part of the main deck is the *forecastle* (pronounced foc'sle), and the back part is the *fantail*.

A ship is divided lengthwise in half by the *centerline*. Everything to the right of the centerline is to *starboard*, and everything to the left is to *port*. The direction from the centerline toward either side is *outboard*, and from either side toward the centerline is *inboard*.

The section of the ship around the midpoint area is called *amidships*. Sightings by lookouts are noted and reported as being off the port or starboard bow or beam, and off the port or starboard *quarter* (area abaft of the beam toward the stern).

You never go downstairs in a ship; you always go *below*. To go up to the main deck or above is to go *topside*. However, if you climb the mast, stacks, rigging, or any other areas above the solid structure of the ship, you go *aloft*.

Ship Structure

The hull is the main body of the ship. It is like a box. Its inner construction might be compared to the girders of a steel bridge. The *keel* is the backbone of the hull; it is on the centerline like an I-beam running the full length of the bottom of the ship, with heavy castings fore and aft called the *stem* and *stern posts*. Girders attached to the keel, called *transverse frames*, run athwartships and support the watertight skin or *shell plating*, which forms the sides and bottoms of the ship. Most Navy ships also have *longitudinal frames* running fore and aft. When covered by plating, the longitudinal and athwartship frames form a honeycomb structure in the bottom of the ship called a *double bottom*. This type of construction greatly strengthens the bottom and makes the ship more resistant to damage from collision or grounding. The spaces between the inner and outer bottoms may form *tanks* or *bilges*, which may be used for fuel and water stowage or ballast (usually concrete or pig iron). If they are empty, they are called *voids* (air spaces).

Many of these tanks are fitted with pumps that can transfer liquids from one tank compartment to another to help keep the ship level or "on an even keel." The tanks at the extreme bow and stern, called the forward (or forepeak) and after *peak tanks*, are used for *trimming* the ship (leveling it fore-and-aft).

The top of the main hull is called the *main deck*. The intersection of the main deck with the shell or side plating is called the *gunwale* (pronounced gun'el). Projections at the joint between the side plating and the bottom plating are called *bilge keels*; their purpose is to reduce rolling of the ship. (A ship *rolls* from side to side; it *pitches* when it goes up and down fore and aft; it *yaws* when the bow swings to port and starboard because of wave action.)

Most warships built today have unarmored hulls. Ships of the last century with armored hulls (the old battleships and heavy cruisers) had vertical armored belts of very thick steel running fore and aft along the sides of the hull to protect engine rooms and magazines from torpedoes, shell fire, and missiles. They also had horizontal armor-steel plates built into exposed decks to protect against plunging bombs, shells, and missiles. The *waterline* is the

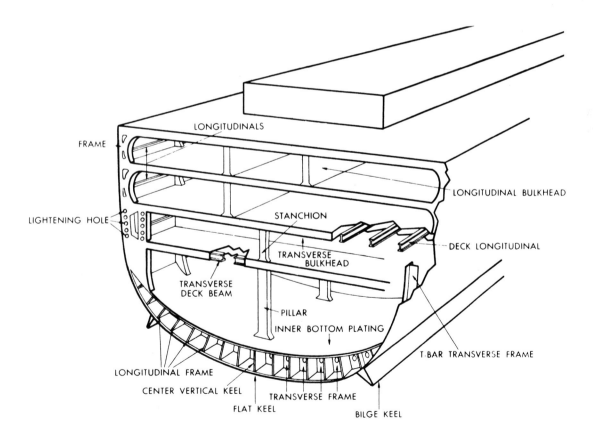

Transverse and longitudinal structure of a ship. Note that transverse beams and bulkheads run athwartships, while longitudinals run the "long way," from stem to stern.

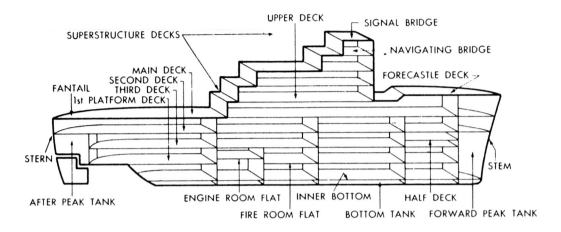

Decks are named by their position in the ship and their function.

water level along the hull of the ship. The vertical distance from the keel to the waterline is the ship's *draft*. *Freeboard* is the distance from the waterline to the main deck.

Decks and Spaces

The "floors" of a ship are called *decks*. They divide the ship into layers in the same way that floors of a building divide it into stories. Decks help strengthen the hull and form the inner *spaces* (rooms) or *compartments*. The undersurface of each deck forms the overhead of the spaces below. Sometimes spaces are called *rooms*, such as the wardroom (officers' dining room), staterooms (officers' bedrooms), and engine rooms, but usually they are referred to simply as compartments. The dining area for enlisted crew members is called the *mess deck*, and their living quarters are called *berthing compartments*. Officers' living spaces are collectively called *officers country*. Bathrooms on a ship are called *heads*. All spaces aboard a ship are identified by standardized compartment numbers that locate them and indicate their use.

The compartments of cargo ships, and main storage spaces of all ships, are called *holds*; holds are normally larger in merchant ships than in naval combatants or civilian passenger ships.

Decks are named by their position in the ship and their functions. Decks that extend throughout the ship from side to side and stem to stern are called *complete decks*. In most ships the uppermost complete deck is called the *main deck*. The next complete deck down is the *second deck*, and the third the *third deck*, and so on.

In aircraft carriers, the uppermost complete deck is the *flight deck*, from which aircraft take off and land, and their main deck is the *hangar deck* below, where aircraft are stowed and serviced.

A partial deck at the bow above the main deck is called the *forecastle deck*. Amidships it becomes an *upper deck*, and at the stern it is a *poop deck*. Main deck areas between the forecastle and poop decks are called *well decks*. Very few Navy ships have forecastle and poop decks today, but these are often built into merchant ships. A *half deck* is any partial deck between complete decks. *Platform decks* are partial decks below the lowest complete deck.

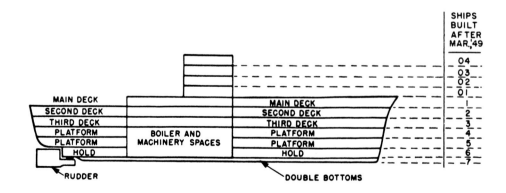

The deck numbering system of all U.S. naval ships is standardized to the system shown here. The main deck is always numbered 1. Decks below are numbered sequentially 2, 3, 4, etc., while decks above are called "levels" and are numbered 01, 02, 03, etc.

The term *weather deck* includes all parts of decks that are exposed to the weather. *Bulwarks* are a sort of low, solid-steel fence along the gunwale of the main deck, fitted with *scuppers*, rubber or metal drains that allow water to run off the deck during rain or heavy seas.

Any deck above the main deck, forecastle deck, or poop deck is called a *superstructure deck*. These decks are generally called *levels*. The first level above the main deck is the 01 (pronounced oh-one) level, the second the 02 level, and so on. These decks may have other names related to their use, such as boat deck, signal bridge, and navigating bridge.

Superstructure

The *superstructure* of a ship includes all structures above the main deck. It will vary according to the type of ship, but most warships have a pilothouse, bridge, signal bridge, chart room, combat information center, "radio shack," and probably a sea cabin for the captain.

The superstructure is topped by the *mast*. It will be at least one vertical pole fitted with a horizontal *yardarm* that extends above the ship and carries flag halyards (ropes) and navigational and signal lights. The mast may also be in the form of a structural tripod. On most ships there also will be electronic devices, radar antennas, radio aerials, and meteorological instruments on the mast or the yardarm. Most Navy ships have only one mast, but many merchant ships and some naval vessels have two. The one forward is called the *foremast*, and the one aft of this is called the m*ainmast*; the mainmast is usually taller than the foremast, making it normally the highest structure above the main deck.

The top of a mast is called the *truck*. The *pigstick* is a slender vertical extension above the mast from which the ship's commission pennant is flown. The *gaff* extends abaft of the mainmast. It is from the gaff that the national ensign is flown when the ship is under way. The small vertical pole at the bow on the forecastle and the slightly raked (diagonal) pole at the stern are called the *jackstaff* and the *flagstaff* respectively. When a Navy ship is at anchor or moored, it flies the jack on the jackstaff, and the national ensign on the flagstaff from 0800 hours to sunset.

The *stack* of a ship supplies air to the main propulsion engines and exhausts smoke and hot gases from them. Nuclear-powered ships do not need stacks, because their reactors require no air for combustion, so they produce no smoke or gas.

Watertight Integrity

In order to prevent the spread of flooding, watertight bulkheads are built in naval ships to divide the hull into a series of watertight compartments. This is called *watertight integrity*, meaning soundness or without leaks. The more watertight compartments a ship has, the more secure it will be from flooding. Watertight integrity is intended to limit flooding, which can cause a ship to *list* (lean) to port or starboard, lose *trim* (be "down" by the bow or stern), *capsize* (tip over), or sink.

Watertight doors and hatches allow access through bulkheads and decks, respectively. Any ship could be made almost unsinkable if it were divided into enough watertight compartments, but too much compartmentation would interfere with the arrangement of mechanical equipment, and ease of movement within the ship. A strong watertight bulkhead at the after end of the forepeak tank

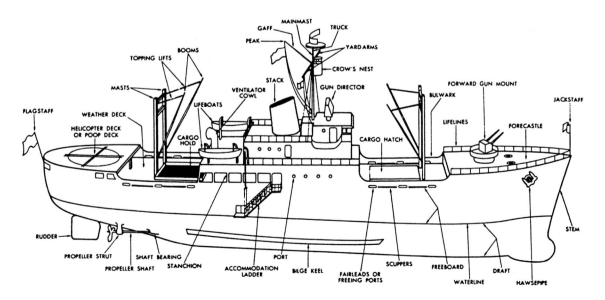

The principal parts of a typical auxiliary ship. With the exception of cargo holds and booms, all of these features are found on warships as well.

is called the *collision bulkhead*. If one ship rams another head on, the bow structure would collapse, hopefully, somewhere forward of the collision bulkhead, thus preventing flooding of compartments aft of it.

Maintenance of watertight integrity is a function of *damage control*. The purpose of damage control is to keep any damage from spreading elsewhere in the ship. All doors and hatches through watertight bulkheads or decks must be watertight. Wherever steam, oil, or air piping, electric cables, or ventilation ducts penetrate a watertight bulkhead or deck, they go through a watertight *stuffing tube* (a cylinder plugged with watertight filler material) or other device to prevent leakage. All watertight doors and hatches carry markings that indicate when they may or may not be opened.

Propulsion Plants

Today's naval ships are propelled mainly by conventional steam plants, gas turbine engines, or nuclear power plants, although the use of diesel engines is steadily increasing. A conventional steam propulsion plant consists of boilers, main engines (steam turbines), reduction gears, propeller shafts, and propellers. Nuclear-powered ships have steam propulsion also, but the steam is produced by heat from a nuclear reactor instead of oil-fired boilers.

A *boiler* consists of a boxlike casing containing hundreds of water-filled steel tubes near the top, which are arranged so that heat from furnace-like fireboxes beneath passes over them, turning the water into steam. Fuel oil, sprayed into the fireboxes under high pressure, ignites and burns intensely, producing the heat.

After being raised to high pressure and temperature in a superheater in another part of the boiler, the steam flows through pipes to turbines, called the "main engines." Fresh water used to produce the steam in the boilers is distilled from salt water by evaporators.

A steam turbine consists of a central rotating shaft, to which are attached several rows of movable blades similar to those of a fan, with stationary blades between. The shaft and blading are enclosed within a thick, airtight casing. As the steam passes through the turbine, it is directed through the stationary blades onto the rotating ones, causing the shaft to spin rapidly.

Because turbines operate most efficiently at speeds of several thousand revolutions per minute (rpm) but propellers are not very effective above a few hundred rpm, *reduction gears* like a transmission in an automobile must be used to make the transition from the high speed of the turbine to the necessarily slower speed of the propeller shafts.

In recent years the *gas turbine engine* has been adapted for ship propulsion. Developed from aircraft engines, this engine powers several classes of destroyers and frigates, Aegis cruisers, minesweepers, Coast Guard cutters, and landing craft. The Navy's new littoral combat ships (LCSs) are powered by a combination of two gas turbine engines and two diesels.

Gas turbines are made up of three basic parts: a compressor, a combustion chamber, and a turbine. The compressor draws in air, compresses it, and sends it under pressure to the combustion chamber, where it is combined with atomized (small droplets) fuel and burned. The combustion gases expand and flow through the turbine blades, causing the turbine to rotate and drive the shaft and propeller.

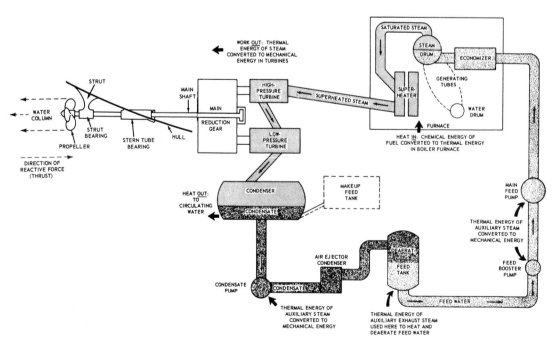

Processes and components of the basic steam cycle of a conventional (oil-fired) steam-driven ship.

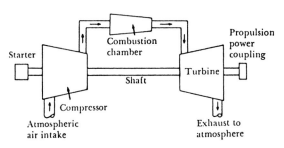

Basic parts of a gas turbine.

The gas turbine has several advantages over a conventional steam plant. It is more compact, lighter, and easier to maintain and repair. Because it has a spark ignition system, much like a car, it can go from "cold iron" shutdown to fully ready to turn the shaft in only one minute, in contrast to the several hours of warm-up time required to bring a steam engine on line.

With a nuclear power plant, the primary system is a circulating water cycle. This consists of the reactor, loops or piping, primary coolant pumps, and steam generators. Heat produced in the reactor by nuclear fission is transferred to the circulating primary coolant water, which is pressurized to prevent it from boiling. This water is then pumped by the primary coolant pumps through the steam generator, where steam to run the turbines is produced, and then back into the reactor, where it can then be reheated for the next cycle. The steam produced in the generator and used to run the turbines circulates in a separate loop outside the reactor, to avoid problems with radioactivity.

Because the generation of nuclear power does not require oxygen, submarines can operate underwater for extended periods of time. Since there are high levels of radioactivity in the reactor during operation, no one is permitted to enter the reactor compartment. Heavy shielding around the reactor protects the crew so well that they receive less radiation than they would from natural sources ashore.

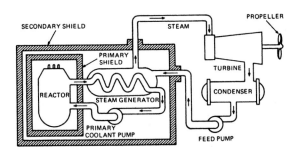

Schematic showing steam flow from a nuclear reactor to the ship's propulsion unit. Nuclear fuel (uranium) in the reactor heats the water to produce steam, much like burning fuel oil does in a conventional boiler. The rest of the propulsion system, with turbines, condenser, and reduction gears, is essentially the same.

However it is produced, propeller shafts carry the power to the propellers. They run from the reduction gears through long watertight spaces called *shaft alleys* in the very bottom of the ship. Propellers drive the ship. Aircraft carriers and many cruisers have four propellers. Most destroyers have two propellers, but many newer ones have only one. They are *variable-pitch propellers*, the blades of which can be rotated on the hub to provide more or less bite into the water for additional control of the ship's speed or to provide reverse thrust.

Shipbuilding

Almost all large ships constructed in shipyards throughout the world today are built in dry docks. The dry docks have a number of large blocks on the bottom upon which the hull is assembled. The blocks under the ship are high enough so workers can work under the hull while the ship is being built. As the hull is built, scaffolding is raised along the sides to make construction easier.

Today large portions of ships are often built in subassembly bays away from the site where the main part of the ship is being built. Here shipbuilders at Bath Iron Works Corporation, Bath, Maine, position the 97-ton upper bow on a new merchant ship.

Today in many shipyards, large portions of the ship are built in subassembly bays away from the main assembly site. As whole sections of the ship are completed, they are carried to the main building site with large cranes, where they are welded together. Some of these sections weigh more than 50 tons. This method of building enables the projects to move along much faster.

The first operation in constructing a ship is erecting the keel sections on the building blocks. After the keel is laid, it is extended in both directions, from the center outboard, and at the same time, forward and aft. Everything is scheduled step-by-step. Early in the construction process the main propulsion plant and major auxiliary machinery and shafting are installed. The whole bow section is usually assembled at a subassembly site and placed in position late in the building schedule. The last step in the prelaunching construction is painting the exterior hull of the vessel.

Launching

A ship can be launched in one of three ways: dry-dock launched, side launched, or float-off launched. In dry-dock launching, the dock is simply flooded to the outside water level and the ship is floated out. Side launching is often done for small ships like tugs and other harbor craft. In the float-off launching method, the ship is constructed on powered pallet cars, which are rolled onto a pontoon with tracks. The pontoon is towed into deep water and ballasted down. When submerged far enough, the ship is towed off to the outfitting docks.

The name of a ship is chosen by the secretary of the Navy upon recommendation of the chief of naval operations (CNO). A female sponsor is selected by the secretary of the Navy according to naval tradition. At the time of launching and christening, the sponsor, naval officers, officials of the shipbuilding company, and the commandant of the naval district in which the ship is being built meet on a flag-decorated platform at the bow of the ship. There may be some speeches, and a chaplain offers a prayer: "May this new vessel of our Navy be guarded by Thy gracious providence and care. May she bear the sword to bring peace on Earth among the nations. Let her be a terror to those who do evil and a defense to those who do well."

The band plays the national anthem, flags and pennants wave, and as the ship begins to move, the sponsor breaks on its bow a gaily wrapped bottle of champagne, wine, or water, saying, "I name you in the name of the United States." She often adds, "May success always attend you."

After the christening and launching, the ship is *fitted out* alongside a pier, where giant cranes hoist the heavy equipment into the ship. Masts, guns, machinery, and electronic components are installed, and spaces are painted and fitted with furniture and equipment. The fitting-out period may take over a year for large ships.

Side-launching the littoral combat ship USS *Freedom* (LCS 1). (Lockheed Martin)

Christening of the littoral combat ship USS *Freedom* (LCS 1). (Lockheed Martin)

Commissioning

When the ship is ready for commissioning, the shipyard commander or another senior officer representing the CNO is ordered to place it in commission. On that day, its officers and crew assemble in dress uniforms. Many dignitaries and guests are usually present, along with the CNO's representative and staff. As the band plays and all stand at attention, the representative orders the national ensign hoisted to designate the ship in the official service of the government, and the commission pennant is unfurled at the mainmast.

The CNO's representative then formally turns the ship over to the prospective commanding officer. The CO reads aloud orders from the Navy Department to command the ship. The first order is "Bring the ship to life and set the watch!" The officers and crew file aboard and take their stations in the new ship.

After commissioning, the ship starts sea trials. The weapons are fired and calibrated. All gear is checked out and tested. The ship goes on a shakedown cruise to verify seaworthiness, speed, endurance, and ability to maneuver as designed. After the ship returns to the outfitting yard, any problems are corrected. More checks and tests are made at sea of fuel consumption, speeds, propeller revolutions, and many other functions. Finally the ship and crew undergo a training cruise lasting from six to eight weeks, usually out of San Diego or Guantanamo Bay, Cuba. Upon successful completion of this cruise, the ship is ready to join the fleet.

Ship Designations

The Navy has some three hundred oceangoing ships operating under their own commanding officers. In addition to these, there are over one thousand service craft, many without crews and some with no self-propulsion.

Navy ships have both a name and a number, called a *designation*, which is a group of letters and numbers that identify the ship. The *letters* tell the ship type and general use; the *hull numbers* indicate the number of ships of that type built, in sequence. These designations are used in correspondence, records, and plans, and appear on ships' boats and ships' bows.

The first letter in a designator is a general classification. The designator letters are as follows:

A	Auxiliary	L	Amphibious, littoral
B	Battleship	M	Mine warfare
C	Cruiser	P	Patrol
CV	Carrier	S	Submarine
D	Destroyer	T	Military Sealift Command
F	Frigate	Y	Yard and service craft

In combatant designations, the letter N means nuclear propulsion and the letter G means that the ship carries guided missiles. Other letters serve to further identify the vessel and its purpose. When a number of ships are built to the same design they make up a *class*, which is named for the first ship in it.

Two examples of ship designations are as follows: the USS *Kidd* (DDG-993) and USS *Ohio* (SSGN-726). The *Kidd* is a guided missile destroyer, DD meaning destroyer and G meaning guided missile. The *Ohio* is a nuclear-powered guided missile submarine, SS meaning submarine, G, guided missile, and N, nuclear powered. The *Ohio* also happens to be the first of the latest class of guided missile submarines, so that group of ships is known as the *Ohio*-class guided missile submarines. All Navy ships can be easily identified as to their type, mission, armament, and propulsion by their designator.

In recent years many auxiliary-type Navy ships have been assigned to the Military Sealift Command and crewed by contract civilians. These ships are identified by a T preceding their designator, for example, the replenishment oiler USS *Neosho* (TAO-143).

STUDY GUIDE QUESTIONS

1. List the major factors considered in the construction of naval ships.

2. Provide the nautical terms for these civilian terms:

   A. Outer walls

   B. Inner walls

   C. Floors

   D. Ceilings

   E. Hallways

   F. Stairs

   G. Entrance hall

3. What nautical names are given to these parts of a ship?

   A. Front part

   B. Back part

   C. Middle of ship, lengthwise

   D. Lengthwise direction

   E. Crosswise direction

   F. Midpoint area

   G. Widest part of ship

   H. Main deck, forward

   I. Main deck, aft

   J. Main deck and above

   K. Below the main deck

   L. Right of centerline

   M. Left of centerline

   N. In the rigging

4. A. What name is given to the girders attached to the keel that support the watertight skin of the ship?

   B. What is the watertight skin called?

   C. What additional strengthening beams run fore and aft?

5. What is another name for the deck edge where the main deck meets with the shell or side plating?

6. How are all compartments in a ship identified?

7. A. How are decks numbered below the main deck?

   B. Above the main deck?

8. A. What name is given to all structures above the main deck?

   B. What is the highest structure above the main deck?

   C. What equipment is installed on this structure?

9. A. What main components does a steam propulsion plant have?

   B. What is the biggest difference between a steam and nuclear-powered vessel?

10. Briefly describe how a gas turbine engine works.

11. What part of the propulsion system actually drives the ship through the water?

12. Why is there heavy shielding around the reactor compartment of a nuclear propulsion plant?

13. Where are ships built?

14. What are the basic steps in building a ship?

15. In what three ways can a ship be launched?

16. Who chooses the name of a new ship?

17. A. Who places a naval ship in commission?

   B. What is the first order of the new commanding officer after he or she reads the orders?

18. What are the purposes of the shakedown and underway training cruise?

19. A. What is a ship's designation composed of?

   B. What are the first-letter designators of major naval vessels?

20. A. What determines a class of ships?

   B. What do the letters G and N indicate in a ship's designator?

   C. What does a T before a ship's designator mean?

CRITICAL THINKING

1. How does the construction of a naval warship differ from a typical dry cargo merchant ship? Why the differences?

2. Research some of the features that have been incorporated in new naval warships built during the 1990s and beyond that make them more resistant to damage than ships built earlier. What provided the impetus for these changes?

3. Briefly describe the different types of propulsion systems found on present-day naval warships.

4. Make a table listing common features of a building such as foundations, walls, doors, as so on, then list in the table the corresponding nautical features in a boat or ship.

VOCABULARY

propulsion plant	weather deck
armament	scuppers
seaworthiness	list, trim
endurance	collision bulkhead
habitability	superstructure
landlubber	mainmast
bulkhead	foremast
overhead	pigstick
quarterdeck	jackstaff
fore, aft	stack
athwartships	reduction gear
bow, stern	rpm
forecastle	propeller shaft
fantail	nuclear reactor
watertight integrity	variable-pitch propeller
amidships	subassembly
port, starboard	christening
beam	commission pennant
quarter	shakedown cruise
keel	hull number
gunwale	ship designator
roll, pitch, yaw	compartment
draft	wardroom
freeboard	head (ship compartment)
stateroom	

2 Damage Control and Firefighting

A ship's ability to do its job may one day depend on its crew's damage control abilities. Damage control covers firefighting, collision and grounding damage, explosion damage, battle damage, and care of the injured. The duties and responsibilities of the ship's damage control organization are outlined in the ship's battle bill and covered in detail in the *Damage Control Manual*. They include routine and emergency maintenance of damage control equipment and closures; control of damage and flooding caused by accident or hostile action; and defense against chemical, biological, and radiological attack.

The Damage Control Organization

The shipboard damage control organization consists of damage control central (DCC), repair lockers, and repair parties stationed in and responsible for various areas of the ship. The engineering officer is the damage control officer. He or she is assisted by the damage control assistant (DCA), who is responsible for preventing and repairing damage, training the crew in damage control, and caring for machinery, drainage, and piping assigned to the damage control organization (such as firemains, foam systems, and water washdown systems). In addition to these key leaders, each department has a damage control petty officer, who coordinates the training of departmental personnel in both damage control procedures and maintenance of damage control fittings and equipment in their departmental spaces.

Damage control central is the headquarters for all damage control activities in the ship's battle organization. It is located in a protected space well within the ship. DCC coordinates all the repair parties for hull, propulsion, electronics, weapons, air operations, and the battle dressing (first aid and emergency operating) stations. It receives reports from damage control parties, assesses the damage, and decides which damage is most in need of repairs. It also advises the commanding officer (CO) on what must be done to keep the ship in fighting shape.

The DCA has a battle station in the DCC, where he or she uses various visual aids to help coordinate plans to contain damage. These include charts and diagrams of the entire ship, its systems, and access routes to different areas. A casualty display board enables the DCA to keep track of the damage sustained and the progress of corrective action, based on repair party reports. The DCA also coordinates the decontamination stations, monitors teams to detect chemical, biological, or radiological (CBR) attacks, and routes casualties to battle dressing stations.

Repair Parties

Repair parties consist of personnel who attempt to make emergency repairs to any vital damaged equipment or ship's structure. They are the main components in the DCA's damage control organization. The number and ratings of crew members assigned to a repair party are determined by the location of its station, the size of the area to be covered by that station, and the total number of people available.

Each repair party will have an officer or chief petty officer in charge, a scene leader to supervise all on-scene activities, a phone talker, messengers, and personnel equipped with special oxygen breathing apparatus (OBA). (For further discussion of OBA, see the section on protective fire clothing.) Repair party personnel are assigned to various teams within each repair party, including investigation teams, hose teams, dewatering, plugging, and patching teams, shoring, piping repair, structural repair, casualty power, interior communications repair, and electrical repair teams. There are also CBR (chemical, biological, and nuclear warfare) monitoring teams and decontamination teams. Besides the general repair parties, on some ships there are special departmental teams to handle aviation fuel repair, aviation crash and salvage, and ordnance disposal.

Repair parties are assigned to each major part of the ship, and to propulsion and electronics repair. Repair parties must be capable of:

- Evaluating and reporting correctly on the extent of damage in their areas

- Controlling and extinguishing all kinds of fires

- Giving first aid and transporting the injured to battle dressing stations

- Detecting, identifying, and measuring nuclear radiation and biological and chemical agents, and carrying out decontamination procedures

- Performing the special duties assigned to their parties, such as propulsion and electronics repairs, and maintaining watertight integrity, structural integrity, and ship's maneuverability

Sailors man Damage Control Central (DCC) on the aircraft carrier USS *Ronald Reagan* (CVN 76) under direction of the ship's damage control assistant (center) during a general quarters drill. Note the protective hoods and gloves worn by all, and the schematic diagrams of the ship's decks posted on the bulkhead to the right. (Aaron Burden)

In addition to repair parties, each ship also has an auxiliary at-sea and in-port fire party organization, consisting of enough on-duty repair party personnel to handle a moderate-sized fire. A large fire requires the crew to go to general quarters (GQ) and all repair parties to be fully manned to fight it.

Battle dressing stations are first aid stations equipped to handle casualties and are manned by medical department personnel. Stretcher cases may be brought directly to a station by the repair party stretcher-bearers. Emergency supplies of medical equipment are placed in first aid boxes at various places throughout the ship in addition to those stored at the battle dressing stations.

Material Readiness Conditions

The success of damage control depends partly on the maintenance of watertight integrity. As discussed in the last chapter, each ship is divided into compartments to control flooding, withstand CBR attacks, protect and strengthen the structure of the ship, and maintain buoyancy and stability. The watertight integrity of a ship may be reduced or destroyed by enemy action, storms, collisions, or negligence.

Navy ships have three basic material conditions of readiness, each representing a different degree of "tightness" and protection. These are conditions: X-RAY, YOKE, and ZEBRA.

Condition X-RAY offers the least protection. It is set when the ship is in no danger of attack, such as when at anchor in a well-protected harbor or secured at home port during regular working hours. During this condition, any closure (door, hatch, valve, and so on) with a black X on it will be secured. X-RAY fittings are also closed for conditions YOKE and ZEBRA.

Condition YOKE provides for a bit more protection than X-RAY. YOKE is set and maintained at sea. In port, it is maintained at all times during war, and outside of regular working hours during peacetime. YOKE closures are marked with a black Y; they are also closed during condition ZEBRA.

Condition ZEBRA provides the highest level of protection possible without securing ventilation. It is set before going to sea or when entering port during war. It is set immediately, without further orders, when general quarters stations are manned. Condition ZEBRA is also set to localize and control fire and flooding when not at GQ. When condition ZEBRA is set, all closures marked with a red Z are secured.

Once a material condition is set, no fitting marked only with that or lower condition symbols may be opened without permission from the commanding officer, given through the DCA or Officer of the deck (OOD). However, to allow for access to critical spaces, certain fittings having a circle around the basic marking; for example, a circle X-RAY may be temporarily opened for access without prior permission. Ventilation fittings marked with a W (WILLIAM) are never closed. Those marked with a circle WILLIAM may be closed to limit air circulation in a space during a CBR attack. ZEBRA (marked with a Z) fittings within a capital D are called DOG-ZEBRA fittings; they are closed for darken ship. It is the responsibility of all hands to maintain whatever material condition has been set for the ship.

Damage Repairs

Battle damage repair is emergency action taken to keep the ship afloat and fighting. Drills and personal qualification training are continuously done to teach everyone how to use damage control equipment. An important part of winning in any emergency is to keep calm, remain alert, and work rapidly with the tools at hand. Unless the damage is very bad, there is much that damage control teams can do to keep the ship afloat and ready for action.

Any rupture, break, or hole in the ship's outer hull plating below the waterline can let in seawater. If flooding is not controlled, the ship will sink. When the underwater hull is pierced, there are only two ways to control flooding. The first is to plug the holes; the second is to establish and maintain flood boundaries using the watertight compartmentation in the ship so flooding will not spread.

Communications

Good communications between different parts of the damage control organization are of vital importance. There are three main communication systems used in the damage control organization: the general announcing system (usually called the 1MC), sound-powered telephones, and messengers.

The 1MC is not the primary means of transmitting damage control information, but it is a way of getting orders, information, and alarms throughout the ship. It may be used to announce the location of a bomb or shell hit, fire, or collision.

Emergency alarms include the general alarm, used to call the crew to general quarters because of impending enemy attack, and general quarters for fire, collision, and CBR attack. The general alarm used for attack or fire is a series of single gong tones; the chemical alarm is a steady tone signal; and the collision alarm consists of a series of three pulses, with a short pause before the next series. Battle stations are manned for all of the emergency alarms.

The ship's battle circuits use sound-powered telephones. They are the principal means of communication throughout the ship. Their advantage over other systems is that they require no external source of power other than the talker's voice. Each repair party has its own circuit connecting it to damage control central, to its roving patrols, and to other stations in its area.

When other methods of communication fail, messengers must be used to relay orders and information. Messengers must learn how to get around the ship to all the repair party stations and other areas. Messengers will often be given written messages for delivery, but they must also be able to deliver oral messages accurately.

Fire and Firefighting

Any person aboard ship who discovers a fire must give the alarm. Another person must be notified to go for help. The fire report may be spread by any means, such as the telephone or other internal communication system. Damage control central is the headquarters area for fighting any fire. Once the alarm has sounded, anyone nearby should act promptly to contain or extinguish the fire. Other personnel in the fire or repair party will arrive quickly on the scene with the necessary equipment to carry on the fight.

Fire is a constant threat aboard ship. All appropriate measures must be continually taken to prevent fires. Any fire of significant size that does occur can threaten the survivability of the ship and everyone aboard. They may start from spontaneous combustion (self-generated heat), carelessness, hits by enemy shells or missiles, explosion, or collision. A fire must be controlled quickly, since it may cause extensive damage or loss of the ship.

In order for a fire to occur, three physical requirements must be met: there must be a burnable fuel, it must be heated enough to burn, and there must be enough oxygen to keep it burning. These three requirements form the *fire triangle*, whose sides consist of *fuel*, *heat*, and *oxygen*. Removing any side of the triangle will result in extinguishing the fire (putting it out). Firefighters must determine the best way to put a fire out—in other words, which side of the triangle to remove. This is not always an easy choice.

Removing the fuel is often not possible. It could be done, however, in an instance where liquid fuel was being fed by a pipeline. Closing the valves would cut the flow of the fuel, and the fire could then be allowed to burn itself out. Sometimes combustible materials can be removed or soaked with water—another way of eliminating fuel.

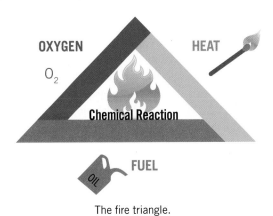

The fire triangle.

Oxygen can be removed in two ways. In a closed space, carbon dioxide (CO_2) can be pumped in to displace the oxygen and starve the fire. Another method is to smother the fire with a blanket of chemical powders, foam, or sand.

Removing the heat side of the triangle, or cooling the fire, is the method most often employed, usually by the use of lots of water, both solid stream and fog (spray), to cool the burning surface rapidly.

Classes of Fires

There are four classes of fires, depending on the type of fuel or material burning and the methods required to extinguish them.

Class A (Alpha) fires involve solid combustible materials such as wood, cloth, or paper. They often leave ashes. Explosives are also in this category. Water is the usual means of putting out Class A fires. Carbon dioxide (CO_2) may be used on small fires, but not on explosives. The flames of a large fire are usually cooled down with fog. Then a solid stream of water is used to break up the material for further cooling.

Class B (Bravo) fires involve flammable liquids such as oil, gasoline, other fuels, cleaning agents, and paints. CO_2 is good for putting out small Class B fires. For larger fires, light water (a mixture of water and chemicals) or water fog or spray should be used. A solid stream of water should never be used on Class B fires; it will only scatter the fuel and spread the flames.

Class C (Charlie) fires are those burning in electrical or electronic equipment such as radios, radars, generators, and electric control panels. The main extinguishing agents are CO_2 and dry chemical extinguishers. Liquids should not be used because they will damage the equipment and may be a shock hazard. If at all possible, electrical gear should be deenergized before any firefighting is undertaken, to eliminate the potential shock hazard. Electricity can travel along wet decks and electrocute firefighters.

Class D (Delta) fires involve combustible metals such as magnesium, titanium, sodium, and in some cases, aluminum. These elements are used in certain parts of ships, aircraft, missiles, some weapons, and computers and other electronic gear. A magnesium aircraft parachute flare, for instance, can burn at a temperature greater than 4,000° Fahrenheit, with a brilliancy of 2 trillion candlepower. Dry powder extinguishing agents containing sodium chloride granules or copper powder are used on this type of fire. Water can excite these fires and make them worse. Firefighters dealing with Class D fires should wear welders' goggles with dark lenses to protect their eyes from the often-intense glare of this type fire.

Fire Prevention

A fire is certain to cause some damage. The most firefighters can do is to minimize the damage and keep the fire from spreading. A main objective, therefore, is to prevent fires from starting. The rules for preventing fires are generally the same anywhere, but special precautions must be taken in the Navy and aboard ships because of the concentration of flammable fuels and explosives.

The first rule is to keep things squared away—clean, in good order, and in their proper places. Flammable materials must be kept away from potential fire starters such as torches, cigarettes, and sparking equipment.

Firefighting equipment must be well maintained. If a fire starts, the right gear must be immediately available and operating properly to prevent the fire from spreading.

One of the more common causes of Class A fires is lighted cigarettes or matches thrown into trash cans. Smoking in bunks is strictly forbidden by regulations, but the regulations have been broken with serious consequences. Through spontaneous combustion, piled up oily rags and papers also commonly cause such fires.

Class B fires are very difficult to predict, especially if fumes leak in voids and tanks aboard ship. Sparking from welding torches, light switches, and even flashlights can be sufficient to cause an explosion and fire with gasoline fumes. Grease fires in galleys are not uncommon if hot oil or grease spills onto burners. The smoking lamp (term for permission to smoke in authorized spaces) is out whenever handling fuels or explosives aboard a ship.

Paint and oils should be kept away from electric wires. Frayed or worn wires and insulation must be repaired or replaced immediately. Dust and dirt should not be allowed to accumulate around electrical equipment. Unauthorized electrical appliances and overloaded circuits, extension cords, and plugs are an open invitation to overheating and fires.

Firefighting Equipment

The fire main system aboard ship is designed to deliver seawater to fireplugs and sprinkler systems, just like a city's fire main delivers water under pressure to the fire hydrants. Two connected 50-foot lengths of fire hose—one end attached to the fire main, the other fitted with a nozzle—are placed on racks at each *fire station* throughout a ship. Additional lengths of hose are rolled and stowed in repair lockers.

Sprinkler systems are installed in magazines, gun turrets, ammunition-handling rooms, spaces where flammable materials are stored, and hangar bays aboard ships that operate aircraft. Some systems are automatically triggered when the temperature in the protected compartment reaches a certain temperature, but most are operated manually by control valves.

Light water used to fight Class B fires acts as a blanket that floats on top of the burning liquid and smothers the fire. It should not be used on Class C fires because of the potential shock hazards involved.

Two types of *portable extinguishers* are common: CO_2 and purple-K powder (PKP). Both are effective in fighting Class B and Class C fires. The CO_2 *extinguisher* is used mainly for putting out electrical fires but is effective on any small fire. Because CO_2 is heavier than air, it forms a smothering blanket over the fire. CO_2 is quick to use and leaves no mess, but carbon dioxide "snow" can be blown away by wind or draft. It is not poisonous, but contact with it can cause painful skin blisters.

Dry chemical PKP extinguishers are mainly for Class B fires. The chemical used is potassium bicarbonate (similar to baking soda). It is called purple-K powder, or PKP. PKP is not poisonous and is four times as effective as CO_2 for extinguishing fires. The dry chemical is an excellent firefighting agent, but its effects are temporary. It has no cooling effect and provides no protection against reflash. PKP should be used sparingly in confined spaces because it will reduce visibility and make breathing difficult.

PKP can be used with light water to produce a highly effective extinguishing agent. The dry chemical beats down the fire, and the light water prevents a reflash.

Dry powder extinguishers are used to combat Class D fires. As previously mentioned, sodium chloride granules or copper powder are used in this type extinguisher. They are often installed in spaces that have materials in them that can be involved in this class of fire.

Protective Fire Clothing

Any clothing that covers the skin will protect it from flash burns and other short-duration flames. In addition to their uniforms, personnel aboard Navy ships and shore stations that may be exposed to flame and heat in emergency conditions are issued flame-retardant hoods and long gloves that are worn whenever warranted. Eyes are protected with antiflash goggles. If clothing catches on fire, one should not run, since this will fan the flames. Lie down and roll up in a blanket, coat, or anything that will smother the flames. If nothing is available, the person should roll over slowly, beating out the flames with his or her hands. If another person's clothes catch on fire, he or she should be put down and covered up (except the head) with a blanket or coat.

Two crew members aboard the guided missile cruiser USS *Vella Gulf* (CG 62) outfitted in fire proximity suits carry a simulated casualty to safety during a flight deck fire drill. The suits do not allow the wearer to enter burning spaces or walk through flames, but only to get close enough to rescue victims or assist in firefighting. (Jason Zalasky)

The *proximity firefighting suit* (close-in suit) consists of coveralls, gloves, helmet, and boots. Its helmet provides a protective cover for the oxygen breathing apparatus (OBA or SCBA) that is normally worn with it. It is lightweight and resists penetration of liquids. The suit allows crew members to enter overheated or steam-filled compartments and to make crash fire rescues. The wearer is not expected to enter burning spaces or walk through flames, only to get close enough to rescue victims or assist in putting the fire out.

The Navy's OBA is a self-contained unit designed to protect the wearer in a place lacking oxygen or containing harmful gases, vapors, smoke, or dust. The wearer breathes in a closed system in which oxygen is supplied by a chemical reaction in a disposable canister. All Navy personnel are trained in the use of the OBA in boot camp and in fleet training schools, as well as aboard ship during repair party training sessions.

A damage control petty officer adjusts the OBA on a trainee in damage control school. The OBA is designed to protect the wearer in places lacking oxygen or containing harmful gases, vapors, smoke, or dust. It is a closed self-contained unit in which oxygen is supplied by chemicals in a canister that purifies exhaled air. A newer model, the SCBA, uses a rechargeable air cylinder vice a canister.

Fighting a Fire

A fire may gain considerable headway before smoke is detected, especially if it has started in an unattended space. The first sign may be smoke coming out of a ventilation outlet or seeping around a door or hatch cover. The smoke may have traveled some distance. Therefore, the first job of a repair or fire party is to locate the fire. This is done by team members called *investigators*, normally the first people to go out to respond to any damage or fire that may have occurred.

The investigators check bulkheads, decks, and vents for heat to see if the fire is in an adjoining compartment. They may have to follow a trail of smoke. Once the fire is located, they check adjoining compartments to be sure it has not spread to them.

As soon as the extent of the fire is determined, a full report is made to damage control central. Upgraded material readiness conditions are set around the entire area.

While the firefighting is under way, the team sets up *fire boundaries* to isolate the fire and keep it from spreading. Fire boundaries are set in several ways. Combustible materials in adjoining spaces are moved or cooled to prevent spread of fire by heat transmission. Since fire can blister and ignite paint on bulkheads in adjoining compartments, fog or sprinklers are used to cool the bulkheads, decks, and overheads in adjoining spaces. Ventilation systems in the area are secured to cut off the oxygen supply to the fire and to limit the spread of smoke and gases to other compartments. Fire watches are posted in surrounding compartments.

When the fire is isolated, electrical circuits in the area should be deenergized to protect against shock. Doors should be checked for heat and pressure behind them before their door dogs (heavy latches) are fully opened.

After the fire has been extinguished, the area must be overhauled to prevent reflash of the fire. All smoldering or charred materials should be saturated thoroughly and removed if possible. The compartments must be checked for explosive vapors or liquids that might remain. Dewatering (removing water used in firefighting) is then begun. At this time, a full report is made to damage control central on fire and smoke damage and flooding. The final step in fighting the fire is to set a *reflash watch* to be sure that the fire does not start again from a smoldering fragment or through vapor ignition. Gases, especially from fuels, can be ignited by heat or sparks if allowed to concentrate in or near an area that has not been properly overhauled.

STUDY GUIDE QUESTIONS

1. A. What does damage control include?

   B. What are the duties of a ship's damage control organization?

2. A. Which officer is the ship's damage control officer?

   B. Who is the principal assistant?

3. A. What is the name given to the control station for shipboard damage control?

   B. What is the name given to the on-scene groups of people who are responsible for damage control in assigned sections of the ship?

4. A. What is the task of a repair party scene leader?

   B. What are the special teams within a repair party?

5. A. What is a battle dressing station?

   B. Who brings stretcher cases to the battle dressing station?

6. A. What are the three basic material conditions of readiness?

   B. What is the extent of protection for the ship in each?

7. What are the two ways to control flooding?

8. A. What are the emergency alarms used aboard ship?

   B. When are they used?

9. A. What is the principal means of internal communication throughout a ship?

   B. What is the particular advantage of this system?

   C. When internal phone and electrical systems fail, what method is used to relay messages?

10. Who should be the first person to report a fire?

11. A. What is the fire triangle?

    B. How can a fire be put out?

    C. What is the method most often used?

12. List the four classes of fires, fuels for each, and best method of extinguishing each.

13. Why must a stream of water never be used to put out fires in electrical or electronic equipment before it is completely deenergized?

14. A. Why must special precautions against fire be constantly observed aboard ship?

    B. What are some of the key rules for shipboard fire prevention?

    C. Why do these rules make sense in your own home?

15. Where are shipboard sprinkler systems used?

16. What should you do if your clothes catch on fire?

17. What is the purpose of the Navy's oxygen breathing apparatus?

18. A. What are the first steps a firefighting party must take in fighting a fire?

    B. Why do they check bulkheads and decks for heat?

19. What is the purpose of a fire boundary?

20. What is dewatering?

CRITICAL THINKING

1. Explain why quick response to damage such as fire or flooding is even more critical on board a ship than in the case of buildings ashore.

2. Summarize the various classes of fires and the extinguishing agents used for each.

VOCABULARY

damage control	sound-powered telephones
DCA, DCC	OBA, SCBA
repair party	fire boundaries
investigator	reflash watch
battle dressing station	dewatering
water fog	reflash
smoking lamp	fire triangle
carbon dioxide (CO_2)	light water
PKP	door dogs
dry chemical extinguisher	dry powder extinguisher

Shipboard Organization and Watchstanding

A naval ship's crew is made up of the officers and enlisted personnel necessary to fight the ship. A ship's organization, then, is set up to meet combat needs. The crew can operate efficiently in peacetime but can adapt quickly to meet wartime needs. Whether in time of peace or war, each crew member has an important job. The chapters in this unit will discuss the way ships' personnel are organized in the U.S. Navy.

Shipboard Organization

The basic shipboard departments are operations, combat systems (weapons), engineering, supply, and, on ships having manned aircraft, air. There may be some other departments as well, depending upon the type and size of the ship.

Each type of ship has what is known as an *administrative organization* for running the ship. The administrative organization described in this chapter is that of a typical naval fighting ship, or *combatant*.

The commanding officer of a guided missile destroyer (right) greets visitors from the Chinese navy. (Matthew White)

Commanding Officer

Every commissioned ship in the Navy operates under the authority of an officer ordered to command it. Regardless of rank, he or she is called "captain." The *commanding officer (CO)* is the line officer in actual command of a ship.

The CO is totally responsible for the command. His or her authority is also total, within the limits set by law and *Navy Regulations* and the reporting senior. Subordinates in the chain of command may be delegated authority to manage the details of running the ship, but delegation of authority in no way relieves the CO of responsibility for the safety and operation of the command.

The CO strives to keep the command ready for war service. He or she is assisted by the executive officer, who has charge of administration and training of the ship. The CO gives directions to the executive officer. That officer then works with the ship's department heads to conduct training, exercises, and drills to keep the crew ready.

The main responsibility of the CO is the safety of the ship. This means, among other things, proper handling and stowage of ammunition, making sure the ship is watertight, careful navigation, posting of proper lookouts, and safe maneuvering and navigation. Since the CO cannot handle all these matters personally, he or she depends on the assistance of good subordinate officers. For example, the navigator must know the ship's position at all times, but the CO is still responsible for the safe navigation of the ship.

During combat, the CO's battle station is that station from which he or she can best fight the ship. In the event of the loss of the ship, the CO waits until all personnel are off the ship before leaving.

The CO supervises everyone under his or her command. He or she must direct the investigation of conduct offenses, and assign punishments under the Uniform Code of Military Justice. The CO, in turn, is held responsible for his or her command by higher authority.

The welfare, morale, and living conditions of the crew are a CO's constant concern. The executive officer and his or her assistants manage these affairs, but the CO must always be concerned also.

Executive Officer

The *executive officer*, often called "the exec" or "XO," is the line officer next in rank to the CO. He or she is the direct representative of the CO. The XO is responsible for all matters relating to personnel, ship's daily routine, and discipline in the ship. All orders issued by the XO have the same force as if issued by the CO.

The executive officer is responsible for:

- Coordination of all departments
- Assignment of personnel and upkeep of their records
- Preparation and maintenance of ship's organization bills and orders
- Supervision and coordination of work, exercises, training, and education
- Supervision of loading and berthing plans
- Navigation (smaller ships only)
- Supervision of ship's correspondence

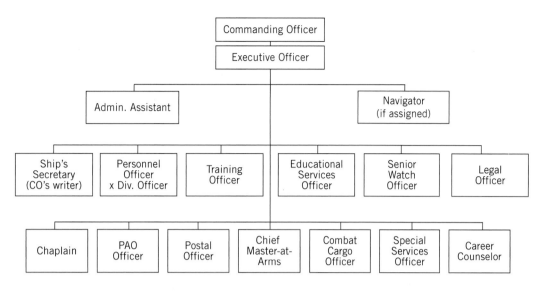

The executive officer's assistants in a typical combatant ship. In smaller ships, many of these tasks are assigned as collateral duties.

With the help of department heads, the XO coordinates all ship's work. This includes drills and exercises, the personnel organization, policing of the ship through the master-at-arms force, and inspections of the ship. The XO is responsible for the cleanliness, good order, and military appearance of ship and crew.

The XO supervises the department heads in the performance of their duties and is in charge of the instruction of junior officers. The XO is responsible for the entries made in the crew's service records. He or she investigates matters involving conduct and discipline of the crew, normally through the executive assistants.

He or she supervises whenever all hands are called for any particular duty, exercise, or evolution, except during combat. When the ship is cleared for action, the XO inspects it, receives reports from the various departments, and reports to the CO the condition of the ship. If the CO is incapacitated or killed, the XO becomes the acting CO. For this reason, the XO's battle station is located some distance from the captain's. In modern ships, the CO often is in the combat information center (CIC), and the XO is on the bridge.

Navigator

The *navigator* is responsible to the CO for the safe navigation and piloting of the ship. In small ships, navigation is an extra duty of the XO. Large ships usually have a separate navigator.

The navigator keeps the CO, XO, and officer of the deck advised on the ship's location and maintains a position plot by celestial, visual, electronic, or other navigational means. He or she must study all charts and other sources of information before entering pilot waters and give careful attention to the course of the ship and the depth of water when near land or shoals.

The navigator's staff maintains records of all observations concerning navigation of the ship. They obtain and correct all navigational charts, sailing directions, light lists, and other navigation publications.

The navigator is responsible for the operation and care of navigational equipment. He or she is also responsible for the care and proper operation of the steering gear, except for the steering engines and motors. In general, the navigator is in charge of the bridge, pilot house, chart room, and wings of the bridge for maintenance and upkeep.

Executive Assistants

Several additional officers and senior enlisted personnel work directly under the XO. The size of the staff depends on the size of the ship. In small ships several of these duties are assigned to one person, or as *collateral duties,* that is, in addition to primary duties. These assistants, and their basic duties, are as follows:

The *administrative assistant* helps the XO in details of administration.

The *personnel officer* assigns enlisted personnel according to the ship's bills. He or she is responsible for the enlisted service records.

The enlisted *career counselor* keeps all crew members informed about career and educational opportunities. He or she counsels all enlisted crew members about any career decisions or career-related problems they may have.

Larger ships may have a chaplain, a legal officer, and a public affairs officer.

The *chaplain* is responsible for religious activities of the command. The chaplain ministers to the spiritual needs of ship's personnel and often helps with personal counseling.

The *legal officer* advises the CO and XO on matters concerning discipline and administration of justice. He or she often serves as an investigator for the XO on disciplinary charges.

The *public affairs officer (PAO)* carries out the public affairs program of the ship. He or she keeps the CO and XO informed on public relations matters and prepares articles and photography for release to the news media (newspapers, radio, and TV).

The *combat cargo officer* in amphibious ships has charge of the loading and unloading of troops, billeting and messing of troops, and the loading, stowage, and unloading of cargo.

The *special services officer* organizes all the welfare, recreational, and athletic activities of the ship. In foreign ports, he or she often arranges tours for members of the crew.

The *senior watch officer (SWO)* is responsible to the CO for assignment of all deck watchstanders, both under way and in port. The SWO prepares the officer deck watch bills, supervises the enlisted watch bills, and coordinates and directs the training of deck watch officers.

The *chief master-at-arms (CMAA),* normally one of the more senior petty officers on board, is responsible for enforcing regulations and keeping good order and discipline. He or she is in charge of supervising most working parties, and is responsible for the security and welfare of any prisoners in the ship's brig. The CMAA may have several assistant petty officer *masters-at-arms (MAAs)* to help carry out these duties.

Command Master Chief

The command master chief, normally the senior enlisted chief petty officer aboard, serves as the principal enlisted adviser to the CO. The command master chief has direct access to the CO on matters that affect the welfare, morale, and well-being of the enlisted crew.

Heads of Departments

A ship's major departments are operations, combat systems or weapons, engineering, supply, and air. Each has a department head, a middle-grade officer in charge of that department. Except in staff departments (medical, dental, supply), the department head is a line officer eligible for command in the event of the loss of his or her superior officers. In aircraft carriers, the operations and air departments are headed by naval aviators.

The head of a department represents the CO in all matters related to the department. All persons assigned to the department are subordinate to him or her. All department heads have equal status. They report directly to the XO for administrative matters, and directly to the CO on matters in their departments affecting overall readiness of the ship, while keeping the XO informed of such reports.

The department heads' duties cover a broad area. They assign, organize, and train their personnel. They are members of the XO's training board. They are responsible for the proper use and care of

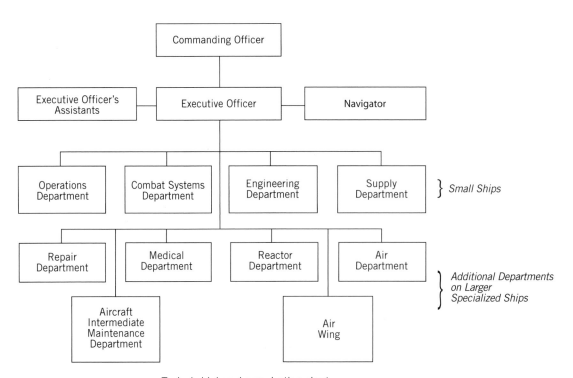

Typical shipboard organization chart.

departmental equipment, as well as the cleanliness and upkeep of spaces assigned.

Heads of departments and their principal assistants are assigned battle stations where they can best supervise their assigned personnel in combat.

An operations specialist monitors air contacts in the CIC of the cruiser USS *Lake Champlain* (CG 57). (Greg Messier)

Operations Officer

The *operations officer* collects, evaluates, and disseminates combat and operational information wherever needed in the command. He or she also is responsible for operations of the ship and assigned airborne aircraft.

The operations department is responsible for:

- Surface, air, and subsurface search (radar and sonar)
- Electronic warfare (listening to and jamming enemy communications and electronics equipment)
- Aircraft when airborne and under combat or operational control of the ship
- Collection, display, analysis, and dissemination of intelligence information
- Preparing operations plans and training schedules
- Planning of seamanship evolutions
- Gathering weather information and informing the command
- Ship's communications, if there is no communications department

Communications Officer

In most ships the *communications officer* is a division officer in the operations department. In some large ships, however, such as aircraft carriers and amphibious command ships, he or she is a department head. The communication officer is responsible for visual and electronic communications and all the communications equipment. He or she is also responsible for the routing of all messages in the ship. He or she must be familiar with all tactical and communications publications. He or she is in charge of communications watch and signal officers, conducting their training, and supervising their watchstanding.

The communications officer supervises cryptographic (encoded communications) operations, and looks after the security of crypto publications and equipment.

Combat Systems Officer or First Lieutenant

Most newer naval warships have either a combat systems or a deck department. Ships mainly concerned with ordnance or aircraft have a combat systems department headed by a *combat systems officer*. Other ships, such as amphibious and logistics ships, have a deck department headed by the *first lieutenant*, who is assisted by a weapons or gunnery officer. (Some older ships have a *weapons department* headed by a *weapons officer*, instead of a combat systems department and officer.)

Aviation units in a ship without an air department are assigned to the combat systems department; they make up the aviation division. These units retain their own basic organization even when so assigned. An embarked Marine Corps detachment is assigned to the combat systems or deck department, also.

The combat systems officer is responsible for the operation and maintenance of the ship's armament and fire-control equipment. He or she must see to the stowage and care of ammunition, including the magazines and sprinkler systems.

The first lieutenant is in charge of deck evolutions and repair and care of the ship's exterior, and in control of the paint, sail, and boatswain's lockers. This officer is in charge of lifeboats and rafts, life jackets, and other survival equipment. He or she sees that all gear about the weather decks is properly secured. The first lieutenant is in charge of all surface underway replenishment operations.

Engineering Officer

Operation and maintenance of the ship's machinery are assigned to the engineering department. Damage control and certain types of repair are also handled by the divisions that make up the department: auxiliaries, repair, boiler, main propulsion, and electrical.

The *engineering officer*, sometimes called the *chief engineer*, is the head of the engineering department. He or she is responsible for the operation, care, and maintenance of all propulsion and auxiliary machinery, electrical-power generators, switchboards, and wiring. Engineering personnel operate the ship's engines, power, light, telephone, ventilation, heat, refrigeration, compressed air, and water systems. The engineering officer is in charge of the stowage, care, and use of fuels and lubricants. He or she maintains the engineering log, engineer's bell book, and other engineering records.

A *damage control assistant* working with the engineering officer maintains the ship's damage control organization, including the control of ship's stability, list, and trim, and the ship's damage control equipment. He or she is responsible for training ship's personnel in damage control, including defensive measures against chemical, biological, and nuclear weapons.

A *main propulsion assistant* assists the engineering officer in all duties pertaining to the maintenance and operation of the ship's propulsion and auxiliary machinery.

Reactor Officer

Nuclear-powered ships have a reactor department headed by a *reactor officer*, whose job is the operation, care, and safety of the reactor plants and auxiliaries.

The reactor officer is a technical assistant to the CO on matters of reactor safety. He or she supervises disposal of radioactive wastes from the ship's reactor plants, is responsible for the operation of the main engines, and maintains the engineer's bell book.

Air Officer

In ships that have an air department, the head of that department is the *air officer*, who directs the launching and landing of aircraft and their handling on deck. He or she is responsible for crash salvage operations and aircraft firefighting. The air officer is in charge of aircraft-handling equipment such as elevators, catapults, and arresting gear, and is responsible for the care, stowage, and issue of aviation fuels and lubricants.

On aircraft and helicopter carriers, the *air wing commander* is the head of the embarked air squadrons. The title usually is *aviation officer* in the case of a helicopter detachment on a nonaviation-type ship.

The air wing commander directs tactical training of the air wing, coordinates and supervises all activities of the embarked squadrons and detachments, and sees to the material readiness of the wing as a whole. The air wing commander works with the ship's operations officer in matters concerning employment, scheduling, training, and tactical air operations.

A member of the Air Department explains to some NJROTC cadets how aircraft are spotted on the flight deck of the amphibious assault ship USS *Wasp* (LHD 1) (Grandby HS NJROTC, Crystal Raner)

Supply Officer

The *supply officer* heads the supply department. He or she is a staff corps officer responsible for ordering, receiving, storing, issuing, shipping, selling, transferring, accounting for, and maintaining all stores and spare parts in the command. He or she is in charge of the equipment in the supply department such as forklift trucks, computers, ice cream machines, and vending machines.

He or she is in charge of the general mess and all food preparation in the command. He or she manages all the ship's services—laundry, barber shop, tailor shop, ship's store, snack bar—and supervises the personnel who take care of the officers' staterooms, wardroom, and food preparation. He or she is in charge of disbursing pay, and maintaining the pay records of all personnel in the command.

Medical Officer

The head of the medical department of a larger ship is the *medical officer*, the senior officer of the Medical Corps serving on board. He or she is directly responsible for the health of personnel of the command. The medical officer advises the CO in all matters affecting health of personnel on board.

Dental Officer

Most large ships and tenders have a dental department with the senior officer of the Dental Corps serving as department head, or dental officer, responsible for the dental care and oral health of ship's personnel. The dental officer and subordinates may be called upon to help the sick and wounded in cases of emergency. In smaller ships the medical and dental departments may be combined.

Division Officers

The departments of a ship are composed of *divisions*. These divisions are organized into sections or watches. The division is the basic unit of personnel on board ship. The number of divisions in a department varies depending upon the size and function of the ship. A division may be very small, or as large as a hundred members or more, such as a deck division on an aircraft carrier.

Each division is headed by a *division officer*. Division officers are responsible to their department heads. The division officer is the first commissioned officer in the chain of command over enlisted personnel. The division officer is a guide, leader, counselor, and supervisor. He or she is the one officer whom division personnel see every day. He or she must show a very personal type of leadership, always finding time for personal contact with assigned personnel.

The assignment as division officer is a often a young officer's first really important assignment. It is his or her first chance to practice leadership skills. A division officer sets the pace and the

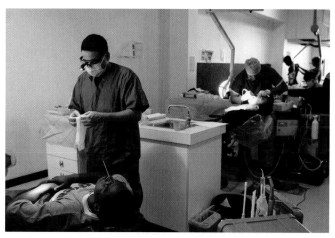

A Navy dentist ministers to a patient aboard the amphibious assault ship USS Kearsarge (LHD 3). (Jilleanne Buda)

example for the division. Almost every duty performed gets instant attention. He or she must issue clear instructions, and give orders in such a way that the morale and spirit of the division is maintained.

Running the training program is one of the most important jobs of a division officer. Because of the rapid personnel changes in today's Navy, it is a continuous job.

Functional Organization

Every ship has a *Ship's Organization and Regulations Manual* and *Battle Organization Manual*; each division has a *Watch, Quarter, and Station Bill*. These documents assign all personnel to their jobs. The purpose is to see that the crew functions as a well-coordinated team in any military situation.

The *Ship's Organization and Regulations Manual* contains the administrative, operational, and emergency bills necessary to handle almost anything that could happen. This manual has the force and effect of *Navy Regulations*. It tells the divisions and departments their normal responsibilities.

The *Battle Organization Manual* sets out the ship's organization for battle conditions. It is an important tool that COs use to prepare their ships to fight. The book has four chapters showing battle stations, conditions of readiness, battle bill, and interior communications systems.

STUDY GUIDE QUESTIONS

1. What are the basic departments in a naval ship?
2. Who has overall responsibility for the safety and operation of a naval ship?
3. What are the main tasks of the executive officer?
4. What is the basic responsibility of the ship's navigator?

5. Why are the battle stations of the CO and XO separated?

6. What is the basic task of a department head?

7. What is the basic responsibility of the operations officer?

8. What is the primary responsibility of the communications officer?

9. What type of ship has a combat systems department and combat systems officer?

10. What is the basic responsibility of the first lieutenant?

11. What is the basic responsibility of the engineering officer?

12. In what kinds of ships would the manning document call for a reactor department and reactor officer?

13. What are the tasks of the air officer?

14. What are the duties of the supply officer?

15. On what matters does the medical officer advise the commanding officer?

16. A. What organization is the basic unit of personnel on board ship?

    B. What is the title of the senior officer of this unit?

17. Why is the division officer's job important?

18. What publication contains the administrative, operational, and emergency bills of the command?

CRITICAL THINKING

1. Research the organizational structure of a large private company and compare and contrast it with the shipboard organization described in this chapter.

2. Compare the organizational structure of your school district headquarters to the organizational structure of a naval ship. What are the key differences?

VOCABULARY

collateral duty	combat systems
auxiliary machinery	department head
command master chief	career counselor
master-at-arms	division officer

2 Watches

A naval ship or shore station can never be left to run itself. Just as equipment such as boilers, water evaporators, and electrical generators must be kept running, so officers and enlisted personnel must stand watches. While at sea, underway watches such as helmsman and lookouts must always be stationed. Other watchstanders keep the ship's equipment operating and propulsion machinery running. In port, watchstanders must be posted to keep the ship secure and to provide needed services. A naval watch may be compared in many ways with a "shift" in an industrial plant.

"Watch" in the Navy is a word with several meanings. It sometimes refers to the location of the person on watch (for example, the bridge watch or comm watch), or to his or her *watch section* (for example, port or starboard, first or second). It may also refer to the individual on watch, such as the lookout watch. Watches take precedence over all normal duties and jobs that a person must routinely do aboard ship or a shore station.

Traditional shipboard watches are normally four hours long, except for two 1600–1800 and 1800–2000 *dogwatches* in the early evening. These divided or "dogged" watches allow crew members to go off watch at 1800 to eat their evening meal, and to rotate the watches so people are not standing the same watch every day. An alternative watch schedule in use on a number of ships today features four five-hour-long watches from 0200 until 2200, then a 2200–0200 mid-watch. This schedule facilitates the morning and evening meals for watchstanders, and eliminates the two early evening dogwatches.

Shore station watches are normally eight or twelve hours long. Watches ashore are usually less demanding and not so frequently stood.

As mentioned in the last chapter, each division is responsible for maintaining a *Watch, Quarter, and Station Bill* for all the personnel in the division. This is based on the ship's or shore station's *Battle Organization Manual* and the *Ship's Organization and Regulations Manual.* They show each person's name, rate, and billet number; the battle station; the duty section assignment; the watch assignments; the station or duty in the event of an emergency such as fire, collision, or man overboard; and cleaning station.

Shipboard Watches

As mentioned above, crew members of a ship are assigned to various watches both at sea and in port. All crew members standing watch at a given time comprise a numbered *watch section.* Underway during routine operations, smaller ships usually have three rotating watch sections; larger ships may have four or more. Sometimes when involved in very demanding operations, ships may go to only two underway watch sections, called "port and starboard," so that roughly one-half the crew is always up on watch at any given time. In port, most ships have four or more rotating watch sections each duty day.

During routine conditions at sea and in port, those persons not on watch are involved in ship's work, drills, recreation, and rest. When the ship goes to general quarters for battle or some other emergency, all watch personnel are relieved and go to assigned battle stations.

Watches must be relieved on time. That does not mean the relief shows up at the exact minute the watch changes, but normally about fifteen minutes before the exact time. This is both a courtesy and a practical procedure. This period allows all pertinent information and instructions to be passed on to the relief from the person going off watch before the watch is relieved. In the case of night watches topside, this period is also necessary for the reliever's eyes to adjust for night vision.

When reporting to the person to be relieved, the relief will say, "I am ready to relieve you." The watchstander then passes on to the relief all the pertinent information and instructions. When the relief understands everything and is ready to assume the watch, he or she says, "I relieve you." After that, the new person is responsible for the watch. When enlisted watches are relieved, and an officer of that watch is present, the change of watchstanders is reported to that officer.

A watch officer or senior petty officer is placed in charge of each watch. Normally, there is a duty officer or petty officer for each duty and watch section of each department. Each duty and watch section is roughly equal in size and in experience.

Command duty officer (CDO). To provide continuity throughout each duty day, most ships appoint a senior officer to act as CDO each day when the ship is in port. This officer represents the CO when he or she is off the ship or otherwise unavailable. The CDO makes sure all events in the XO's plan of the day (POD) for the ship are carried out.

Officer of the deck (OOD). The OOD is the officer on watch in charge of the ship. He or she must have good knowledge of the policies of the CO, XO, and CDO and must make decisions. The

Part of the underway watch team on the bridge of the aircraft carrier USS *Ronald Reagan* (CVN 76). (Kathleen Gorby)

safety and well-being of the ship depends, to a large extent, on the OOD. Under way, the OOD is on the bridge and can give orders to the helmsman at the wheel. Or the OOD may delegate this to the junior officer of the deck (JOOD) in order to train that person for OOD responsibilities. In port, the OOD stands watch on the ship's quarterdeck.

The OOD is assisted by several other watch officers and enlisted watchstanders on duty on the bridge, other topside areas, and throughout the ship. All ship's departments will have duty personnel "on watch," both under way and in port, handling the responsibilities of the department. The operations/communications department has watch sections on duty at all times in the radio room, signal bridge, and CIC while under way and reduced watches in these spaces in port. There is always a duty hospital corpsman. The engineering department has a number of watches in its engineering spaces: boilers, main engines, generators, auxiliaries, and so on, as the situation requires. The supply department has personnel assigned to handle spare parts. The primary enlisted topside watches will be described below. The other departmental watches are not described in detail here, since most of them require specialized training and qualifications.

Topside Watches Underway

There are two basic types of enlisted watches in a topside underway watch section: deck watches and navigational watches.

The makeup of a standard traditional enlisted underway watch section is described below. On newer ships outfitted with high-tech ship control and navigation systems, several of these watch assignments may be eliminated or combined.

Boatswain's mate of the watch (BMOW). The BMOW is the petty officer in charge of the topside watch. His or her principal deck watchstanders include the helmsman, the lee helmsman, the messenger, the bridge sound-powered telephone talkers, lookouts, and when stationed, the lifeboat watch. The navigation watches include the quartermaster of the watch and the after steering watch. The BMOW is the main enlisted assistant to the OOD. He or she sees that all deck watch stations are manned, and that all in the off-going watch are relieved. He or she must see that all watchstanders are instructed and trained in their duties. He or she must be a qualified helmsman.

Helmsman. The helmsman must be fully qualified to steer the ship. He or she steers courses ordered by the *conning officer*, the officer who gives orders to the helm.

Lee helmsman. The person who stands watch at the engine-order telegraph on the bridge is called the lee helmsman. This person rings up the conning officer's orders to the engine room on the telegraph and sees that all bells are answered correctly. He or she should be a qualified helmsman. The helm and lee helm watches often alternate when on watch in order to spell each other and to keep alert. On ships with automatic propulsion control systems, the helm and lee helm are in the same console, and both are operated by the same watchstander.

Messenger. The messenger stands watch on the bridge and delivers messages, answers telephones, and carries out other duties assigned by the OOD.

Bridge sound-powered telephone talkers. A number of bridge sound-powered telephone circuits must always be operating when the ship is under way. Talkers relay messages over these circuits between the OOD and all stations on the circuit. It is very important that all stations "get the word" about all important events taking place during the watch.

Lookouts. Lookouts stationed on the ship's superstructure report aircraft sightings and all surface sightings of ships, craft, obstructions, and so on. They report on the condition of the ship's navigational lights every half-hour at night. The after lookout is stationed on the fantail with a lifebuoy close at hand in the event of a man overboard. Additional lookouts may be posted during periods of fog or low visibility. Each lookout will have a sound-powered telephone set to relay all sightings to the bridge.

Lifeboat watch. Lifeboat watches enable fast recovery of any person in the water. Ships conducting air operations, on plane guard detail behind an aircraft carrier, or engaged in other potentially hazardous operations like underway replenishment, muster a ready lifeboat crew for each watch, so the ship can launch a lifeboat on short notice. The watch usually does not have to remain on the lifeboat station. But it must be on call, up and awake and ready for fast action.

Quartermaster of the watch (QMOW). The QMOW maintains the *Quartermaster's Notebook*, which records among other things all orders to the helm or lee helm, and assists the OOD in navigational matters. The QMOW is a qualified helmsman.

After steering. This watch is stationed in an emergency steering station in the after part of the ship. This person is able to take

over the helm in the event of a casualty to the bridge. He or she has direct control of the steering gear. Usually the OOD directs actual shift of steering control to the after station several times each day. This guarantees that all gear is working correctly and keeps watchstanders alert.

In-Port Watches

The in-port shipboard watch is similar in some ways to the underway watch, but there are important differences. In the first place, the primary watch station is shifted from the bridge to the quarterdeck. The quarterdeck is located on the main deck of the ship, usually at the head of the brow (access) through which persons board or leave the ship. The OOD stands watch on the quarterdeck.

Another major difference between watches in port and under way is that because much of the ship's equipment is shut down (secured) while the ship is in port, not as many duties and watchstanders are required. The ship's company is therefore divided into several rotating *in-port duty sections*, normally three while deployed overseas, and from four to six while in U.S. ports and naval bases. Each person in a duty section must remain on board throughout the twenty-four-hour period his or her section is on duty. Those personnel not in that day's duty section are free to go on liberty after working hours and on weekends. Each day's watchstanders are drawn from that day's duty section.

The enlisted in port deck watch section is generally headed by the petty officer of the watch (POOW). This is a senior petty officer qualified to lead the enlisted watch. The rest of the watch section consists of the brow watch, security watches and patrols, messenger, duty MAAs, and side boys as required. These will all be described below.

Petty officer of the watch (POOW). The POOW is the OOD's primary enlisted assistant in-port. He or she supervises and instructs sentries and messengers and carries out the daily routine and orders as the OOD directs. When neither the OOD nor any junior officer of the watch (JOOW) is near the brow, the POOW returns salutes of those leaving and arriving. The POOW calls away boats in accordance with the boat schedule, calls away evolutions scheduled in the plan of the day, and assembles liberty parties for inspection by the OOD. If a QMOW (see below) is not assigned, the POOW maintains the deck log and requires the messenger to make calls listed in the call book.

Brow watch. A brow watch is sometimes posted at the foot of the brow on the pier. This person maintains security of the brow and will attend to military and ceremonial duties for visiting dignitaries.

Security watches and watrols. These watches may be posted to increase the security of the ship. Duties include being alert for evidence of sabotage, theft, or fire; checking security of weapons magazines; making soundings of tanks and spaces; inspecting damage control fittings; and making hourly reports to the OOD.

A quartermaster plots course changes while standing bridge watch aboard amphibious assault ship USS *Essex* (LHD 2). (Nardelito Gervacio)

Quartermaster of the watch (QMOW). When assigned, the QMOW will maintain the deck log, handle absentee pennants of the CO and any embarked officials, check anchor and aircraft warning lights, hail boats, and assist with the rendering of honors. He or she takes bearings when at anchor, and takes temperature and barometer readings every hour. If a QMOW is not assigned, these duties will be carried out by the POOW, the messenger, and the duty quartermaster in the navigation division.

Anchor watch. When the ship is at anchor, this watch is posted near the ground tackle (pronounced tay-cul; the anchor and anchor chain and associated equipment). He or she keeps a continuous watch on the anchor chain to check the strain and how the chain is tending. The anchor watch talks by sound-powered phone to the QMOW and the OOD. Special alertness is called for if the ship is moored to a buoy, since the buoy may drag.

Side boys. When high-ranking officials are expected to arrive or depart on official visits to the ship, side boys are mustered, inspected, and instructed in their duties by the POOW. They are stationed on either side of the quarterdeck to render honors to the arriving or departing officials. When the POOW pipes the side on the boatswain's pipe, two to eight side boys, depending on the rank of the honored officer, will form a passageway to or from the brow. They salute on the first note of the pipe and drop their salute together on the last note.

Side boys must be smart in appearance and grooming, with polished shoes and immaculate uniforms. Enlisted women may be detailed to this duty, but they are still called "side boys."

Duty master-at-arms (MAA). The duty MAA is a watch of the executive department. This person is a regular member of the MAA force who stands duty under the direction of the XO. He or she also performs the duties of the sergeant of the guard in ships without Marines. In this job, the duty MAA is responsible for brig sentries and orderlies.

Watches Ashore

All major naval stations and bases, like ships, have watches that are stood by officers and enlisted personnel assigned to duty there. However, with the exception of forward bases supporting operations in places like Iraq and Afghanistan, the pace of activity ashore is usually not as fast as that on board ship, so watch and duty assignments are usually not so frequent, except during special exercises or times of increased readiness.

Because they are not so often stood, nor as demanding as most shipboard watches, most shore station watches are longer than those on board ship, usually eight or twelve hours duration. On occasion, especially during evening hours and on weekends, duty

Secretary of the Navy Donald Winter passes through side boys during a ship visit. (Daniel Viramontes).

personnel not on watch may be allowed to stand their duty on call in quarters or at home.

Major shore staffs and stations usually have an officer assigned as CDO for each day, and they may also have an OOD, who stands his or her watches in a duty office. These may be assisted by several enlisted watchstanders, including a duty MAA, communications watch, and, on larger stations, a shore patrol watch.

Barracks Security Watch

The *barracks security watch* is a watch maintained in all shore station barracks for protection against fire, for the safety of personnel and material, and for carrying out routines. This watchstander is responsible for fulfilling the provisions of the fire bill, emergency bill, and barracks regulations. The barracks watch is also responsible for keeping order and discipline.

All NJROTC cadets must be aware of the need for a barracks security watch, and learn how to stand one. Why? Because NJROTC cadets are normally scheduled to attend "mini-boot camps" as part of their Naval Science program. These mini-boot camps are held at various military bases around the country. While there, cadets normally stay in barracks at the base.

NJROTC units also routinely visit naval bases and installations around the country. During these visits cadets are often housed in barracks as guests of the base commander. NJROTC units are responsible for the security, cleanliness, and discipline of the barracks that they occupy.

STUDY GUIDE QUESTIONS

1. A. What is a "watch"?
   B. What is meant by "dogging" a watch?
2. A. How long does a traditional shipboard watch last?
   B. A typical shore station watch?
3. What is meant by "relieving the watch on time"?
4. What are the two basic types of enlisted watches in a topside underway section?
5. Who is the main enlisted assistant to the OOD?
6. A. What do lookouts report during their watches?
   B. When should additional lookouts be posted?
7. A. What is the purpose of the lifeboat watch?
   B. What does it mean to be "on call"?
8. What are the duties of the QMOW?
9. How many duty sections is a ship's crew normally divided into:
   A. When visiting a foreign port while deployed?
   B. When in U.S. ports and naval bases?
10. What name is given to the primary shipboard watch station in port?
11. Who is the primary enlisted watch assistant of the OOD in port?
12. What is the purpose of the security watch and patrols?
13. What is the purpose of side boys?
14. A. What is the purpose of the barracks security watch?
    B. Why should NJROTC cadets be aware of barracks watch requirements?

CRITICAL THINKING

1. In the future many of the watchstanders described in this chapter may be replaced with automated systems. Describe which watchstanders might be replaced on board a typical Navy ship of the year 2020, and which positions if any will probably still be manned by humans.

VOCABULARY

watch	working hours
dogwatch	watch section
night vision	duty section
deck watches	conning officer
BMOW, QMOW	after steering
helm	quarterdeck brow
lee helm	POOW, JOOW
lookout	plan of the day (POD)
OOD, JOOD	ground tackle
CDO	side boys
shore patrol	boatswain's pipe
	barracks

Basic Seamanship

The first requirement of everyone who sails in the ships of the U.S. Navy is seamanship. Seamanship has three main components: the art and skill of handling a vessel, skill in the use of deck equipment, and the care and use of various kinds of line, called *marlinspike seamanship*. On board ship, the people most concerned with seamanship every day are those in the deck department. Sailors who work in the ship's office, radio shack, or engine room may not be called upon for much seamanship in their normal everyday duties. This does not mean, however, that seamanship is unimportant for them.

Seamanship is the skill that ties every member of the Navy together. Whether an admiral or a seaman, a Navy person wears a uniform that says he or she is familiar with the art of seamanship. Regardless of what job specialty a Sailor selects, that Sailor first becomes a seaman, then a technician. The pride with which a person performs seamanship duties will carry over into the specialty ratings.

Many times, especially in smaller ships, everyone must help the deck force. Enlisted persons may have to carry stores on board, assist in replenishment, or help in mooring or unmooring the ship. Officers are expected to be able to supervise all such activities. In emergencies or general quarters, all hands may have to do all manner of seamanship evolutions from manning guns, standing lookout watches, or handling boats, to fighting fires. All departments must keep their spaces (compartments) clean and painted, exercise good safety procedures, and do preventive maintenance of their equipment.

1 Deck Seamanship

Skills used in the conduct of shipboard evolutions such as cargo handling, underway replenishment, and mooring, requiring the use of lines, anchoring gear, and other such equipment, are collectively referred to as deck seamanship. As mentioned earlier, most of these evolutions are carried out by personnel of the deck department aboard large ships and the deck division aboard smaller ships.

We have already talked about the first lieutenant in an earlier chapter on shipboard organization. That officer is in charge of the deck department or division. The title goes back to the early days of British naval sailing ships. Then, the captain was served by a number of lieutenants, each in charge of a division. The first lieutenant was the most senior and knowledgeable in the business of working and maneuvering a man-of-war under sail. He therefore was the specialist in seamanship. This title has survived to this day. The first lieutenant, assisted by the ship's boatswain, is in charge of all deck seamanship evolutions, as well as the care and maintenance of most of the ship's exterior.

Deck Personnel

The personnel under the first lieutenant who carry out most seamanship duties are members of one or more deck divisions, depending upon the size of the ship. Most large surface ships have three deck divisions. The first division has charge of the forward part of the ship; the second, the ship's boats and boat decks; and the third, the after part of the ship.

On ships having aviation personnel aboard, nonaviation personnel, especially those in the deck department, are traditionally referred to as "blackshoes," while aviation personnel are collectively called "brownshoes." These nicknames refer to the shoe colors of surface line officers who wear black shoes, as opposed to naval aviators who by custom wear brown shoes with their khaki uniforms.

The seaman apprentice (SA) reporting on board ship from boot camp (recruit training) is usually assigned to one of the deck divisions. These new personnel do the physical work that must be done by the deck force in any ship. This includes upkeep of ship's compartments, living areas, decks, and external surfaces. Also, it includes the deck watches such as helmsman, lookout, messenger under way and in port, and other special watches such as sentry duty and anchor watches. During general quarters, seamen are members of gun crews and damage control parties. During seamanship tasks, they will operate small boats, booms, cranes, and winches.

Before a seaman apprentice (E-2) can become a striker for advancement to a specialty rating, he or she must first satisfy the requirements for seaman (E-3). To qualify for this rate, the E-2 must prove competent at marlinspike, deck, and boat seamanship. He or she must be able to do these things to the satisfaction of the leading petty officers and division officer, receive their recommendation for advancement, and take a written exam on deck seamanship.

Boatswain's Mates

The enlisted supervisors of the deck force are boatswain's mates. They direct and train seamen in military duties and in all activities that have to do with marlinspike, deck, and boat seamanship.

A boatswain's mate supervises as an inflatable boat is about to be lowered into the water. (Brett Morton)

They also act as petty officers in charge of gun crews and damage control parties during general quarters. Under way, they stand boatswain's mate of the watch on the bridge; in port they stand petty officer of the watch on the quarterdeck. During replenishment operations under way, boatswain's mates have most of the key jobs at the transfer stations.

The boatswain's mates on board ship have much influence on their enlisted. They spend most of their day supervising seamen. They have the responsibility of training, and working with, almost every new person reporting on board ship. Many people receive their first impressions of shipboard life in the deck division. The work is often hard, and the hours are long. Seamen are often in the open, exposed to the weather. The life of a deck seaman is demanding, so the leadership provided by boatswain's mates is very important.

In larger ships, the first lieutenant often has a chief warrant boatswain as an assistant, in addition to deck division officers. In such cases, this officer is called the *ship's boatswain*. The senior boatswain's mate will serve as the leading boatswain's mate, and assists the ship's boatswain. First-class boatswain's mates normally serve as division petty officers.

Marlinspike Seamanship

The *marlinspike* is a tapered steel tool used for separating strands of rope. It is the basic tool of the seaman, and has become the symbolic "tool of the trade."

Marlinspike seamanship concerns the use and care of fiber line and wire rope used at sea. It includes every kind of knotting and splicing, as well as all fancywork done with rope, twine, and cord. It takes knowledge and skill to become proficient in marlinspike seamanship. A good seaman has a real appreciation for a sound piece of line or a good square knot or splice. One look at the way a person handles a line tells experienced people whether or not that person is a seaman. It is not a difficult art, but to learn it well takes time, patience, and practice. Knowledge of marlinspike seamanship is the real test for deck Sailors, and is most important to their chances for advancement.

The rest of this chapter will deal with the types, care, makeup, and use of rope. Many NJROTC cadets will want to try their hand at tying knots, and some may even wish to do some fancy or ornamental work. It can be fun, as well as practical.

Rope and Line

Rope is a general term that can be applied to both fiber and wire. In the Navy, though, fiber rope is called *line*. Fiber rope is called rope as long as it is still in its original coil. Once the rope has been uncoiled and cut for use, it is not called rope anymore. Rope made from wire is called wire rope, or just *wire*.

Line is made from either natural fibers of various plants (manila, sisal, hemp, cotton, and flax), or synthetic fibers such as nylon and Kevlar. Of the natural fibers, *manila* is the one most often used aboard ship. It is strongest and most expensive. It is made from the fibers of the abaca, or wild banana plant, raised chiefly in the Philippines (hence the name manila). At one time most all line used on Navy ships was made from manila.

Today, however, nylon and Kevlar line has replaced manila for almost all shipboard applications in the Navy except high-line transfer of personnel between ships at sea. Although nylon line is more expensive than manila, it is much stronger and lasts longer. For these reasons, nylon and Kevlar line is often cheaper in the long run, even though its initial cost is greater than that of manila.

Nylon does not rot or age as rapidly as natural fiber, so it keeps its strength better throughout its life. It is also less bulky, requires less stowage space, and is more flexible, making it easier to handle. Nylon is practically waterproof. It does not decay, and resists marine fungus growths. But nylon also stretches more than manila under load. This is why it is not used for transferring people or cargo from ship to ship by highline. Nylon will stretch about 50 percent before breaking, but when it does, it snaps like a rubber band, so it can be very dangerous under heavy strain.

Although wire rope has not been in general use for some years, some ships still use it for situations where extra strength is required, such as when storms or high winds are expected. Because such rope tends to form spurs or burrs on the surface over time, people handling it should always wear heavy leather work gloves. They should take care not to rub against it, since the sharp burrs can easily pierce light clothing and inflict severe cuts.

Regardless of the material from which it is made, all line is formed in basically the same way. The natural or synthetic fibers are twisted together in one direction to form *yarns* or *threads*. These yarns or threads are twisted together in the opposite direction to form *strands*, which are in turn twisted together in the opposite direction to form the line. General-purpose line made in this manner is known as *plain-laid*.

The degree of twist of the strands or the type of lay of the strands will cause the strength of different types of line to vary. For instance, hard twisting increases the friction that holds the line together and makes it less likely to absorb moisture. But too many twists reduce

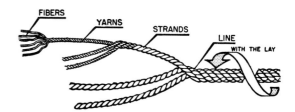

The construction of line. Note how successive twists of the fibers, yarns, and strands are always opposed. Line formed in this way is called plain-laid.

the strength of the fibers. Most line used on board ship is three-strand, plain-laid, and has a right-hand twist or lay. *Right-laid* line must always be coiled down right-handed or clockwise.

Single- or *double-braided* nylon and Kevlar line is also carried on board ship for such things as hoisting signal flags (halyards) and mooring lines. Braided line will not unlay or untwist when it is free to rotate on swivels as signal halyards must do. Plain-laid line will tend to unlay or untwist under similar conditions. Kevlar mooring lines will not stretch under heavy strain and will not recoil if they break as nylon does, making them much safer to use than nylon mooring lines.

Length of line is normally measured in fathoms, feet, or meters (1 fathom equals 6 feet). However, the *size* of a line is its circumference, measured in inches. The size of wire rope is its diameter, measured in inches across the widest part.

The largest line used for general shipboard purposes in the Navy is 10-inch, normally referred to as a *hawser*. A hawser is the name given to any line larger than 5 inches in circumference that is generally used for towing or mooring. Five-inch manila is used for personnel high-line transfer rigs in most cases. Any small stuff less than six-thread is called by name rather than by the number of threads.

Line less than 1¾ inches in circumference is called *small stuff* and is identified by the number of threads in the line. Twenty-four thread, with about 1¾-inch circumference, is the largest small stuff. Other sizes of small stuff are twenty-one thread (1½ inch), fifteen thread (1¼ inch), twelve thread (1⅛ inch), nine thread (1 inch), and six thread (¾ inch).

Marline is the most common small stuff referred to by name. It is made of two-stranded, left-laid, tarred hemp. It is not much larger than ordinary household wrapping cord. It is most often used for *serving*, or covering a larger line for protection from abrasion. *Seizing stuff* is similar to marline, though stronger because it is three-stranded and right-laid. *Small white line* is made from cotton or flax and is used for lead lines, flagstaff halyards, and the like. It is like household clothesline.

Handling Fiber Line

When preparing to use any line larger than small stuff, it is usually a good idea to lay it out on deck in one of several established ways. Doing so will help in handling the line, plus help to avoid kinks in the line as it is run out. It also contributes to the shipshape and seamanlike appearance of the ship or boat.

Coiling down a line means to lay it in circles on the deck, roughly one coil or circle on top of the other. Right-laid line is always coiled down in a clockwise direction, and left-laid line in a counterclockwise direction. Coiling down in the wrong direction results in annoying and possibly dangerous kinks and twists. When a line is coiled down, the end on top is ready for running. Coiling is the fastest way of making up line or wire, and the most common.

Faking down a line is to lay it out in long, flat rows on the deck, one alongside the other. The main advantage of working with line that is properly faked down is that it runs off with little chance of fouling or kinking. Mooring lines are commonly made ready by flaking them down before coming in to a pier.

A third method used for laying down short lengths of line is *flemishing*. To flemish down a line is to lay it down in a flat helical coil on the deck, somewhat like a wound clock spring, with the *bitter end* (end of the line) in the center. The line is laid down loosely and wound tight to form a "mat" by placing the hands flat on the line and twisting in the direction the line is laid.

Most rope and line on board ship is stowed in the *boatswain's locker*. This is a storage compartment, usually in the forward part of the ship, which holds all the line, wire, and tools used by the deck force.

Coils of line are stored on shelves or platforms clear of the deck so they will stay dry. They should not be covered, but should be open to the air, since natural fiber is apt to mildew and rot if damp. Small stuff is stored on a shelf in order of size, with the starting end of the line out for easy reach.

The bitter end of a line should always be *whipped* to prevent it from unlaying, or fraying. A good seaman cannot stand to see a good piece of line frazzled out. To prevent such fraying, a temporary plain whipping can be put on with a piece of small stuff. The whipping line is laid down along the line and bound down with a couple of turns. Then the other end of the whipping should be laid on the opposite way and bound a couple of turns from the bight of the whipping and pulled tight.

Faking down a line.

Flemishing down a line. The bitter end is in the center.

A permanent whipping is put on with a palm and needle. A *palm* is a tough piece of leather that fits into the palm of the seaman's hand, serving somewhat the same purpose as a thimble. This is rarely done to line or rope smaller than 1¾ inches, but normally is done with larger lines.

The bitter end of a nylon line is usually secured by taping the end of each strand and then taping all strands together and fusing the end of the line with a hot iron or torch. The heat will melt and fuse the line together.

A good rule to remember with any line is that all loose ends must be whipped, cut, or tucked in order for the ship to maintain a smart, shipshape appearance. Attention to such detail is important; the ship that takes care of such details usually performs well.

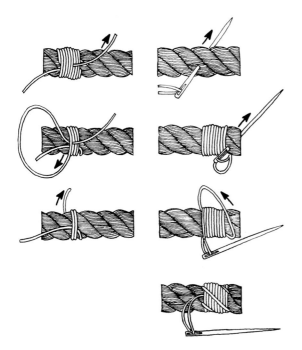

Whipping lines. The bitter end of a line should always be whipped (wrapped) to prevent it from unlaying. Whipping is done with a palm and needle.

Wet fiber lines should be dried thoroughly before stowing. If this cannot be done, the line should be faked out on gratings under cover so it can dry as quickly as possible. All fiber lines shrink when wet and stretch again when dried out. For this reason, wet lines in use should be slackened when the weather becomes damp or lines become wet with rain.

A line with a kink should never be placed under strain. A heavy strain on a kinked or twisted line will cause permanent distortion or damage, seriously weakening the line. When a kink has been forced into each strand, it is impossible to work it out.

Line will weaken with use and exposure. Nylon line will gradually change its color from yellowish-white to gray. It is necessary to inspect the inner part of a line to determine its real condition, though. The strands are unlaid either by hand or with a *fid*, a pointed, round, tapered wooden tool designed for splicing fiber lines. If weakened, the yarns will show bristles and a decrease in diameter. Lines in such weakened condition should not be used and certainly never for supporting people aloft or over the side.

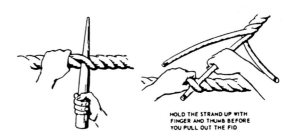

HOLD THE STRAND UP WITH FINGER AND THUMB BEFORE YOU PULL OUT THE FID

Using a fid to separate and splice lines.

Natural fiber line under heavy strain will make cracking noises as the strands work against the strain. When such noises increase in intensity, this is a warning that the line may part. A visible sign of such strain will appear in the form of a steamlike vapor over a weakening area if the line is wet. Nylon may not emit such noises unless against a cleat or bitt, but will stretch and eject the steamlike vapor. Natural fiber line will stretch very little, even under heavy strain. It will lose about 30 percent of its strength over a two-year period with normal careful use.

Knots, Bends, and Hitches

The term "knot" is often used as an all-inclusive term, but experienced seamen distinguish between knots, bends, and hitches. *Knots* are used to form eyes (loops) or to secure a cord or line around an object such as a package. Generally they are intended to be permanent, so they are hard to untie: *Hitches* are used to fasten a line to or around an object such as a ring or stanchion (a metal or wooden pole) or another piece of line. *Bends* are used to secure lines together.

Most Navy men and women are expected to know how to tie the square knot, bowline, and single and double becket bends, and the round turn and two half hitches. Most also should know the clove hitch. These knots are explained and illustrated here to give you some guidelines to go by in your own seamanship practice. Besides that, it's fun!

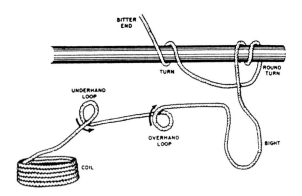

Terms used in tying knots, bends, and hitches.

The *square knot*, also called the reef knot, is the best-known knot for bending two lines together. It can also be made to secure small stuff around a package. It can sometimes slip and can jam under strain. It can be loosened by pulling first one and then the other end.

A landlubber trying to tie a square knot often comes out with a *granny knot*. For a square knot, both parts of the line must be under the same bight (half-loop).

Here is the proper way to tie a square knot: Take the end in your right hand, and pass it over and under the part in your left hand. With your right hand, take the end that was in your left, and pass it under and over the part in your left hand.

The *bowline* is one of the most useful knots. It has many variations. The chief use of the bowline is to form an eye at the end of a line, but it also can be used to secure a line to a ring or pad-eye (a deck fitting resembling a vertical steel plate rounded on the top and welded to the deck along the bottom, with a hole near the top), to form a loop around a stanchion or other object, or to bend two lines together. The bowline neither slips nor jams, and it ties and unties easily. It is the best knot to use for bending a heaving line or messenger to the eye of a hawser or cable because it is quick to tie and easy to get off.

The method of tying a bowline is as follows: Form a small horizontal loop in the line about where you want the eye to be formed, with the standing part (long side) of the line underneath. Pass the bitter end up through the loop, around behind the standing part, and back down through the loop (i.e., up, around, and down). Tighten the knot by applying some strain to the eye with the standing part of the line.

The chief value of the *becket bend* is to bend together two lines of different sizes. If there is a great difference in sizes, or the strain on the line is to be great, a *double becket bend* should be used. A becket bend is as good as a square knot, and much easier to untie after strain.

To fashion a single becket bend, make a bight on one line and run the bitter end of the other line up through it. Pass the bitter end around behind both parts of the bight and back under itself. The third step, to make a double becket, is made by taking another turn around the bight.

The *clove hitch* is the best all-around knot for bending a line to a ring, spar, or anything else that is round or nearly round. The clove hitch can be easily tied, and it will hold as long as there is a strain on it. Once the strain is taken off, however, the hitch must be checked and tightened to prevent the bitter end from pulling out when the strain is reapplied. For that reason, it is a good idea to put a half hitch on the end of it.

To tie this hitch, take a turn around the object with the bitter end, pass the end across the standing part, and take another turn. (Notice that both turns go around in the same direction.) Then pass the bitter end under itself alongside the standing part, and the hitch is complete.

Another way to make the clove hitch is to form two underhand loops. Lay the second loop on top of the first. This method is often used to form the hitch when it can be slipped over the end of the object to which the line is to be secured.

Since the clove hitch may slide along a slippery object, the *round turn with two half hitches* is often used instead. The chief advantage of the round turn and two half hitches is that it will not slip along the object to which it is secured. If the angle of pull is acute (less than 90 degrees), this hitch should be used. The round turn and two half hitches is especially useful on a spar (pole) because it grips tightly and holds its position.

This hitch is made by taking a round turn around the object and then making two half hitches around the standing part. (The two half hitches actually consist of a clove hitch formed around the standing part of the line.)

Securing for Sea

Knots, bends, and hitches are necessary to ensure the safety of people working, for many seamanship evolutions, and for securing equipment to prevent damage during rough seas. You can never underestimate the force of the sea!

Lines must be in good shape and strong enough to hold the gear and people who depend on them. For heavy weather, all objects must be lashed tightly against something solid. The lines should be taut so the object will not "work" with the pitch and roll of the ship. *Chafing gear*, consisting of a padded sleeve or canvas, should be placed around lines to prevent wearing on sharp corners and rough surfaces. Lines should never be tied to electric cables, small piping, or other movable objects.

Safety first is always the rule when working with lines and wire rope.

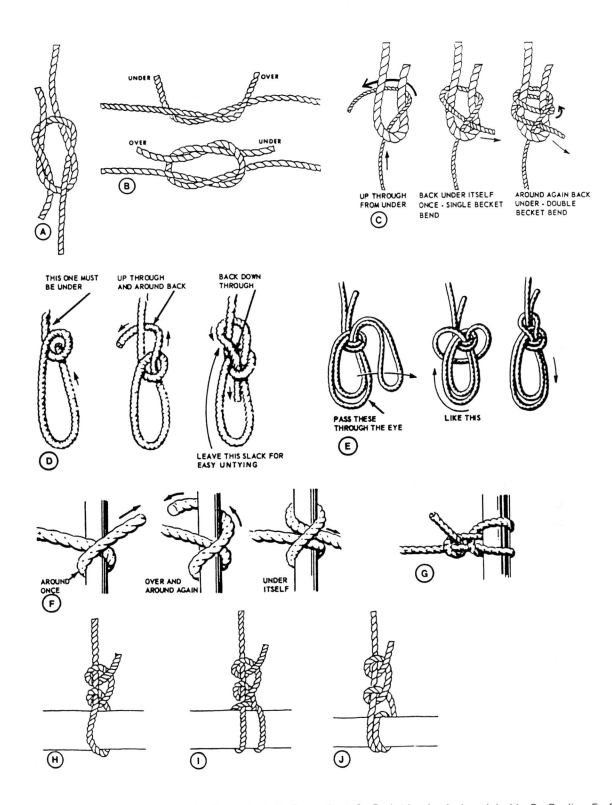

Diagrams of various knots, bends, and hitches. A—Granny knot. B—Square knot. C—Becket bends, single and double. D—Bowline. E—Bowline on a bight. F—Clove hitch. G—Clove hitch and single half hitch. H—Two half hitches. I—Clove hitch with two half hitches. J—Round turn with two half hitches.

STUDY GUIDE QUESTIONS

1. What is the first requirement for those who sail in naval ships?

2. A. What is seamanship?

   B. Which shipboard department is concerned with seamanship as its primary duty?

3. What is meant by the statement that "one is first a seaman, and then a technician"?

4. Which officer is in charge of the deck department?

5. What must a seaman apprentice accomplish in order to advance to pay grade E-3?

6. What are the main duties of the ship's boatswain?

7. What is marlinspike seamanship?

8. A. What is rope?

   B. When does the term *line* come into use in the Navy?

   C. What materials is line made from?

9. A. What is the strongest of the natural fibers?

   B. What is its principal use aboard Navy ships?

10. A. Why is nylon line the most common kind of line used in the Navy today?

    B. What is a disadvantage of nylon line?

11. What special safety precautions should be observed when handling wire rope?

12. A. How is the length of line measured?

    B. How is the size of line denoted?

13. What is the name given to line larger than 5 inches in circumference?

14. What is line under 1¾ inches in circumference called?

15. What is marline, and what is it used for?

16. What is seizing stuff?

17. What is the bitter end of a line?

18. Where are most rope and lines stowed in a ship?

19. What is the purpose of whipping a line or rope?

20. Why should loose ends of line be whipped or tucked?

21. A. What is a fid?

    B. What is it used for?

22. What is the difference between a knot, a bend, and a hitch?

23. What is the best knot for securing small stuff around a package?

24. What is the bight of a line?

25. What is the best knot for bending together two lines of different sizes?

26. What is chafing gear?

27. What is always the rule when working with lines and wires?

CRITICAL THINKING

1. Demonstrate your knowledge of at least four of the various types of knots, bends, and hitches described in this chapter.

VOCABULARY

deck seamanship	splicing
boatswain's mate	knots
marlinspike	bending a line
rope	hitches
line	hawser
wire rope	small stuff
yarn	marline
clockwise	seizing stuff
counterclockwise	bight of line
halyard	square knot
manila	bowline
circumference	chafing gear
faking down	bitter end
flemishing down	padeye
fid	standing part of a line
eye of a line	

Deck equipment consists of all equipment used in deck seamanship. This equipment is normally operated by the deck force. The anchors and chains and all equipment associated with anchoring are fundamental to the business of deck seamanship; they are called *ground tackle*. Other deck equipment has to do with mooring the ship, including the deck fittings to which lines are made fast. A third major group of deck equipment is the rigging and booms, which are used to handle cargo.

This chapter will discuss some of the basic information about these most important equipments. Different size ships will have different size equipments, but all ships have this basic gear.

Ground Tackle

Ground tackle is the equipment used in anchoring and mooring with anchors. It includes anchors, anchor cables and chains, and all chain cable parts such as chain stoppers, shackles, detachable chain links, mooring swivels, and the tools used to work this and other chain parts. It also includes the anchor windlass, the machinery used to lift, or *weigh*, the anchor and its cable.

Before the development of anchor chain, anchors were raised and lowered by fiber hawsers and wire ropes. Thus, the large pipe through which the cable passes from the deck to the ship's side received its name: *hawsepipe*. This is not to be confused with the *chain pipe* through which the chain runs from the windlass down into the *chain locker*.

Anchors

Anchors used by the Navy today are grouped into four types: the patent or stockless anchors, the mushroom anchor, the lightweight type anchor, and the two-fluke, balanced-fluke anchor.

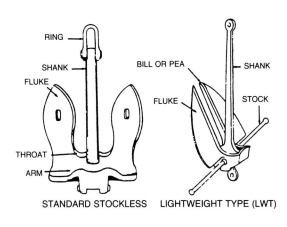

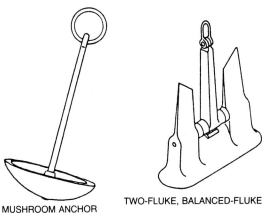

The four major types of anchors used by U.S. naval ships.

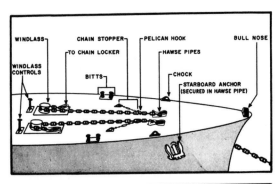

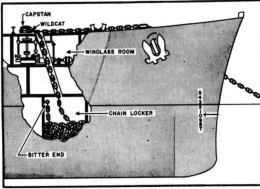

The ground tackle in the forecastle of a typical ship.

The guided missile destroyer USS *Stetham* being positioned for a Med-type moor. (Nardelito Gervacio)

When a ship has one anchor down, it is *anchored*. When it has two anchors down and swings from a mooring swivel connected to both, it is *moored*. (A ship secured to a pier with lines or to a buoy with an anchor chain is also moored.) In a type of mooring common in the Mediterranean (called a *Med moor*), a ship usually has the stern tied up to a pier, and an anchor out on each side of the bow.

Most naval ships have *patent* or *stockless anchors* because they are easy to stow and handle. They can be raised directly into the hawsepipe because there is no long stock. Stockless anchors are also called *bower anchors* because they are always carried on and used from the bow. The arms, or *flukes*, of this kind of anchor can swing to either side to permit the anchor to dig into the harbor bottom. The largest stockless anchors weigh 30 tons and are used on aircraft carriers.

Submarines are equipped with a *mushroom anchor* so they can anchor even when submerged. The mushroom is also used to anchor buoys and barges.

Lightweight type (LWT) anchors are relatively new, and have been used mostly for small craft until recently. The LWT anchor has a short stock, which makes it easy to stow in the hawsepipe. The LWT anchor tends to bury itself deep in the bottom when under strain, and has better holding power than the stockless anchor. Also, a LWT anchor only half the size of a stockless has the same holding power as a stockless anchor. This makes the cost of the anchor and the gear to handle it much lower. Most new destroyers, frigates, and cruisers have LWT anchors that are bower anchors.

The two-fluke, balanced-fluke anchor is used for anchoring some new surface ships and the newest submarines. It is housed in the bottom of the ship. It is used on board some surface ships in place of a bower anchor, in order to prevent interference with the ship's bow sonar dome.

Anchor Chains and Related Equipment

Even though it is made up of links, an anchor chain is usually called an *anchor cable* by custom. Modern naval anchor chain is made of high-strength steel links. The size of chain varies according to the size of the ship and its anchors. All links are studded, that is, a solid piece is welded in the center of the link to prevent chain kinking.

To give you some idea of the weight of a large anchor chain, a single link of a large aircraft carrier chain weighs about 250 pounds! Most ships are equipped with two anchors and two chains.

The lengths of chain that make up the ship's anchor cable are called *shots*. A standard shot is 15 fathoms, or 90 feet, long. Shots are connected by *detachable links*, painted in a red, white, and blue sequence to let the anchor detail know how much chain has run out.

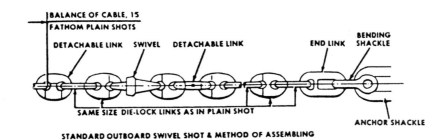

STANDARD OUTBOARD SWIVEL SHOT & METHOD OF ASSEMBLING

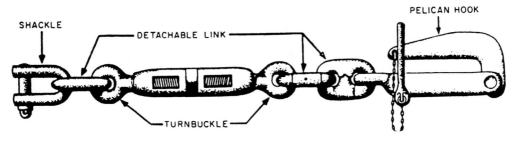

The swivel shot, or bending shot (top), used to attach the anchor chain to the anchor. The chain stopper (bottom) is used to hold the anchor tight in the hawsepipe, or to hold the anchor if it is detached from its chain for any reason.

Adjacent links to each side are painted white. The number of adjacent links painted white indicates the shot number. Each link of the next-to-last shot is painted yellow. The entire last shot is painted red. This is to warn that the chain is out almost to its bitter end.

On most ships, standard short *swivel shots* called "bending shots" attach the anchor chain to the anchor (see illustration). These swivel shots consist of detachable links, regular chain links, a swivel, an end link, and a *bending shackle*. The bending shackle is attached to the anchor shackle.

Chain stoppers (see illustration) are made up of a *turnbuckle* inserted in a short section of chain. A *pelican hook* is attached to one end of the chain, a shackle at the other. Chain stoppers are used for relieving stress on the windlass when anchored, holding the anchor taut in the hawsepipe, or for holding an anchor and its swivel shot when they are disconnected from the chain.

Anchor Windlass

An *anchor windlass* is the machine used to hoist a bow anchor. A ship with a stern anchor has a stern-anchor winch to hoist it. On combatant ships the anchor windlass is a vertical-type winch with control, friction brake handwheel, capstan, and wildcat above deck, and an electric and hydraulic drive for the wildcat and capstan below deck (see illustration). Auxiliary ships have a horizontal windlass that is above deck, with two wildcats, one for each anchor. The *capstan*, or warping head, is the line-handling drum on top of the shaft of the anchor windlass. Just below the capstan is the drum or *wildcat*, which contains teeth (whelps) that grab the links of the anchor chain and prevent it from slipping. The wildcat is fitted with a brake to stop the chain at the desired length (scope) in the water.

A seaman painting a huge 15-ton stockless anchor of a LSD. (Spike Call)

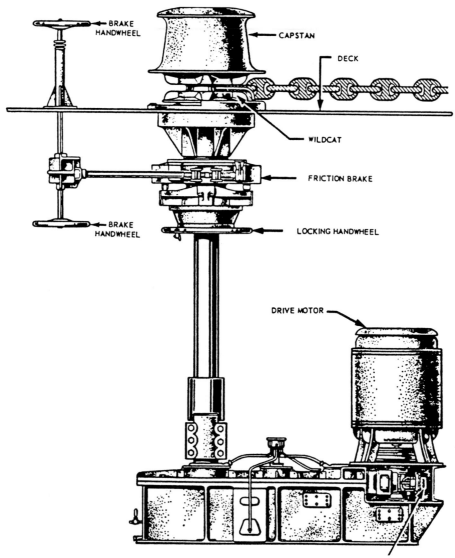

The anchor windlass is the machine used to hoist a bow anchor. The wildcat under the capstan has teeth (whelps) that engage the links of the anchor chain.

Anchoring

The first lieutenant is in charge of the *anchor detail* on the forecastle while anchoring and weighing anchor. Either the ship's boatswain or a senior boatswain's mate assists the first lieutenant. A person from the auxiliary machinery division and an electrician's mate, both from the engineering department, are in the anchor windlass room to handle any problems with the equipment. The first lieutenant is in direct contact with the bridge by sound-powered telephone.

Letting go. In preparing to anchor, all but one of the chain stoppers are removed, and the brake is released so the anchor in the hawsepipe is supported only by the remaining stopper. Sometimes the anchor may be walked out (slowly lowered) to a position just above the water surface by the windlass before the restrain-

ing stopper is attached. With all in readiness, the first lieutenant orders all hands (except a person with a sledgehammer to release the last stopper) to stand clear of the chain. This is a safety precaution because nothing will stand in the way of the rapidly moving chain once the stopper is released. On the order "Let go!" relayed from the bridge, the pelican hook is knocked open with the sledgehammer, and the anchor and chain plunge with a roar through the hawsepipe into the water.

As the chain runs out, reports are made of the amount, strain, and angle relative to the bow. For example: "Thirty fathoms out; chain tending at six o'clock; no strain." The word "tend" indicates the direction of the chain relative to the bow, given in terms of clock direction (e.g., six o'clock would be tending aft, nine o'clock would be tending 270 degrees to port). Strain on the chain may be reported as light, moderate, heavy, or no strain.

Sailors on a ship's forecastle making ready to anchor. Note the two chain stoppers securing each anchor in place.

Scope of chain. The amount of chain payed out (veered) is known as the *scope of chain* used to anchor. Usually a ship anchors in water less than 20 fathoms deep. Under favorable sea conditions, the common practice is to use a scope of chain that is five to seven times the depth of the water, with six times the depth being a common rule of thumb. More chain may be payed out if rough weather is expected.

With the chain veered to the proper scope, it should hang in a slight catenary (downward curve). Normally a stopper is attached, and the ship will be slowly backed down to imbed (set) the anchor into the sea floor. If too little chain is let out, the flukes will not dig well into the bottom, and the anchor is apt to drag. Loud rumbles will be heard if the anchor drags on a rocky bottom, and a series of vibrations may be felt on a mud bottom.

Weighing anchor. Before the anchor is hoisted (weighed), the windlass engine is tested. The wildcat is engaged, the brake released, a strain is taken on the chain, and the stoppers are cast loose. Just before the ship gets under way, the anchor is usually heaved in to *short stay*. This is a condition in which there is the minimum amount of chain out that keeps the anchor from breaking loose from the bottom; the chain is nearly vertical in the water. Only the officer of the deck can order heaving to short stay, and then only after receiving permission from the captain.

When the ship is ready to get under way, the anchor is heaved in as ordered from the bridge. Status reports are made to the bridge from time to time, usually when the various shot markers become visible at the water's edge. (Examples: "Fifteen fathoms at the water's edge"; and when the anchor is at short stay, aweigh [broken loose from the bottom], in sight, and secured for sea or ready for letting go.)

As the chain comes in, it is hosed off to remove mud. Often, the shot markings are repainted. Some links of each shot are tested by

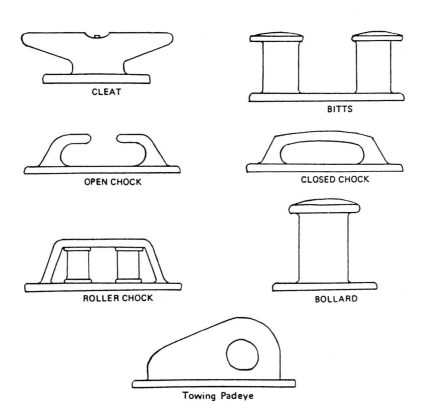

CLEAT

BITTS

OPEN CHOCK

CLOSED CHOCK

ROLLER CHOCK

BOLLARD

Towing Padeye

Deck fittings used for handling lines. All the fittings shown are common on ships and boats except for the bollard, which is a pier fitting. The towing padeye is used as the attachment point for a towing hawser.

A boatswain's mate passes the eye of a second bow line from a Navy destroyer over a bollard on a pier. Note the stockless anchor dangling from the hawsepipe, ready to be let go if the ship had difficulty while maneuvering into its berth. (Douglas Morrison)

striking them with a hammer. All links are tested if the chain was subjected to a heavy strain. If a link rings, it is all right; if it sounds flat, it may be damaged, and in this event, it must be marked for later replacement.

Mooring

A ship is *moored* when it is made fast to a mooring buoy, when it is swinging on a bight of chain between two anchors, or when it is secured by lines to a pier or another ship. Mooring a ship to a pier, buoy, or another ship, and unmooring, are some of the most basic jobs of the deck department. These tasks require skillful use of mooring lines and deck winches. Deck fittings such as cleats, bitts, bollards, chocks, and towing padeyes are used in the process (see illustration). Quick, efficient line handling when coming alongside or getting under way is one of the marks of a smart ship.

Deck and pier fittings. The fittings used in mooring and unmooring are important to the use of mooring lines. Sailors must know when and how to use these fittings to do a smart job of line handling.

A *cleat* is a device welded to the deck that looks like a pair of projecting horns. It is used for fastening a line or wire.

Bitts are cylindrical objects made of steel implanted in the deck. They are arranged in pairs, each pair mounted on a separate footing. Usually there is a set of bitts forward and aft of each mooring chock, for use in securing mooring lines.

A *mooring chock* is a heavy fitting on the deck edge with smooth rounded surfaces through which mooring lines are led. Mooring lines are run from bitts on deck through chocks to bollards on the pier when a ship is moored. Chocks are of three kinds: (1) *open chock*, a mooring chock open at the top; (2) *closed chock*, a mooring chock closed by an arch of metal across its top; and (3) *roller chock*, a mooring chock that contains a set of rollers for reducing friction.

A *bollard* is a strong mushroom-shaped fitting on a pier, around which the eye or bight of a ship's mooring line is placed.

A *towing padeye* is a large padeye of extra strength located on the stern that is used in towing operations.

Mooring Lines to a Pier

Ships are moored to piers, wharves, and other ships with a set of mooring lines. In general, they are as light as possible to ease handling. They are also strong enough to take a big strain during mooring, and to hold a ship in place when secured.

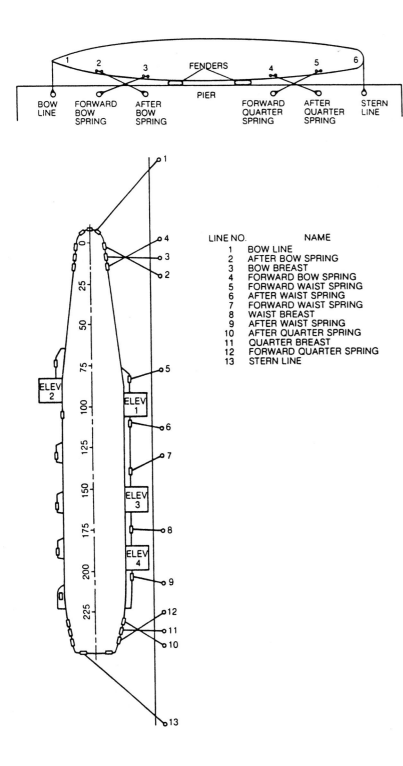

LINE NO.	NAME
1	BOW LINE
2	AFTER BOW SPRING
3	BOW BREAST
4	FORWARD BOW SPRING
5	FORWARD WAIST SPRING
6	AFTER WAIST SPRING
7	FORWARD WAIST SPRING
8	WAIST BREAST
9	AFTER WAIST SPRING
10	AFTER QUARTER SPRING
11	QUARTER BREAST
12	FORWARD QUARTER SPRING
13	STERN LINE

The standard mooring patterns and their names for a large ship such as a carrier and a small one such as a destroyer.

Mooring lines are numbered from forward to aft in the order that they are run out from the ship. Many ships are normally moored with six lines, though large ships may use seven or eight, aircraft carriers thirteen, and small ships as few as four. In any event, the lines are grouped according to their use as bow, stern, spring, or breast lines.

The *bow line*, line one, is the mooring line that runs through the bull-nose or chock nearest the bow of the ship. For larger ships this line is led well up the pier to stop the ship from moving aft; similarly the last line, the stern line, is led aft to stop any forward motion of the ship. For smaller ships, however, the bow and stern lines lead directly to the pier to serve as breast lines, explained below. Bow spring lines lead fore and aft at an angle and control the fore-and-aft movement of the ship. Quarter spring lines do a similar job from the ship's quarter.

Breast lines are at a right angle to the ship and control the distance to that part of the ship from the pier. Breast lines are designated bow, waist, or quarter breast lines.

The size of mooring line used depends on the type of line and size of ship. Destroyers normally use 5-inch nylon. Smaller Navy ships use 4-inch nylon, and large ships like aircraft carriers use 8-inch nylon. If manila is used for mooring lines, the next larger sizes of manila line are used.

When the ship is secured, the mooring lines are normally doubled up. To double up a line, an additional bight of it is passed around the fitting on the pier or other ship to which the line is attached. Then slack is taken out until the two parts of the bight are alongside the original part of the line. Thus, three parts of the line absorb the strain, rather than just one. Often with a line to a pier, the three parts are bound together with small stuff, and a conical *rat guard* is placed about midway up the line, with the open end facing the pier, so that rats and mice cannot crawl up the line onto the ship.

Towing

Most routine towing in the Navy is handled by harbor tugs, fleet tugs, salvage vessels, and submarine rescue vessels. Such vessels are especially fitted for this task. All ships, however, must be able to tow or be towed in an emergency.

On the stern of most Navy ships, a towing padeye is located on the centerline. The towing assembly has a large pelican hook that is shackled to the towing pad and made fast to a towing hawser. The hawser is attached to one of the towed ship's anchor chains, which is let out through the bull-nose and veered to about 20 fathoms.

The length of the towline—hawser and chain—is adjusted to hang in a deep catenary. This catenary helps to relieve surges on the line caused by movements of the two ships. Proper towing technique requires that the towline be of such scope that the two craft are "in step." Both must reach the crest of a wave at the same time, or the towline will be whipped out of the water under terrific strain. Once properly rigged, the towing vessel must barely get under way as the towed vessel begins to move. A sharp start or jerk may part the towing hawser. Speed is gradually increased to about 5 or 6 knots for the duration of the tow.

Cargo Handling

Cargo is loaded or offloaded by ship's gear, or dockside winches and floating cranes when in port. At sea the ship's gear is used for underway replenishment (UnRep) either by another ship (ConRep), or by helicopters (VertRep), in which case very little ship's gear will be used. Amphibious and mobile logistic ships have heavy-lift cargo systems. In such ships, deck seamanship is mainly concerned with heavy-cargo handling. Sailors in these ships need to know about all the parts of cargo gear and the various "rigs" for handling cargo.

Rigging. The term *rigging* is used for all wires, ropes, and chains supporting masts or kingposts (vertical poles), and operating booms and cargo hooks. *Standing rigging* includes all lines that support masts or kingposts but do not move, such as stays and shrouds. *Running rigging* includes all movable lines that run through blocks, such as lifts, whips, and vangs, described below.

Booms. A *boom* is a long pole built of steel. The lower end is fitted with a gooseneck, which supports the boom in a boom step bracket. The free end is raised or lowered and held in position by a cable called a *topping lift*. Booms range in capacity from 5 to 75 tons.

Booms are moved into position, and cargo is moved into and out of holds by running rigging. Topping lifts move the free end of the boom vertically and hold it at the proper height. Inboard and outboard guys, or *vangs*, move the boom horizontally or hold it in working position over a hatch or dock. The cargo hook is raised or lowered by *cargo whips* running from winches.

Underway Replenishment

In addition to anchoring and mooring, one of the more frequent deck seamanship evolutions done by the deck personnel of naval ships is underway replenishment (UnRep) while alongside another ship (ConRep). Such operations may involve the transfer of fuel, cargo, ordnance, and sometimes personnel by *highline transfer*. Normally the ship receiving the transfer maneuvers alongside the supplying ship. Once alongside, light heaving

When a ship is secured to a pier, the mooring lines are usually doubled up, as shown here. Then light line is used to bind the parts together, and conical rat guards are put in place so that rats and mice cannot crawl up the lines onto the ship.

Several booms and their rigging are shown in use by this oiler during an underway replenishment of another ship alongside.

lines are first passed to the supplying ship, then thick transfer wires (manila line in the case of personnel transfer) are attached to messenger lines and passed back to the receiving ship, where they are fastened to appropriate fittings. Slack is removed from the wires or highline until they are taut. Then fuel transfer probes and hoses, or in the case of cargo or ordnance transfer, pallets suspended from moveable trolleys, are slid along the taut span wires from the supplying to the receiving ship. For personnel transfers, a *boatswain's chair* is suspended beneath the manila highline. Upon completion of the replenishment or personnel transfer operations, the wires or highlines are detached and retrieved, and the receiving ship maneuvers away from the supplying ship.

Often vertical replenishment by helicopters (VertRep) will take place simultaneously with ConRep, or sometimes independently. Except for ships not having an air detachment, deck personnel are not normally much involved with this, as that is the province of the air department personnel.

STUDY GUIDE QUESTIONS

1. What is all of the equipment associated with anchoring called?
2. What is the machinery used to hoist the anchor and its cable called?
3. What is the large pipe through which the cable passes from the deck to the ship's side called?
4. What are the four types of anchors used by the Navy?
5. Describe a Mediterranean moor.
6. What is the most common anchor in use in the Navy today?
7. What are anchors carried on the ship's bow called?
8. What are the advantages of LWT anchors?
9. A. How many fathoms and feet are in a shot of chain?
   B. How are shots connected to each other?
10. What is the identifying color scheme of detachable links and shots?
11. A. How is strain on the chain reported to the bridge?
    B. What is the common reference used to describe the direction in which a chain tends?
12. What is the common rule of thumb used to determine the proper amount of chain to be veered in an anchorage?
13. What does it mean to "heave in the anchor to short stay"?

14. Describe the following:
    A. Cleat
    B. Bitts
    C. Chock
    D. Bollard
15. What are names of the lines in a standard six-line moor?
16. What is the purpose of breast lines?
17. Why must all naval ships be prepared to tow or be towed?
18. With respect to cargo handling, what does the term "rigging" include?
19. What do underway replenishment operations alongside another ship involve?

CRITICAL THINKING

1. Describe the complete sequence of anchoring a vessel from initial preparation through setting the anchor.
2. Describe the complete sequence of raising an anchor from a mooring until it is in final position in the hawsepipe.

VOCABULARY

ground tackle	LWT anchor
anchor windlass	chain shot
mooring	detachable link
hawsepipe	fathom
chain pipe	towing padeye
Mediterranean moor	mooring lines
stern anchor	bull-nose
stockless anchor	swivel shot
mushroom anchor	fluke (anchor)
scope (of chain)	chain stopper
veer (chain)	pelican hook
catenary	wildcat
weigh anchor	capstan
short stay	standing rigging
cleat	running rigging
bitts	boom
chock	topping lift
bollard	vang

3 Small Boat Seamanship

At some time or another during unit visits to naval bases and ships or in recreational activities, you will be concerned with small boat seamanship. In this chapter we will discuss the particular characteristics of small boats, including nomenclature (vocabulary), boat handling, and boat etiquette. Most of our discussion of boat handling will be concerned with powerboats, as opposed to sailboats, because that is the type of boat with which most NJROTC cadets will come into contact during their training.

Boat Nomenclature

The first thing that anyone who will be in or around a small boat needs to know is the nomenclature that applies to it. There are two basic kinds of small boats with which we will be concerned: powerboats and sailboats. A *powerboat* is any vessel that is propelled through the water by some type of motor or engine. A *sailboat* is a vessel that is propelled mainly by the wind, through the use of some type of sail. Some boats, called *motor-sailers*, are designed to be propelled by both power and sail at the same time, but under the rules of the road, and for purposes of our discussion, they are considered power-driven vessels.

A powerboat, like this captain's gig being made ready alongside the USS *Boxer* (LHD#4), is any vessel propelled by some type of motor or engine.

The Hull and Its Parts

The hull is the largest part of a boat and is the structure that floats in the water. There are two basic hull designs:

- the *displacement* type, which plows through the water
- the *planing* type, which skims on the surface

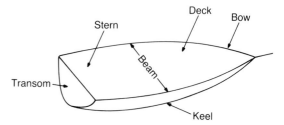

A drawing of a small boat hull, showing the principal parts.

Most sailboats and many powerboats have displacement hulls, while high-speed powerboats usually have planing hulls. But regardless of the type of hull, the basic nomenclature used to describe them is the same for both sailboats and powerboats.

Like a ship, the pointed forward portion of the hull is called the *bow*, and the opposite rear portion is the *stern*. The extreme back end of the stern, usually fairly flat in a powerboat, is called the *transom*. At the bottom of the hull is the *keel*. The keel is usually fairly deep in a sailboat and relatively shallow in a powerboat. On the top of the hull is the *deck*. The depth to which the hull sinks in the water is the *draft* of the hull, and its maximum width is the *beam*. The line the water makes with the hull is the *waterline*.

Boats that have two fairly shallow-draft V-shaped hulls connected together by the boat's upperworks are called *catamarans*, and those having three such hulls are *trimarans*.

Upperworks

Structures placed on the hull, corresponding to the superstructure of a ship, are called *cabins*. Vertical openings in the cabin are called *doors*, and horizontal openings in the cabin and deck are *hatches*. Windows, particularly in a sailboat, are called *ports*. The forward window or sets of windows in a powerboat are the *windshield*.

Larger boats have a kitchen, or *galley*, and one or more bathrooms, called *heads*. Separate bedrooms on a boat are called *staterooms*.

Sailboats, like the two-masted one shown here, have a low upper-works to allow for free movement of the sails. All except the very smallest usually have some sort of auxiliary engine for propulsion when the sails are down.

The position of the steering gear for the boat, which may be inside or outside the cabin, or in some cases both, is called the *helm*. In many sailboats, the helm is located in the *cockpit*, a depressed area aft of the cabin, or, in some cases, amidships between two cabins. The edge of the deck, called the *rail*, usually has vertical metal stanchions that support one or more rows of *lifelines*. In the front of the bow on most sailboats and many powerboats is the *pulpit*, a wooden platform that overhangs the bow and provides room to handle the forward sail and anchor. It may be supported underneath by the *bowsprit*, a beam that extends from the bow beneath the platform. Some powerboats have an auxiliary helm and engine controls on a platform elevated for better visibility called a *flying bridge*.

Sailboats have one or more vertical poles called *masts* used to support one or more sails, collectively called the *rig* of the sailboat. A powerboat may have a short stubby mast for the radar and radio antennas, and on some types called *trawlers* these may even be high enough to carry a steadying sail. If a sailboat has two or more masts, one is the *main*, and the other the *mizzen* (if aft of the mainmast) or *foremast* (if forward of the mainmast). The position of the mainmast may vary according to the type of rig the boat has. Metal wires, rods, or lines used to support the masts are the *standing rigging*, and the various lines used to support and control the sails are the *running rigging*. Horizontal supports near the top of the masts that support the standing rigging are the *spreaders*, and horizontal poles near the base of the masts used to support the bottom of the sails are *booms*.

There is a great deal of other nomenclature peculiar to sailboats that we will not include here. Any basic text on sailing will usually contain a section on sailboat nomenclature, which can be referred to if the need arises.

Propulsion and the Rudder

The propulsion machinery on a powerboat is called the *engine*, and on a sailboat, the *auxiliary*. Boat engines may be either gasoline- or diesel-fueled. They transmit their power to the propeller or screw under the stern via the *propeller shaft*, which corresponds to a drive shaft on a car. Most powerboat propellers are three-bladed; some sailboats have a two-bladed propeller that can be aligned with the back of the keel to reduce drag through the water while operating on sail alone. Powerboats may have one or more engines; they may be permanently installed inside the hull, in which case they are called *inboard*, or they may be semiportable and on the stern, in which case they are called *outboard*. Most Navy small boats have engines of the inboard type. Near the propeller is the *rudder*, or in some cases two rudders, that control the direction of travel of the boat.

Types of Boats

There are hundreds of different types of sailboats and powerboats, collectively called *pleasure boats* if they are operated mainly by civilians as leisure-time activities. In the Navy, most powerboats, called *small craft*, with which NJROTC cadets will come into contact fall into one of only a few categories: amphibious craft, utility boats, officers' boats, and inflatables.

A landing craft utility (LCU) makes ready to offload a group of Marines. (Geronimo Aquino)

Amphibious craft include such boats as landing craft of several sizes and types, some of which are equipped with bow ramps that can be lowered to discharge troops or cargo when the boats reach shore. They also include various types of control boats that look like traditional powerboats and other specialized types of craft such as hovercraft and tracked amphibians that can swim ashore and then climb the beach to discharge their troops and cargo inland.

Utility boats, like this personnel boat, are used for transporting people and light equipment.

Utility boats are essentially open powerboats of sizes ranging from about 25 feet to about 75 feet, designed for hauling personnel and light cargo between ships and fleet landings ashore. Most have a single screw and rudder.

Officers' boats are smaller, traditional-looking powerboats with cabins intended to carry senior officers and other ship's officers. They are usually of less capacity than comparably sized utility boats. Most ships have only one or two of these, reserved for use primarily by the ship's captain or higher-ranking officers who may be embarked on the ship. The captain's boat is called a *gig*. A boat used by an officer of higher rank than the ship's captain is called a *barge*.

Modern inflatables come in many shapes and sizes. Traditional double-ended whaleboats of years past have largely been replaced by rigid hull inflatable boats (RHIBs) to fill the small boating needs of most Navy ships. The latest RHIBs are water jet propelled, eliminating the need for a propeller and rudder.

Coxswain

The person in charge of handling a civilian boat, regardless of its size or type, is customarily called the boat's *captain*. This tradition is followed almost universally in both commercial and pleasure boating. In the Navy, the person in charge of a sailboat is also called the captain, but in the case of powerboats of all sizes and types, the person in charge of the boat, its crew, and any passengers is called the *coxswain* (pronounced coc'-sun). The coxswain is responsible for the maneuvering and safety of the boat under all circumstances except when a commissioned line officer is embarked as either a boat officer or passenger; these officers may then give directions under certain circumstances to the coxswain.

Boat Handling

In order to become a good boat handler, a person must understand the forces that act on the boat and cause it to move in one way or another. These forces can be broadly classified into two types: those that are controllable by the boat handler, such as the propeller force and rudder pressure, and those that are uncontrollable, such as wind and current. It is the interplay of all forces acting simultaneously that determines how a boat will react in any given situation.

Propeller Forces

Generally speaking, a boat is moved by forces resulting from pressure differences. For all practical purposes, water is incompressible; therefore, when a propeller or screw rotates, high- and low-pressure areas are created on opposite sides of the propeller blades. This force, called *propeller thrust*, is transmitted along the propeller shaft from the high-pressure area toward the low-pressure area. When a right-handed propeller, the type normally used on a single-screw boat, is rotating clockwise as viewed from astern, the low-pressure area is on the forward face of the propeller blades, resulting in forward movement of the boat. When the propeller rotates counterclockwise, an opposite effect occurs, and the boat backs.

Next in importance to propeller thrust is *side force*, which tends to move the boat's stern sideways in the direction of propeller rotation. The upper blades exert a force opposite to that of the lower blades, but the lower blades are moving in water of greater pressure. Consequently, the force of the lower blades is greater. It is as though the lower blades were touching the bottom and pushing the stern to the side. When going ahead the stern tends to starboard, and when backing, to port. Side force is greatest when the

Rigid hull inflatable boats (RHIBs) have become the workhorses among the small craft of the fleet, doing duty as lifeboats, personnel boats, fast patrol craft, and utility boats.

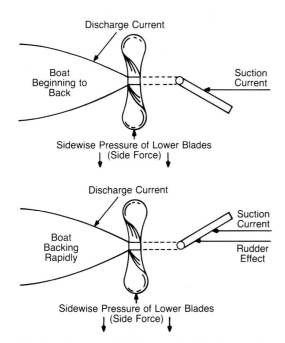

The screw (discharge) current, side force, and rudder forces all combine to determine how a boat will respond, as in the backing situation depicted here.

boat begins moving from a stationary position, or nearly so, and decreases rapidly as the boat's speed increases. Side force is greater when backing than when going ahead.

Screw current, caused by the action of a rotating propeller, consists of two parts. The portion flowing into the propeller is the suction current, and the portion flowing away from the propeller is the discharge current. Suction current is a relatively minor force in boat handling. Discharge current is a major force in two main respects: it is a strong force acting on the rudder with the screw going ahead, and it is a strong component of side force when the screw is backing because of the discharge current acting against the boat's hull.

Single-screw ships and boats have a single rudder mounted directly behind the propeller. Twin-screw ships and boats usually have a rudder mounted directly behind each propeller, but some have a single rudder mounted between and just behind the propellers. Basically, a rudder is used to attain or maintain a desired heading. The force necessary to do this is created by dynamic pressure against the surface of the rudder. The magnitude of this force and the direction in which it is applied produce the rudder effect that controls stern movement and, through it, the boat's heading. Factors having a bearing on rudder effect include rudder size, rudder angle, rudder location, boat's speed, direction of propeller rotation, headway, sternway, suction current, discharge current, and side force. The diverse effects of all of these factors can be lumped together under a single term, *resultant force*, which indicates the direction and amount of net force exerted on a boat's stern.

A single-screw vessel is most difficult to maneuver at very low speeds where rudder effect is minimal, while at the same time propeller side force is greatest.

One of the most notable characteristics of a single-screw boat or ship is its tendency to back to port. Four distinct forces affect a boat's steering when backing:

- The discharge current from the propeller (which tends to throw the stern to port)
- The suction current caused by the propeller drawing in water from astern (which adds to the steering effect of the rudder, although not by any great amount)
- The sidewise pressure of the blades (which forces the stern to port)
- The normal steering effect of the rudder

Typical Situations

Let us examine the effect of the forces just described in a few typical situations. We will assume there is no wind, tide, or current, except in certain instances where it is so stated.

Boat and screw going ahead. When a boat is dead in the water, with right rudder on, and the screw starts turning over, the screw current hits the rudder and forces the stern to port. With left rudder on, the stern moves to starboard. As the boat gathers way, the effect of the screw current diminishes and the normal steering effect of the rudder controls the boat's head.

When the boat is proceeding ahead in the normal manner and the rudder is put right, the boat first falls off to port. If the rudder is put left, the boat goes to starboard. The entire boat is thrown slightly (almost imperceptibly) to the side, but the stern gives way to a greater extent. The boat advances two or three boat lengths along the line of the original course before it commences to gain ground in the desired direction. At higher speeds, this advance is slightly less than at lower speeds, and turns are executed more quickly. Because of the advance, trying to execute a turn to avoid an obstacle only a short distance ahead can result in disaster.

Boat and screw backing. When backing down, four distinct forces are involved in steering. They are discharge current, side force, suction current, and rudder effect. The combination of these forces is such that it is almost impossible to back in a straight line.

Because discharge current (from the propeller) and side force tend to throw the stern to port, most single-screw boats tend to back easiest in that direction. The relatively weak suction current acts to throw the stern to the side on which the rudder is, but suction current is negligible at slow speeds, so the rudder tends to be ineffective. As the boat gathers sternway, the water through which the boat is moving acts on the rudder and increases the effect of suction current, so the rudder becomes more effective. This usually slows, but does not necessarily stop, the stern's swing to port. When backing long distances, it usually is necessary to occasionally reverse the rotation of the screw and shift the rudder long enough to straighten out the boat.

Strong winds affect backing ships and boats. Ships with high superstructures forward, as well as many boats, will back into strong winds, because their upperworks act as weathervanes.

Until you discover differently, assume that a boat will more easily back to port.

Boat going ahead, screw backing. A boat going ahead with the screw backing is an important illustrative case, for it is the usual condition when danger is discovered close aboard. One might assume that the rudder would have its usual effect in such a situation, *but this is not true.* As soon as the propeller starts backing, the forces discussed earlier combine and begin to cancel rudder effect.

If the rudder is left amidships (centered), the head falls off to starboard and the boat gains ground to the right as it loses way. This is because both side force and discharge current force the stern to port.

If the rudder is put hard right at the instant the screw starts to back, the boat changes course to starboard. The stern continues to swing to port unless, as the boat gathers sternway, the rudder effect is great enough to take charge.

If the rudder is put hard left at the instant the propeller backs, the boat's head goes to port at first, and as the speed decreases, the head usually falls off to starboard. Some boats and ships, however, back stern to starboard for a while if there was a distinct change in course to port before the screw started backing.

Boat going astern, screw ahead. With the boat going astern, the screw going ahead, and the rudder amidships, side force and screw current are the strongest forces. They oppose each other; hence the resultant effect is difficult to determine. You must try it on each boat to obtain the answer. If the rudder is put hard right, the discharge current greatly exceeds the side force and the normal steering effect of the rudder, and the stern swings rapidly to port. Throwing the rudder hard left causes the stern to fall off to starboard.

Making a Landing

Many books on boat handling tell the beginner to make a landing heading into the wind, if possible, or to make it on the side of the pier where wind or current will set the boat down on the pier. This is good advice, but any Sailor knows that a boat coxswain often has few chances to select landings. Consequently, the coxswain must learn the effects of the elements on each boat and to control the boat under any condition. The coxswain will be then able to get under way or make a landing when and where necessary in a smart, seamanlike manner. With experience, the coxswain eventually will be able to adjust to any circumstances and handle the boat correctly in an almost second-nature manner.

The pointers that follow, plus a firm understanding of the preceding section, will assist a person learning the basics of boat handling. A boat handler should remember, though, that boats do not

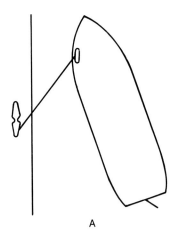

A

Making a landing can be simplified with the proper use of lines and current. This diagram shows a port-side-to landing using a spring line.

always respond exactly as theory predicts and there is no substitute for actual experience.

Throughout this section, we assume that the boat handler knows how far the boat, going at various speeds, will travel before a reversing screw stops the boat or changes its direction. We also assume that the boat handler knows how far the boat will fetch (glide) with the screw in neutral.

Making a landing usually involves backing down. For this reason, procedures for landing port-side-to differ from those for a starboard-side-to landing. Let us first consider a port-side-to landing.

Port-side-to landing. Making a port-side-to landing is easier than making a starboard-side-to landing because of the factors previously discussed. With no wind, tide, or current with which to contend, the approach normally should be at an angle of about 20 degrees with the pier. The boat should be headed for a spot slightly forward of where you intend to stop. Several feet from that point (to allow for advance) put your rudder to starboard to bring your boat parallel to the pier, and simultaneously commence backing. Quickly throw the bow painter (bow line) over. Then, with the painter around a cleat to hold the bow in, you can back down until the stern is forced in against the pier.

If wind and current are setting the boat off the pier, make the approach at a greater angle and speed. The turn is made closer to the pier. In this situation it is easier to get the stern alongside by using hard right rudder, kicking ahead, and using the bow line as a spring line. To allow the stern to swing in to the pier, the bow line must not be snubbed too short.

If wind or current is setting the boat down on the pier, make the approach at about the same angle as when being set off the pier. Speed should be about the same as or slightly less than when there is no wind or current. The turn must be begun farther from the pier because the advance is greater. In this circumstance, the stern can be brought alongside by either of the methods described, or the boat can be brought parallel to the pier and allowed to drift down alongside.

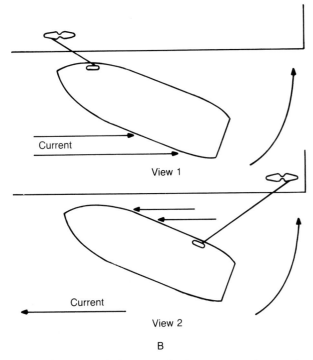

A diagram of a starboard-side-to landing in a current using a spring line.

Starboard-side-to Landing. Making a starboard-side-to landing is a bit more difficult than a landing to port. The angle of approach always should approximate that of a port-side-to landing. Speed, however, should be slower to avoid having to back down fast to kill headway, with the resultant swing of the stern to port. A spring line should be used when working the stern in alongside the pier. Get the line over, use hard left rudder, and kick ahead.

If you cannot use a spring line (as when approaching a gangway), time your turn so that, when alongside the spot where you intend to swing, your bow is swinging out and your stern is swinging in. When it looks as though the stern will make contact, back down; as you lose way, shift to hard right rudder.

Making use of the current. If there is a fairly strong current from ahead, get the bow line to the pier and the current will bring the boat alongside. If the current is from aft, the same result can be achieved by putting over a stern line first. Care must be taken during the approach, because a following current decreases rudder efficiency, and steering may be slightly erratic:

Twin-Screw Boats

On twin-screw boats, the starboard screw is right-handed and the port screw is left-handed. The lateral (sidewise) forces produced by one screw cancel those of the other when both are going ahead or astern. When one is going ahead and the other is going astern, however, the forces complement each other, and the effect is doubled. For this reason, maneuvering a twin-screw boat is consider-

ably easier than maneuvering a single-screw boat. You need not worry about the separate forces or their combined effect; think of it as a lever with a force (screw) at each end and the load (boat) in the middle. Thus, you can readily see how much more quickly a particular maneuver may be accomplished by using the correct propeller combinations along with the appropriate rudder angle. For example, to turn your boat 180 degrees to starboard from a dead stop, use right full rudder, port engine ahead, and starboard engine astern. The boat will make the turn in little more than its own length, whereas a single-screw boat would require considerably more space to complete the same turn. It is also much easier to get into a short berth or other confined space with a twin-propeller boat.

Almost all the maneuvers required of a boat can be accomplished by varying the direction and speed of the engines and without using the rudders. An experienced coxswain also can maintain a fair course by varying the number of turns of the propellers.

Boat Etiquette

In the Navy the observance of proper boat etiquette is second in importance only to safety aspects of boat handling when it comes to judging the competence of a boat's coxswain and crew. Boat etiquette is concerned with customs, honors, and ceremonies observed by the boat coxswain and crew. Most of these are traditions that have been passed along through the years since the founding of our Navy over two hundred years ago.

The customs that have been established promote the smooth loading of passengers, help govern boat traffic, and expedite the movement of boats at gangways and piers. Proper boat etiquette is a sign of good seamanship. It also makes a lasting impression on all who observe it. Clean boats and sharp, courteous crews draw favorable comments.

The following few rules of boat etiquette, established by custom and regulations, should serve as a guide to proper conduct when in boats. Passengers in a boat should observe them closely, and insist that others do likewise.

Rendering Honors

Hand salutes are rendered to boats carrying officers and officials in much the same way as salutes would be made when passing such individuals while walking on land. Junior boats salute the senior first, and the senior returns the salute. It is not the size or type of boat, but the rank of the officer aboard that determines a boat's seniority. Thus, a small boat carrying a commander is senior to a large boat carrying a lieutenant. Usually it is possible to tell by the officer's uniform or by the flag flown which boat is senior. In cases of doubt, however, it is best to go ahead and salute.

Boat salutes are rendered by a boat's coxswain and by the senior officer embarked. The engine of the junior boat should be idled during the salute, and after the return of the salute, speed may be resumed. Coxswains always rise to salute unless it is dangerous or impractical to do so. Officers generally do not rise to salute, but do so from a seated position if visible to the other boat.

During morning or evening colors, a boat's engine should be idled or stopped and the clutch disengaged. The boat officer (if assigned) and the coxswain stand at attention and salute in the direction of the ceremony if it is possible to do so without losing control of the boat.

A coxswain in charge of a boat salutes when officers enter or leave his boat if the situation allows. For example, when a boat is alongside a ship's accommodation ladder, the coxswain oftentimes is too busy maintaining control of the boat to salute.

Finally, men working in a boat or working on the ship's side from a boat do not salute unless "Attention" is sounded.

Courtesy Aboard Boats

Through the years, certain courtesies have come to be practiced by the crews and passengers of boats. The basic rule in Navy manners, as in civilian life, is to make way for a senior quickly, quietly, and without confusion.

The procedure for boarding and leaving boats is as follows: juniors board boats first, and leave after seniors, unless the senior officer gives orders to the contrary. The idea is that the senior officer should not have to wait in a boat for anyone. The senior gets out first, because normally his business is more important and pressing than that of the personnel of lower rank. Generally, seniors take the seats farthest aft; in boats with no officers embarked, the after part of the boat (or stern sheets) is usually reserved for chief petty officers.

Subject to the requirements of the rules for preventing collisions, junior boats must avoid embarrassing senior boats. At landings and gangways, juniors should give way to seniors. Juniors should show deference to their seniors at all times by refraining from crossing the bows of their boats or ignoring their presence.

Under ordinary circumstances, enlisted personnel maintain silence when they are passengers in boats with officers aboard.

Boat Flag Etiquette

The national ensign and personal flags and pennants of officers are properly displayed from small boats as described below.

National ensign. The national ensign is displayed from boats of the Navy at the following times:

- When under way during daylight in a foreign port
- When ships are required to be dressed or full dressed
- When going alongside a foreign vessel
- When an officer or official is embarked on an official occasion

- When, in uniform, a flag or general officer, a unit commander, a commanding officer, or a chief of staff is embarked in a boat of his or her command or in one assigned to his or her personal use
- At such other times as may be prescribed by the senior officer present

Personal flags and pennants. When embarked in a boat of the naval service on official occasions, an officer in command, or a chief of staff when acting for him or her, displays from the bow of the boat his or her personal flag or command pennant or, if not entitled to either, a commission pennant.

STUDY GUIDE QUESTIONS

1. With what type of boat will most NJROTC cadets come into contact while on visits to Navy ships and shore stations?
2. Identify the following boat parts:
   A. Hull
   B. Transom
   C. Waterline
   D. Pulpit
3. What are the two types of fuel used in powerboats?
4. What is the difference between a personnel boat and a gig?
5. What is the person in charge of a powerboat in the Navy called?
6. What forces determine how a boat will handle in any given circumstance?
7. What is the effect of propeller side force on a vessel's stern?
8. When is it most difficult to maneuver a single-screw boat?
9. In what direction will a single-screw boat be easiest to turn when backing?
10. When a boat is proceeding ahead and the rudder is put over to one side, what happens to the stern initially?
11. What happens in respect to the rudder when a propeller starts backing?
12. When making a normal landing, at what angle should the boat approach the pier?
13. On twin-screw boats, in which directions do the two screws turn when going forward?
14. How does a twin-screw boat handle as compared to a single-screw boat?
15. With what is boat etiquette concerned?
16. By whom are boat salutes rendered on board a boat?

17. What is the custom for embarking officers and enlisted personnel on a boat?

18. When should the national ensign be displayed from boats?

CRITICAL THINKING

1. In what ways is handling a small boat the same as handling a larger vessel in a seaway? In what ways is it different?

VOCABULARY

displacement hull	personnel boat
planing hull	gig
catamaran	trimaran
transom	coxswain
keel	side force
draft	screw current
beam	headway
waterline	sternway
hatch	boat etiquette
port (window)	pennant
pulpit	mizzenmast
bowsprit	flying bridge

Marine Navigation

Navigation is the art and science by which mariners find a vessel's position and guide it safely from one point to another. Most of you would know how to guide yourself, or a watercraft, by following a magnetic compass needle. The problem is finding your location in the first place. This is the navigator's first job: to locate the vessel exactly on the Earth. The navigator can then recommend a course to be steered in order to arrive safely at the destination.

To find out where we are now, we must locate ourselves in relation to something else. For instance: your desk is 20 feet from the back door and directly in front of the teacher's desk. Or your house is on the corner of Elm Street and Western Avenue. Using a road map, we can say that the town of Jefferson is on Highway 26,15 miles south of Watertown.

We have now used a tool that is important in locating places: a map. In this unit, we will talk about maps of the Earth, particularly, maps that show on a flat surface the locations of places important to the mariners of the world. The type of map used to navigate on the water is called a *nautical chart*. The charts we will talk about may be defined as "pictures of the navigable waters of the Earth." Charts are what the navigator uses when plotting courses and finding positions of his or her vessel. The navigator cannot refer to a highway, a crossroads, or towns. There has to be a way of locating the vessel on the ocean. The following chapters will describe how this is done.

1 Introduction to Navigation

Navigation is a fundamental nautical science. Like seamanship, a knowledge of navigation is basic to operating on water. Navigation enables the mariner to locate his or her position and to get from one place to another.

The Terrestrial Sphere

To discuss navigation and nautical charts, we must first understand the Earth. In navigation, the Earth is called the *globe* or *terrestrial sphere* (this latter term comes from the Latin word *terra*, which means "earth"). Our planet is spherical. Actually, our Earth is a little flattened at the poles instead of being perfectly spherical. But this can be disregarded in most cases in navigation.

There are several reference points for locating objects on the Earth. The *north pole* and *south pole* are located at the ends of the axis on which the Earth rotates. The imaginary lines running through the poles and around the Earth are called *meridians*. They divide the surface of the Earth into sections much as you might cut an orange for easy peeling.

The imaginary line that runs around the center of the Earth, cutting every meridian in half and dividing the Earth into top and bottom halves, is called the *equator*. It is formed by passing an imaginary plane horizontally through the center of the Earth,

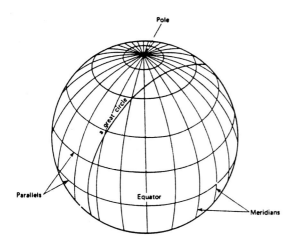

The globe with meridians of longitude and parallels of latitude. Any line that cuts the globe into equal parts is a great circle. A random great circle is shown cutting the meridians. The other great circles in this drawing are the meridians and the equator.

perpendicular to its axis. The word "equator" implies "equal parts." It lies exactly halfway between the north and south poles. The top half of the globe is called the *Northern Hemisphere* (northern "half-sphere"), and the lower half is the *Southern Hemisphere*.

Great Circles

Meridians and the equator are called *great circles* because they each divide the globe into two halves. Any circle drawn around the Earth so as to divide the world into equal parts, or hemispheres, is called a great circle.

The concept of the great circle is very important, so it should be clearly understood. A great circle is any circle formed on the Earth's surface by passing a plane through its center, dividing it into two halves.

Look at the globe. You will note that all meridians are great circles. Of all the lines going around the globe from east to west, however, only the equator is a great circle. The other lines are called *parallels*, since they go around the globe parallel to, and north and south of, the equator. They are all smaller circles than that made by the equator. Of the parallels, only the equator cuts the globe into two hemispheres.

You can also see that a great circle does not have to be a meridian or the equatorial parallel. A great circle is *any* circle whose plane passes through the Earth's center, no matter what direction.

What is the significance of the great circle in navigation? Just this: the shortest distance between two points on the Earth (or any sphere) lies along the path of a great circle passing through those two points. This path, or segment of a great circle, is an arc on the Earth's rounded surface. It has to be an arc, because a straight line between two points would go under the surface!

Circular Measurement

You already have learned in your math classes that a circle's *circumference* (the distance around) contains 360 degrees (°). Regardless of the size of the circle, whether it is the size of a ping-pong ball or of the globe, the circumference has 360 degrees. Each degree contains 60 minutes ('), and each minute contains 60 seconds ("). Measurement along a meridian or parallel is expressed in terms of degrees, minutes, and seconds of arc (the curve of the circle).

Meridians

There are an infinite number of meridians running from pole to pole, but rarely are they drawn more often than one for each degree around the Earth. On the average globe, map or chart, meridians are usually drawn every 5 or 10 degrees. More will sometimes be drawn on enlarged navigation charts. The starting point for numbering these meridians is the meridian on which the Royal Observatory at Greenwich, England, is located. The Greenwich meridian, therefore, is numbered 0, or 0°, and is called the *prime meridian.*

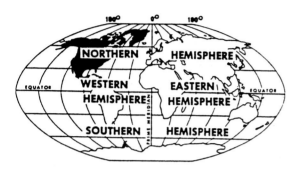

A projection of the globe showing the four hemispheres, divided by the equator, the prime meridian, and the International Date Line.

Halfway around the globe from the prime meridian is the 180th meridian. The 180th meridian is the other half of the 0 meridian; together they make a great circle that divides the globe into the *Eastern* and *Western Hemispheres.* The Eastern Hemisphere is that portion of the globe between 0° and 180° east of the prime meridian, and the Western Hemisphere is that part between 0° and 180° west of the prime meridian. The 180th meridian is called the *International Date Line,* which will be discussed further in chapter 4. Meridians between the prime meridian and the date line are numbered from 0° to 180° east (E) or west (W), depending on how far east or west they are from the prime meridian. For example, a location in the Western Hemisphere might be at 70°W, while one in the Eastern Hemisphere might be at 120°E. In navigation these meridians are called *longitude* lines.

Parallels

We learned earlier that the equator is a great circle formed by bisecting the Earth on a horizontal plane. Since the Northern and Southern Hemispheres are equal halves of the globe, there must be 90 degrees in the arc from the equator to a pole. However, parallels drawn around the Earth get smaller and smaller as you get closer to the poles. But remember, no matter how small a circle it is, it still contains 360 degrees. What this means, then, is that the distance represented by a degree of longitude measured along the parallel circles becomes ever smaller as you get nearer the poles.

The starting point for numbering the parallels is the equator, the 0° parallel. Parallels are numbered from 0° at the equator to 90° north (N) at the north pole, and from 0° to 90° south (S) at the south pole. A place in the Northern Hemisphere, for example, might be located at 35°N, while one in the Southern Hemisphere might be at 50°S. In navigation, the parallels are called *latitude* lines.

Latitude and Longitude

We have seen that there is a network of meridians and parallels all the way around the globe. Thus, every spot on Earth may be located at the intersection of a meridian and a parallel. The navigator describes every location on the Earth in terms of its corresponding latitude and longitude. Latitude is the distance of arc north (N) or south (S) of the equator. It is expressed in degrees, minutes, and seconds, measured along the meridian of the place. Longitude is the distance in degrees, minutes, and seconds of arc east (E) or west (W) of the prime meridian, measured along the parallel of latitude. Let's state it again: latitude is always measured north or south from 0° through 90°, and longitude is always measured east or west from 0° through 180°.

For example, the position of Washington, D.C., is 38°58'N latitude, 77°01'W longitude. This is spoken as "thirty-eight degrees, fifty-eight minutes north; seventy-seven degrees, one minute west." Seconds are used only if very exact locations are required. Every spot on Earth can be located precisely by this method. You should become very familiar with locating places on the globe this way.

Nautical Measurements

Distance. In talking earlier about degrees of arc, we were actually talking about nautical distance, or distances at sea. The nautical mile is used to measure nautical distance. It is about equal to one minute of arc measured along the equator, or any other great circle. That is about one and one-seventh statute or land miles. A nautical mile is about 6,076 feet; for most applications in the Navy, we consider this to be 2,000 yards. A land mile is 5,280 feet, or 1,760 yards.

Since meridians of longitude are great circles, they may be used as distance scales. Distance is measured along the meridian, using a tool called *dividers.* One minute of latitude along any meridian equals 1 nautical mile. (Distances are not measured on parallels of latitude, because one minute equals 1 nautical mile only along the equator.)

Speed. The word *knot* is a seagoing speed term meaning nautical miles per hour. It is incorrect to say "knots per hour," except when referring to increases or decreases in speed. The term comes from old sailing days, when ships determined their speed through the water by running out a line knotted at fractions of one nautical mile. The line was attached to a flat piece of wood called a chip log. The amount of line (numbers of knots) run out in two or three minutes gave an estimate of the ship's speed, from which the number of nautical miles covered per hour could be figured.

Nowadays ship speed through the water is determined by use of a *speed log* (like a speedometer), either mechanical or electronic. Mechanical speed logs have a small propeller that extends down beneath a vessel's hull. The water streaming past the hull rotates the propeller, and the vessel's speed is proportional to the speed of rotation. Others have a *pitot tube* that measures the speed of the water stream by pressure differences. Electronic speed logs measure vessel speed electronically by projecting sound beams down into the water.

Direction. *True nautical direction* is measured from true north (north pole) as located on a globe. This used to be given in olden days by *points* on the *compass rose*, such as north, north by east, north-northeast, and so on. Modern navigators use a system of circular measurement using 360 degrees of arc, which is more accurate and convenient. A compass card shows the readings of degrees of arc. The true bearings of the so-called *cardinal points* are north, 000°; east, 090°; south, 180°; and west, 270°.

A direction is always expressed in three figures, regardless of whether three digits are necessary. In other words, it is not 45° (forty-five degrees), but 045° (spoken "zero four five degrees").

The direction in which a ship is facing at any moment is called its *heading*. The direction that a ship is steered through the water is called its *course*. Because they are directions, headings and courses are always expressed in three digits. There is usually some difference between the two because of wind and wave and current action and the like.

Most larger naval ships and aircraft are fitted with an instrument called a *gyrocompass* that always points toward true north. It is used as the basis for all true direction and course measurements. However, a gyrocompass is expensive and needs a power supply to operate. Therefore, most smaller vessels, boats, aircraft, and many ground vehicles use a relatively inexpensive *magnetic compass* as a directional reference, similar to those you may have used as a Boy

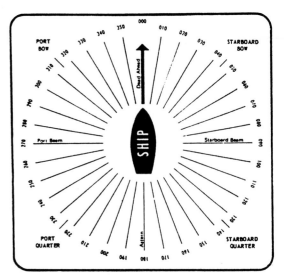

Relative bearing card showing numerical and descriptive relative bearings from a ship.

or Girl Scout or in a science class. Directions referenced to the magnetic compass are called *magnetic* or *compass* directions.

Magnetic compasses point to the Earth's northernmost magnetic pole, presently positioned at about 80 degrees north latitude in northern Canada. Its location wanders as much as 80 kilometers each day, and it has been moving northerly at an average rate of about 10 kilometers per year. Because it is at a distance from the true north pole, there is usually an angle between magnetic and true north at all locations on Earth. This angle is called the *variation angle*. If the magnetic compass points east of true north, the variation angle is labeled east. If the magnetic compass points west of true north, the variation angle is labeled west.

One type of direction can be converted into the other very simply. To convert from magnetic to true, just add or subtract the variation at your location to the magnetic bearing. Westerly variations are subtracted, and easterly variations are added. For example, if your ship were heading 090° magnetic in a region where the variation was 10° east, the true heading would be 090° + 10°, or 100° true. If you wanted to proceed on course 270° true in the same region, you would steer 270° − 10° or 260° magnetic. The size and direction of the variation can easily be obtained from the nautical chart of the area in which you are operating.

It is important to be able to make these kinds of conversions because nautical charts and land maps are drawn up based on true directions, but small ships, boats, and land vehicles are most often fitted with magnetic compasses, necessitating navigation using magnetic courses and bearings described below.

A *bearing* is the direction of an object from an observer, measured clockwise in one of three standard ways. A *true bearing* is the direction of an object measured clockwise from true north. A *magnetic bearing* is the direction of an object measured clockwise from magnetic north, and a *relative bearing* is the direction of an object measured clockwise from the ship's head (bow).

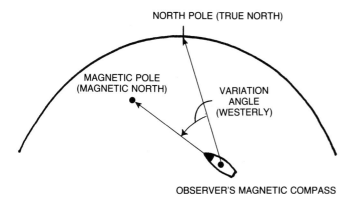

A diagram showing the relationship between true and magnetic north. The angle between the two directions is called the variation angle. Here, the variation angle is westerly, because at the observer's location the magnetic compass needle points to the west of true north.

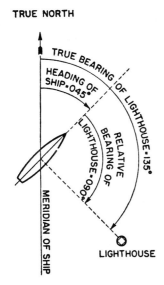

TRUE NORTH

TRUE BEARING OF LIGHTHOUSE·135°

HEADING OF SHIP·045°

RELATIVE BEARING OF LIGHTHOUSE·090°

MERIDIAN OF SHIP

LIGHTHOUSE

A comparison of true and relative bearings, showing the relationship between them.

Bearings are given in three digits, as with nautical direction. When recording a bearing, it is assumed to be a true bearing unless followed by the letters M or R. For example 030°M means 30° to the right of magnetic north, spoken "zero three zero degrees magnetic," while 030°R means 30° off the starboard bow, spoken "zero three zero degrees relative." Objects seen by lookouts are reported in terms of relative bearing by degrees. Note the following relative bearings: dead ahead, or bow, 000°R; starboard beam, 090°R; dead astern, 180°R; and port beam, 270°R.

Sometimes a three-digit true bearing is followed by the letter T to emphasize that it is a true bearing, as, for example, 030°T, spoken "zero three zero degrees true."

To go from a relative to a true bearing, just add the ship's true course to the relative bearing of the object sighted. If the sum is less than 360°, that sum is the true bearing of the object. If the sum is more than 360°, subtract 360° from the sum, and that difference will be the true bearing of the object.

Nautical Charts

A *nautical chart* is a standardized drawing representing part of the navigable waters of the Earth. A chart has shading on it to show water areas and nearby land outlines to help a ship's navigator find his or her way at sea. Nautical charts give a great deal of information to the navigator. This is called *hydrographic information*. Charts display water features such as depth and overhead obstructions, and they have symbols representing navigational aids such as buoys, lights, and anchorages.

The globe is a spherical, three-dimensional (length, width, and height) object, but it is not practical to work navigation problems or chart courses on a round surface. It is necessary, therefore, to convert the round surface of the globe to one that is flat and two-dimensional (having only length and width) — in short, a flat piece of paper on which a chart is drawn.

Cartographers (map and chart makers) have used math to work out chart projection techniques. These techniques make it possible to create charts with a minimum of distortion from the actual spherical globe.

Mercator projection. The best-known map or chart projection is called the *Mercator projection*. It is the one your teachers generally use to locate geographic places when they display maps in the classroom. It is the projection used for road maps on land.

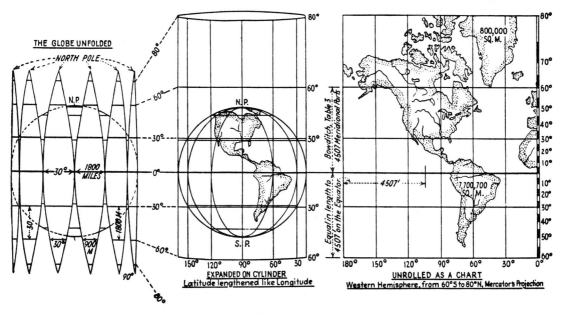

THE GLOBE UNFOLDED

NORTH POLE

N.P.

30° 1800 MILES

1800 M.

30°

900 M.

EXPANDED ON CYLINDER
Latitude lengthened like Longitude

UNROLLED AS A CHART
Western Hemisphere, from 60°S to 80°N, Mercator's Projection

800,000 SQ. MI.

4507'

7,700,700 SQ. MI.

Bowditch, Table 3. 4507 Meridional Parts

Equatorial length to 4507 on the Equator.

A Mercator chart is made by projecting the spherical globe onto a cylindrical surface tangent at the equator. In effect this cuts the globe up much like an orange peel might be sliced. Distortion is minimal near the equator, but increases rapidly as the poles are approached.

The Mercator projection was developed by a Dutch cartographer, Gerardus Mercator, in the sixteenth century. It is the most widely used of all chart projections for navigation. In this projection, the spherical globe is projected onto a cylinder-shaped piece of paper, wrapped around the globe at the equator. Then, the cylindrical paper is spread flat, after cutting it at convenient meridians. A Mercator projection of the world, for instance, is usually cut vertically near the International Date Line so the continental land areas are shown almost unbroken.

Because of the method of projection, increasing distortion occurs the farther the area on the Mercator chart is from the equator. However, this distortion is made uniform in both latitude and longitude, so the finished chart is usable for navigation even at high latitudes. The space between parallels increases with latitude, but the distance represented by 1 degree of latitude is always the same, 1 nautical mile. Because of the distortion at high latitudes, the island of Greenland appears much larger than the United States on a Mercator projection. In actuality the reverse is true.

The meridians on a Mercator chart appear as straight lines, north and south, parallel to and equidistant from one another. They represent the imaginary curved meridian lines that come together at the poles on a globe.

Scale of charts. The *scale* of a chart refers to a measurement of distance. It is a comparison of the actual distance or size of a feature with that shown on the chart. The scale of a chart or map is normally printed near the legend in the form of a ratio, such as 1:5,000 (meaning that the feature shown is actually 5,000 times larger than its size on the chart). Said in another way, an inch or centimeter or other measurement on the chart represents 5,000 identical units on the real Earth's surface. The smaller the ratio, the smaller the scale of the chart. A chart with a scale of 1:5,000 is on a much larger scale than one whose scale is 1:4,500,000, for example. Small scales are used to depict large areas on a chart, and large scales are used to depict small areas.

Another way of expressing scale, called the *numerical scale*, is in inches, miles, or kilometers to the nautical mile. This is shown near the legend as a bar scale (linear scale) with both compared measurements shown, one on either side of the bar. By using a pair of dividers, set to the linear scale desired, you can find distances by "walking" the dividers across the chart and using simple arithmetic. For example, if an inch on the chart represents 50 miles, 5 inches would represent 250 miles.

Remember, the larger the scale, the smaller the area shown on a given chart or map. Large-scale charts show areas in greater detail. Features that appear on a large-scale chart may not show up at all on a small-scale chart of the same area.

Types of charts. Nautical charts, as described above, are those with the necessary information for safe navigation. They have standard symbols, figures, and abbreviations that tell the depth of water, type of bottom, location of navigational aids, and so forth.

Harbor charts are large-scale charts that show harbors and their approaches in detail. *Coastal charts* are intermediate-scale charts used to navigate a vessel whose position may be determined by landmarks and lights, buoys, or soundings offshore. For navigating inside outlying reefs or shoals, or well offshore in large bays of sizable inland waterways, a coastal or harbor chart may be used.

General ocean sailing charts are small-scale charts showing the approaches to large areas of the coast. These charts show offshore soundings, principal lights and outer buoys, and any natural landmarks visible at a distance.

Scattered all over water areas of any nautical chart are many tiny italicized figures called *soundings*, each representing the depth of water in that particular place. Depths may be given in feet, fathoms (6 feet to 1 fathom), or meters. A notation under the title of the chart is the key; for example, "Soundings in feet at mean low water." Most charts also contain dotted lines called fathom curves, marking the limits of areas of certain depths. Most newer charts will give water depth, heights of lights, and land contours in meters as well as in feet.

Nautical charts are available for purchase at nautical supply stores in most coastal cities and towns throughout the United States. In addition to traditional paper charts, *electronic charts* on computer data storage media that can be projected onto computer screens and various types of electronic plotters are coming into widespread use in marine navigation.

Plotting

In order to use the nautical chart for navigating, you must know something about how courses, bearings, and lines of position are plotted on it.

The basic instruments used in plotting are parallel rulers, some kind of protractor, and dividers. The *parallel ruler* consists of two straightedges connected by pivoted metal straps near each end. The straps allow the two straightedges to be opened and closed, while always remaining parallel to each other. By placing the edge of one straightedge along a line of bearing and "walking" the ruler carefully across the chart to a compass rose (a graphic used as a reference for both true and magnetic directions on a chart), the true bearing of the line may be determined. *Dividers* are a plotting instrument used for measuring chart distances along a suitable scale on a chart.

A *protractor* does just about the same thing as parallel rulers. A simple protractor consists of a graduated arc on a piece of clear plastic. Another kind of protractor has a ruler that pivots on the center of the curvature of the arc. The protractor's arc is graduated like the upper half of a compass rose. Horizontal and vertical reference lines on the plastic can be lined up with the meridians or parallels, and any course or bearing can be easily plotted by swinging the ruler to the desired degree mark on the arc.

Fixes and Lines of Position

In plotting a ship's location on a chart, a fix is an accurate position determined without reference to any previous position, using visual, electronic, or celestial observations. A fix position is the intersection of two or more *lines of position (LOPs)* obtained at the same time.

Two examples of visual gyro bearing LOPs.

In clear-weather navigating near land, lines of position (lines along which a vessel must be located) are obtained by taking visual magnetic or gyrocompass bearings to objects or landmarks whose position is known and printed on a chart of the area. Lines corresponding to the bearings are plotted on the chart, extending to the chart symbols representing the objects or landmarks used. Such lines are called *bearing LOPs*. They are labeled with the four-digit time of observation above the line.

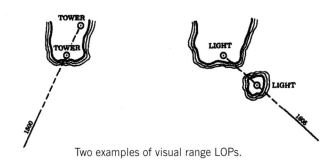

Two examples of visual range LOPs.

A special kind of bearing LOP is the *visual range*. A ship is said to be on a visual range when two landmarks or navigation aids are observed in line one behind the other. Such an LOP is considered one of the most accurate obtainable. Visual ranges are extensively used when navigating in narrow waters such as canals.

LOPs for fixes can also be obtained by electronic means such as radar, or by observation of celestial bodies. Each of these will be discussed in more detail later in this chapter.

A *distance arc* is a circular line of position. When the distance from an observer to an object is known, a line of position can be drawn with the object as the center. The radius is equal to the measured distance. The entire circle need not be drawn, because the navigator normally knows the ship's position well enough so that drawing an arc of the circle is sufficient. The arc is labeled with the time above, expressed in four digits, and the distance below, in nautical miles (and tenths). The distance to a landmark may be

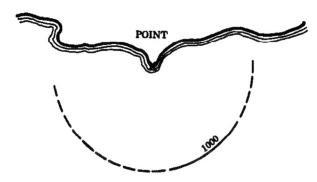

An example of a distance arc LOP.

measured by using radar, a *stadimeter* (an optical distance-measuring device that operates by measuring the distance of an object of known height, such as the masthead on a ship), or a sextant.

In selecting objects from which to determine lines of position for fixes, the navigator must consider the number to be used and the angle of intersection of their lines of position. The closer LOPs come to crossing at right angles, the less error there generally will be. Also, for fixes it is best to have at least three LOPs, since each acts as a check on the other. If all LOPs cross in a pinpoint or form a very small triangle, the fix may be considered reliable. If a larger triangle or some other geometric shape is formed, the fix position is generally assumed to be in the center of it.

In summary, fixes may be obtained by means of the following combinations of lines of position (the first three are much more commonly used than the latter three):

- Two or more lines of bearing
- A distance arc and a line of bearing
- Two or more distance arcs
- A visual range and a distance arc
- A visual range and a line of bearing
- Two simultaneous visual ranges

A watch officer measures the distance to another ship with a Brandon sextant-type stadimeter. The stadimeter measures the distance to an object of known height, such as the masthead of a ship. (Emmitt Hawkes)

The symbol for a fix is a small circle or triangle around the point of intersection. For identification, it is labeled horizontally with the time in four digits.

Navigation plotting symbols and their meanings are shown in the accompanying graphic. When the symbols depicted are used, it is not necessary to label the position (except for time), since the symbol tells what type of position is shown.

SYMBOL	DESCRIPTIVE LABEL	MEANING
⊙ △	FIX	AN ACCURATE POSITION DETERMINED WITHOUT REFERENCE TO ANY PREVIOUS POSITION. ESTABLISHED BY ELECTRONIC, VISUAL, OR CELESTIAL OBSERVATIONS.
⌂	DR	DEAD RECKONING POSITION. ADVANCED FROM A PREVIOUS KNOWN POSITION OR FIX. COURSE AND SPEED ARE RECKONED WITHOUT ALLOWANCE FOR WIND OR CURRENT.
⊡	EP	ESTIMATED POSITION. IS THE MOST PROBABLE POSITION OF A VESSEL, DETERMINED FROM DATA OF QUESTIONABLE ACCURACY, SUCH AS APPLYING ESTIMATED CURRENT AND WIND CORRECTIONS TO A DR POSITION.

Standard plotting symbols are used by navigators, quartermasters, and CIC personnel to mark the ship's position along its track.

Piloting

Piloting means determining position and directing the movements of a ship by using landmarks, constructed navigational aids, and water depth readings made by a *fathometer*, described below. Piloting is the primary means of navigation when entering or leaving port and in coastal navigation. In piloting, the navigator gives warnings of danger (rocks, shoal water, wrecks, etc.), fixes the ship's position frequently and accurately on the basis of sightings taken of aids and land features, and recommends what course to take to the commanding officer and conning officer.

Navigational equipment used in piloting includes the compass, to determine the ship's heading; a speed log, either mechanical or electronic, to indicate ship's speed; the bearing circle, to determine the direction of land features, buoys, and so on; charts, which show the outlines of the shore, as well as the position of land and seamarks, aids to navigation and the depths of water; various electronic devices; and various plotting instruments like parallel rulers and dividers.

Also used is the *fathometer*, or *echo sounder*, which determines the depth of water under the ship's keel by measuring the time it takes a sound signal to reach the bottom and return to the ship. These operate on the basis of the fact that sound travels through water at about 4,800 feet per second. (This speed varies with temperature, salinity, and depth but is a good average figure.) A depth finder sends out a sound signal, which bounces off the ocean floor and returns to the ship much like an echo. Then, half the time in seconds required for the sound to make the round trip, multiplied

by 4,800, is the distance in feet to the bottom. The depth is normally displayed both digitally and graphically on a small screen.

Increasing use during piloting is being made of the satellite-based global positioning system described in the next section. Modern GPS receivers and plotters incorporating them are capable of continuously fixing the ship's position to accuracies of 10 meters or better, and projecting highly accurate electronic plots of the ship's future track. Such displays may in the future completely replace the traditional manual plot kept on paper charts as the primary navigation plot during piloting.

Electronic Navigation

As discussed above, traditional piloting is dependent on obtaining lines of bearing and ranges from objects seen visually for the most part. *Electronic navigation*, on the other hand, uses lines of position obtained by the use of radio waves to determine a ship's position.

The advantages of navigating by radio waves are several. A ship's position may be fixed electronically in fog or heavy weather when it is impossible to take visual bearings. Electronic gear can get ranges and bearings from stations or points far beyond what people can see from on board ship. But as marvelous as modern electronics equipment is, it can still malfunction, or its power supplies may fail. It is subject to jamming or destruction in wartime. And even in today's environment of continually decreasing cost for most electronic gear, such equipment is more expensive than most traditional manual navigation equipment. Therefore, even with excellent electronic reception and equipment, the navigator must still be able to make visual and celestial observations to establish the ship's position if necessary.

A quartermaster on the aircraft carrier USS *John F. Kennedy* (CV 67) uses a *bearing circle* to obtain a true bearing to an object. (Anthony Riddle)

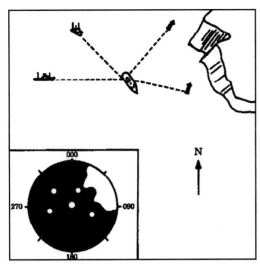

A radar PPI presentation oriented to true north.

Radar. Radar, an acronym derived from the first letters of each word in the phrase "**ra**dio **d**etection **a**nd **r**anging," was developed originally as a means for detecting surface ships and aircraft. Later improvements and refinements led to its becoming a valuable electronic navigational device. Its operation is based on the fact that, like sound waves, radio waves are reflected from solid objects. Its great advantage over other means of electronic navigation is that it does not require external transmitting stations. Radar's chief disadvantage, however, is that its maximum range is currently limited to slightly more than line-of-sight. Extensive research has been under way for years to extend radar ranges to distances over the horizon, and some breakthroughs have been made.

Radar involves sending out a narrow beam of very high frequency radio waves. Upon striking any object in their path, they are reflected and return to the transmitter as "echoes." Exact measurement of the time of return of each yields the distance, or range, to the object. The bearing can be determined by the position of the antenna, which is indicated with a bright line called a sweep on a radarscope. Targets appear as bright spots of light, called pips. The form of scope most often used is the plan position indicator (PPI), which gives a bird's eye view of the area covered by the radar, with the transmitting ship in the center.

Radar has a number of important advantages as a navigational device. It can be used at night and during periods of low visibility. A fix can be obtained from a single object. It is very accurate and rapid. It can also be used to locate and track other vessels and storms, and thus is important for ship safety.

Loran. Loran is a term derived from the first letter(s) in each word of the term "**lo**ng **ra**nge **n**avigation." Loran is a system of radio signals broadcast by groups of transmitting stations of known position. A loran fix is determined by a loran receiver from the intersection of lines of position obtained from these signals.

Because of GPS, loran coverage is no longer available in much of the world. But in areas it does cover, mostly in and around North America, it is a highly reliable system still used by many, including first responders to emergencies in places where the weaker GPS signals are not receivable. The Department of Homeland Security has proposed keeping an upgraded enhanced version of the system (eLoran) in operation in the United States as a back-up to GPS, and the British government has proposed the same for areas around the British Isles.

GPS. The newest electronic navigation system to have been developed by the United States is the Global Positioning System (GPS). It consists of a constellation of some twenty-four operational satellites circling the Earth in 10,900-mile-high circular orbits, and their supporting ground stations. GPS can provide continuous three-dimensional positioning data on land, sea, and air, accurate to within ±10 meters (132.8 feet) everywhere on Earth.

GPS can yield even better accuracy when corrections to its positioning information are determined by land-based receivers and transmitted to users in the surrounding area. This enhancement is called *differential GPS*, and it is capable of producing positions accurate to within ±1 meter (13.28 feet). Differential GPS signals are broadcast throughout the United States by transmitters operated by the Coast Guard, and by many foreign governments worldwide.

GPS has revolutionized the practice of navigation. When it became fully operational in 1994, it was at first used for position-finding mainly by mariners and the military. But since then its use has exploded. GPS is now the basis of operation of a wide variety of electronic plotters and high-tech marine navigation systems. It has an amazing variety of civil and commercial applications, including navigation and tracking systems for boats, cars and trucks, aircraft navigation and landing systems, surveying, and much more. Many cell phones and laptop computers now come equipped with GPS-based navigational systems for personal use. In addition to position finding, military applications now include hands-off control of aircraft and ground vehicles, and guidance systems for many of today's precision weapons, cruise missiles, and unmanned aerial vehicles (UAVs). There is also a Russian version of the GPS system called GLONASS under development, whose capabilities may rival those of the U.S. GPS system within the next several years.

Ship's inertial navigation system (SINS). SINS is mainly a navigational aid for submarines and aircraft carriers, although modern more compact models are coming into use in smaller vessels, AUVs, land vehicles, and aircraft. In essence SINS uses highly precise gyroscopes along with a computer to track the platform's motion with great accuracy. It is a completely self-contained system, so it would be an especially valuable wartime navigation aid.

SINS produces extremely accurate and continuous dead reckoning positions from the last good fix position. The DR positions can be displayed on an electronic chart, along with the desired track. Although most SINS systems are routinely updated every few hours using external systems such as GPS, they can maintain accu-

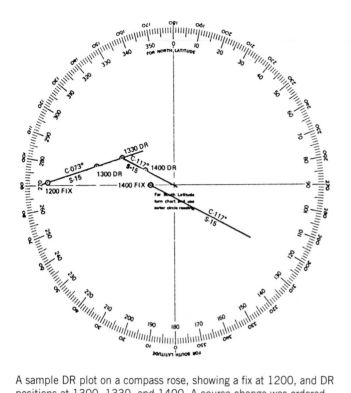

A sample DR plot on a compass rose, showing a fix at 1200, and DR positions at 1300, 1330, and 1400. A course change was ordered at 1330. At 1400 a new fix was taken and the ship's position was updated accordingly.

rate positioning information without such updates for up to seven to ten days or more. This makes them ideal for use in submerged submarines when GPS signals cannot be received, such as when cruising under Arctic ice, or on extended submerged patrols.

Celestial Navigation

Piloting, dead reckoning, and electronic navigation systems determine position by reference to objects or localities on the Earth or in near-Earth space. The remaining branch of navigation, in which position is determined by the aid of heavenly bodies such as the Sun, Moon, and selected stars and planets, is called *celestial navigation*. A precise altitude observation of any of these celestial bodies yields an accurate line of position. Navigation by such lines of position has been the key to navigating on the oceans for much of the past two hundred years. The widespread availability of GPS in recent years, however, is fast making celestial navigation at sea a vanishing art.

The instrument used in celestial navigation to measure the angle (altitude) between a heavenly body and the visible horizon is the *sextant*. After finding the altitude of several bodies, or of a single body like the Sun over an extended time period, the navigator can work out the ship's position using various almanacs, tables, and sight reduction forms or electronic calculator or computer.

Dead Reckoning

When a ship is out of sight of land, or electronic navigation is not available and bad weather prevents taking celestial observations, the ship must be navigated by dead reckoning. *Dead reckoning* means determining a position from the direction and distance theoretically traveled from a known starting point, normally the last good fix.

In dead reckoning, a line called a *course line* is drawn on a nautical chart from every new fix in the direction in which the ship is proceeding. The direction, or course, is labeled above the line, and speed in knots below the line. Then, future positions called *DR* (dead reckoning) *positions* are computed, plotted, and labeled along this line as required for safe navigation. This is the *dead reckoning (DR) track* for the ship. But a ship under way is moving through water, a very unstable element. Wind and current may cause the ship to drift from the presumed course, or its speed to vary from what is set, even though the helmsman has very carefully tried to steer the exact course. For this reason, dead reckoning positions are only approximate, and their accuracy decreases over time.

A quartermaster on the amphibious assault ship USS *Bonhomme Richard* (LHD 6) maintains the ship's DR plot for the navigator while entering port at Seattle, Washington. (John Ciccarelli)

Plotting a ship's DR track from one fix to the next is a continuous process while under way. A constant check on approximate position helps the navigator to locate an assumed position for celestial observations reasonably close to the ship's actual position. At sea, navigators using celestial navigation will obtain and plot fixes at least every morning, noon, and evening. In piloting waters, the navigator and quartermasters will normally be on the bridge plotting numerous fixes as often as every three minutes whenever usable navigation aids come into sight.

As mentioned previously, electronic plotters incorporating continuous fix updates from GPS or loran, and projecting current ship's position and the DR track onto an electronic chart projection on a computer screen, are becoming ever more widely used in marine navigation. For many navigators such plotters eliminate the need to maintain a manual DR plot during normal operations. The know-how to do a manual plot is still a necessary skill for every navigator to have, however, in the event that a power loss, equipment failure, or damage renders the electronic plotter unusable. Even when electronic plotters are in use, therefore, many navigators keep a manual DR plot on a paper chart as a backup and for practice, especially when in piloting waters.

STUDY GUIDE QUESTIONS

1. What is navigation?
2. What is a chart? How does it differ from a map?
3. What is the terrestrial sphere?
4. What are the imaginary lines that run through the poles around the Earth?
5. What name is given to the imaginary line formed by a horizontal plane passing through the center of the Earth, cutting every meridian in half?
6. What is a great circle?
7. What is the shortest distance between two points on a globe?
8. What are the lines going around the Earth parallel to the equator called?
9. A. What is the circumference of a circle?
   B. How many degrees does it have?
10. Into what units may degrees be divided?
11. A. Where is the reference place for the prime meridian?
    B. What is the meridian exactly opposite the prime meridian on the other side of the globe called?
    C. What two hemispheres does this great circle line create?

12. Using an atlas or other reference book, locate the following places in terms of their latitude and longitude, in degrees and minutes:
    Washington, D.C.
    Chicago, Illinois
    San Diego, California
    Honolulu, Hawaii
    Colon, Panama
    Gibraltar
    Baghdad, Iraq
    Tokyo, Japan
    Sydney, Australia
13. How are distances measured at sea? Compare a land or statute mile with a nautical mile.
14. How is nautical direction or course measured?
15. What are the true bearings of the cardinal points, N, E, S, W?
16. Compare and contrast a true bearing, a magnetic bearing, and a relative bearing.
17. If a ship is on course 050°T, and a lookout sights an object on the starboard beam at 090°R, what is the true bearing of the object?
18. If a lookout sights a merchant ship at 285°R, forward of the port beam, and own ship's course is 135°T, what is the true bearing of the contact?
19. What does the hydrographic information on a chart consist of?
20. A. Which projection is used for almost all nautical charts?
    B. Where is the greatest distortion on this kind of projection? Why?
21. What is meant by the scale of a chart?
22. What tool is used to determine distance on a chart with a linear scale?
23. A. What are soundings?
    B. How are they shown on a nautical chart?
24. What is a navigational fix?
25. What are lines of position?
26. A. What is piloting?
    B. When is it used?
27. What kind of shipboard device is used to determine depth of water?
28. A. What are some of the advantages of radar?
    B. What is radar's chief disadvantage?

29. A. What is the newest U.S. worldwide satellite navigation system called?

    B. How is it affecting the practice of marine navigation?

30. What does the ship's inertial navigation system do?

31. A. What is celestial navigation?

    B. What instrument is used to obtain celestial sights?

32. What is meant by dead reckoning?

CRITICAL THINKING

1. In what ways is navigating on the water the same as navigating on land? In what ways are they different?

2. Draw a globe and show the following on it: longitude lines, parallels of latitude, the equator, the north and south spin axes, and the prime meridian.

3. Describe the steps that a sailor of a small boat might go through in preparing to navigate his or her boat on an extended ocean voyage. Include the navigation equipment that might be brought along on such a voyage.

VOCABULARY

navigation
sphere
meridian
parallel
great circle
nautical mile
longitude
latitude
cardinal points
magnetic compass
gyrocompass
dividers
fix (position)
true bearing
relative bearing
echo sounder
fathometer

soundings
loran
radar
global positioning system (GPS)
variation angle
parallel ruler
stadimeter
nautical chart
hemisphere
knot (of speed)
hydrographic information
chart projection
Mercator projection
ratio
fathom (of depth)
visual range

2 Aids to Navigation

Piloting is one branch of marine navigation. In traditional piloting, a ship's position is mostly determined by bearings taken on visible objects whose exact locations are shown on a chart. Some of these objects may be natural landmarks, such as hills, rocks, islands, or cliffs. Others may be large buildings, smokestacks, television towers, church steeples, and so on, which are located close to shore where they can be easily spotted by navigators.

Most aids to navigation, though, are specially constructed to assist in the safe navigation of vessels. These include lighthouses, light towers, navigation lights, buoys, and daybeacons. Most harbors and well-traveled coasts are well marked with these aids to navigation. Elsewhere, these kinds of aids may or may not be present to assist the navigator. When specially constructed aids are not available, or when they become inoperative or out of position, then natural landmarks must be used.

This chapter will discuss the major types of constructed navigational aids found in international and inland waters. All who operate watercraft in rivers, lakes, harbors, the Intracoastal Waterway, and along seacoasts must know about these navigation aids, just as one who drives a car or truck on the nation's highways must be able to interpret road signs.

Lights

Vessels under way operate at night as well as by day. Therefore, navigation lights are important aids to night navigation. These lights are identified primarily by their color, pattern of flashes, and timing interval (period). Of these, the timing interval is considered the most valuable for identification purposes, since that is least likely to be confused if several navigational lights are present in a given area. These identifying attributes, together with height and nominal visibility, are usually printed in abbreviated form near the light symbol on the nautical chart. Other details are set forth in publications called light lists that are available for purchase in most nautical supply stores.

Light Characteristics

There are three principal general patterns of flashes, called *characteristics*, of navigational lights: fixed, flashing, and occulting. *Fixed* lights burn steadily. *Flashing* lights show single flashes of light at regular intervals, with the duration of light less than the duration of darkness. There are variations of these called *fixed and flashing*, with the fixed light intensifying at intervals with two or more bright flashes; and *group flashing*, in which two or more groups of flashes are shown at regular intervals.

Occulting lights are totally off at regular intervals, the duration of light always being greater than the duration of darkness. *Group occulting* lights have two or more off periods at regular intervals.

Variations of these principal light characteristics include *equal interval*, in which the duration of light equals that of darkness; *Morse code*, where the light flashes represent a Morse code character (usually the letter A); and *alternating*, in which rhythmic lights show different colors during each sequence.

The Fort Story lighthouse, Virginia Beach, Virginia. (Eric Clement)

The most important navigation lights are usually either flashing or occulting, since these patterns are the most easily identified.

Visibility of a Navigation Light

The *visibility* of a light is the distance, in nautical miles, a mariner can see the light at night. The distance at which a given navigation light may be seen depends on its intensity and height above sea level, the height of eye of the observer, and the existing *meteorological visibility conditions* (weather). Information about the intensity and height of navigation lights can be found in publications called *light lists*. A navigator will usually know his or her height of eye at different positions on the vessel from which he or she normally makes observations, and can estimate the meteorological visibility conditions in any of several ways. With this information, the navigator can compute the exact visibility of a light using various tables. A good approximation of the distance at which a light may be seen is printed on nautical charts beside the light symbol. This *charted range* is the distance a light will shine in clear weather and is about the distance a mariner in a small boat can usually expect to see the light.

Lighthouses and Light Towers

There are many lighthouses along the coasts of the United States and the Great Lakes and along many interior waterways. They are placed wherever a powerful light, called a *primary light*, may be of assistance to navigators, or where very dangerous water requires a warning beacon of long-range visibility. Since the range of visibility of a light increases with its height, the main purpose of a lighthouse is to increase the height of a light above sea level.

The Ambrose Offshore Light Tower, 7 miles east of Sandy Hook, New Jersey. Its primary light has a high intensity of 6 million candlepower with a charted range of 18 miles.

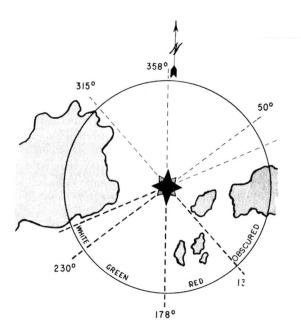

A navigation light with white, red, and green sectors. The bearings shown at the bottom are those from the light. In a light list the bearings given would be the reciprocals, as would be seen from a vessel proceeding clockwise around the light. In this case, the description of the light would read obscured from land to 315°, red thence to 358°, green thence to 050°, white thence to land.

A lighthouse may have fog-signaling and radio-beacon equipment in addition to the light itself. At one time, most such lights were run by keepers who lived at the lighthouse. Now, however, the lights in lighthouses are mostly automatic, with no keepers required. The towers of lighthouses are usually painted distinctive colors and patterns to make them easier to identify in the daytime. These may be solid colors, bands, stripes, or squares.

At some locations, primary navigation lights are placed atop large structures of girders, painted similarly to lighthouses. Some powerful offshore primary lights are mounted either on large buoys or a tower on stilts embedded in the ocean bottom. These *light towers* often house a crew, and they have a powerful light, radiobeacons, oceanographic research equipment, and a helicopter platform. Like lighthouses ashore, their increased height allows their lights to be seen for greater distances, and their crew ensures that these important lights will always be on. Secondary, minor, and automatic lights are located in structures ranging in size from towers to a single pile supporting a battery box and the light.

Some lights have *sectors* of red glass placed in their lanterns to show danger bearings. Danger bearings on a chart show a vessel when it is in danger of running aground on rocks, shoals, or some other hazard. Arcs over which the red light shows are the danger sectors. The red color shows only within the danger zone; other light characteristics remain the same. Some lights also show a green sector, which indicates a turning point or the best water across a shoal. All sector bearings are true bearings to the light.

Buoys

Navigational buoys are moored, floating markers placed to guide ships and boats safely along channels and in and out of ports. Buoys on water are like street signs for motorists on land. They also warn vessels away from hidden dangers and lead them to anchorage areas. They may be of various sizes and shapes, but it is mainly their coloring that indicates their purpose. Buoy symbols are printed on harbor charts, so buoys can be used for determining positions in piloting.

A system of buoyage called the IALA (International Association of Lighthouse Authorities) System B is used on all navigable waters of the United States. Under this system, the coloring, shape, and lighting of buoys all indicate the direction of danger. These characteristics and the numbering of buoys have been standardized on the basis of what their direction is when coming from seaward.

In offshore channels, the lateral buoyage system considers the following directions as coming from seaward in U.S. waters: in a southerly direction along the Atlantic Coast; a northerly and westerly direction along the Gulf Coast; and a northerly direction along the Pacific Coast. All coastal buoys on the right are red, even-numbered buoys when proceeding in those directions. Left-hand buoys are green and are marked with odd numbers. The Intracoastal Waterway is so marked, proceeding from the North Atlantic states to the lower coast of Texas.

Buoys are valuable aids to navigation, but they must never be depended upon alone. They may drag their moorings in heavy weather or may be set adrift if hit by a passing ship. Lights on them may go out, and whistles, bells, and gongs may fail to function.

Types of Buoys

A buoy's type has no special navigational significance but can help identify it. There are eight main types of buoys used in U.S. inland waters, described as follows:

- *Spar buoys* are upright wooden poles, or tubes of steel, which are often used to mark obstructions.
- A *can buoy* is shaped like a cylinder, much like an oil drum. If unlighted, green left-hand channel buoys must be can buoys.
- A *nun buoy* has a conical shape. If unlighted, red right-hand channel buoys must be nun buoys.
- A *bell buoy* has a framework supporting a bell. Older bell buoys are sounded by the motion of the sea. Newer types are operated automatically by compressed gas or electricity.
- A *whistle, or horn, buoy* is similar to a bell buoy in shape but it carries a whistle sounded by the sea's motion or horns that are sounded at regular intervals by mechanical or electrical means.
- A *gong buoy* is also similar to a bell buoy in shape but it has a series of gongs, each with a different tone, with hammers that are moved by the motion of the sea.

- A *lighted buoy* carries batteries or gas tanks and has a framework that supports a light.
- A *combination buoy* is one in which a light and sound signal are combined, such as a lighted bell, gong, or whistle buoy.

Coloring of Buoys

As stated previously, in the inland waters of the United States, red buoys mark the right side of a channel, and green buoys the left side, coming from seaward. Of great help in remembering this placement of buoys is the jingle "red-right-returning." Unlighted red channel buoys are always cone-shaped nun buoys. Unlighted green channel buoys are always can buoys.

Green and red horizontally banded buoys, called *preferred-channel buoys*, mark obstructions or channel junctions. They may be passed on either side, but it is wise to give them a wide berth. If the top band on a preferred-channel buoy is red, the best channel is to the left of the buoy, coming from seaward. If the top band is green, the preferred channel is to the right.

Red and white vertically striped buoys, called *safe-water buoys*, mark the middle of a channel or fairway.

Some special buoys are not meant to be used for navigation. White-painted buoys, for instance, mark anchorage areas. Buoys with black and white horizontal stripes are sometimes used to mark fish trap areas. A white buoy with a green top usually designates a dredging area. A yellow buoy signifies a quarantine anchorage, where ships go to await customs clearance. Cylindrical white buoys with orange markings are informational buoys marking restricted areas, speed limits, and the like.

Types of buoys used in the inland waters of the United States.

Buoy Numbering and Lights

Red buoys marking the right side of a channel bear even numbers, starting with the first buoy from seaward. Green channel buoys, to the left of the channel coming from seaward, have odd numbers. Banded or striped buoys are not numbered, but some have letters identifying the name of the buoy, such as Governors Island West End Shoal Bell Buoy (GI) and East Rockaway Inlet Bell Buoy (ER).

Red lights are used only on red channel buoys. Green lights are only for green channel buoys. White lights are the only lights used on preferred-channel (junction) or safe-water (mid-channel) buoys.

Characteristics of lights on lighted buoys are as follows:

- A fixed light may be on either a green or a red channel buoy.

- A flashing light, at regular intervals, not more than thirty flashes per minute, may also be on either a green or red buoy.

- A quick-flashing light, no fewer than sixty flashes per minute, may be on either a green or red buoy at a turning point or junction where special caution is required.

- An interrupted quick-flashing light (repeated series of quick flashes, separated by four-second dark intervals) may be on a red and green horizontally banded preferred-channel buoy.

- A Morse A flashing light (short and a long flash, recurring at the rate of about eight per minute) may be on a red and white vertically striped safe-water buoy.

Daybeacons and Ranges

Unlighted structural aids to navigation are called *daybeacons*. A daybeacon may consist of a single wooden pile, or dolphin, with a square or triangular *daymark* shape on top of it, a metal or concrete tower supporting a daymark, or other similar structures. They are colored to distinguish them from their surroundings. Daymarks on beacons marking channels are colored and numbered like channel buoys. Those on the right coming from seaward are triangular, and those on the left are square. Many have reflectors that show the same colors as lighted buoys would at night.

Two daybeacons, located some distance apart on a specific true bearing, make up a daybeacon *range*. When a ship reaches a position where the two beacons are seen exactly in line, the ship is "on

Drawings of daymarks that mark a channel. Red triangular daymarks with sequential even numbers mark the right side coming from seaward, and green squares with sequential odd numbers mark the left side.

Daybeacon ranges in the Gaillard (Culebra) Cut of the Panama Canal. Pilots conning ships transiting the canal do much of their steering through the canal on these daybeacon ranges.

the range." Ranges are valuable for pilots and conning officers who must guide ships along narrow channels. For example, much steering through the Panama Canal is done on ranges. Similarly, ranges are used often on the Columbia River in the Pacific Northwest.

Intracoastal Waterway

The U.S. Intracoastal Waterway is an inland channel in which a light-draft vessel can navigate along the U.S. Atlantic and Gulf coasts from the Chesapeake Bay almost to the Mexican border without going into the ocean. The vessel can remain inside natural or artificial breakwaters for almost the entire length of the trip.

Every buoy, daymark, or light structure along the Intracoastal Waterway has part of its surface painted yellow. Buoys have a yellow band at the top. Daymarks and other structures have a band or border of yellow. Red buoys and daymarks are to the right, and green to the left, as one proceeds from the Chesapeake Bay toward Mexico. Standard colors, numbers, and lights are used with navigation aids in the waterway. Because the numbers would become large in such a long line of buoys and daymarks, they are numbered in groups of about two hundred, starting again at "1" at natural dividing points.

Chart and Map Symbols

The publication *Nautical Chart Symbols, Abbreviations, and Terms, Chart No. 1*, available at most marine supply stores, contains explanations of the numerous symbols used on charts to identify prominent features of coastlines, buildings and structures, bottom features, hazards to navigation, and depth contours. It also gives information on the identification of danger signals, buoys, daybeacons, lights, and radio and radar stations. NJROTC units have a supply of *Chart No. 1* for practical work in charting and piloting.

STUDY GUIDE QUESTIONS

1. A. What are the four main categories of constructed navigational aids?

   B. What is their purpose?

2. A. What are light lists?

   B. What is their purpose?

3. What are the three principal characteristics of navigational lights? Briefly describe each.

4. What is the visibility of a light?

5. What is the purpose of a lighthouse?

6. What is a light tower?

7. What is the purpose of buoys?

8. Why must buoys alone not be depended upon for piloting?

9. What are the eight main types of buoys?

10. A. How are buoys colored in the United States?

    B. What is the jingle used as a reminder for red buoys?

11. A. How are buoys numbered?

    B. How are channel buoys lighted?

12. What is a daybeacon?

13. A. What is a range on a channel?

    B. Where are ranges used a great deal for piloting?

14. A. What is the name of the inland channel in which light-draft vessels can navigate from the Chesapeake Bay almost to the Mexican border without going into the ocean?

    B. What is the significant color identifying all buoys, daymarks, or light structures along this channel?

CRITICAL THINKING

1. List the attributes of an ideal night navigation aid.

2. What are the similarities between land navigation aids, such as signs alongside a highway, to navigation aids along a channel through water?

VOCABULARY

light tower
daybeacon
daymark
period (of light)
light characteristic
buoy

Intracoastal Waterway
chart symbols
spar buoy
can buoy
nun buoy
combination buoy

Time and Navigation

You probably have not given much thought to the study of time. The navigator of a vessel, however, needs to know the exact time in order to determine the vessel's position at sea.

If you have ever taken a long plane trip across the country, or to Hawaii or Europe, you have felt the effects of time zone changes. It often takes a day or two to get one's body adjusted to the new time schedule—when to get up, when to eat, when to go to bed. This condition is called *jet lag,* a term used to describe the effect of rapid time zone changes on the body, as for example when you take a long east-west plane flight. It occurs because your body is used to reckoning time based on the relationship of the Earth and the Sun. As we will see later in this chapter, this means that your day becomes considerably longer if you are traveling in a westerly direction, and shorter if you are traveling easterly.

In this chapter we will discuss how time is reckoned, the instruments the Navy uses for timekeeping, and how to deal with time zone changes around the world.

Time and Timepieces

Everyone is familiar with watches and clocks. In the Navy, time and timekeeping are of great importance, both because the routine of shipboard life is often fast-paced, and because time is essential in navigation and operation of the ship. As part of their duties in most Navy ships, every couple of days the quartermasters check and reset as necessary all ship's clocks to the correct time, so that everyone can be sure they are using an accurate time in their log entries, tactical plots, messages, and all other phases of their daily routine.

In addition to the usual types of watches and clocks, there are more specialized timepieces found on board ship. These are called *chronometers.* A chronometer is an extremely accurate timepiece used in navigation. It is made to withstand shock, vibration, and temperature variation. Years ago ship chronometers were mechanical clocks, but nowadays they are electronic quartz clocks. They are set to Greenwich Mean Time (GMT), the basic time used in fixing position by celestial navigation, and the time used as a reference in all message traffic and many other things aboard ship.

Radio stations in Colorado and Hawaii broadcast time signals every five minutes, twenty-four hours per day. Time signals are also obtainable from GPS and loran. The ship's chronometer is periodically checked against these time signals by the quartermas-

ters. Any error is recorded, and the navigator must take it into consideration during celestial navigation.

Military Time

We all know how to tell time by watches and clocks. We know that the new day begins a fraction of one second after midnight, and concludes twenty-four hours later at midnight. The time between midnight and noon is labeled "A.M."; these letters mean *ante meridiem,* or before the middle of the day (noon). The time between noon and midnight is labeled "P.M.," meaning *post meridiem,* or after the middle of the day. We are comfortable with this system of timekeeping in civilian life, because we can simply look out the window, so to speak, to see if it is morning or afternoon. We do not confuse 5:00 in the evening with 5:00 in the morning, to say nothing of 1:00 in the morning and 1:00 in the afternoon.

But it has long been a custom in the Navy and other military services to tell time by the twenty-four-hour clock. There are several reasons for this. It is done to avoid confusion in message communications, all of which are identified by the date and Greenwich Mean Time of transmission. Also, this is a common way to tell time in many European countries, including England, where many of our military customs began. It is also another way to avoid the confusion that might happen if the A.M. or P.M. were accidentally left out of directions or orders.

So the Navy, and other military services, uses the twenty-four-hour clock. In this way of keeping time, the day begins with a fraction of a second after midnight, 0000 (zero hour), and continues past 0100 (1:00 A.M.) and 0200 (2:00 A.M.) toward noon, 1200. The time after noon continues with 1300 (1:00 P.M.), 1400 (2:00 P.M.), and so forth until 2400, midnight. The terms "o'clock," A.M., or P.M., are not used, nor is a colon used to separate hours from minutes. Rather, we speak in terms of "hundred." For example, 0100 is "zero one hundred," 1000 is "ten hundred," 1800 is "eighteen hundred," and 2130 is "twenty-one thirty."

All NJROTC cadets should learn to use the twenty-four-hour clock. Mathematically, it is very easy to figure out; simply add all P.M. time numbers to 1200 (noon). For example, 2:25 P.M. becomes 1425, and 10:30 P.M. is 2230. You should memorize the twenty-four-hour clock so it becomes second nature when telling time:

Morning (a.m.)		Afternoon (p.m.)	
0100	1 a.m.	1300	1 p.m.
0200	2 a.m.	1400	2 p.m.
0300	3 a.m.	1500	3 p.m.
0400	4 a.m.	1600	4 p.m.
0500	5 a.m.	1700	5 p.m.
0600	6 a.m.	1800	6 p.m.
0700	7 a.m.	1900	7 p.m.
0800	8 a.m.	2000	8 p.m.
0900	9 a.m.	2100	9 p.m.
1000	10 a.m.	2200	10 p.m.
1100	11 a.m.	2300	11 p.m.
1200	12 p.m./noon	2400/0000	12 a.m./ midnight

While 0000 and 2400 are exactly the same time, it is common practice to start each day at 0001 and end it at 2400.

Ship's Bell Time

Another custom on board ship is to mark the passage of time by bells. Before timepieces such as watches or chronometers were common, time on board ship was reckoned by a so-called *hourglass*, which ran out its sand from one end to the other every thirty minutes. The glass would then be turned over to start measuring another thirty minutes, and a bell would be struck so all hands would know a half hour had passed. It was struck once at the end of the first half-hour of each four-hour watch, twice at the end of the second, and so on, until eight bells were struck at the end of the fourth hour. After eight bells were struck, the series started over again.

The practice still continues on board some Navy ships, in spite of the use of clocks and watches. The bells are rung in pairs; that is, if there are two or more bells to be rung, they are rung closer together than the odd bell. For example, five bells would sound like "ding-ding, ding-ding, ding." An odd number of bells marks half past the hour, and an even number marks an hour. When used, bells are rung only from reveille to taps, but not during divine services or when fog requires that the bell be used as a fog signal.

There are also commercially available ship's clocks in gift shops and the like that have chimes that can be set to go through the bell sequence described above.

Time and Arc

From ancient times to the present, people have reckoned time according to the travel of the Sun once around the Earth each day. Of course, since the time of the medieval astronomer Copernicus in the sixteenth century, we have known that it is really the Earth's rotation that makes the Sun seem to move. But for navigation, and to make it easier for us to understand how time works, it is often helpful to imagine the Earth as standing still at the center of the universe, with the Sun, as well as all the other celestial bodies, moving around the Earth.

The Sun thus appears to make one complete 360-degree revolution around the Earth during each twenty-four-hour day. Actually, as we will see below, on any specific day during the year it will usually take a few minutes more or less than twenty-four hours for the Sun to complete its journey. But on the average over a year, we can say that it takes exactly twenty-four hours.

Now, because the Sun goes 360 degrees around the Earth in twenty-four hours on the average, we can say that there is a definite relationship between arc as measured in an east-west direction on the surface of the Earth (which we saw in the first chapter in this unit is longitude) and time. If we divide 360 degrees of arc around the Earth, or longitude, by twenty-four hours, we see that it takes the Sun one hour to go 15 degrees of arc, or longitude. And, since it travels 15 degrees in one hour, the Sun must go 1 degree (60 minutes of arc) in four minutes ($1/15 \times 60$ minutes = four minutes). Thus, 1 degree of longitude can be thought of as being equivalent to four minutes of time. This relationship is of basic importance both in navigation and in keeping time, as we will see.

Kinds of Time

The Sun is the most convenient reference for reckoning time. Time measured by the Sun is *solar time*. Solar time, or Sun time, is based on the apparent motion of the Sun around the Earth.

Apparent time. Time based on the apparent position of the Sun from our position is called *apparent time*. If the Sun is directly over the meridian we are on, we say that it is noon, local apparent time. When it is directly over the meridian 180 degrees away from ours, it is midnight local apparent time.

If the Earth stood still in space, and the Sun orbited in a circle around it, all the days reckoned by apparent time would be exactly the same length. But the Earth travels around the Sun in an elliptical orbit (like a race track); the Earth's axis is inclined with respect to the plane of its orbit around the Sun; and the Earth's speed along its orbit varies. Therefore, the time required for a complete rotation of the Earth on its axis relative to the Sun—or in other words, the length of a solar day—varies continually according to the position of the Earth in its orbit.

Mean time. Time keeping would be confusing if some days had more, and some fewer, minutes because of the Earth's revolution. To eliminate this confusion, an average solar time is used; this is called *mean solar time*. It is calculated from the motion around the Earth of an imaginary or *mean Sun*, which always makes the 360-degree circuit in exactly twenty-four hours. So if your watch says it is 1200 local mean time (LMT), the *mean* Sun is over your meridian, not the *actual* Sun.

In November of each year the actual Sun is about 16½ minutes ahead of the mean Sun, and by February it has fallen behind by some 14 minutes. The difference between apparent time and mean solar time at any moment is called the *equation of time*. It is tabulated in navigational publications called *almanacs*, and must be taken into account for certain tasks in celestial navigation at sea.

Atomic time. Besides the above kinds of time that are based on the relationship of the Earth and the Sun, there is one other more modern base for time that is coming into ever wider use because of its extreme accuracy. This is *atomic time*, called *universal coordinated time*, abbreviated as UTC. This time is based on the frequency of vibrations of the radioactive cesium atom. Because cesium is a fairly common element, it is readily available to be used in *atomic clocks* as a time standard everywhere on Earth. Since GMT is based on the changing relative motion of the Earth and the Sun, and UTC is based on the unchanging cesium frequency, GMT and UTC can differ at certain times by as much as nine-tenths of a second. But the difference is usually smaller, and can be disregarded for most navigational purposes. For more precise needs, the amount of difference at any time is readily available; so the user can easily correct UTC to GMT, or vice versa.

Zone time. Zone time (ZT) = standard time. Since local mean time is based on the relationship between one's own meridian and the mean Sun, a slight difference in longitude between two places would result in a slight difference in time kept. Though not very significant in days of old, this difference would be very impractical in our modern world. For example, if we set our watches to local mean time (LMT), we would have to reset them every few blocks along an east-west street. In New York City, for instance, a difference of about nine seconds LMT occurs between one end of 42nd Street and the other end.

To eliminate this problem, *standard time zones* have been established around the world. All clocks and watches within a standard time zone are set to the same time, and there is a difference of one hour between one time zone and the next. Because there are twenty-four hours in a complete day, and 360° of longitude around the Earth, each standard time zone is 15 degrees of longitude wide (360 ÷ 24 = 15). The standard time zone system is fixed by international agreement and by law in each country.

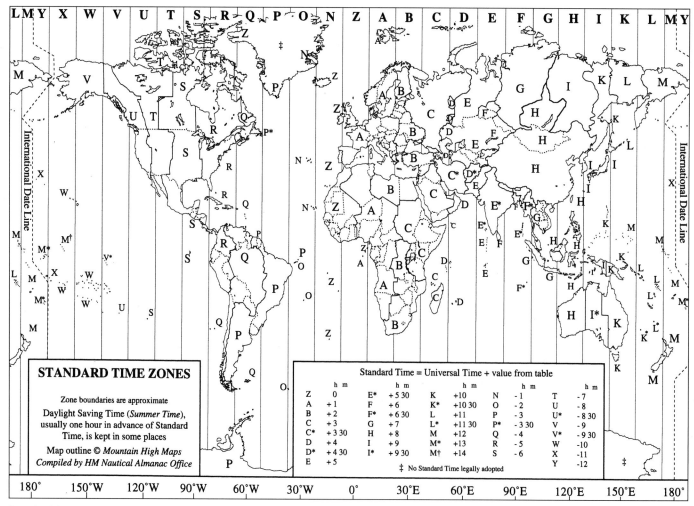

STANDARD TIME ZONES

Zone boundaries are approximate

Daylight Saving Time (*Summer Time*), usually one hour in advance of Standard Time, is kept in some places

Map outline © *Mountain High Maps*
Compiled by HM Nautical Almanac Office

Standard Time = Universal Time + value from table

	h m		h m		h m		h m		h m
Z	0	E*	+ 5 30	K	+10	N	- 1	T	- 7
A	+ 1	F	+ 6	K*	+10 30	O	- 2	U	- 8
B	+ 2	F*	+ 6 30	L	+11	P	- 3	U*	- 8 30
C	+ 3	G	+ 7	L*	+11 30	P*	- 3 30	V	- 9
C*	+ 3 30	H	+ 8	M	+12	Q	- 4	V*	- 9 30
D	+ 4	I	+ 9	M*	+13	R	- 5	W	-10
D*	+ 4 30	I*	+ 9 30	M†	+14	S	- 6	X	-11
E	+ 5							Y	-12

‡ No Standard Time legally adopted

Standard time zone chart of the world. The prime meridian (0°) is the central meridian for the Zulu (Z) time zone. Successive time zones lie every 15 degrees to the east and west. Each time zone has a letter designator as indicated on the chart. The numbers in the inset table must be added to Universal (Greenwich) time to find standard (zone) time. Their inverse values are the zone descriptions of the various time zones. (Chart reproduced by permission of HM Nautical Almanac Office @ Copyright Council for the Central Laboratory of the Research Councils)

The standard time zones begin at the Greenwich meridian (0°). Since the Earth rotates toward the east, time zones to the west of Greenwich are earlier; to the east, the zones are later. Every meridian east and west of Greenwich that is a multiple of 15 degrees (15°, 30°, 45°, 60°, and so on) is a standard time meridian. Each standard time meridian is at the center of its time zone, and the zone extends 7½ degrees (half of 15 degrees) on either side of the meridian. Some standard time zones ashore vary somewhat from this, to make life easier for the people living there.

Local mean time along each standard time meridian is *zone time*, or standard time, for that entire time zone. Zone time in navigation is abbreviated ZT. Each time zone is identified by an alphabetical letter and by a negative or positive number from 1 to 12, east or west of the prime meridian. The number is called the *zone description (ZD)* of the zone, and the letter is called the suffix. Time zones to the east of Greenwich have negative zone descriptions, and time zones to the west have positive ones.

To separate one day from the next, the 180th meridian in the mid–Pacific Ocean has been designated the *International Date Line*. On both sides of the line, the time of day is the same, but west of the line it is one day later than it is to the east.

The continental United States has four standard time zones. The East Coast keeps +5 Romeo (R) time, called Eastern Standard Time (EST). Central Standard Time is +6 Sierra (S), Mountain Standard Time is +7 Tango (T), and Pacific Standard Time is +8 Uniform (U). All of Alaska keeps + 9 Victor (V), and Hawaii keeps +10 Whiskey (W).

Daylight savings time. A is simply zone time set ahead one hour to extend the time of daylight in the evening, usually in summer, is done strictly for convenience ashore in some localities. Daylight savings time is not used in navigation.

Zone time and GMT. Greenwich Mean Time (GMT) is the ZT at the Greenwich meridian. The Greenwich meridian is the standard time meridian for the time zone numbered 0. It has the zone description suffix letter Zulu (Z). Most information in navigational tables and naval communications uses GMT, so you must know how to convert the time in any zone to GMT, and vice versa.

Remember that the solar day has twenty-four hours, and each time zone represents one hour. Beginning with the 0 zone (Greenwich), time zones run east and west from zone 1 to zone 12, with zones east of Greenwich being minus, and those west of Greenwich being plus. (Note that the +12 and −12 zones each extend over only 7½ degrees of longitude.) The zone description (ZD) tells you the difference in hours between your zone time and GMT. To convert the time in any time zone to Greenwich Mean Time, you must *add* the zone description number algebraically to the zone time. To convert from GMT to zone time, you must *subtract* the zone description. This procedure can be represented by the following simple algebraic formulas:

$$GMT = ZT + ZD \text{ and } ZT = GMT - ZD$$

When using the formulas, you must be careful to remember to use the rule of algebra that two minuses together make a plus. For example, if we were at a position in a time zone east of Greenwich where the zone description was −5, and we wanted to convert a GMT of 0600 to our standard zone time, we would set up the formula like this:

$$ZT = GMT - ZD$$
$$ZT = 0600 - (-5) = 1100$$

Standard time zones are also described by letter suffixes, as we noted earlier. In writing naval time, it is generally required that a time zone's suffix letter be placed after the numbers. For instance, eleven o'clock in the morning in Norfolk, Virginia, zone time, would be written 1100R; 3:30 P.M. in San Diego would be written 1530U. This avoids confusion for the person reading that time.

Date/Time Group

Another aspect of naval time involves the date, the month, and the year in naval communications. Messages and other data keep coming twenty-four hours a day, every day of the month, and every month of the year. Therefore, there must be some way to identify exactly when a communication was originated or received. To do so, the Navy uses what is called the *date/time group*.

Let us assume that a message was originated at 1635Z on 15 April 2010. This would be placed in the message heading as 151635Z APR 10. The first six numbers and letter Z show the date, the time, and the ZD suffix (usually Z for GMT). For further clarification, the month and year are also added. All messages are subsequently filed and referenced by their originator and the date/time group.

STUDY GUIDE QUESTIONS

1. Why do you suffer jet lag if you take a long east-west plane flight?
2. A. What is a chronometer?

   B. To what time is a ship's chronometer usually set?
3. What do A.M. and P.M. mean?
4. Why do the Navy and other armed services use the twenty-four-hour clock?
5. What would the following times be on the twenty-four-hour clock?

   A. 8:30 A.M.

   B. 5:45 P.M.

   C. 11:15 P.M.

   D. Midnight

6. A. How did telling time by ship's bell originate?

    B. What is the maximum number of bells struck?

7. What is the basic relationship between longitude (arc) and time?

8. Why does the length of each solar day vary slightly?

9. What is mean solar time?

10. A. How have people made time setting and time keeping more practical?

    B. How many degrees of longitude are in each standard time zone?

11. How is each time zone identified?

12. How do the dates on each side of the International Date Line differ?

13. What is daylight savings time?

14. What are the four standard time zones in the continental United States? Identify each with its alphabetical suffix and numerical ZD.

15. Convert the following zone times to Greenwich Mean Time:

    A. 1200 at San Francisco (ZD = +8)

    B. 1700 at Norfolk (ZD = +5)

    C. 0600 at Rome, Italy (ZD = –1)

16. Convert the following Greenwich Mean Times to zone time at the locations in the previous question:

    A. GMT 0800

    B. GMT 1600

17. What are the date/time groups for the following:

    A. 0835 local time in Norfolk, Virginia, on 23 March 2010?

    B. 7:30 P.M. in San Diego, California, on 17 May 2010?

CRITICAL THINKING

1. Why is an accurate timepiece of great importance in celestial navigation as sea?

2. What are the advantages of keeping zone time as opposed to a single standardized time throughout the world? Would you prefer to keep time according to your local zone time, or keep a standard time such as Greenwich Mean Time? Justify your answer.

VOCABULARY

jet lag	standard time
chronometer	local mean time
solar time	zone time
mean time	zone description (ZD)
apparent time	Greenwich Mean Time (GMT)
equation of time	universal coordinated time (UTC)
almanac	date/time group
rotation (of Earth)	daylight savings time
revolution (of Earth)	mean Sun

Rules of the Road and Maneuvering Board

Just as there are rules for drivers of vehicles on land, so there are rules for those who handle ships and boats on the water. The automobile and truck driver must know traffic signals and signs, highway markings, and the rules of the road for motor vehicles. The ship and boat "driver" must know the buoyage systems, lights and signals, and nautical rules of the road governing traffic afloat on the waters of the world. Chapter 1 of this unit will introduce you to the basic nautical rules of the road that must be followed by all those operating a watercraft on either inland waters of the United States or on the world's oceans.

When maneuvering a ship or boat either to comply with the rules of the road or for other purposes, there are two primary safety objectives: (1) do not hit anything (such as another vessel or other object), and (2) do not run aground (i.e., hit bottom or shore). In pursuit of the second goal, all those involved in directing the movements of vessels study the subject of marine navigation as summarized in the previous unit of this text. A valuable aid in achieving the first goal is a diagram called a *relative motion plot*—actually a printed sheet—called a *maneuvering board*. Chapter 2 of this unit will introduce the fundamentals of the maneuvering board.

1 Nautical Rules of the Road

The nautical traffic laws are contained in several sets of rules. These are commonly known as the nautical rules of the road. There are two main sets of rules: the international rules, and the U.S. inland rules. Most provisions are identical, but there are some differences.

Where Rules Apply

The international rules must be obeyed by all vessels of all nations that travel on the high seas. These rules were first established in 1897 by all the maritime nations of the world. There have been several major revisions since then, the latest of these being in 1972. The full official name for the international rules of the road is *The International Regulations for Preventing Collisions at Sea, 1972*, often abbreviated to "the COLREGS." These rules were drawn up by the Inter-Governmental Maritime Consultative Organization of the United Nations, now known simply as the International Maritime Organization (IMO). They became law in the United States with their ratification by Congress in 1977.

The U.S. inland rules must be obeyed by all vessels of all nations that navigate the bays, harbors, and rivers of the United States. These rules were established by Congress under the *Inland Navigational Rules Act of 1980*. They are also known as the unified rules because they combine three sets of rules formerly in effect in U.S. waters.

Purpose of the Rules

The purpose of the rules of the road is to prevent ship collisions. Ship collisions can result in the loss of millions of dollars through damage or sinking. Also, lives may be lost in such collisions.

The rules govern all waterborne traffic. As defined in the rules, a power-driven vessel means any vessel propelled by machinery, even though it may also have sails up. Any vessel under sail alone is considered a sailing vessel whether propulsion machinery is aboard or not. Because they are more easily maneuvered, power-driven vessels must usually give way to sailing vessels. On the other hand, in harbors and narrow channels, small craft and sailboats must avoid collisions by standing clear, since larger vessels do not have as much freedom of movement.

The nautical rules of the road have one purpose—to prevent ship collisions. A Coast Guard plane flies over the collision of the containership *Transhawaii* and the passenger-cargo ship *Republica de Colombia* east of Cape Hatteras, North Carolina. The collision caused the death of one man, injuries to four others, and the loss of 24,000 gallons of diesel oil.

A vessel is "under way" when not at anchor, when not moored to a dock or buoy, or when not aground. So a ship stopped dead in the water can still be under way. In such a situation, the phrase used is "under way but with no way on."

Both international and inland rules cover vessel lights and day shapes, sound signals, steering and sailing rules, and distress signals.

In the event of a collision on water, the applicable international and inland rules are used by the courts to decide who will pay for the damages. Unless the vessels are equally at fault or there was nothing more that either one could have done, the courts must split the damages according to degree of fault (one vessel 30 percent at fault, the other 70 percent at fault, etc.).

Rules for Lights

Proper lights must be shown by all vessels from sunset to sunrise and during times of reduced visibility due to fog, smoke, storms, or other causes. Lights that could be mistaken for required lights must not be shown. The word "visible" when applied to lights means visible on a dark night with a clear atmosphere.

Running Lights

White, red, and green lights shown by all vessels under way at night or in poor visibility conditions are called *running lights*. The white light in the fore part of a ship is called the *masthead light*; it is required for all oceangoing vessels. The white light on an after-mast is called the *range light*; it is required only on vessels 50 meters (feet) or more in length. The *port sidelight* is red, and the *starboard sidelight* is green. A vessel under way must also display a white stern light.

The purpose of these lights is to warn vessels of the presence or approach of other vessels and to show in which direction they are going. On a dark night, it is nearly impossible to see anything of a ship or boat except the running lights. The sidelights are arranged so that when both the red and green sidelights are seen, you are looking at the bow, and the vessel is heading directly toward you. When only the green sidelight is seen, you are looking at the starboard side, somewhere from the bow to slightly behind the starboard beam. When only the red sidelight is seen, you are looking at the port side, somewhere from the bow to abaft the port beam. The masthead and range lights have the same arcs of visibility as the sidelights, and reinforce the ability to determine what aspect of the vessel you are seeing (See the diagram of the arcs of visibility.)

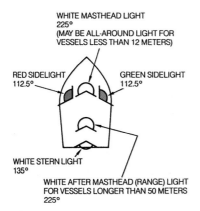

Diagram of the arcs of visibility for masthead, sidelights, and stern lights, for both international and inland rules.

The observed pattern of the white masthead and range lights, together with the sidelights, indicate the course of a sighted ship or boat. The white stern light warns overtaking vessels that another vessel is ahead. On oceangoing vessels 50 meters or more in length, the upper white lights must be visible from a distance of at least 6 miles. The port and starboard sidelights and the stern light must be visible at least 3 miles away. Running lights on smaller vessels have somewhat lower range requirements.

The international rules and the inland rules agree in the arcs of visibility required of the lights shown. Power-driven motorboats require similar lights, but the range light is optional.

Other Lights and Day Shapes

In addition to the normal underway lights described above, there are several other special combinations of lights and *day shapes* (geometric shapes like balls, cones, and diamonds, made from canvas stretched over metal ribbing) for vessels engaged in certain activities or in a special status.

Most harbors require large ships to take aboard a pilot who is thoroughly familiar with the harbor, berthing instructions, and the handling of local tugboats, to take the ship into port. When entering port at night, an officer of the deck (OOD) or conning officer of a ship will want to know the instant the pilot boat is sighted so it may be signaled alongside. "White over red, pilot ahead" is the little memory aid to use when looking for the special identifying lights of a power-driven pilot boat at night.

All vessels over 7 meters (23 feet) long at anchor must show anchor lights, according to the rules. Vessels less than 50 meters in length at anchor show an all-around white light forward. If more than 50 meters, a similar light aft must be shown also. The forward light should be higher than the one aft, usually on the top of the jackstaff at the bow of a ship. Powerboats and sailboats typically display their anchor light from their mast-top.

In the daytime, all vessels over 7 meters long at anchor must display a black ball day shape. The black ball is displayed in the forward part of the vessel, usually from a crosstree of the mast where it is clearly visible from all directions.

Vessels towing must display two masthead lights in a vertical line. If the tow extends beyond 200 meters (656 feet) astern of the towing vessel, a third light must be displayed below the second light. By day, if the length of the tow exceeds 200 meters, a black diamond shape is hoisted on the towing vessel (international rules) and the tow where best seen.

In both sets of rules the term "not under command" refers to ships and craft that are disabled and cannot operate in accordance with the rules. A vessel not under command at night must show two red lights, one over the other. If a power-driven vessel with headway, the vessel must show the not-under-command lights instead of the masthead light, as well as its sidelights and stern light. During daylight, a merchant ship hoists two black balls. A naval vessel hoists the "5" flag if it is not under command and will also hoist two black balls as a warning to any merchant vessels if in international waters.

Other lights and day shapes are prescribed for various specialized operations such as commercial fishing, cable laying, underwater or diving operations, and dredging. The interested student may find all these rules in books covering the complete rules, published by both private publishers and the Coast Guard, available at most nautical supply stores and large libraries and bookstores.

Special Rules for Naval Vessels

Many naval vessels, because of their special construction, cannot comply exactly with the rules for running lights. In such cases, the vessels must meet the requirements of the rules as nearly as possible. Any departures from the rules of the road for naval vessels are provided for by U.S. law.

Some examples of these variations are the following:

- The horizontal separation of the white lights on destroyers and smaller ships is often less than that required by the rules.

- The white lights on aircraft carriers are usually on the super-structure and off the centerline.

- Special lights such as speed lights, carrier landing lights, and colored recognition lights may be shown on naval vessels during certain operations.

- During certain exercises, naval vessels may show no lights at all. In peacetime, however, the officer in tactical command will usually order navigation lights turned on if a merchant ship approaches the formation. Departure from the rules of the road for exercises is not a good idea if it could result in a collision with a merchant vessel.

- Special lights and day shapes are required for minesweepers when they are engaged in sweeping operations.

- U.S. submarines are specially authorized to display an amber-colored intermittent flashing beacon—three seconds on, three seconds off—when running surfaced, in addition to other required lights.

Whistle Signals

Whistle signals are required by both sets of rules for vessels maneuvering within sight of one another. Under inland rules, a whistle is a signal of *intent*, sounded before any maneuvers are made. The vessel that sounds a signal in inland waters does not execute a maneuver until the other vessel makes the same signal in reply, meaning that it understands and agrees. If the other vessel does not understand the signal, or considers the proposed maneuver dangerous, it replies with the danger signal, a signal consisting of not less than five short, rapid blasts.

Whistle signals in international waters are signals of *execution*, sounded when a vessel is starting a maneuver. No replies are necessary. Since international waters are not as crowded as inland waters, international rules for whistle signals are not as demanding as inland rules. Whistle signals are absolutely essential to safe navigation, however. The principal international whistle signals are the following:

- One short blast: I am altering my course to starboard.
- Two short blasts: I am altering my course to port.
- Three short blasts: My engines are going astern.
- Five or more short blasts: Danger signal.

Confusion over whistle signals is probably responsible for more collisions than any other part of the rules of the road. Though all the rules are important, the steering and sailing rules are the ones most essential to avoiding collision. The rules are designed to keep vessels clear of one another.

Risk of Collision

Both international and inland rules govern situations in which two vessels are approaching each other with the risk of collision. There are three basic approach situations: meeting, overtaking, and crossing. The situation depends upon the relative position of the two vessels when they first sight each other.

Vessels do not need to maneuver if they will pass clear by simply maintaining their courses and speeds. But when two ships or boats approach each other and there is a risk of collision, at least one must keep out of the way of the other. This may be done by altering course or by slowing, stopping, or backing engines. The vessel that must keep out of the way of the other is called the *give-way* vessel. The other ship is required to maintain course and speed, and is called the *stand-on* vessel.

The rules say that risk of collision can be determined by carefully watching the compass bearing of an approaching vessel. If the bearing does not appreciably change as the range decreases, such risk should be considered to exist. Therefore, when in a constant bearing decreasing range situation, the vessel is said to be on a "collision course." There is a saying among mariners: "A collision at sea can ruin your whole day." There is no mariner who does not take the possibility of collision very seriously.

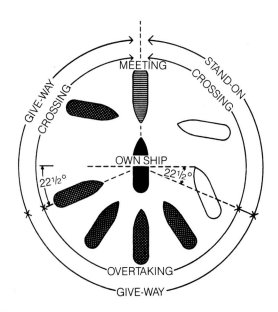

Typical meeting, crossing, and overtaking situations as viewed by own ship.

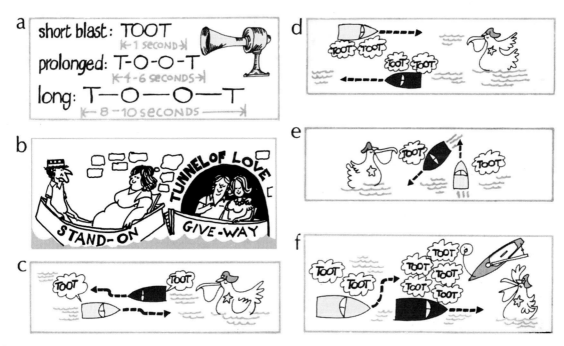

Summary of inland rules whistle signals. A—Lengths/duration of whistle signals. B—Crossing situation. Stand-on vessel is on starboard hand (to the right) of give-way vessel. Stand-on vessel must maintain course and speed; give-way vessel must maneuver, slow, or stop to allow stand-on vessel to pass ahead. C—Meeting head-on. Both vessels must give way. Vessels exchange single short blasts and maneuver to pass port to port. D—Meeting situation, but clearly safely separated, allowing for starboard to starboard passage with no maneuvering. Vessels exchange two short blasts. E—Crossing situation. Stand-on vessel allowed to pass ahead after exchange of one short blast. F—Overtaking situation, danger to port. Overtaking vessel proposes overtaking to port with two short blasts, stand-on vessel replies with five or more short blasts, indicating to give-way vessel that it may not pass to port because of danger in that direction.

Meeting Situation

In a *meeting* situation, both vessels are give-way. In all waters, power vessels meeting head-to-head or nearly so are required to pass port to port. To do so, both vessels must alter course to starboard. International rules authorize only a port-to-port passing and are silent on a starboard-to-starboard passing. Therefore, it is implied that a starboard-to-starboard passing is proper under international rules only when there is no risk of collision, and no maneuvering is required. In U.S. inland waters, starboard-to-starboard passing is authorized only if the vessels are not meeting head-to-head and safe passage is assured without any maneuvering.

In a port-to-port meeting situation in inland waters, one vessel gives one short blast on its whistle, telling the other vessel that it intends to come right to make the passage. After the other vessel has answered with a single short blast, indicating understanding and agreement, both vessels turn smartly to the right. The turn should be large enough to clearly show the action to the oncoming vessel (normally from 5 to 10 degrees in a channel, and about 15 degrees in open waters). Under inland rules, after agreement has been reached and the turns have been executed, no further sound signals are required during maneuvering to make a safe passage, or to return to the original courses.

In international waters, each ship sounds one short blast as they are executing the right turn. The vessels may choose to sound

the appropriate action signals when maneuvering back onto their original courses, but these signals are commonly omitted, since the danger of collision has passed.

In a meeting situation in international waters in which the vessels are not head-on, where no course change is necessary for safe passage, no whistle signals are made. Both ships will maintain course and speed and pass clear. However, the inland rules for the same situation require that if vessels are to pass port-to-port, regardless of whether or not a course change is required, the one-short-blast signal must be exchanged. If they are going to pass starboard to starboard, whether or not change of course is required, the two-short-blast signal must be exchanged.

Under both sets of rules, starboard-to-starboard passages are discouraged, since misunderstandings can easily lead to a collision. There is another old nautical saying that warns: "Two short blasts are the first two notes of the collision waltz."

Crossing Situation

A *crossing situation* on the water is analogous to a four-way stop situation on land. In both sets of rules, the power vessel having the other to starboard is the give-way vessel. The vessel to starboard is the stand-on vessel and must maintain course and speed. The give-way vessel is required to maneuver if necessary to avoid crossing ahead of the stand-on vessel. This may mean reducing speed, stopping, altering course to starboard, or backing down. Vessels are prohibited from turning left in order to cross ahead of the stand-on vessel.

In international rules, the give-way vessel must sound one short blast for a turn to starboard, two for a turn to port. Signals are not sounded unless course changes are made. In inland waters, the give-way vessel must sound a short blast to indicate its intent to leave the stand-on vessel to port. The signal is answered with a short blast to indicate agreement. The give-way vessel then maneuvers if necessary to pass astern of the stand-on vessel.

Overtaking Situation

In an *overtaking situation*, in both sets of rules the overtaking vessel is the give-way vessel. The overtaking vessel must keep clear of the overtaken vessel. In international waters, a ship that can pass another without a change of course may do so without a signal. If it must change course to pass, it sounds one short blast if turning to the right, or two short blasts if turning to the left, and does not have to wait for an answer. If the overtaken vessel considers the maneuver dangerous, it sounds the danger signal of five or more short blasts, warning that the action is too dangerous and may involve risk of collision.

In inland waters, an overtaking vessel cannot pass another until signaling on which side it intends to pass. The overtaking vessel sounds one short blast if proposing to pass the other vessel on its starboard side, and two if proposing to pass on its port side. The overtaking vessel must give a signal whether or not it must change course to pass, and it may not pass until it hears the agreeing signal from the vessel ahead.

If the ship being overtaken considers the proposed maneuver risky, it sounds the danger signal of five or more short blasts, followed by a signal for what it considers the safer procedure. The overtaking vessel then may answer this signal, and pass on the recommended side.

Channels, Bends, and Leaving a Berth

Both inland and international rules say that powered vessels must keep to the starboard side of a narrow channel. Both sets of rules provide that a powered vessel approaching a bend in a channel, if unable to see for at least half a mile ahead (defined as a blind bend), must sound a *prolonged blast* of four to six seconds duration on the whistle. This must be answered with a prolonged blast from any approaching vessel that hears it. If no answer is received, the first vessel may consider the channel ahead clear and may proceed with customary caution. After vessels are in sight, the usual signals for meeting and passing should be given.

A vessel leaving its dock or berth (change of status) also sounds a prolonged blast in inland waters. This is sounded whether or not vision is obscured beyond the slip or berth. If the ship is backing

from its berth, it will sound three short blasts, indicating that the ship has sternway. The backing signal follows the prolonged blast for change of status.

Avoiding Collisions

The stand-on vessel normally has the right-of-way, that is, the legal responsibility to maintain course and speed in crossing and overtaking situations. In unusual instances, however, this might not be the thing to do if a collision is to be avoided. For example, in a driving situation on land, the driver of an approaching car may fail to stop at a stop sign or red light, either by mistake or because the brakes failed. Under such circumstances, it would not show good judgment to keep on going and plow into the car because the law gave you the "right-of-way." In fact, the court would be apt to judge such a driver guilty of driving without control of his or her vehicle.

Similarly, both inland and international rules of the road require a vessel's captain to take action to avoid collision even if this might violate the rules. International and inland rule number 8 says, "Any action taken to avoid collision shall, if the circumstances of the case admit, be positive, made in ample time and with due regard to the observance of good seamanship." Therefore, a vessel may depart from the requirements of the rules of the road when there is imminent danger of collision. Such a danger of collision is called "in extremis."

A departure from the rules of the road is permissible only when an immediate danger or special circumstance exists, or when the ordinary practice of seamen dictates a departure from the rules—for example, when more than two vessels are approaching one another. Otherwise, the rules must be strictly followed.

Fog Signals

Under both sets of rules, audible *fog signals* are sounded in any condition that reduces visibility to under the range of a sidelight in any direction around a vessel under way or at anchor. Such reduced visibility conditions may be caused by a number of things, including fog, falling snow, mist, or heavy rain. Signals are sounded both day and night in such weather. In addition, running lights are turned on if under way, and anchor lights are turned on if anchored or moored.

A power-driven vessel sounds a prolonged blast of from four to six seconds duration on the whistle at least every two minutes when it has way on in a fog. If stopped but under way (not anchored, moored, or aground), it sounds two prolonged blasts, two seconds apart, at least once every two minutes. If anchored, a bell is rung for about five seconds at intervals of not more than one minute. If the ship is over 100 meters (feet) in length, the bell is sounded in the forward part of the ship, followed by the sounding of a five-second gong in the after part of the ship. If the anchored ship believes there is possibility of collision, it may sound three blasts (one short, one prolonged, and one short) to warn each approaching vessel of its position.

If at any time a vessel hears a fog signal forward of its beam and cannot tell from where the signal is coming, it must reduce speed to bare steerageway (the minimum speed at which the rudder is effective). If necessary, it must take all way off.

A whole list of special fog signals exist for sailing vessels, vessels aground or towing, fishing, and certain other situations. These will not be covered in this text but may be found in the rules.

Distress Signals

Both inland and international rules provide a list of acceptable common distress signals that may be used to call attention to a vessel in special need. Vessels in distress may use one or more of these signals whenever necessary.

There exists a common misunderstanding that the national ensign hoisted upside down is a signal of distress. A man-of-war would not subject the national colors to this indignity, but the belief is widespread among those with private or recreational craft. Therefore, if a craft is seen with its ensign hoisted upside down, it probably is in distress.

Distress signals specified under inland rules are as follows:

- In the daytime, a continuous sounding with any fog signal apparatus, or firing a gun.
- At night (a) flames from a burning tar or oil barrel; (b) a continuous sounding of any fog signal, or firing of a gun.

International rules provide for the following distress signals:

- A gun or other explosive signal fired at intervals of about one minute
- A continuous sounding with any fog signal
- Rockets or shells, throwing red stars, fired one at a time at short intervals
- The signal group (SOS) in Morse code
- Radiotelephone (voice) signal "Mayday"
- A flaghoist flying the flags November Charlie (NC)
- A flaghoist flying a square flag with a ball or anything resembling a ball either above or below it
- Flames, as from a burning tar or oil barrel
- A rocket parachute flare or a hand flare showing a red light
- A smoke signal giving off orange-colored smoke
- Slowly and repeatedly raising and lowering arms outstretched to each side

STUDY GUIDE QUESTIONS

1. A. What are the two sets of rules governing the nautical rules of the road?

   B. Where is each in effect?

2. What is the purpose of the rules of the road?

3. What designation is given to any vessel propelled by machinery?

4. A. When is a vessel "under way"?

   B. If a vessel is stopped in the water but not anchored, what is its status?

5. A. What running lights must a vessel show at night?

   B. What is the purpose of these lights?

6. Why is a pilot required for large ships in most harbors?

7. A. What anchor lights must be shown according to the rules?

   B. What day shape is used to show that a vessel is at anchor?

8. A. What is meant by the term "not under command"?

   B. What are the lights and day shapes that indicate this condition?

9. Why can some U.S. naval vessels not comply exactly with the rules of the road? Give some examples.

10. What is the basic difference between whistle signals in inland and international rules?

11. If a ship does not understand a whistle signal, or considers a proposed maneuver dangerous, what signal must that ship sound?

12. What are the three basic possible situations when there may be risk of collision when two vessels are approaching in sight of each other?

13. Under the rules, what are two vessels in an approach situation called, depending on their relative position?

14. When a bearing of an approaching vessel remains constant (does not change significantly), what situation is developing?

15. A. In a meeting situation, what is the responsibility of both vessels?

    B. What are the preferred maneuvers?

16. What is the rule in a crossing situation?

17. What is the rule in an overtaking situation?

18. A. What is the sound signal for approaching a blind bend in a channel?

    B. What is the sound signal for leaving a berth (or changing status)?

19. What term defines a situation in which collision is imminent?

20. Under what conditions must fog signals be sounded?

21. What kinds of signals may be sounded or shown to call attention to a vessel in special need of assistance??

CRITICAL THINKING

1. Compare and contrast the nautical rules of the road for the crossing, meeting, and overtaking situations with similar situations when driving on land.

2. List the fundamental differences in maneuvering situations between the international and inland rules of the road.

VOCABULARY

rules of the road

COLREGS

inland rules

under way

"not under command"

signal of intention

running lights

masthead light

range light

arc of visibility

pilot (ship)

day shape

give-way vessel

stand-on vessel

in extremis

prolonged blast

sidelight

anchor light

2 The Maneuvering Board

During your years as an NJROTC cadet, you have occasion to be concerned with maneuvering boats and ships. On training cruises or visits to naval bases, you may find yourself on board either a boat or a ship for training purposes. It is to be hoped that you will have a chance to participate in maneuvers, either as an observer or possibly as a junior watchstander.

In this chapter we will introduce you to the basic concepts of the maneuvering board and how to use it to construct a relative motion plot to solve problems involving wind and the maneuvering of ships and boats. The specific problems with which we will be concerned are finding the closest point of approach (the CPA) of other vessels to yours, finding their courses and speeds, and determining the speed and direction of the true wind. Such information is needed to assist in avoiding collisions in various approach situations, and to put the ship on the proper course and speed for flight operations with aircraft or unmanned aerial vehicles (UAVs). There are also many more advanced types of problems that can be solved using the maneuvering board. As part of their formal training, enlisted operations specialists and line officers who stand deck watches spend many hours learning to solve all kinds of maneuvering problems with the maneuvering board.

Relative Motion

You know both from observations of the world around you and from math and physics courses you may have taken that there is no such thing as absolute rest or absolute motion. Rather, all states of rest or motion are said to be relative to some reference point in space or location on Earth. In driving a car, for example, the reference for how fast it is going is the road on Earth's surface (or sometimes the police officer's radar or laser gun). In a passing situation, the reference for how fast another car is passing you is you in your car. And the reference for parallel parking is the car in front and the car behind the empty space you want.

At sea, the reference for what other vessels and the wind are doing relative to your vessel is your boat or ship. To determine these things, it is helpful to construct a relative motion diagram on a standard plotting sheet called a *maneuvering board*. For those who have taken math courses or physics, you may recognize the relative motion diagram drawn on the maneuvering board as being a kind of *vector diagram*.

A *vector* is a plotted line used to represent any quantity that has both magnitude (size) and direction. Since vessels have courses (direction) and speeds (magnitude) of travel, and winds have directions and speeds at which they blow, vessel courses, vessel speeds, and winds can be conveniently represented by vectors drawn on the maneuvering board.

The Maneuvering Board Plot

The maneuvering board is a type of plot called in mathematics a *polar plot*, wherein all quantities are plotted using their magnitudes and directions, as opposed to their x- and y-coordinates as would be the case on a standard x-y rectangular type plot. The maneuvering board features a reference position in the center called the *pole*, a series of concentric circles drawn around the pole at uniform intervals, and a 360-degree "bearing circle" printed around the outside circle. On the left and right margins are scales that can be used to represent lengths of vectors or distances between the concentric circles, and on the bottom is a logarithmic speed-time-distance device called a *nomogram*, the use of which will be described later.

The polar plot on the maneuvering board can be used to plot both *vectors*, representing vessel courses, speeds, and tracks, or wind speeds and directions, and *points*, representing locations of your own and other vessels.

To use the maneuvering board, you will need the following plotting instruments: a pencil to draw vectors and plot points; a parallel ruler and a triangle to assist in drawing vectors and to pick off directions; and navigator's dividers or a drawing compass to pick off distances between two points.

In order to construct a maneuvering board plot, it is first necessary to decide the frame of reference for the plot you are going to construct. For most purposes, this will be your own vessel. So the first step is to plot a point on the pole to represent your boat or ship; it is labeled with a capital R, for *reference vessel*.

Next, your vessel's course and speed need to be represented by a vector drawn on the diagram. To do this, first choose a suitable scale to represent the magnitude of the speed from among those in the left and right margins; usually either the 3:1 or the 4:1 scale is a good choice, as this will produce a nice-sized vector to work with on the plot. Now, using a straight-edge or the parallel ruler, lay off a line for the vector, using the pole as the origin, toward the

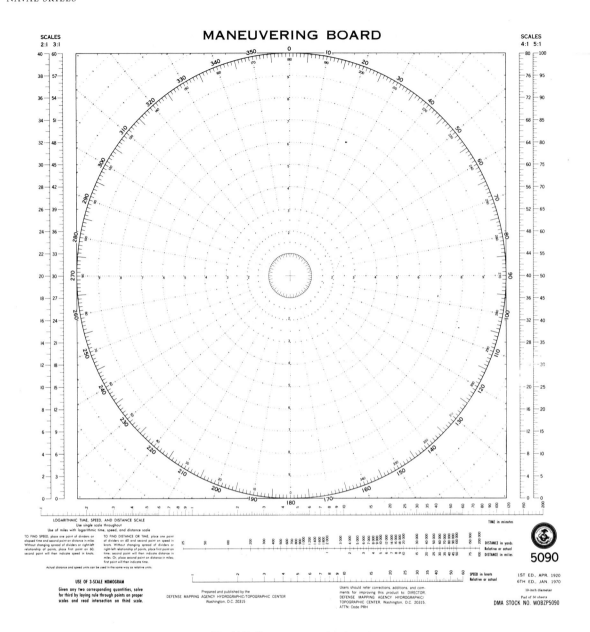

The U.S. Navy maneuvering board.

appropriate bearing on the perimeter corresponding to your vessel's heading. Finally, using the dividers, lay off the scaled length of the vector representing your vessel's speed from the pole, and place an arrowhead on the end of the line. Customarily, the base or tail of the vector at the pole is labeled with a lowercase e, and the head defined by the arrowhead is labeled with a lowercase r, so that the vector er represents the reference ship's course and speed.

As an example, suppose your vessel is on course 125 degrees at a speed of 15 knots. If the 3:1 scale is selected to represent the magnitude of the speed, the dividers are set for this value by placing one point at 0 at the bottom of the 3:1 scale and opening them until the other point is over the mark representing 15 on the scale. The spread of the dividers now represents a magnitude of 15

knots. Now, using a straight-edge or parallel ruler, a line is drawn from the pole toward the 125-degree mark on the perimeter of the outer circle. One point of the divider is placed at the pole, and the other pricks a small point on the line in order to lay off the scaled 15-knot distance. To complete the plot, an arrowhead is drawn at the head of the vector, and labeled with a lowercase r. The foot or tail of the vector at the pole is labeled with a lowercase e (see the illustration on page 223).

Once your own ship has been plotted at the pole or center of the maneuvering board, and the vector representing its course and speed has been plotted, you are ready to solve any of the basic kinds of maneuvering board problems.

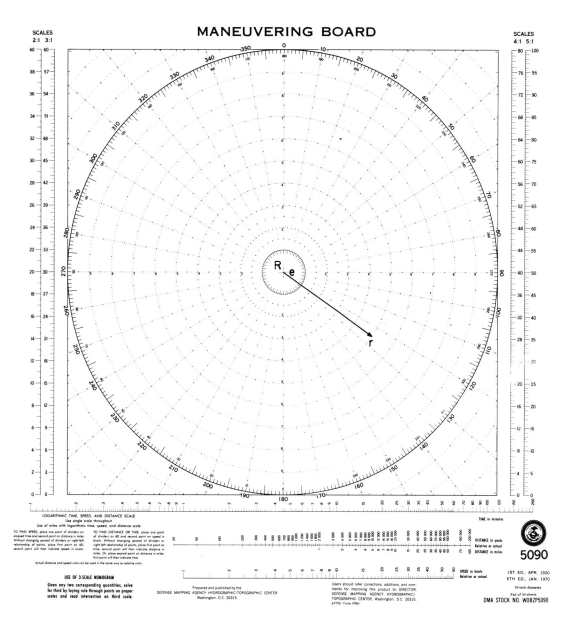

Reference ship's course and speed vector plotted on a maneuvering board for a course of 125°T and a speed of 15 knots.

The CPA Problem

As stated in the beginning of this unit, a major concern of those in charge of a vessel is to avoid hitting other vessels or things in the water. To assist in this endeavor, it is very helpful to be able to determine their projected closest points of approach (CPAs) and their true courses and speeds. Once this information has been determined, appropriate actions can be taken if required to prevent a hazardous situation from developing or to comply with the rules of the road. The maneuvering board can be used both to find the other vessels' CPAs and courses and speeds and, if required, to determine the course and speed changes that could be made by your own vessel to open the CPAs to suitable safe distances.

To find the CPA of a vessel approaching your own vessel, it is necessary to construct its relative track on the maneuvering board. To do this, several ranges and bearings to it, usually taken three minutes apart over a period of several minutes, are plotted on the maneuvering board and labeled M_1, M_2, and so on (for maneuvering vessel). The resulting points, when connected with an extended line, define the *relative motion line (RML)* of the approaching vessel relative to your own.

The CPA to your vessel will be the smallest distance from the pole, where your vessel is, to the extended RML line. Since by geometry we know that the smallest distance between a point and a line is the perpendicular distance between them, it is only necessary to pick off the perpendicular distance on the plot with the

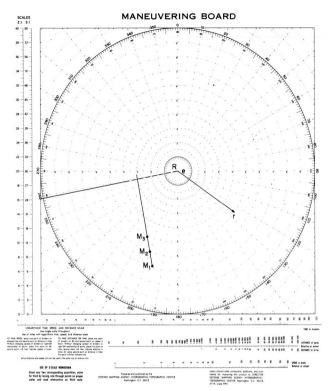

Relative motion line for a maneuvering ship, with the CPA to the reference ship in the center indicated.

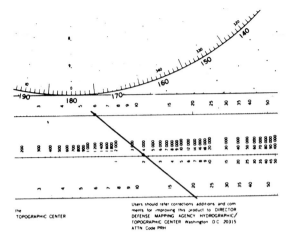

A maneuvering board nomogram, set up to find the relative speed, given a distance of relative movement of 4,000 yards and a time of six minutes.

triangle and the dividers and then move the dividers to the distance scale in use to determine the distance of CPA. In the example shown, the 2:1 scale was used for distance, so the CPA distance is about 6,000 yards. To determine the bearing at CPA, just extend the perpendicular distance line to the outer bearing circle. Here, the bearing at CPA will be 259 degrees. By convention, CPAs are normally given in terms of bearing and distance from one's own vessel to the maneuvering vessel.

Now, to determine the other vessel's true course and speed, we need to complete the construction of a vector diagram that will allow us to solve for the other vessel's true course and speed, given our own vessel's true course and speed vector (which we've already plotted) and the other vessel's relative course and speed vector.

To determine the other vessel's relative course and speed vector, we make use of the RML we plotted to find the CPA. The relative speed is the rate at which the other vessel is proceeding along its RML; the relative course is the direction of the RML.

To find the relative speed, we use the speed-time-distance nomogram at the bottom of the maneuvering board, which can be thought of as a sort of paper computer. To use the nomogram, place a mark on the central *distance* scale of the nomogram, corresponding with the distance traveled along the RML between any two points, say, M_1 and M_3. Note this scale is graduated in either yards along the top, or corresponding nautical miles along the bottom. In our example, the other vessel traveled 4,000 yards between M_1 and M_3, so we put a mark at 4,000 on the distance scale. Next,

put a mark over the elapsed time between M_1 and M_3 on the upper *time* scale of the nomogram, which is graduated in minutes. Here, since six minutes elapsed between the range and bearings obtained for points M_1 and M_3, we put a mark at 6 on the time scale. Finally, draw a straight line through the two marks using a straight-edge, and extend it down onto the lower *speed* scale. The point on the speed scale thus defined is the relative speed—20 knots, in this case (see the illustration).

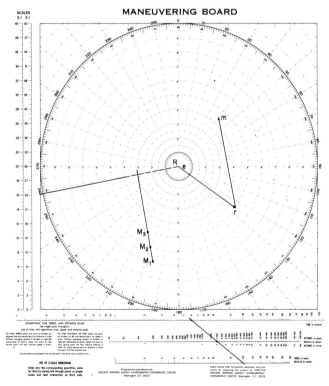

Vector diagram on a maneuvering board set up to find the maneuvering ship's course and speed (the *em* vector), given the reference ship's course and speed (the *er* vector) and the relative course and speeed (the *rm* vector).

Alternatively, if you have an electronic calculator, you could find the relative speed by solving the formula speed = distance ÷ time, making sure you use distances in miles and time in fractions of an hour. Or you could use either the *three-* or *six-minute rules.* The three-minute rule is the distance traveled in yards in three minutes ÷ 100 equals speed in knots. The six-minute rule is the distance traveled in miles in six minutes × 10 equals speed in knots.

In practice, bearings and distances to maneuvering ships used to plot points M_1, M_2, M_3, and so on are generally taken three or six minutes apart, so the two rules above can be quickly applied to find the relative speeds between M_1 and M_2 or M_2 and M_3, and so on.

Having determined the magnitude of the relative speed, we can now plot the relative course and speed vector from the head of our own ship's true course and speed vector, and then determine the resultant other vessel's true course and speed vector. To do this, lay one side of the parallel ruler along the RML, and position the other side at the tip *r* of our own ship's vector. Now draw a line from *r* in the same direction as the RML. Lay off the relative speed along this line with the dividers, being sure to use the same speed scale as was used earlier to plot your own ship's vector, the 3:1 scale in this case (if different scales were used, the resulting vector diagram would not be usable). Place an arrowhead at the end of the relative speed vector, and label it with a lowercase *m.* Vector *rm* now represents the relative motion speed vector (see the illustration on page 224).

To complete the problem, the *em* vector representing the maneuvering (other) vessel's true course and speed is formed

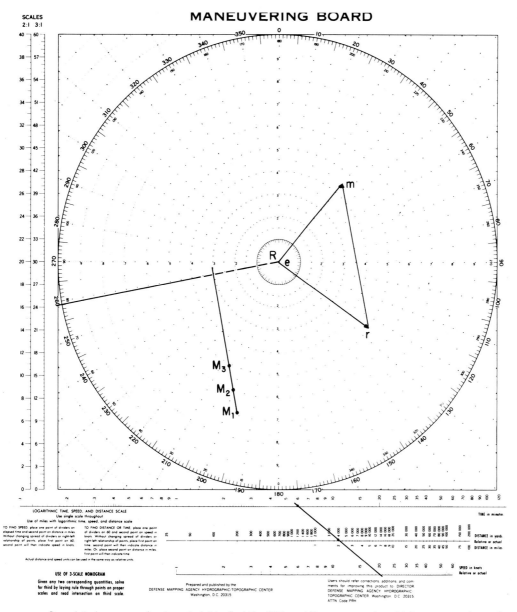

Completed maneuvering board plot to find the CPA and the maneuvering ship's course and speed.

by drawing a line from the pole *e* to the end of the relative speed vector(see the illustration on prvious page).

The bearing of the vector *em* is the true course—040° in this case—and its length, measured by the dividers along the 3:1 scale, is the speed—14½ knots.

The Wind Problem

Since the *relative wind* that a person feels across a vessel's deck is the result of the wind created by the motion of the vessel plus the actual or *true wind*, which can both be represented by vectors on a vector diagram, the maneuvering board can be used both to determine the true wind, given the ship's true course and speed and the relative wind, given the ship's true course and speed and the true wind.

To determine true wind on the maneuvering board, a vector representing the direction toward which the relative wind is blowing and its speed (determined by a vessel's anemometer) is plotted from the head of the ship's true course and speed vector. Again, for consistency the same speed scale is used throughout; the head of the relative wind vector is labeled with a lower case *w*, so that vector *rw* is the relative wind.

The true wind vector *ew* is then formed by drawing a line from *e* at the pole to the head of the relative wind vector *r*. Since winds are defined according to the direction from which they are blowing,

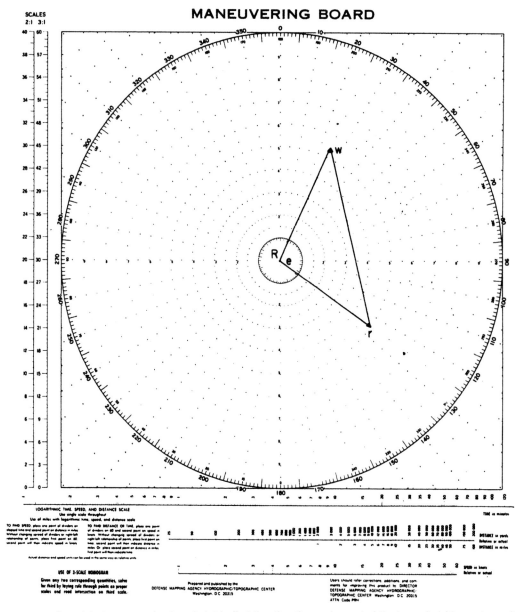

Completed maneuvering board plot to find the direction and speed of the true wind (the vector *ew*).

the reciprocal (opposite) of the bearing of vector *ew* is read using the small numbers inside the perimeter of the maneuvering board.

To solve for relative wind given the ship's course and speed and true wind, a reverse procedure to that described above is followed. First, the ship's and true wind vectors are plotted. The resulting vector *rw* then defines the relative wind. Its direction is specified relative to vector *er*, and its velocity is obtained by measuring its length along the speed scale being used for the problem.

STUDY GUIDE QUESTIONS

1. What is the maneuvering board used for?

2. At sea, what is the reference for what other vessels and the wind are doing relative to your vessel?

3. A. What is normally placed at the center of a maneuvering board, and how is it labeled?

   B. What does vector *er* represent on a maneuvering board?

4. What does the relative motion line (RML) in a CPA-type problem indicate?

5. A target ship *M* is tracked on your ship's radar with the following results:

time	bearing	range (yds)
0908	276°	10,000
0911	269°	8,300
0914	258°	6,800
0917	244°	5,800

   A. What is ship *M*'s speed of relative movement?

   B. What are the bearing and range of the CPA?

6. Your own ship is on course 150°, speed 15 knots. Ship *M* is observed as follows:

time	bearing	range (yds)
1100	255°	20,000
1106	260°	15,700
1112	270°	11,200

   A. What is the CPA of ship *M*?

   B. What is the course and speed of ship *M*?

7. Your own ship is on course 090°, speed 10 knots. You sight a ship *M* on course 270°, speed 15 knots. What are the magnitudes and directions of the following vectors:

   A. The *er* vector

   B. The *em* vector

   C. The *rm* vector

8. Your own ship is on course 025°, speed 12 knots. You sight a ship *M* on course 000°, speed 15 knots. What are the magnitudes and directions of the following vectors?

   A. The *er* vector

   B. The *em* vector

   C. The *rm* vector

9. Your own ship is on course 122°, speed 15 knots. At 0400 a target ship, *Skunk M*, bears 144°, 27,000 yards. *Skunk M*'s course is 020°, 30 knots. What will be the bearing and range of *Skunk M* at CPA?

10. Your own ship is on course 285°, speed 18 knots. At 0800 a target ship *M* bears 310°, 9,000 yards. Ship *M*'s course is 215°, speed 15 knots. What will be the bearing and range of *M* at CPA?

11. You are aboard a boat heading 060°, speed 25 knots. Your anemometer indicates the relative wind to be from 330°R at 35 knots. What are the direction and speed of the true wind?

12. You are on a boat heading 350°, speed 15 knots. The true wind is 10 knots from 240°. What are the direction and speed of the relative wind?

CRITICAL THINKING

1. Compare and contrast a maneuvering board solution for the course and speed of a maneuvering vessel with the conventional head-to-tail graphic solution for the sum of two vectors.

VOCABULARY

maneuvering board	CPA
relative motion	relative motion line (RML)
vector	anemometer
vector diagram	true wind
polar plot	relative wind
nomogram	three-minute rule
six-minute rule	

Naval Weapons and Aircraft

Sea power is that portion of a nation's overall power that enables it to use the sea in furtherance of its interests, objectives, and policies. A major part of this is sea control: the ability to use the sea for oneself and one's allies and to deny that use to an enemy. Another major aspect is the ability to project naval power to inland areas of conflict far from our shores whenever necessary.

The naval power that can best bring its airborne and waterborne weapons to bear on a given area of the sea, land, or air controls that area. Naval weapons have played and will continue to play an important role in achieving victory in battle, both on land and sea. The navy of John Paul Jones's day used muzzle-loaded guns, cannon balls, and Marine sharpshooters in the rigging. Its ability to project power ashore was pretty much limited to the range of a cannon shot. Today, the U.S. Navy has highly accurate gun projectiles, missiles, torpedoes, bombs, and rockets and a variety of ships and aircraft can deliver them. The ability to project naval power far inland with sea-based intercontinental ballistic missiles (ICBMs), naval aircraft, and long-range cruise missiles makes naval weaponry an important consideration in both the strategic and the tactical planning done by national political and military leadership.

1 Introduction to Naval Weapons

Before the invention of gunpowder, naval battles were fought with oar-powered galleys. The principal tactic was to outmaneuver enemies and attempt to ram them, overturn them, or set them on fire. Other alternatives were to board enemy vessels after securing them with grappling hooks, or to shave off oars with a close run alongside. Fighting was basically hand-to-hand combat with the same weapons used on land: swords, bows and arrows, and spears. Gradually, crossbows, catapults, and spring- or torsion-powered artillery did allow some battle action before actual ship contact, but speed and maneuverability remained the best offense and defense.

The first recorded use of naval gunfire occurred when the Spanish fired on a Turkish fleet in 1453. This action showed that an adversary could be destroyed at a distance. Eventually, pistols, muskets, cannon, and rudimentary rockets arrived on the scene. Even so, the use of grapples and boarding parties normally concluded a ship-to-ship naval action until well into the nineteenth century. There was no fire control in the modern sense until the late nineteenth century. Early naval guns with their solid and grape shot depended for effectiveness on close range and skillful seamanship.

The United States Navy defeated the Spanish at Manila Bay and Santiago de Cuba in 1898 in classic naval battles, with battle cruisers and battleships outfitted with large-caliber guns. By the early twentieth century, rifled barrels and detailed studies of projectile motion increased gun ranges to 9 miles, at which ranges the famous British-German naval battle off Jutland was fought in World War I.

During World Wars I and II, destroyers assumed the primary role in the deadly business of antisubmarine warfare (ASW), or undersea warfare (USW) as it is called today. Depth charges were used in both wars, and forward-thrown projectiles called hedgehogs were launched in circular patterns against U-boats in the latter war. Concurrently, the submarine perfected tactics for the use of the torpedo. By the end of World War I, the British had built their first aircraft carrier, a ship type that would be developed further along with its main battery, the airplane, during the interim between the wars. When the Japanese opened World War II in the Pacific with carrier-based air attacks on Pearl Harbor, and then destroyed the two British battleships HMS *Repulse* and HMS *Prince of Wales* with land-based aircraft, the era of the battleship as the main fighting ship of world navies was over. Except for the extremely important gunfire support mission in amphibious assault, the attack carrier with its aircraft as the main weapon became the principal fleet unit. Battleships and cruisers built or refitted during World War II were outfitted with extensive antiaircraft batteries so that they could serve as defensive gunnery platforms protecting the carriers.

Since World War II, naval weapons development has concentrated on improved lightweight rapid-fire guns, a whole arsenal of subsurface, surface and air-launched missiles, and extremely sophisticated electronic fire-control radars, weapons control systems, sonars, and guidance systems. The development of the atomic bomb in 1945 ushered in a whole new family of weapons, including the strategic ICBMs with ranges in excess of 4,000 miles. It is clear that naval weaponry remains a dynamic technology.

Basic Weapons Terminology

Ordnance is a general term for weapons and related physical equipment. This can be further broken down into *explosive ordnance*, which includes gun ammunition, missiles, torpedoes, mines, bombs, and rockets, and *inert ordnance*, which includes projecting devices such as guns and launchers and all equipment needed to operate and control weapons. Aboard ship, all these elements come under the general term *ship's armament*. A *battery* of weapons on a ship consists of all armaments of a similar type and size, for example, all 3-inch guns, or all antiaircraft missiles.

Traditionally, *gunnery* is the art and science of using guns, while *weaponry* is concerned with the practical use of all ordnance. *Ballistics* is the science of projectile motion and is normally used in relation to the motion of projectiles fired from guns. *Internal ballistics* relates to the motion of a projectile within the bore or barrel of a gun, and *external ballistics* concerns the action of the projectile in flight along its *trajectory*, the curved path traveled by the projectile.

Naval Weapons Organization

Any military organization must make provisions for the procurement of weapons and their ammunition, as well as their installation on vessels, vehicles, or aircraft, and their maintenance. These responsibilities are handled at three levels in the U.S. defense establishment: the Department of Defense for all military services, the Department of the Navy for its fleet and shore facilities, and the individual activity's weapons department.

Aboard warships, the combat systems department has responsibility for all matters pertaining to ordnance. The department head is called the combat systems officer. Depending on the ship type, that officer will have a number of assistants, among which are the fire-control officer, missile officer, gunnery assistant, and USW officer.

On ships whose tactical characteristics are not primarily related to ordnance or aircraft, deck responsibilities take precedence over weapons. These are the auxiliary ships in the amphibious and mobile replenishment forces. In such ships, the first lieutenant is assigned as head of the deck department, and one of the assistants may be the gunnery officer. Enlisted personnel assigned to the combat systems or gunnery department/divisions are the gunner's mates, fire-control technicians, torpedomen, and missile technicians, again depending on the ship's armament.

Range of Weapons

From the earliest guns, which had ranges of only a few hundred feet, the range of naval guns increased to more than 40,000 yards (20 miles) by the end of World War II. Since then, rocket-propelled projectiles, aircraft, and guided missiles have increased weapon ranges greatly beyond this.

The most significant results of the increased range of seaborne weapons have been an increase in the importance of naval firepower in land warfare, an increase in the effectiveness of naval as compared with land-based firepower, and an increase in the importance of amphibious warfare. Modern naval gunfire, missiles, and aircraft can reach many miles inland to attack specific targets, to supplement land artillery in supporting land forces, and to support amphibious operations.

Increases in weapons range have steadily extended the distances between combatant forces in battle. The extreme in this trend toward greater separation between attacker and target is represented by modern missiles, which can cross whole oceans to reach their targets.

The development of nuclear fission and fusion revolutionized not only weapons but also war itself, in light of the possible adverse effects on human beings in general. One can point out, however, that warfare has often been revolutionized before. The discovery of gunpowder, for example, was once thought to forecast the end of civilization.

The increased lethal range of nuclear weapons has required the introduction of the tactic of dispersion of military forces to minimize combat damage. Also, improvements in aircraft, undersea craft, and missiles have forced the development and use of early warning systems involving both ships and aircraft on patrol far from the main area of operations.

Ship Weapons Selection

The primary consideration that governs what type of weapons a ship will have is its combat missions. A guided missile cruiser (CG) employed in escorting and protecting aircraft carrier strike groups (CSGs) will carry a balanced armament of antiair warfare, antisurface warfare, and undersea warfare weapons. An amphibious ship such as a dock landing ship (LSD) will carry only such self-defense weapons as the Phalanx close-in weapons system and machine guns, because the ship is not designed to be a weapons platform but a carrier of troops and vehicles. Small patrol vessels, destroyers, and cruisers may carry surface-to-surface missiles for attacks against surface ships. They may also carry antiaircraft guns and missiles to protect against the air threat, and machine guns for defense against small craft. Destroyers, frigates, and cruisers carry antisubmarine torpedoes for use against submarines.

Two tactical concepts are of major importance in the design of gun and missile systems.

Area defense. If a ship's primary mission is to provide defense as far distant from a formation of ships as possible, its sensors and weapons will be designed to cover an area extending some distance from it. The weapons of ships of this kind provide protection for the entire formation, and the weapons are therefore called *area defense weapons*. Guided missile destroyers and cruisers are ships of this type. They can cover a large area with their air and surface search and fire-control radars, and they have weapons capable of engaging any target that enters this defensive envelope. Likewise, destroyers and frigates provide area defense against enemy submarines.

Point defense. The concept of point defense involves providing self-protection for a single unit, regardless of the ship type. A ship armed for point defense will attempt to destroy any target that penetrates a close defensive perimeter centered on the ship. Its guns and missiles must be effective at very close ranges to prevent the attacker from damaging the ship. Almost all combatant ships and many fleet auxiliaries are armed with short-range, point-defense weapons.

Weapon Systems

A weapon system is the combination of a weapon, or weapons, and the equipment used to bring it to bear against the enemy. The weapon system, taken as a whole, must include the following:

- Elements that detect, locate, and identify the target (for example, radar and sonar equipment)
- Elements that deliver or initiate delivery of the destructive payload of the weapon to the target (for example, a gun delivers a projectile to the target and a mine itself explodes when a passing ship detonates it)

Watchstanders monitor the tactical situation in the command and control center of the cruiser USS *Cowpens* (CG 63). (Lowell Whitman)

- Elements of fire control that guide a weapon, set the fuse of its explosive payload, or "program" it to reach the target (for example, a torpedo or surface-to-air guided missile)

- A destructive payload capable of destroying the target when exploded on contact with it, or in close proximity to it

The effective use of any naval weapon requires that a payload, usually an explosive device, be delivered to a target, which most often is moving. Accuracy in determining the location and velocity of the target is vital to the success of the attack. Moreover, the threat to our ships posed by modern air, surface, and subsurface weapons is such that today, to be effective, all defensive weapons must be capable not only of individual use, but also as part of a total weapon system.

The trend in recent times has been toward design and procurement of complete weapon systems. This is especially so in the case of the newer missile systems, with their complex guidance and propulsion components.

Any weapon system or component designed today must effectively address two basic questions:

- What is the system or component unit supposed to do?
- How well is the system or component supposed to do it?

The answer to the first question is called the *military requirement*. It is a statement of the nature of the equipment and its capabilities. Some examples of this might be the range and rate of fire of a gun, the range, accuracy, and sensitivity of a radar, or the speed, accuracy, and limits of operation of a missile control computer.

The answer to the second question concerns general requirements that are applicable to all weapon systems, regardless of the nature of the system or its components. Some of the current general requirements are described below.

Reliability and flexibility. The system must be able to function satisfactorily in spite of some failures in its power supply, or with certain components disabled and others substituted.

Safety. The system should reduce hazardous conditions by interlocks or other means; it must not endanger friendly ships and aircraft, or its own ship's structure or personnel.

Simplicity of operation. Even though modern weapon systems are complex, they should be designed for uncomplicated operation by average, trained human beings.

Maintainability. This requires not only the use of long-life components, but also convenient or nearly automatic testing and trouble-diagnostic capability, integrated into the system if possible. Failed parts should be able to be replaced quickly with spares, so that the equipment will not be out of commission for an extended period of time.

Before a weapon system is accepted for the fleet, it must go through many tests and tactical evaluations to ensure that all of the military and general requirements are met.

Naval weapon systems, both seaborne and airborne, can be broadly classified into guns, missiles, torpedoes, and mines. Naval guns will be described in the next chapter; aircraft and missiles, torpedoes, and mines will be covered in the next chapters, followed by a brief discussion of chemical, biological, and nuclear weapons and warfare.

Weapon Control System

The need for rapid handling and evaluation of target data from detection to destruction has brought into being a system concept more sophisticated than the traditional fire-control system, which was designed to control only one particular battery. Modern computer equipment has changed this concept to that of a total weapon control system (WCS). The WCS integrates all ship's batteries and can operate them in close coordination with those of other ships in company. The weapon control system is composed of a weapon direction system, a tactical data system, and one or more fire-control systems. The WCS concept has, in most cases, relocated the commanding officer from the bridge to the ship's combat information center (CIC) in an interior compartment as the location from which that officer is best able to direct the batteries and "fight" the ship.

The WCS acts as a clearinghouse for target information, to provide early acquisition and designation of a target. The tactical data system is closely related to the ship's weapon direction system, but it receives input from other ships and aircraft as well. It is made up of data processing, display, and transmitting and receiving communication modules. The tactical data system makes it possible to exchange target information instantaneously with all ships in the force, so each ship's weapons become part of the total array of weapons available to the task force commander. He or she can designate the ship or ships best equipped and positioned to engage the target.

For example, if an incoming cruise missile were detected by one ship, it would automatically pass all target information obtained by its sensors to the other ships via the tactical data links. Every ship's weapon direction system would then be able to feed the target data to its own fire-control system, for dissemination to each missile and gun battery. The batteries then would have the necessary preliminary information to acquire and track the incoming missile. Orders to fire can be given by the task force air warfare commander or by an individual ship's commanding officer, as the tactical situation requires.

Aegis cruisers and *Arleigh Burke*–class destroyers are equipped with the most sophisticated shipboard combat system developed to date. The Aegis WCS is designed to provide area air defense in a high density, high threat, antiship missile environment. The major capabilities of the system include long detection range, automatic detection and tracking of multiple targets, automatic special threat alert, and high resistance to electronic countermeasures.

STUDY GUIDE QUESTIONS

1. Why is naval weaponry an important part of both strategic and tactical planning at the highest levels of government?
2. What capability did naval gunfire provide in naval warfare when it was introduced?
3. What factors increased naval gun range to 9 miles by the time of World War I?
4. What major missions remained for the battleship after the emergence of the carrier as the principal fleet unit in World War II?
5. What types of naval weapons have received the greatest attention since World War II?
6. What are the three most significant results of the increased ranges of seaborne weapons?
7. What tactical requirement has resulted from the increased destructive range of nuclear weapons?
8. What is the main consideration that governs the selection of weapons for a ship?
9. What kinds of weapons are used to provide protection for an entire formation of ships?
10. What kinds of weapons provide self-protection for a single ship?
11. Briefly, what must a weapon system include?
12. What is the advantage of having a combat system like Aegis within a force of ships?

CRITICAL THINKING

1. Research and describe how a modern battle force consisting of an aircraft carrier and its screening cruisers and destroyers might be dispersed because of the threat posed by nuclear weapons.
2. Research the effects of modern computer technology on modern weapon systems insofar as their response times and capabilities are concerned.

VOCABULARY

ordnance	battery (of weapons)
arsenal	projectile
armament	fire control
ballistics	payload
internal ballistics	weapon system
external ballistics	weapon control system (WCS)
area defense	point defense

Almost all naval ships and many kinds of naval aircraft are fitted with various kinds of guns. Guns may be used against surface, shore, and air targets. Ship guns designed for engaging both air and surface targets are termed *dual-purpose systems*. Most guns in use today are *automatic*; that is, the recoil of the gun ejects the fired powder case and reloads the gun.

Gun Nomenclature

A *gun* is basically a tube or *barrel* closed at one end, from which a projectile is ejected at a high speed by gases produced by a burning propellant. The inside or *bore* of the barrel is *rifled* with grooves having a right-hand twist of uniform diameter from one end to the other. Rifling causes the projectile to spin in flight, which keeps the projectile from tumbling after it leaves the barrel, thus providing greater accuracy and range.

The size of naval guns is expressed in one of several ways. Inside or bore diameter, measured from the tops of the *rifling lands* (high side of the rifling grooves), may be specified in millimeters (mm) or, for older guns, in inches. For guns less than 3 inches in bore diameter, their barrel width is often referred to as their *caliber*, expressed in millimeters or decimal fractions of an inch. A 20-caliber machine gun, for instance, is a machine gun whose bore diameter is 20 millimeters. A 32-caliber revolver is a handgun whose bore diameter is .32 inches. For guns larger than 3 inches in bore

Guns like this 25-mm chain gun comprise the secondary batteries aboard ships like the guided missile destroyer USS *Mason* (DDG 87), monitoring a vessel captured by pirates off Somalia late in 2008. (Michael McCormick)

diameter, however, the diameter is specified in either millimeters or inches, and the *length* in calibers. Caliber for these guns is defined as a number equal to the length of the gun in inches divided by the diameter of the gun in inches. For example, a gun having a bore diameter of 3 inches and a barrel 150 inches long is designated 3-inch, 50-caliber. Similarly, a 5-inch-diameter gun 270 inches in length is called a 5-inch/54-caliber gun.

The *arc of elevation* is the total vertical arc through which a gun barrel can be raised and lowered. The *arc of train* is the total horizontal arc through which a gun mount may be rotated. If a gun were mounted well forward on the bow, it could have a clear field of fire up to about 320 degrees, but a gun mounted aft might have only a 180-degree arc astern. Electrical and mechanical *cut-out cams* are incorporated in gun circuits and on mounts, which prevent guns from being fired when they are pointed at a part of a ship or aircraft's structure.

The *mount*, or *gun mount*, is the entire structure between the gun and the ship or aircraft's structure. It supports and secures the gun, and provides for the gun's elevation, train, and recoil.

A *battery* of guns is a group of gun mounts of the same size, normally controlled from the same point. The main battery of a ship consists of the largest size guns on board. The secondary battery consists of dual-purpose guns, or guns of the next smaller size.

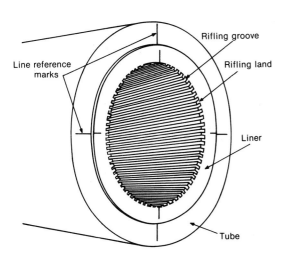

Diagram of the barrel of a rifled gun, showing lands and grooves.

A 5-inch/54-caliber gun of a Navy cruiser fires a round during a live firing exercise. (Joshua Scott)

On ships having both guns and missiles, the most capable system may be designated the main battery, and the other the secondary.

The range at which a gun is effective against surface and air targets (the *effective range*) is an important characteristic of a gun system. It is dependent on the initial velocity imparted to the projectile by the propellant, the weight of the projectile, the caliber of the gun, and the ability of the sensors and fire-control systems to detect and track the target. The ranges of larger caliber naval gun projectiles have been extended somewhat by the addition of rocket assistance. These rocket-assisted projectiles (RAP) have a solid-propellant rocket motor incorporated in the shell casing.

Naval guns are categorized as major (8 inches or larger), intermediate (less than 8 inches and larger than 4 inches), and minor (less than 4 inches in diameter).

The biggest naval guns available today are the 127-mm (5-inch)/54- and 62-caliber automatic, dual-purpose, single-mount guns fitted on *Burke*-class destroyers and *Ticonderoga*-class cruisers. These guns are completely automatic, and are loaded, controlled, and fired from remote positions without any need for a gun crew to enter the mount. The gun can fire twenty rounds per minute to a maximum range of 13 nautical miles. The shell weighs 72 pounds.

The Oto Melara 76-mm (3-inch) /62-caliber rapid-fire, dual-purpose mount was developed in Italy for NATO use in the late 1960s to combat high-speed aircraft and the cruise missile. Because of its light weight, it is suitable for installation on frigates. It is a water-cooled single mount, with a rate of fire of eighty rounds per minute and a maximum range of 17,800 yards (19,200 meters). The mount is not manned and requires only three ammunition handlers to reload the magazine.

The Phalanx close-in weapon system (CIWS) is a 20-mm gun system designed to be a ship's last-ditch weapon against an antiship cruise missile. The system is a complete unit containing search and tracking radar, a fire-control system, and a magazine. The Phalanx system is capable of automatically detecting and engaging any missiles that penetrate the other task force defenses. The gun is a six-barrel Vulcan Gatling gun capable of firing three thousand rounds per minute to a range of about 1 mile. The Phalanx search radar input is fed directly into a computer, which will identify the target, lock the gun on, and fire it until the target is destroyed, whereupon the system will automatically cease firing and begin searching for another target. A follow-on CIWS system to Phalanx called the Sea-Ram uses a magazine of eleven rolling airframe missiles (RAM) vice a Gatling gun to engage close-in targets. It is installed in littoral combat ships.

Types of guns on today's naval aircraft will be discussed in the following chapter.

Gun Ammunition

The principal components of a full round of gun ammunition are a *propelling charge* (propellant) and a *projectile*. The propelling charge provides the thrust that ejects the projectile at the desired velocity from the muzzle of the gun. The propelling charge assembly includes an ignition system, the propellant, and the container. The payload or projectile assembly includes the detonating fuse, the booster, and the burster charge.

In a naval gun, the propellant charge is packed behind the projectile, either in bags or in metal cartridge cases. If the propellant is packed in bags, the ammunition is called *bag ammunition*; if it is packed in a case, it is called *case ammunition*. The huge 16-inch guns of the old retired battleships used bag ammunition, but all modern naval guns on active ships today use either semifixed or fixed case ammunition. *Semifixed* ammunition refers to a round that consists of a projectile and a separate case charge loaded one after the other. This type of round is used in most 5-inch guns. *Fixed* ammunition refers to a round in which the projectile and powder case are permanently attached, as with a rifle cartridge. Such ammunition is used in 3-inch and smaller guns.

Propellants are chemical compounds that burn at a rapid rate rather than detonate or explode. The initiating stage in a propel-

The Phalanx close-in weapon system is a 20-mm fully automatic gun system designed as a ship's last-ditch weapon against antiship cruise missiles. The gun is a six-barrel Vulcan Gatling gun capable of firing three thousand rounds per minute to a range of about 1 mile. (Philip McDaniel)

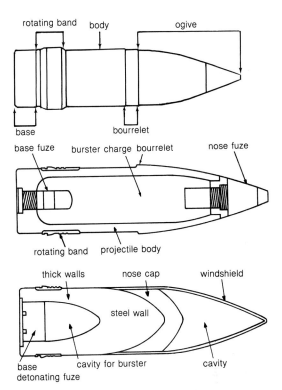

Diagrams of a naval gun projectile, showing the external features (top), the internal construction of an antiaircraft common projectile (middle), and the internal construction of an armor-piercing projectile (bottom).

lant train or series is called a *primer* or *detonator*; it produces a hot flame that sets off the next stage, called the *igniter* or *booster*. The igniter, in turn, sets off the main burster charge.

Gun Projectiles

The projectile is the part of a round that is expelled at high velocity from the gun bore by the burning propelling charge. Projectiles used in small weapons often consist of solid metal; projectiles used in larger guns, however, are assemblies of several components. The three main parts of a projectile are its metallic body, the fuse that sets off the main charge, and the explosive burster charge. A solid bullet damages by impact alone. Naval high-explosive projectiles inflict damage primarily by blast and fragmentation. This type of projectile is designed to break up into many fragments of specific dimensions upon detonation.

Projectiles are cylindrical in shape, with pointed noses called *ogives*. Such a shape makes the projectile stable as it spins about its long axis in flight, with a minimum resistance to air. As previously mentioned, the bores of modern naval guns are rifled in order to impart this spin to the projectile as it travels the length of the bore.

Various projectiles have different designs, because the targets they are intended for differ in character. There are three general classes of projectiles: penetrating, fragmenting, and special purpose.

Penetrating projectiles include armor-piercing shells designed to penetrate heavy armor such as that of a ship before exploding. The "AP armor piercing" projectile is an example of a projectile of this type. The burster charge must be insensitive to the shock of impact, to permit penetration and subsequent detonation by a delay fuse.

Fragmenting projectiles are designed to damage by blast effect and fragmentation. Fragmentation is the breaking up of the projectile walls into high-velocity shrapnel. These projectiles have relatively thin walls and large burster charges. The most commonly used projectiles of this type are called HE-PD (high explosive–point detonating) projectiles. They are used against lightly armored surface targets such as torpedo boats, shore installations, or personnel. Since no penetration is required, the bursting charge is sensitive to impact. Most antiaircraft projectiles are of the fragmentation type; some such as the widely used "AA common" projectile, are normally fused to detonate in the proximity of the aircraft, and the fragments penetrate the skin.

Special purpose projectiles have a variety of applications, including illumination, smoke, chaff, and target practice. They are not intended to inflict damage by blast or fragmentation. Whatever small amount of explosive may be in the shell is there only to expel the contents to achieve the designed purpose.

Illuminating projectiles, often called *star shells*, contain a bright flare attached to a parachute. The flare is intended to illuminate an enemy target or terrain as it slowly descends under the parachute.

Incendiary projectiles contain white phosphorus. They can be used to set fire to flammable targets such as fuel and ammunition dumps, to mark the fall of shot during shore bombardment, and to create chaos and confusion among enemy troops. Once released by the exploding projectile, the fragments of burning white phosphorus are almost impossible to extinguish.

Chaff projectiles contain metal foil strips that are scattered into the air by a small burster charge. The foil strips can confuse enemy search and fire-control radar by causing interference that can mask the intended target.

Nonfragmenting projectiles produce bursts of various colored smoke for antiaircraft gunnery practice. *Target projectiles* contain sand or other inert material to simulate the weight and balance of burster charges; they are used for surface gunnery practice.

Once a projectile has hit the target or has come within close proximity of it, a device called a *fuse* detonates the burster charge. A fuse can be either a mechanical or electrical device. Fuses are classified according to their function as impact, time, or proximity. They may be located either in the nose or the base of a projectile, again depending on their intended function. Various physical forces of flight, impact on or proximity of target, or passage of a set time can cause the fuse to initiate the explosive train.

Proximity-fused (VT-fused) shells were introduced in 1943. A VT fuse contains a radio transceiver that emits pulses of radio energy and receives a reflection of those pulses back from the target. It is designed to detonate the projectile at a position that will cause the greatest damage to the target. If the projectile comes within 100 feet of the target, the returning pulse is strong enough to set off the fuse. In the case of a projectile fitted with a VT fuse, therefore, a near miss can be nearly as effective as a direct hit. VT fuses are commonly used in fragmentation shells. A more recent innovation is the *controlled variable time fuse* which delays for a set time after the projectile is fired before becoming active (arming), allowing the weapons officer to choose the time at which the fuse arms and begins radiating. For example, if a ship were firing over friendly ships, the arming would be delayed until the projectile was well past those ships.

The mechanical time fuse contains a clock mechanism that explodes the projectile after a preset amount of time elapses. Projectiles containing this type of fuse were commonly used in the 5-inch, 40-caliber, and 20-caliber antiaircraft guns of battleships and cruisers during World War II, which put up flak screens to protect fast carrier task forces during enemy air attacks. Flak is heavy antiaircraft barrages through which aircraft must fly to attack the defended targets.

Naval Surface Fire Support

Bombardment of enemy shore installations was common in World War II. Techniques have been continually improved through experience gained in successive amphibious landings in that war, and later in surface gunfire support missions in Korea, Vietnam, and several operations in the Middle East, including Desert Storm against Iraq.

Naval surface fire support can mean the difference between success or failure in an opposed amphibious assault. But in order for it to be effective, naval gunfire support for amphibious operations must be carefully planned in advance and executed with precision and timeliness. Naval surface fire is vitally important both before the assault to neutralize beach defenses and after the troops have landed to support them before adequate field artillery can be brought ashore and put into action.

Naval surface fire may also be called upon for other support roles, in addition to those connected with amphibious warfare. It can be of prime importance in mine warfare activities, air-sea rescue missions, reconnaissance and demolition operations, feints, raids, and flak suppression during air strikes. It can be used in interdiction of coastal roads, railroads, airfields, and troop assembly areas.

STUDY GUIDE QUESTIONS

1. What is the purpose of rifling in a gun barrel?

2. A. How is the caliber of a gun measured?

   B. How is the caliber of guns with 3-inch barrels and larger expressed?

3. A. On what does the effective range of a gun depend?

   B. What is the purpose of the RAP innovation in naval gun projectiles?

4. A. What gun is carried by most post–World War II destroyers and cruisers?

   B. What is the range of this gun in miles?

5. A. What is the close-in shipboard weapon in wide use today?

   B. How does it operate?

6. What are the two principal components of a round of gun ammunition?

7. From the standpoint of the propellant, what kind of gun ammunition is used most in the active fleet today?

8. What is the sequence of the propellant train, and what does each stage do?

9. A. What is the projectile in naval ammunition?

   B. What are the three main projectile parts?

10. List five kinds of special purpose projectiles.

11. What is the proximity-fused shell designed to do?

12. What are some important tasks that may be assigned to naval surface fire support?

CRITICAL THINKING

1. Research and trace the evolution of the modern naval large-bore gun from the smooth-bore cannon of the fifteenth century to the rifled gun of the twentieth century.

2. Describe the process of firing a projectile from a naval gun in terms of the chemical reaction of the burning propellant charge and the physics of the resulting forces on the projectile. Explain how Newton's Laws come into play during the firing process.

VOCABULARY

rifled barrel	gun mount
effective range	dual-purpose system
main battery	arc of train
propellant	arc of elevation
fuse	caliber
burster charge	rifling lands
RAP	fragmenting projectile
recoil	illuminating projectile
case ammunition	star shell
fixed, semifixed ammunition	chaff
shrapnel	controlled variable time fuse
projectile	proximity fuse
ogive	flak

3 Naval Aircraft and Missiles

In this chapter we will take a brief look at naval aircraft, their weapon systems, and guided missiles used in the U.S. Navy.

Naval aircraft, like aircraft in general, fall into three main groups: fixed-wing, rotary-wing, and lighter-than-air. *Fixed-wing* airplanes have wings that are the primary lifting devices of the airplane. *Rotary-wing* craft, primarily helicopters, have two or more rotor blades that lift the aircraft into the air. *Lighter-than-air* craft, such as blimps, depend on casings filled with light gas, primarily helium, to provide their lifting power.

Fixed-wing aircraft have many roles in the Navy:

- *Attack planes* are used for low-level bombing, ground support, or nuclear strikes. They carry heavy payloads (fuel, bombs, and missiles) and can remain on station long enough to support ground troops.

- *Fighters* are high-performance aircraft used to gain air superiority. They may be used defensively as interceptors, offensively as escorts for bombers, or on ground support missions. Some can carry bombs and other precision weapons for limited attack missions.

- *Patrol aircraft* are land-based, long-range multiengine planes used mainly for antisubmarine patrol. They can detect, locate, and destroy submarines. They can also escort surface convoys, conduct photographic missions, and lay mines from the air.

- *Electronic warfare (EW)* aircraft detect and jam enemy radars to protect the strike group (attack and support aircraft) from being targeted by enemy missiles, guns, or interceptor aircraft.

- *Reconnaissance aircraft* are aircraft that have been specially configured to gather intelligence.

One of the newest military aircraft in the U.S. inventory is the V-22 Osprey, expected to fill the medium-lift needs of the Marine Corps for at least the next decade. With the engines positioned as shown here, the aircraft can take off and land vertically. Once airborne, the engines rotate 90 degrees forward, converting the V-22 into a high-speed turboprop aircraft. (Mike Jones)

- *Airborne early-warning (AEW)* aircraft maintain stations far from a fighting force, to provide early warning of approaching enemy aircraft and cruise missiles, and to direct interceptors into position.

Rotary-winged helicopters serve a variety of roles in the Navy, among which are cargo and personnel transportation, undersea warfare, observation and reconnaissance, search and rescue, and mine countermeasures. In the other services they are often used in ground-attack roles.

For many years following World War II, lighter-than-air craft fell into disuse in the Navy, but in recent years their stability and ability to hover on station for long periods of time have caused renewed interest in them. A new type of USW patrol blimp has been proposed and may possibly join the fleet in the future.

Naval Aircraft Weapon Systems

Until the end of World War II, most of the armament of naval fighter-type aircraft consisted of small- to medium-caliber machine guns of one sort or another, augmented at times by unguided rockets suitable for use against land targets, ships, and surfaced submarines. To these were added bombs of various sizes and types, incendiaries in the case of fighter-bomber and attack aircraft, and torpedoes. In the years after the war, the advent of nuclear weapons caused several models of Navy attack planes such as the A-3, A-4, and A-5 to be developed specifically to deliver nuclear bombs. Fortunately these capabilities were never called upon in practice, so eventually they were fitted with conventional weaponry or converted to use as unarmed tanker and reconnaissance aircraft.

During these same years, guided missiles were developed for fighter aircraft, and these saw some use in aerial combat in both the Korean and Vietnam Wars. Most aerial dogfight engagements in both these wars, however, continued to be decided with bow or wing-mounted machine guns. Rapid-firing Gatling-type (rotating barrel) machine guns mounted in detachable pods beneath the fuselage began to appear in the late 1960s. These were intended primarily for use against ground targets by contemporary fighter-bomber and attack aircraft, several models of which had not originally been fitted with any guns at all, in the mistaken belief that they were no longer needed—a notion proved very wrong during the Vietnam War. Almost all fighter and attack aircraft developed since have been fitted with some type of integrated gun system.

In the 1980s and 1990s, however, improved guidance systems and better propulsion systems did ultimately cause more and more reliance to be placed on the guided missile as the main armament for most modern jet-powered naval fighter-type aircraft. Cruise missiles and precision weapons like smart bombs play major roles in the case of today's attack aircraft. Modern USW helicopters use air-launched homing torpedoes as their principal weapon against enemy submarines. Carrier- and ground-based aircraft attacks against enemy buildings, tanks, ground equipment, and fortifications during Operation Desert Storm in 1991, similar attacks later in Operation Enduring Freedom in 2001–2002, and in many other military operations since have shown how devastatingly accurate today's precision-guided weaponry has become.

Nevertheless, as a result of the combat experience in Vietnam and later conflicts, new fighter aircraft such as the F-16 Falcon and the F/A-18 Hornet were designed from the beginning to incorporate fuselage-mounted 20-mm Gatling guns among their armament, the six-barreled version of which can fire one hundred rounds per second. These fuselage-mounted guns are more accurate, especially against airborne targets, than the older pod-mounted versions were.

All things considered, while guided weapons now predominate, it is likely that some form of gun will remain an important part of naval aircraft armament for many years to come.

Guided Missiles

A *missile* is any object that can be projected or thrown at a target. This includes stones and arrows as well as gun projectiles, bombs, torpedoes, and rockets. Today, however, the term usually refers to a *guided missile*, an unmanned, self-propelled vehicle with a guidance system that controls its flight to the target. By contrast, the term *smart bomb* has come into common use to describe non–self-propelled air-dropped munitions fitted with guidance systems that can control the flight path to the target. A *rocket* differs from a guided missile in that it does not have an internal guidance system. A guided missile can carry either a conventional explosive or a nuclear warhead.

The Navy's homing torpedoes are self-propelled weapons having elaborate guidance systems that hunt for a target and steer for it on a collision course. They are not technically regarded as guided missiles, since they do not travel above the Earth's surface. They will be discussed briefly along with guided missiles, however, because they are so important in the fleet's advanced guided weapon systems.

There is a standardized three-letter DOD designation system for the various types of guided missiles, similar to the designation system for Navy ships. The first letter designates the launch environment: A is for air launched; R is for surface ship launched; and U is for underwater launched. The second letter designates the mission, such as G for surface attack, I for aerial intercept, Q for drone, and U for underwater attack. The third letter designates the type: M for guided missile, R for rocket, and N for probe. The three designation letters are followed by a design number. Most missiles are also given names by which they are commonly identified throughout their service lifetimes, regardless of any modifications they may go through. For example the RIM-156 Standard 2 missile is the one hundred fifty-sixth design of ship-launched, aerial intercept guided missile. It is still named the Standard missile, even though it is several models later than the original design, the RIM-66 Standard 1 missile, phased out of U.S. service in 2003.

Missile Components

Each guided missile has four basic parts: the airframe, the propulsion system, the guidance system, and the warhead. The *airframe* of a missile is the streamlined body that contains the other parts plus the fuel. Missile airframes are made of aluminum alloys, magnesium, and high-tensile steel sheet, all of which are lightweight materials capable of withstanding extreme heat and high pressure.

The propulsion system must propel the missile at speeds sufficient to minimize its vulnerability while maximizing the probability of intercepting a target. Most missiles designed to operate at supersonic speeds, or partially above the atmosphere or in the water, are equipped with liquid- or solid-fuel propulsion systems containing an *oxidizer* (oxygen-carrying agent). Subsonic air-breathing "cruise" missiles carry only a petroleum-based fuel and draw their oxygen from the atmosphere, which limits their operating altitude to about 70,000 feet.

The warhead is the high-explosive payload of the missile. It may be either conventional or nuclear or, in the case of a practice missile, may contain telemetry equipment.

Most Navy guided missiles have one of five types of guidance systems: preset gyro, inertial, homing, command, or beam rider. GPS-based guidance systems are coming into use on some newer models of Tomahawk cruise missiles and precision ordnance.

Preset gyro guidance uses gyroscopes to keep the missile on a set course, with an on-board computer constantly checking angle of climb and acceleration. When the missile attains the preset course and velocity, power is shut off and it continues to the target as a free (ballistic) projectile.

Inertial guidance makes use of a predetermined flight profile programmed into an onboard missile computer. Missile speed and course are checked constantly, and the computer initiates corrections to keep it on track.

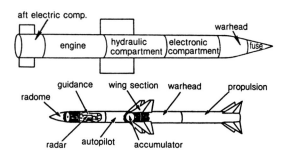

Sectional drawings of typical missiles, showing the usual location of the various modules (top), and an active homing missile (bottom).

Homing guidance depends on the missile picking up and tracking a target by means of radar, optical, or heat-seeking devices. The homing system will follow any evasive maneuvers attempted by the target, and the missile is fast enough to overtake most targets trying to outrun it. There are several types of homing guidance. In *active homing* guidance, a radar transmitter and receiver are both located in the missile. The transmitter emits a signal that is reflected off the target back to the receiver. Active homing is completely independent of the launching ship or aircraft. In *semiactive homing* guidance, a radar transmitter is located on the launching ship or aircraft, and a receiver is in the missile. In *passive homing* guidance, the missile picks up and tracks a target by detecting some form of energy emitted by it. Sources of energy used for passive homing include light, sound, or heat. Like active homing, passive homing guidance is completely independent of the launching ship or aircraft.

Command guidance involves missile control by signals from the launch station. After the missile is launched on an intercept course, a computer tracks both missile and target and transmits to the missile orders to change its track in order to hit the target even though the target might take evasive action.

Beam rider guidance requires the missile to follow a radar beam to the target. A computer within the missile keeps it centered within the radar beam; several missiles may ride the beam simultaneously. If the missile wanders out of the beam, it will automatically self-destruct.

Uses of Guided Missiles

The development of modern guided missiles has added a new dimension to the attack and defense capabilities of the U.S. military. While missiles cannot perform all the functions of guns, they can have greater range, accuracy, and payloads. Sea control remains a primary mission of the Navy, but with the advent of the Polaris, Poseidon, and, in the 1980s, the Trident intercontinental ballistic missiles (ICBMs), the sea also has become a hiding and launching place for our nation's most potent seaborne strategic power-projection system. Modern cruise missiles launched from the sea can also project the Navy's power far inland.

The current fleet ballistic missile (FBM), the Trident ICBM, has a range of over 4,000 nautical miles. With such a range, even the most remote place on Earth can be reached by submarine-launched Trident missile warheads. The Air Force has several models of ICBMs with ranges of over 3,000 nautical miles; the Minuteman is the most powerful of these, having a range of over 5,000 miles. All of these ICBMs have nuclear warheads.

Certain missiles are designed to intercept incoming enemy ballistic missiles and destroy them before they can reach their targets. These are the *antiballistic missiles* (ABMs). They must have great acceleration and long range in order to intercept enemy ICBMs. To date the United States has never deployed a fixed ABM system because of arms control agreements negotiated with the Soviet Union in the late 1970s. The Navy has developed an ABM version of the ship-launched Standard surface-to-air missile, to protect against future potential ballistic missile threats to the fleet and to the United States mainland. It may also be used in the future to provide protection to NATO countries and other allies either in addition to or in lieu of ground-based ABM systems.

Although not originally designed to be an ABM missile, the Army's mobile Patriot missile system was extensively used to knock down incoming Iraqi Scud missile warheads fired against Israeli and Saudi Arabian targets during Operation Desert Storm in 1991. It has been continuously improved since.

Modern military aircraft fly so high and fast that conventional antiaircraft guns are ineffective against them. The surface-to-air guided missile, however, can successfully intercept attacking aircraft at great heights and ranges.

Guided missiles have become the main weapon used in aerial combat. When two jet aircraft are approaching each other head-on, the range can close at speeds in excess of a mile per second. Under these conditions, it is difficult even to see an approaching enemy aircraft, and hitting it with gunfire under these conditions would be just a matter of luck. But the air-to-air missile can "lock on" the hostile aircraft while it is still miles away and pursue and hit it in spite of any evasive maneuvers.

The defense of a naval force against air attack is somewhat similar to the defense of a city against air attack. The incoming enemy air attack would probably be detected by long-range search radar and AEW aircraft while still hundreds of miles away. The first line of defense would probably be interceptor fighter aircraft, which would attack the enemy planes or cruise missiles with air-to-air missiles. A second line of defense might consist of long-range surface-to-air missiles fired by destroyers and cruisers, which can intercept an incoming target at ranges from 100 to 200 miles. A third line of defense would be medium-range missiles designed to intercept between 40 to 90 miles, and antiaircraft guns with ranges

A Tomahawk cruise missile. (Daniel McClain)

up to 10 miles. Point defense missiles and gun systems like Phalanx would be employed against any incoming aircraft or cruise missiles that got past these outer defenses.

Protection against underwater attack is afforded by weapons such as ASROC (antisubmarine rocket) that delivers a homing torpedo to a water entry point in close proximity to a detected enemy submarine.

Navy Submarine-Launched Ballistic Missiles

Since the initial deployment of the Polaris A-1 submarine-launched ballistic missiles (range of 1,200 nautical miles) in 1960, both the SSBN submarines and the missiles they carry have steadily improved in operational capability and flexibility. The U.S. fleet ballistic submarine force, a major component of our nation's strategic defense system, currently consists of fourteen Trident submarines, each of which can carry twenty-four 4,000-nautical-mile-range MIRV (multiple independently targeted reentry vehicle)

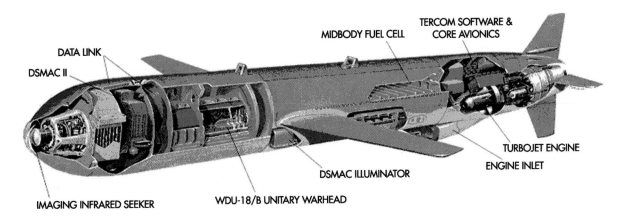

DATA LINK
DSMAC II
MIDBODY FUEL CELL
TERCOM SOFTWARE & CORE AVIONICS
TURBOJET ENGINE
ENGINE INLET
DSMAC ILLUMINATOR
IMAGING INFRARED SEEKER
WDU-18/B UNITARY WARHEAD

Cutaway drawing of a Tomahawk cruise missile.

Two 500-pound laser-guided "smart bombs" and a Sidewinder missile on the wing of a F/A-18 Hornet.

ballistic missiles. The submarines are based at King's Bay, Georgia, and Bangor, Washington.

Ballistic missiles have a two-stage flight path. During the first stage, the guidance system makes corrections to the flight path of the missile to give it the proper trajectory to hit the target. The second stage of the flight, the larger part, has a ballistic free-fall trajectory, although some missiles like the Trident have warheads containing multiple cone-shaped reentry vehicles, each of which can be programmed to hit different targets.

Navy Cruise Missiles

The Harpoon, the Navy's antiship cruise missile, is designed to be launched from ships, submarines, and aircraft. It is the primary antiship weapon system for U.S. naval forces and is carried by cruisers, destroyers, frigates, nuclear attack submarines, carrier-based attack aircraft, and shore-based P-3 Orion maritime patrol aircraft.

The missile features over-the-horizon (OTH) range, a low-level subsonic cruising trajectory (thus the name cruise), active

guidance, counter-countermeasures, and a large payload. It is powered by a turbojet engine. After launch, it descends to 100 feet above the water. This sea-skimming flight profile, along with active terminal guidance radar, ensures a high probability of penetrating enemy defenses and hitting the target. The sea-launched missile is 15 feet long and weighs 1,400 pounds; the air-launched version is 12 feet long. It has a maximum range of over 60 nautical miles, with a 500-pound conventional warhead.

The Tomahawk is an all-weather, long-range, subsonic cruise missile. It can be launched from submarines, ships, land, and aircraft. The Tomahawk is capable of delivering either a conventional or nuclear warhead to ranges in excess of 700–1,350 nautical miles, depending on the model. The land-attack Tomahawk flies at very low altitudes and has terrain masking and infrared guidance features, making defense against it extremely difficult. The latest version has GPS guidance, and can be reprogrammed in flight to an alternate target if deemed necessary. The Tomahawk has been used to great effect over the past twenty years in actions such as Operations Desert Storm and Iraqi Freedom in the Persian Gulf region, and in attacks against al Qaeda terrorists and the Taliban in Operation Enduring Freedom in Afghanistan.

The standoff land attack missile (SLAM) was developed in the late 1980s to give the Navy a surgical strike capability against high-value land targets and ships. Originally used in Iraq in Operation Desert Storm in 1991, it has been continuously improved and upgraded since its introduction. The SLAM can be launched from a variety of Navy fighter, attack, and patrol aircraft. It has a range in excess of 150 nautical miles.

Navy Air-to-Air Missiles

The front line of defense for a naval task force is its combat air patrols (CAP), which range far out from the fleet to meet incoming enemy air threats with highly capable air intercept missiles (AIM).

The AIM-9 series Sidewinder missile is carried by both Navy and Air Force fighter and attack aircraft and is designed for use in close-range, dogfight-type air engagements. The missile is an infrared homing heat-seeker air-to-air missile. It varies in weight from 160 to 210 pounds depending on the version, has a speed of Mach 2.5, a range of about 2 miles, and is capable of operating against high-performance aircraft at altitudes from sea level to over 50,000 feet. The improved fuse, warhead, and maneuverability of the latest model provides U.S. pilots with the best possible advantage in close combat.

The AIM-120 advanced medium-range air-to-air missile (AMRAAM) is the latest in the Navy inventory. It was developed jointly by the United States and several NATO nations. It is a follow-on to an older missile series called the Sparrow. It has active radar guidance and an on-board computer system that makes the missile independent of the fire-control system of the launch-ing aircraft. Once the missile closes in on the target, its active radar guides it to intercept. This enables the aircraft pilot to aim and fire several missiles at once at multiple targets, and then perform evasive maneuvers while the missiles guide themselves to the targets. The missile has a high-explosive fragmentation warhead.

Navy Surface-to-Air Missiles

During the 1960s and 1970s, the second line of fleet defense was centered on the "3 Ts," the Navy's first surface-to-air (SAM/RIM) guided missiles: Terrier, Tartar, and Talos. The RIM-2 Terrier was the Navy's first operational SAM missile. Weighing 3,000 pounds, it was a solid-fuel missile with a range exceeding 10 miles at a speed of Mach 2. Tartar was similar to Terrier but weighed half as much.

The Talos missile was for many years the Navy's largest shipboard surface-to-air missile. It was designed for launching from cruisers, for long-range air defense. It weighed 7,000 pounds and was propelled by a ramjet engine. Its longest-range version exceeded 100 miles, with a ceiling of 80,000 feet. It was phased out in the late 1970s.

Numerous improvements were made in the Terrier and Tartar missiles over the years, culminating in the Standard missile series, featuring both medium-range (MR) and extended-range (ER) versions. Presently the Standard-2 (SM-2) is the Navy's primary surface-to-air air defense weapon. It is an integral part of the AEGIS weapon system (AWS) aboard *Ticonderoga*-class cruisers and *Arleigh Burke*–class destroyers, and is launched from the MK 41 vertical launch system (VLS). The Standard-2 MR, 15½ feet long and weighing some 1,500 pounds, has a range in excess of 90 miles and a ceiling greater than 80,000 feet. The Standard-2 ER, 21½ feet long and weighing some 3,200 pounds, has a range exceeding 200 miles

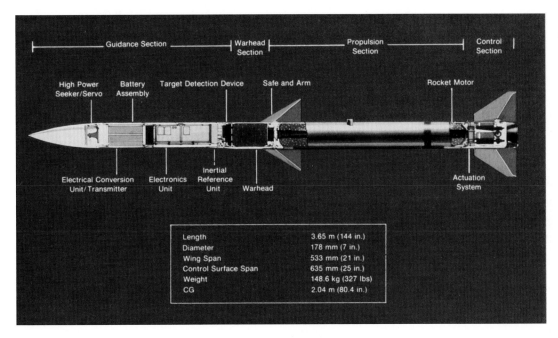

Cross-section of the AMRAAM air-to-air missile.

This SM-3 Standard missile launched from the Aegis cruiser USS *Lake Erie* (CG 70) successfully brought down an errant U.S. satellite high over the Pacific Ocean in February 2008.

A Sea Sparrow surface-to-air missile launches from the aircraft carrier USS *Theodore Roosevelt* (CVN 71). (Nathan Laird)

and a ceiling of 110,000 feet. The newest version, the Standard-3 ER, about the same size and weight as the Standard-2 ER, has a range of over 270 miles, a ceiling in excess of 150 miles, and was developed for use as an ABM. An upgraded version of the Standard-2 ER, the SM-6 ERAM (extended range active missile), is slated to become operational in 2010. It will have improved capabilities against agile cruise missiles and over-the-horizon targets.

In February 2008 a Standard-3 ER was used to intercept and blow up a falling 1,000-pound National Reconnaissance Office satellite some 130 miles above the North Pacific. Launched into a polar orbit at 17,000 miles per hour, the satellite failed soon after orbital insertion, and was threatening to impact possibly populated areas as its orbit degenerated. The SM-3 missile, launched from the cruiser *Lake Erie* (CG-70), successfully detonated near the school/bus–sized satellite, blowing it apart into some eighty pieces, which then fell harmlessly into the Pacific.

The RIM-7 Sea Sparrow is a radar guided surface-to-air missile adapted from the earlier air-to-air version for point defense for surface combatants. The latest version, called the ESSM (evolved Sea Sparrow missile), is 12 feet long and weighs about 500 pounds. It is used on only a few ship types including CVAs and LHAs in the U.S. Navy, but is a primary air defense weapon aboard many NATO surface warships. It provides excellent defensive capabilities against high performance aircraft and cruise missiles.

Navy Air-to-Surface Missiles

The Navy has several different types of air-to-surface missiles (AGM) and other guided ordnance designed to attack a wide range of surface targets, including armor, air defenses, ground transportation, and ships.

The AGM-65 Maverick missile is used for close air support of friendly ground forces, interdiction of enemy forces, and suppression of enemy weapon systems. It has two types of warheads. One has a contact fuse in the nose so that it will detonate on impact, and the other has a delayed fuse that allows the missile to penetrate well into hard targets before exploding. The AGM-88 HARM (high-speed antiradiation) missile is designed to home in on and destroy enemy radars used to locate and track U.S. aircraft, missiles, and ships. The AGM-114 Hellfire missile is a laser guided subsonic missile intended mainly for launching by Navy Seahawk helicopters against tanks or other types of enemy armored vehicles. It can also be used as an air-to-air weapon against helicopters or slow-moving fixed-wing aircraft.

Another more recently developed air-to-surface weapon is the AGM-154 joint stand-off weapon (JSOW). It is a large glide bomb developed by a joint Navy–Air Force program to allow aircraft to attack surface targets while remaining at safe stand-off distances, thus greatly increasing aircraft survivability. The JSOW has a range of from 12 to 40 nautical miles, depending on the altitude at which

A Navy Seahawk helicopter fires a Hellfire missile. (Mark Leonesio)

it is launched. A powered version has a range in excess of 120 nautical miles.

There is also a guidance kit called the joint direct attack munition (JDAM) that converts conventional 1,000- and 2,000-pound bombs into precision-guided munitions using the satellite-based GPS system for guidance. Weapons of this type are often referred to as *smart bombs*, to distinguish them from older unguided bombs that follow ballistic trajectories after being released from the delivering aircraft.

An aviation ordinanceman arms a Maverick missile on a F/A-18 Hornet. (Gretchen Roth)

Navy Undersea Warfare Weapons

Today, the Navy's primary operational undersea warfare (USW) weapons are antisubmarine rockets (ASROC) and antisubmarine torpedoes.

The ASROC is a supersonic, solid-fueled, antisubmarine ballistic missile, carried by Aegis cruisers and *Arleigh Burke*–class destroyers, and fired from vertical launch tubes. The purpose of ASROC is the destruction of enemy submarines at long ranges. It does this by the delivery of a homing torpedo through the air to a point in the water from which it can begin a search pattern to find and home in on the target submarine. An ASROC-equipped USW ship can launch its weapons before the submarine is even aware that it is under attack.

In addition to ASROC, the Navy has several other models of USW torpedoes that can be launched by surface ships and by helicopters. All of these are homing torpedoes guided by the sound of the vessel being attacked or by reflected echoes from it. They are powered by electric motors and batteries. They contain acoustic homing devices, operating either in an active or passive mode. The *active acoustic torpedo* is not dependent upon the sound emitted from the target for its homing information. The torpedo itself generates and transmits acoustic pulses, some of which are reflected from the target. The returning echoes guide the torpedo to the target. The *passive acoustic torpedo* homes in on the noise emitted from the target. It can often be evaded by the use of simple noise-maker-type countermeasures, or the submarine can reduce speed or stop in order to quiet sources of noise. Homing torpedoes of both types can be launched from submarines, surface vessels such as destroyers and cruisers, and helicopters.

Guided Missile Trajectories

The *trajectory* of a missile is its path from launch to impact or destruct. There are two basic types of missile trajectories: ballistic and aerodynamic. A number of other trajectories are named according to the path traveled, such as glide, powered flight, terminal, and standard, among others.

In a *ballistic* trajectory, the missile is acted upon only by gravity and aerodynamic drag after the propulsive force is terminated. Gun projectiles have a purely ballistic trajectory. The major part of the trajectory of ballistic missiles is of this type. An *aerodynamic* trajectory is one in which aerodynamic forces (thrust, drag, weight, and lift) are used to maintain the flight path.

Missile trajectories include many shapes or types of curves. The exact nature of the curve is determined by the type of guidance and the nature of the control system used. A *hyperbolic* trajectory, for instance, will occur with a missile using a hyperbolic guidance system. The missile will first climb to the desired altitude, then follow an arc of a hyperbola before diving on its target.

A *pursuit curve* is followed by most homing and beam rider missiles. At any given instant, the missile is pointed directly toward the target. If such a missile pursues a crossing target, the missile must follow a curved trajectory. In some cases, the extreme curvature required by the pursuit course as the missile nears the target may be too sharp for the missile to follow. In this case, a highly maneuverable aircraft with a proficient pilot may be successful in

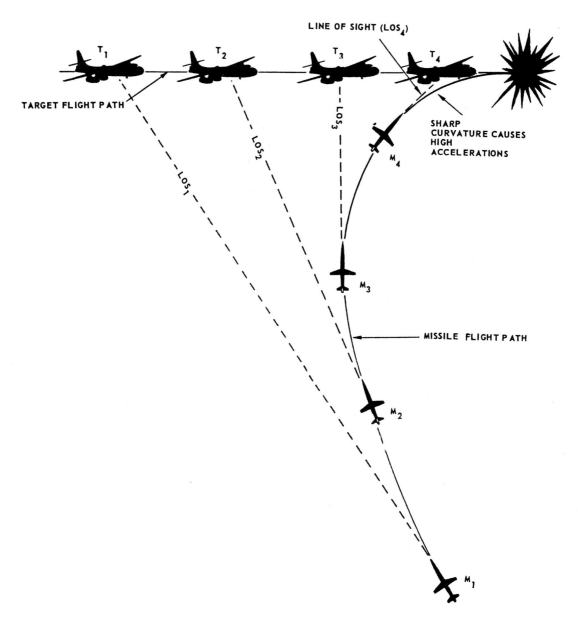

The pursuit homing or zero-bearing missile intercept path followed by most homing and beam rider missiles.

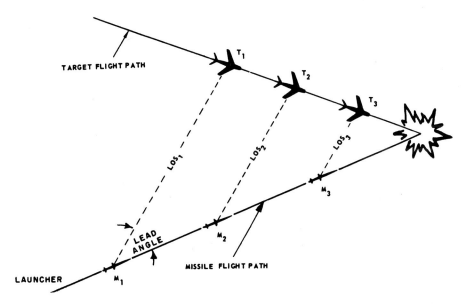

The lead angle modified pursuit missile intercept path.

executing radical maneuvers that will "lose" the missile pursuer. American pilots became adept at outmaneuvering Soviet-made surface-to-air missiles fired from the Hanoi area in North Vietnam during the latter days of the Vietnam War.

Some homing missiles follow a *modified pursuit course*, flying not toward the target but toward a point in front of it. The missile thus develops a *lead angle*, and the curvature of its course is decreased. A refinement of the lead angle course involves a computer, either in the missile or at a control station, that can use known information about the missile and target to calculate a point of intercept that missile and target will reach at the same instant. The computer will compensate for changes in target course, and calculate new intercept points.

ICBMs such as Trident are launched vertically so they can get through the densest part of the atmosphere as soon as possible. At a certain computed altitude, which is controlled by preset guidance, the missile inclines to a more gradual climb. After booster burnout or shutdown of the propulsion system, the missile coasts along a ballistic trajectory to the target.

Combination trajectories are followed by ASROC weapons. The ASROC is fired from a ship and boosted into the air by rocket thrust. After rocket burnout, the torpedo goes through the air in a ballistic trajectory until striking the water. After water entry, the torpedo dives to a preset depth and then begins its homing target search. When it detects an echo from the target, it follows a pursuit path to attack it.

A missile's trajectory is, of course, greatly affected by the design of the missile and its guidance system. But natural external forces affect the trajectory also. These include wind, gravity, magnetic forces, and the Coriolis effect. All of these factors must be taken into account with any long-range missile. Modern computers and guidance systems are usually able to compensate for these effects and keep the missile on a correct course to its target.

STUDY GUIDE QUESTIONS

1. What are the following types of planes principally used for?

    A. Attack plane

    B. Fighter plane

    C. Patrol plane

    D. Reconnaissance plane

2. What type of weapon has become the main armament on most of today's naval fighter and attack aircraft?

3. What are the four basic parts of a guided missile?

4. A. What is the high-explosive part of a missile called?

    B. What kind of high explosive may it be?

5. What are the five types of guidance systems used by most Navy guided missiles?

6. What Navy missile is a part of the nation's strategic defense system?

7. What is the purpose of an antiballistic missile?

8. A. What is the Harpoon missile?

    B. What are its principal features and range?

9. A. What is the Tomahawk missile?

    B. What are its capabilities?

10. What are the three Ts that provided the surface Navy with its principal antiair defensive capability during the 1970s and 1980s?

11. What are the capabilities of the three Standard missile versions presently in use?

12. A. How do homing torpedoes operate?

    B. What are the two types of homing torpedoes?

13. What are the two basic types of missile trajectories?

14. A. Describe a missile pursuit curve.

    B. How may a pilot evade such missiles?

15. What kind of a trajectory is followed by most long-range ballistic missiles?

16. What natural external forces affect a missile's trajectory?

CRITICAL THINKING

1. Are naval aircraft designed for a specific weapon system or is a weapon system adapted to fit an airplane? Give evidence to support your answer.

2. Research three current naval aircraft and identify their weapons capabilities.

3. Research and describe some of the possible tactics that could be used by an aircraft seeking to evade radar-guided air-to-air or surface-to-air missiles.

VOCABULARY

guided missile
warhead
ballistic missile flight path
FBM
lock on
evasive maneuvers
cruise missile
over-the-horizon (OTH)
homing torpedo
acoustic homing

AMRAAM
air-to-surface missile (AGM)
antiradiation missile
ASROC
ICBM
ABM
lead angle
pursuit curve
air-to-air missile (AIM)
surface-to-air missile (SAM/RIM)

4 Mine Warfare

A *mine* as used in naval warfare is a device containing a charge of explosive in a watertight casing, floating on, moored in, or planted under a waterway for the purpose of blowing up an enemy vessel that strikes it or passes close by it. Mine warfare may be divided into defensive and offensive mining, and mine countermeasures. *Defensive mining* is that which is done to protect a nation's own harbors and shorelines. *Offensive mining* may be used to bottle up enemy harbors, to render their shipping routes dangerous or impossible to use, and to make the enemy divert ships, equipment, and personnel to minesweeping chores. By spreading minefields over as wide an area as possible, and by using several different types of mines, the problem of removing or *sweeping* them is made formidable, and safe shipping routes become more and more difficult to maintain. Offensive minefields also force enemy shipping to go through areas where it may be more readily attacked.

Mine countermeasures constitute all methods of countering an enemy's mines. These measures include self-protection for ships, as well as the sweeping of mines.

Evolution of Mine Warfare

During the American Revolution, David Bushnell attempted to break the British blockade of the Delaware River at Philadelphia with floating kegs filled with gunpowder and equipped with con-

tact-firing devices. An unfortunate current caused the kegs to go astray, and red tape in Congress prevented additional expenditures on the concept. In the early nineteenth century, Robert Fulton, the inventor of the steamship, contributed to a slowly developing concept in naval warfare by demonstrating that a ship could be sunk by an underwater explosion.

By the time of the Civil War, "torpedoes" moored in harbors and rivers were considered a prime naval weapon, especially by the Confederates, who used them to defend against the much larger Union Navy.

Admiral David G. Farragut's attack at Mobile Bay in 1864 remains one of the more dramatic episodes in the history of mine warfare. The Confederates had planted some two hundred mines, then called torpedoes, to force Union ships into a channel covered by shore batteries, an early use of a mining tactic that later became standard. When the Union monitor *Tecumseh* hit a submerged mine, blew up, and sank, the Confederate batteries opened fire. Progress into the harbor became confused, and the Union force seemed in danger of defeat. At this crucial point, however, Admiral Farragut personally ordered his force ahead with the famous quotation "Damn the torpedoes—full speed ahead!" taking a calculated risk that no additional mines would explode because of saltwater deterioration. He was right, and the battle was won. With a more reliable mine, the Confederates might have frustrated the

An American mine storage depot at Inverness, Scotland, in World War I. Mines were assembled here to await deployment by the mine squadrons that laid the North Sea barrage.

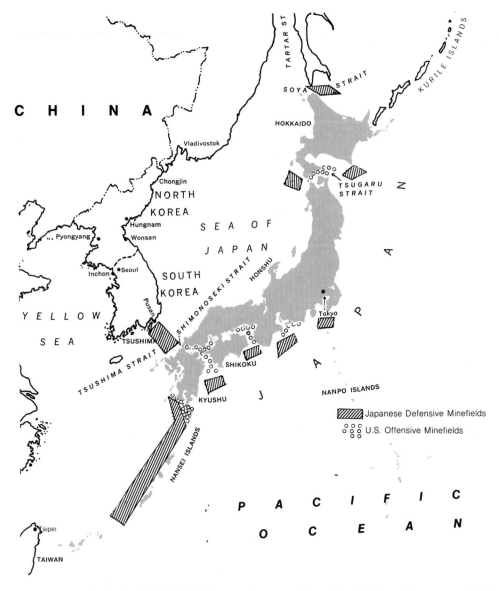

Mine laying in Japanese waters was extensive during World War II. This map shows positions of both U.S. and Japanese minefields in the Shimonoseki Straits and the Sea of Japan.

Union attempt to close the last major Southern port, won a major naval victory, and prolonged the war. Thus was dramatized the problem of mine deterioration, a baffler that modern science has not yet entirely solved.

Mines were considered only a defensive weapon until the Russo-Japanese War of 1904-5. The Japanese sowed offensive minefields across entrances to Russian harbors and then enticed the Russian fleet out with a show of inferior forces; the mines sank six ships. The Russians mined defensively with even more success, sinking nine Japanese ships. After the war, several ships of other nations were sunk by free-floating mines that had broken loose from their wartime moorings, giving rise to the 1907 Hague Convention concerning floating mines. The convention sought to restrict the use of floating mines unless they could self-deactivate after a time.

International law, however, imposes few other restrictions on mine warfare. Moored or bottom mines need not be made to deactivate automatically after a prescribed time.

These developments called attention to mines and opened up new uses for them, but it was not until World War I that offensive use of mines was actively pursued.

The most extensive effort involving mines in World War I was the great Allied North Sea mine barrage laid between northern Scotland and the Norwegian coast. It was designed to keep German U-boats confined in the North Sea and allow the Allies to use Atlantic shipping routes in comparative safety. American minelayers planted some 57,000 of these mines, and the British planted over 13,000. They were the anchored contact type, spherical and studded with "horns." There is no definitive information as to the success of this field in sinking U-boats, but that it kept them bottled up to a considerable extent is certain. This damaged German submariners' morale and simultaneously boosted the morale of American and British merchant seamen upon whom wartime logistics depended.

Postwar statistics reveal that mines sank more ships than did torpedoes and gunfire combined during World War I. The cost of the North Sea barrage was determined to be equal to the cost of prosecuting the war for one day, so if it shortened the war by even that much, it was a good investment.

Mine warfare of World War II featured offensive mine-laying by both submarines and aircraft. Defensive mining was carried out mainly by conventional types of surface minelayers, and mine clearance was done primarily by surface craft equipped with special minesweeping gear. Countermeasures included novel devices for protection and detection.

In the opening months of the war, Nazi submarines and aircraft sowed extensive minefields off the English and Scottish coasts. A number of British ships were sunk by this mine barrage, which was especially heavy in the Thames estuary. Early in the war, however, the Germans lost one of their secret weapons, an influence mine designed to be triggered by the magnetic field of a passing steel-hulled ship. The mine, dropped by an airplane, overshot its mark and landed intact in a mud bank. The British recovered the mine and shortly thereafter produced a successful countermeasure, doubtlessly saving countless Allied ships.

Japanese minefields in the Pacific during the war were also quite extensive. They used defensive minefields to protect their major bases and harbors. Their minefields west of the Nansei Shoto protected shipping in the East China Sea throughout the war. Until the last months of the war, the Sea of Japan was effectively sealed off from American submarine and surface ships by Japanese fields in the straits leading into that body of water from the Pacific. Both the Americans and the Japanese laid offensive fields to destroy or divert enemy shipping.

During the Korean and Vietnam wars, Communist forces floated mines down rivers into harbors and out to sea. Several

This ship was the victim of a Viet Cong mine floated down the Long Tau River leading to Saigon during the Vietnam War.

Allied ships were sunk by mines during the former conflict. The Viet Cong also used improvised controlled mines in the rivers of South Vietnam, which they would detonate from shore whenever a suitable target came within range. Later, drifting mines caused damage to ships of several nations in the Persian Gulf during the Iran-Iraq War in the 1980s, and to several U.S. warships during Operation Desert Storm in 1991.

Mine Classification

Mines are classified according to the method of planting (surface, aircraft, or submarine), the final planted position (moored, bottom, or drifting), the mode of operation (controlled or automatic), and the detonating or actuation mechanism (contact or influence).

Method of planting. Mines can be planted by surface craft when secrecy is not of prime importance. High-speed minelayers can carry many mines and can lay a large minefield in a relatively short time. Presently, however, the U.S. Navy has no minelayers in commissioned service.

Planting mines by submarine can be accomplished with great secrecy and at great distances from home ports. Once the minefield has been laid, however, friendly submarines cannot navigate in the area during the armed life of the planted mines.

Aircraft-planted mines can be carried and released like bombs or torpedoes. A parachute is attached to the mine to slow its descent; the parachute separates from the mine case and sinks on impact with the water. Aircraft can carry mines into enemy-held areas, and the field can be replenished, if necessary, without danger from previously planted mines. There is little secrecy in planting aerial mines, though night-flying planes can be used to some extent. Aircraft can mine coastal and shallow waters that no other platform could possibly mine. Blockading enemy shipping lanes and harbors can be very effectively accomplished by this type of mining.

Planted position. Moored mines have buoyant cases containing the explosive charge. They are kept at a predetermined depth by mooring cables attached to an anchor. Because the depth of the mines can be controlled by the length of their mooring cables, the mines can be deployed in shallow water against small craft, or in deeper water against major surface ships and submarines. The main disadvantage is that they may be cleared with comparative ease by mechanical sweeping gear.

For that reason, bottom mines were developed. They can be planted by any type of craft, and because they lie on the bottom, they require costly minesweeping gear to detect and remove them, both difficult tasks. They cannot be planted in water depths greater than 30 fathoms, unless intended as antisubmarine weapons.

Drifting mines are not actually planted, in the true sense. Often, however, a drifting mine is a moored mine that has broken loose from its mooring cable and has become a hazard to all international navigation, neutral and belligerent alike.

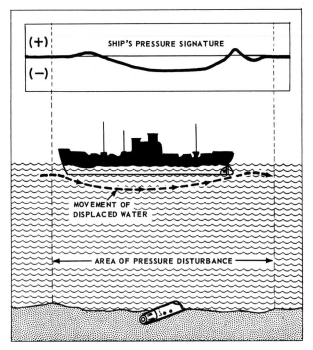

A pressure mine is detonated by the change in water pressure caused by a ship passing over it. The movement of displaced water as the ship passes is called the ship's pressure signature. This type of mine is the most difficult to sweep.

Mode of operation. Controlled mines are no longer used by the United States Navy, but many varieties of them were used in rivers by the Vietcong in Vietnam. They are manually detonated by a person on shore when an enemy ship is near the mine. Most mines today are designed to detonate automatically when a firing mechanism detects a ship nearby.

Method of actuation. Actual contact of a ship with a mine or its antenna is required to detonate a *contact* mine. One common contact mine is equipped with lead horns encasing glass tubes containing an electrolyte. When a horn is struck and bent, the glass tube is broken and the electrolyte flows into a battery cell, generating enough current to detonate the mine. Another type closes an "inertia switch," which completes an electric circuit.

There are three basic types of *influence* mines: magnetic, acoustic, and pressure. The firing mechanisms of two or all three of these maybe interlocked in the case of a combination mine, making it more difficult to sweep. Influence mines are normally of the bottom type. The *magnetic* mine is triggered by the target ship's magnetic field. When a ship passes, the firing circuit is actuated and the mine detonates. The *acoustic* mine is triggered by the noise produced by a passing ship's propellers, machinery, or hull vibrations. The firing mechanism can be set to react only to specific sounds, so it will not be actuated by any normal sea sounds. The *pressure* mine is triggered by the change in water pressure caused by a ship passing over the mine. It is the most difficult of the three basic influence types to sweep.

A *combination* mine, detonated by the simultaneous actuation of two or all three of the foregoing types of firing mechanisms, is more effective because it is less susceptible to activation by false targets and harder to sweep. In order for such a mine to detonate, for example, the pressure influence of a ship may have to close a switch at the same time as its magnetic field influences a coil. The U.S. arsenal contains mines detonated by simultaneous actuation of all three mechanisms. Such mines are almost impossible to sweep.

In addition to the combination of various influence mechanisms, "counters" have been installed in some mines. These are designed to cause the mine to remain inert until the actuation process has occurred a preset number of times. This is intended to give the enemy a false sense of security, by setting up the mines for activation after minesweeping operations have been "successfully concluded" without mishap.

Perhaps the most unusual "mine" in the Navy arsenal is not really a mine at all. Called the CAPTOR (encapsulated torpedo), it consists of an acoustic homing torpedo moored to the bottom with about 300 meters (feet) of cable. Primarily a USW weapon, the torpedo, upon identifying a submarine acoustic signature, is automatically released to home in on and destroy the submarine.

Mine Countermeasures

Mine countermeasures (MCM) include all actions taken to protect friendly shipping against mines. The three major types of mine countermeasures are ship treatment against magnetic and acoustic mines, minesweeping, and mine hunting.

The two principal methods of treating a steel-hulled ship to decrease the magnetic effects that actuate magnetic influence mines are *deperming* and *degaussing*. The hull of a steel ship normally acquires a significant permanent magnetic field during construction. This occurs because the steel plates of the hull are constantly being heated, riveted, and hammered during building, causing the iron molecules to align themselves with the Earth's magnetic field. A ship also has an induced magnetic field caused by the interaction of the moving ship with the Earth's magnetic field.

The purpose of deperming is to reduce a ship's permanent magnetic field to a minimum. Done by means of wrapping the hull with electric coils after the completion of construction, this process is essentially a large-scale version of demagnetizing a magnet. Degaussing was developed by the British during World War II to defeat the aforementioned German influence mine. It neutralizes the strength of both the induced and permanent magnetic fields of a ship by means of an arrangement of electric coils installed within the hull of the ship. Basically, a direct current is sent through the coils to produce a magnetic field in exact opposition to that generated by the ship itself, thus nullifying any magnetic effects.

The MCM 1 *Avenger* mine countermeasures ship.

Though these measures can greatly reduce the magnetic signature of a steel-hulled ship, some residual magnetic field is always generated by all steel vessels. Consequently, minesweeper hulls are built of wood, fiberglass, aluminum, or other nonmagnetic materials.

Very little can be done to protect a ship from acoustic mines. Most underwater noise generated by ships is caused by the movement of the screw blades with respect to the water. This effect is called *cavitation* because of the bubbles of water vapor that are formed and collapse at sonic or subsonic frequencies around the tips of the blades. Some noise also is produced by water flowing over sharp surfaces on the hull and by machinery inside the ship. Beyond the *Albacore* hull design of nuclear submarines, it appears

that little more can be done to change substantially the acoustic characteristics associated with a ship's hull. Research is ongoing to develop a screw shape that would reduce cavitation, at least to some degree. For now, however, underwater ship noise can be reduced only by slowing the speed of the ship, using special noise-reducing mountings for machinery that must operate, and shutting down nonvital noise-producing machinery.

Minesweeping is done by traversing a mined area with mechanical sweeps that set moored mines adrift by cutting their mooring cables, and with influence sweeps that simulate the necessary characteristics to cause detonation of influence mines. The sweeps can be dragged through the area either by minesweeping ships or, in some cases, by a helicopter. Minesweeping helicopters were developed in the 1970s, and have been extensively used as sweeping vehicles in most mine-clearing operations conducted by the U.S. Navy since.

The Navy's primary mine countermeasure force is the fourteen-ship *Avenger*-class of mine countermeasures ships built during the 1980s. They are made of wood sheathed in fiberglass, and can find, classify, and destroy moored and bottom mines. They have both conventional minesweeping gear and newer devices such as remotely operated underwater vehicles to seek out and destroy mines. The Navy's new littoral combat ships also have a minehunting capability.

Mine Hunting

Mine hunting is the methodical detection, location, and neutralization of mines. It involves searching an area with mine-detecting gear to locate mines and then removing them by the use of divers or

A mine countermeasure Sea Stallion helicopter tows a magnetic minesweeping sled past an Egyptian merchant ship while sweeping the Suez Canal during Operation Nimbus Star in 1974. The canal had been closed for seven years by Egyptian mines laid during the Arab-Israeli wars of the 1960s.

One of several models of newly developed autonomous underwater vehicles (AUVs) that can hunt for submerged mines.

A Navy Marine Mammal Program dolphin named Kdog doing mine-hunting work in the Persian Gulf during Operation Iraqi Freedom. The dolphins in the program are trained to report back to their handlers if they detect a mine or a swimmer.

destroying them with explosive charges. Highly trained personnel operate devices called ordnance locators to find the mines; there is a small version of this equipment that can be carried by a diver.

In recent years several experimental versions of self-propelled *autonomous underwater vehicles* (AUVs) have been developed that can be programmed to search for mines automatically after being launched by a mine-hunter vessel. They resemble long torpedoes, but are fitted with electronic mine detection gear and follow search tracks beneath the water. Some have self-contained (SINS) guidance systems that use GPS to determine their position. Sea testing of several models has been conducted and may result in their becoming operational over the next several years.

For many years there has been an ongoing effort to use trained dolphins to search for mines and enemy swimmers as part of the Navy Marine Mammals Program. They work with human handlers in much the same way as police dogs do on land. Dolphins from the program were used in the Persian Gulf in both Operations Desert Storm and Iraqi Freedom, and performed well. There are currently some seventy-five dolphins in the program at Navy bases on the Gulf and West Coasts.

Mine Warfare Capabilities

Of all the aspects of mine warfare, none is as significant as the profound psychological effect of the mine. Almost invariably the danger of mines is judged to be much greater that the actual physical threat. Because a minefield is hidden, unknown in extent, and difficult to assess, there is a usual tendency to overestimate the threat. It is not the calculation of the minefield's effectiveness by the minelayer, but the enemy's estimate of the threat that is important.

In addition to the tactical effects of mine warfare, there is no question that the use or threat of use of mines has had a strong effect on political and military strategy. Mines possess a number of unique qualities that make them very significant in strategic planning.

Mines are versatile. They can do direct damage to military units, but they can also attack the enemy's economy. Ships carry the large bulk of international trade goods, and they are vulnerable to attack and total loss. Mines can destroy a nation's merchant marine. They can increase damage to enemy forces by restricting their area of operations, thereby making their ships more susceptible to attack.

Mines are passive weapons. The target comes to the mine. This has a number of advantages. The mine maintains its vigilance for a considerable amount of time, without continued commitment of forces. The enemy is faced with a choice between confrontation of the minefield and acceptance of a blockade situation.

Mines are selective weapons. They can be set to be detonated only by a very specific size or class of target, and can be selective in depth or range. Mines are flexible in duration and times of activation. They can be rendered harmless during selected time intervals or after a set time duration. They can also, in effect, change the geography of the battlespace, by making certain areas impassable to ships. An area that has been declared dangerous because of the use of mines is usually treated with great respect and avoided as though it were land.

An effective mine blockade may aid significantly in gaining a victory over an enemy country. Such a blockade can destroy the enemy's economy, cause food shortages, enable conservation of friendly attacking forces, psychologically destroy the enemy morale and will to resist, and prevent sortie of enemy forces from their harbors.

Other strategic advantages of mine warfare that might accrue to a belligerent using it effectively are:

- Forcing the enemy to engage in mine countermeasures, tying up personnel and resources at little cost to the minelayer
- Delay of shipping and disruption of cargo-handling facilities at ports on both ends of a supply line, even if no ship is sunk
- Demoralization of both ship and shore crews faced with confronting a minefield
- Cost-effective potential physical, political, and psychological damage to the enemy
- The potential for mine blockade without direct harm to the local populace can be a useful weapon to force settlement of disputes without actual combat, or to constrain a limited war.

STUDY GUIDE QUESTIONS

1. What are the three principal aspects of mine warfare?

2. How is defensive mining used?

3. How is offensive mining used?

4. Where was the first American attempt at mine warfare in the Revolutionary War carried out?

5. Who conducted research in the early nineteenth century demonstrating that ships were vulnerable to underwater explosions?

6. A. What was the famous Civil War sea battle in which mines played a crucial part?

   B. Who was the Union naval commander, and what was his famous directive?

7. Following the Russo-Japanese War, why was there an attempt to place international legal restrictions on some aspects of mine warfare?

8. A. What was the most extensive Allied mining effort in World War I?

   B. What was it designed to do?

9. What two new offensive minelaying methods were employed during World War II?

10. What secret German mine was captured early in World War II, enabling the British to develop countermeasures against this major German weapon?

11. Where were Japanese defensive mining operations conducted in the Pacific during World War II?

12. What are the major methods by which mines can be planted?

13. A. How are moored mines kept at predetermined depths so they may be used against either small craft or major vessels?

    B. What is their main disadvantage?

14. A. Why was the bottom mine developed?

    B. What are its major limitations?

15. A. What are the three basic types of influence mines?

    B. What is a fourth type that complicates sweeping?

16. What are the two methods of treating a ship's steel hull to decrease magnetic effects that actuate magnetic mines?

17. What new type of platform was developed for minesweeping operations in the 1970s?

18. What marine mammal is used by the Navy to hunt for mines?

19. What is often the most profound impact of the mine on an enemy?

20. How can mines be used to change the geography of the ocean battlespace?

CRITICAL THINKING

1. Research the ways in which modern mines might be laid by both open and covert means in order to effectively blockade an enemy port.

2. Describe why and how a credible threat of a minefield can be as effective in controlling enemy shipping and diverting enemy mine-clearing assets as an actual minefield.

VOCABULARY

mine
deterioration
mine countermeasures
minesweeping
contact mine
deperming
degaussing
magnetic mine

pressure mine
acoustic mine
CAPTOR mine
actuation mechanism
AUV
mine hunting
passive weapon
combination mine

5 Chemical, Biological, and Nuclear Warfare

The previous chapters of this unit have discussed various types of weapons and weapon systems with which the naval forces of the United States and other countries of the world are equipped. Most of these weapons depend for their effectiveness on the delivery of some type of high-explosive warhead or explosive device. Such weapons are collectively called *conventional weapons*. In addition to these, there are other potentially far more devastating types of weapons in the arsenals of many of today's military forces. These are collectively referred to as *CBR weapons* (chemical, biological, and radiological or nuclear), or sometimes *special weapons* or *weapons of mass destruction*, to differentiate them from conventional weapons. They can inflict massive destruction over a large area, or mass casualties among a population.

Although they are often thought of along with nuclear weapons as being relatively new concepts, in actuality chemical and biological agents (substances) have been in use in warfare for many centuries. Even in ancient times it was common practice to disrupt an enemy's food-production capability by spreading salt on agricultural fields, or contaminate the water supply by dumping dead animals or vegetation into it. More lethal chemical weapons such as mustard (blister) gas were developed and used in the trench warfare of World War I, and the use of smoke of various kinds to mask movements at sea was a major tactic until well after the advent of radar in the mid-1940s.

Fortunately, the widespread use of chemical and biological warfare agents in World War II and in more recent conflicts since has been held in check for the most part by threats of retaliation and international accords limiting their use, but many nations still have some of these kinds of weapons. Their use by unprincipled nations against weaker foes unable to retaliate has been documented several times in recent decades, as for example Iraq's use of blister gas against Iranian forces during their protracted war of attrition in the 1980s, and Soviet use of blister and possibly nerve gas against rebel Afghan forces during the same years.

Iraq's Saddam Hussein threatened to use chemical and possibly biological agents against U.S. and other coalition forces, as well as against Israel, during Operation Desert Storm in 1991. His forces set fire to most of the oil wells in Kuwait following the Iraqi withdrawal, the smoke and soot from which greatly hindered occupying coalition forces for months thereafter. In late 1995, a group of Japanese terrorists used a nerve-gas agent in an attack against civilians in a Japanese subway, incapacitating all those exposed. More recently,

anthrax-laced mailings were sent to several private and U.S. government buildings following the terrorist attacks of 11 September 2001, allegedly by a disgruntled government research scientist.

The age of nuclear weapons began in 1945 with the Allied use of the American-built atomic bomb against the Japanese cities Hiroshima and Nagasaki in the closing days of World War II, followed by the development of the hydrogen bomb shortly thereafter. The end of the war ushered in a fifty-year-long era of nuclear confrontation and stalemate between the Soviet Union and the United States and their respective major power allies called the Cold War, which did not end until the dissolution of the USSR in the early 1990s.

An expanding circle of radioactive material sweeps out over target ships moored at a mid-Pacific test site at Bikini atoll in 1946.

Fortunately much progress has been made since then with disarmament negotiations and international accords among the remaining world powers that has done much to limit the spread and diminish the stockpiles of CBR weapons. Nevertheless, some threat of potential use of these weapons persists, especially by countries who might develop and use them to blackmail their neighbors into submission if allowed to do so, and by extremists and terrorists who manage to obtain weapons of this type. Thus, even in the post–Cold War era, the United States and its allies are required to maintain strong deterrent capabilities in order to try to discourage any aggressive use of CBR weapons in the future.

The following sections summarize current capabilities in CBR warfare, and some of the damage control measures that could be taken in the event of their use in any future conflict.

Chemical Warfare

Chemical warfare (CW) is the military use of any chemical to harass or cause casualties among enemy forces. Chemical warfare agents are poisonous chemicals that can cause death, injury, or irritating effects. They may be gases, vapors, powders, or liquids, and include screening smokes and incendiaries. Though they can be deadly, chemical warfare agents are often unstable and difficult to produce and store, and can be dispersed and rendered ineffective by weather and sunlight.

Chemical warfare agents can be difficult to detect and some are lethal in very small concentrations. Upwind dispersal of chemical agents could contaminate a large area with devastating results. Chemical smoke screens have been used to hide one's own ships or forces, or to confuse enemy forces. The smokes can be combined with other chemical agents as well. Incendiaries—chemical compounds that burn with terrific heat—may be dropped by aircraft, fired in shells, or used with flamethrowers. They include napalm, jellied gasoline, and thermite and magnesium bombs. But the most dangerous CW threat is the use of casualty and harassing agents against troops or civilian populations.

CW gases cause bodily damage according to the type used. The most common types of CW agents are nerve gases, blister gases, blood gases, choking gases, psycho gases, and vomiting and tear gases. A protective gas mask can protect the eyes and lungs against many of these agents, and specially treated garments will protect the skin.

Nerve gases are the most deadly of the CW agents. They were developed by the Germans in World War II but never used in that war. Entering the body through the nose, skin, or mouth, they are quick killers. Protection against nerve gases depends on speed in detection, masking, and self- or first-aid. These are the most probable CW agents to be used in the future, according to many analysts.

Blister gases cause blisters on the skin. A type of blister gas called mustard gas was used extensively in World War I; it caused many casualties on both sides. Either in liquid or vapor form, these gases cause painful burns and blisters on the skin and can damage the eyes even more seriously. If breathed into the lungs, blister gases will inflame the throat, windpipe, and lungs, often resulting in pneumonia and death.

Blood gases directly affect heart action and interfere with the absorption of oxygen by the body. The body tissues suffocate and die. A mild exposure will produce headache, dizziness, and nausea, followed by recovery within a few hours. Heavy exposure will cause

a speedy death. These gases have not been successfully used in war because they are very light and dissipate quickly. They would probably not be used by themselves.

Choking gases (lung irritants) act on the respiratory system and are often fatal. Chlorine and phosgene are two common types. Phosgene was used in World War I and caused casualties second only to mustard gas. These gases cause the lungs to fill with liquid, causing death due to lack of oxygen.

Psycho gases produce a mentally confused state that includes hallucinations, anger, and inability to sleep. They may also cause physical symptoms such as dizziness, blurred vision, fainting spells, and severe muscle weakness. These gases make people completely ineffective, but they do not kill. Their effects last from eight hours to four days. According to some analysts, psycho gases could be widely used in future wars.

Vomiting gases and *tear gases* produce unpleasant symptoms, but usually for only a short time. They are not intended to cause death. They are used to control riots, to force people out of buildings or caves, or to capture enemy forces without serious injury. They are often used in training exercises. Because they are really vapors, protective gas masks give complete protection if used quickly and correctly. Mixture of these agents with more lethal gases is possible, however; if that were done, many casualties could quickly occur.

All of these chemical warfare agents can be delivered via gun projectiles, missiles, or aircraft bombs or spray tanks.

Biological Warfare

Biological warfare (BW) is the use of living organisms (bacteria, spores, or fungi) or toxins (powerful biologic poisons) to reduce the ability of an enemy to wage war by destroying or contaminating food or water supplies or by spreading epidemic disease. A BW attack would most probably consist of an aerosol spray (fog-like droplets) released into air currents or water supplies, or a powder that people might ingest. BW agents can be released by aircraft, bombs, and missiles, or even by enemy agents or terrorists. Like certain chemical agents, it only takes a very small amount of many of these agents to do serious harm.

A slow laboratory testing process is necessary to detect biological warfare agents, which are very difficult to identify. Many people could become casualties by the time the agent is identified. Once identified, however, diseases caused by most BW agents can be successfully treated. Most BW agents die or lose their effectiveness after a few days of exposure to sunlight and ordinary weather conditions. Food and clothing suspected of being contaminated should be boiled before use. Canned goods are normally considered safe to use.

Vaccines are available against many potential BW agents such as anthrax and plague, and can be administered to military personnel and civilians in danger of being exposed to this kind of attack. Several kinds of antibiotics are effective in treating the effects of many kinds of BW agents after exposure.

Nuclear Warfare

Nuclear warfare involves the use of weapons or devices armed with nuclear warheads, or improvised "dirty bombs" with radioactive materials dispersed by conventional explosives.

When a nuclear warhead detonates, a tremendous shock wave is released, along with intense pulses of light, heat, and electromagnetic and nuclear radiation. These effects, though devastating, last only a few seconds. Subsequent radioactive fallout from this kind of attack can continue for days, and spread over large areas if carried by wind or water currents.

The shock wave, or blast, from a nuclear detonation, just as with any explosion, can smash ships, level buildings, and cause casualties for miles. The light pulse can blind anyone within miles. The thermonuclear heat, called thermal radiation, is so intense that any metal near ground zero (the site of the explosion) may melt, and flammable objects will burst into flame. Soft body tissue of anyone nearby will vaporize, and serious burns to exposed skin can occur out to as far as 25 miles away. The electromagnetic pulse (EMP) can fry electronics for miles around.

The *initial nuclear radiation*, or first radiation, cannot be seen or felt, but it can be as deadly as any of the other effects. This radiation is made up of alpha (like a helium nucleus) and beta (high-energy electron) particles, high-speed neutrons, and gamma rays. All these particles and rays are lethal to human tissue. Alpha particles can be stopped by a sheet of paper; beta particles can be stopped by a thin sheet of aluminum. The others are much more difficult to stop with anything less than heavy lead shielding or some other dense substance.

Residual radiation, or *fallout*, consists of radioactive materials produced by the explosion, plus dust contaminated with alpha and beta particles. It may be deposited for days over a large area by wind and weather. This fallout can be detected and measured by special instruments called radiacs (Geiger counters). If it is present in hazardous concentrations, the area must be decontaminated (washed clean) before unprotected personnel can enter the area.

Ships may be exposed to three types of nuclear bursts: an air burst, in which the fireball does not touch the Earth; a surface burst, in which the fireball touches the surface; and a subsurface burst, in which the explosion is underwater. An air burst produces blast, heat, intense light, and initial radiation, but little fallout requiring decontamination. A surface burst will produce the same effects, plus much residual radiation. The fallout will spread radioactive contamination over a wide area downwind from the explosion. The subsurface burst normally produces little heat or light and very little initial radiation. The biggest danger in this type of burst is the intense underwater shock wave resulting from the

explosion, and heavy residual radiation from the highly contaminated base surge. This is the wall of heavy mist at sea, or cloud of dust on land, created around ground zero when the column of water or dirt formed by the explosion falls back to the surface.

In the case of radioactive material dispersed by a conventional explosive, there will be some shock and heat damage in close proximity as with all such detonations, but the most troublesome effect is the radioactive material that can be spread for some distance. Anyone or anything near the site of such an attack can be contaminated with this material. The site itself may be unusable for a long time until complete decontamination can be accomplished, if ever.

The effect of nuclear radiation on people depends on the intensity of the radiation and the time of exposure. The amount of radiation received is called the *dosage*, and is measured by devices such as film badges called *dosimeters*. The effects of radiation exposure are most severe on soft tissues in the body. They can vary from short-term illness and nausea, to hair loss, immune system deficiencies, sterility, long-term genetic defects, skin lesions, leukemia and other cancers, mental impairment, and severe sickness, delirium, and death within days or weeks, depending on the dosage received and the time interval over which it occurs. Moreover, the effects of radiation dosage are *cumulative*, meaning that even

When a CBR attack is anticipated, a ship will activate the water washdown system in order to wet all exposed surfaces to make the decontamination process after the attack easier. Here, a rainbow forms as a crew member checks out the system aboard the amphibious assault ship USS *Boxer* (LHD 4). (Rudy Pulach)

small exposures repeated often over time can have the same effects as large doses received all at once.

CBR Damage Control

The crew of a naval ship can do much to minimize the damage and casualties that might result from an attack with CBR weapons, except where a ship is at or near the point of impact (ground zero) of such weapons. Tests have shown that ships not receiving direct effects of such attacks have a very good chance of survival with relatively few casualties and with weapons systems still operable.

Before an attack, ships normally would be at general quarters (GQ), so the ship should be pretty well "buttoned up." Water washdown systems that spray salt water through sprinkler heads are turned on to wet all topside surfaces so most contaminants will tend to wash overboard. All nonvital openings of the ship are closed and Circle-William ventilation fittings are shut to maintain as complete a gas-tight envelope as possible. Protective gas masks are distributed to personnel who must breathe outside air. Topside personnel in exposed positions wear protective clothing as well as masks.

After the attack, trained personnel conduct surveys both topside and below deck throughout the ship using specialized equipment to determine the extent and location of contamination. Decontamination is then done in three phases. The first two, called *tactical decontamination*, take place immediately, at sea. They reduce contamination so the ship can carry out its mission without exposing the crew to dangerous levels of radiation or other contaminants.

Phase one is gross decontamination by saltwater washdown, done with firehoses by crew members wearing protective gear. It will eliminate 98 percent of the contamination if the surface was wet before the attack and washdown begins while it is still wet. If the surface has dried, only half of the contamination will be removed.

The second phase is detailed decontamination conducted by repair-party personnel and others of the ship's crew topside. They use a steam lance or hose, scrub brushes with detergents, scrapers, and flame torches to try to remove any remaining concentrations of contamination (called hot spots), and wash it overboard.

The final phase of decontamination would normally be conducted at advanced bases by repair ships and tenders using flame burning, acid dips, and sandblasting.

Decontamination of personnel is done with fire hoses or jury-rigged topside showers. All contaminated clothing and protective gear is discarded. Personnel scrub thoroughly with soap and water and dress out with uncontaminated clothing.

Crew members wearing full CBR protective gear conduct a topside contamination survey during a CBR warfare training exercise. (John Becman)

STUDY GUIDE QUESTIONS

1. What are conventional weapons?
2. What are some examples of the use of chemical and biological warfare in ancient times?
3. What has tended to keep the use of chemical and biological agents in check in modern warfare?
4. What events began the age of nuclear warfare in the closing days of World War II?
5. Who poses the greatest threat in the use of CBR weapons today?
6. What is chemical warfare?
7. What are the most common types of CW agents?
8. What is biological warfare?
9. What does nuclear warfare involve?
10. What are the effects from the explosion of a nuclear warhead?
11. What are the three types of nuclear bursts to which a ship may be exposed?
12. What are the three phases of shipboard CBR decontamination?

CRITICAL THINKING

1. In the summer 2002 hit movie *Sum of All Fears*, a nuclear device was detonated by terrorists in the city of Baltimore, Maryland. Research the likely effects of the explosion of a 10-kiloton nuclear device in or near a city the size of Baltimore in the United States. What would be the lethal radius of such a device, and how might the citizens of the place prepare to defend themselves against the effects of such a blast if some advance warning was received?
2. Research why an effective large-scale chemical or biological attack would be very difficult to effectively plan and carry out under most circumstances.
3. Research some of the modern devices that could be used to give warning of an attack by chemical weapons. What are some of the countermeasures that can be used against such an attack by troops on the ground and ships at sea?

VOCABULARY

conventional weapons	psycho gas
special weapons	tear gas
weapons of mass destruction	"dirty bomb"
CW agent	aerosol
BW agent	thermal radiation
nerve gas	fallout
blister gas	base surge
blood gas	dosimeter
radiac	EMP

Glossary of Naval Skills Terms

AGM—a military designation for an air-launched guided missile designed to attack surface targets.

AIM—a military designation for an air-launched air-intercept guided missile.

airfoil—surface of a body in flight.

airframe—all external parts of an airplane or missile.

air-to-air missile—a missile designed to be used in air-to-air warfare.

air-to-surface missile—a missile designed to be fired from airborne platforms against ground targets.

almanac—a periodic publication of variable astronomical information.

anchorage—an area assigned for anchoring ships.

antiballistic missile (ABM)—missile used in defense against incoming ballistic missiles.

antiradiation missile—missile designed to home in on radiations emitted from enemy weapons or tracking sites.

area defense—protection of an entire formation of ships or land or sea area.

armament—weapons of a ship or aircraft.

ASROC—antisubmarine rocket, fitted with either a homing torpedo or nuclear depth bomb warhead.

atomic time—time reckoned by the use of an atomic clock, usually cesium-based.

attack plane—multiweapon aircraft that can carry bombs, torpedoes, or rockets.

autonomous underwater vehicle (AUV)—a self-propelled underwater vehicle that can perform underwater searches for mines or other objects without external guidance.

ballistic missile—missile that goes on a free-falling path after a powered and guided ascent.

ballistics—the study of flight characteristics of projectiles in free fall.

barge—in the case of boats, any small craft used for transporting officers senior to a ship's captain; in cargo hauling, a long large craft, usually flat-bottomed, unpowered, and towed by other craft, used for transporting raw materials, freight, or liquids.

base surge—the initial surge of radioactive spray, debris, and dust caused by the explosion of a nuclear weapon on or near Earth's surface.

beam—extreme width of a ship or boat.

bearing—direction of an object from an observer, measured clockwise from one of three reference directions: true north, magnetic north, or the ship's head.

biological warfare—the military use of living organisms or toxins to infect target personnel.

boat etiquette—the naval customs and traditions pertaining to small boats.

boat officer—embarked officer in charge of a small boat under certain circumstances.

bollard—a single large post on a pier, used in securing a ship's mooring lines.

bridge—one or more platforms or compartments on the upper superstructure of a ship from which the operations of the ship and its aircraft are directed.

caliber—in naval guns up to 3 inches in diameter, the diameter of the bore in inches or millimeters; in guns larger than 3 inches, the length of the gun in inches divided by the bore diameter.

capstan—a rotating drum of a winch that raises an anchor cable or other heavy weight.

captor mine—a mine consisting of an encapsulated homing torpedo suspended above the sea bottom, activated by the acoustic or magnetic signature of a passing ship or submarine.

case ammunition—propellant charge for naval guns packed in a metal case, placed in a gun barrel just behind the projectile.

cavitation—disturbance around rotating propeller blades and their shafts and struts, caused by collapse of pressure bubbles resulting from water flow over their surfaces.

CBR warfare—chemical, biological, or nuclear (radiological) warfare.

chaff—an air burst of magnetic or aluminum foil strands or fragments, designed to interfere with the passage or orderly reflection of radar beams.

chemical warfare—the military use of any chemical to harass or cause casualties among target personnel.

chock—a metal fitting on board a ship, through which mooring lines are passed.

chronometer—a precise timepiece used for recording the exact times of celestial observations at sea.

cleat—an anvil-shaped deck fitting for securing lines on a boat, ship, or pier.

closest point of approach (CPA)—the distance and bearing from a reference ship to a maneuvering ship at the point where they make the closest approach to each other.

combat systems—any electronic equipment, weapons, or sensors related to a ship's offensive or defensive capabilities.

conventional weapons—weapons that use other than nuclear energy or biological or chemical agents. They mostly depend on explosive chemical energy.

coxswain—a person in charge of a small boat.

cruise missile—an air-breathing surface attack guided missile.

damage control—measures or equipment used to limit damage to a ship from enemy action, fire, flooding, and smoke.

damage control assistant (DCA)—the officer on board a ship charged with running the damage control organization.

daybeacon—an unlighted structural aid to navigation.

dead reckoning—a method of deducing the position of an air, land, or water craft by using the courses and speeds traveled since the last established position or fix.

degaussing—the neutralization of a ship or electronic equipment's magnetic field, usually by means of passing energized electrical wiring around it.

deperming—reduction of the magnetic signature of a ship by energizing coils temporarily placed vertically around it, usually during a yard-upkeep period.

depth charge—a USW explosive dropped from ships, as opposed to depth bombs dropped from airplanes.

detonate—to explode or cause to explode.

deviation—deflection angle between magnetic north and the north axis of a magnetic compass, caused by the presence of metal.

dirty bomb—a conventional explosive laced with radioactive material that disperses upon detonation; a nuclear weapon containing components that will produce an extraordinary amount of radioactive fallout upon detonation.

dosimeter—an instrument used to measure personal cumulative exposure to radiation; carried by all personnel working around nuclear machinery, or participating in decontamination efforts following a nuclear incident.

draft—depth to which the hull of a vessel sinks beneath the waterline, measured vertically.

dual-purpose weapon system—a weapon system designed to be effective against both air and surface, and in some cases against subsurface, targets.

echo sounder—a sonic device used to obtain water depths by measuring the time required for a sound pulse to make a round trip to the sea bottom and back.

effective gun range—the range at which a gun has a high probability of hitting a desired target, as opposed to the maximum range, which is the maximum distance a gun will deliver a projectile.

electromagnetic pulse (EMP)—an electromagnetic pulse of high intensity and energy often associated with the detonation of a nuclear weapon or device.

elevation (of a gun)—the vertical angle that the axis of a gun bore makes with the horizontal.

fathometer—an alternative name for a depth sounder; See also echo sounder.

fighter plane—an aircraft intended primarily for engaging in combat with other aircraft or airborne weapons.

fix—a position determined by the intersection of two or more simultaneous lines of position.

fixed-wing aircraft—aircraft that have wings that are the primary lifting devices for the aircraft.

gig—a ship's boat designated for use by the commanding officer.

gimbals—a mounting device consisting of two rings supported by mutually perpendicular axes so that an object suspended within them will remain horizontal regardless of the motion of the vessel or vehicle.

give-way vessel—a vessel that must maneuver to avoid another vessel during an approach situation while under way; See also stand-on vessel.

great circle—any circle formed by the intersection of a plane passing through Earth's center with Earth's surface.

Greenwich Mean Time (GMT)—time based on the relationship of the mean Sun to the prime meridian passing through Greenwich, England.

ground tackle—any equipment having to do with a ship's anchors, anchor cable, or handling gear.

gun emplacement—a mounting or protected site for the support and operation of a gun.

gyrocompass—an electromechanical compass aligned with true north by means of a spinning gyroscope.

gyro repeater—a remote readout of the position of a ship's gyrocompass card.

hatch—horizontal opening in the deck of a ship or boat.

hawsepipe—heavily built pipes in a ship or boat hull through which an anchor cable runs on its way from the deck to the water.

hawser—a thick line used for towing or high-line transfer.

homing torpedo—a torpedo that uses a self-contained guidance system usually based on sound detection or terminal guidance.

hull—the body or shell of a ship or seaplane.

ICBM—intercontinental ballistic missile.

IED—an improvised explosive device such as a remote-controlled bomb.

incendiary—causing or capable of causing fire.

keel—central longitudinal beam of a ship from which the frames and hull plating rise.

knot—a nautical speed unit equivalent to 1 nautical mile (2,000 yards) per hour.

latitude—the angular distance of a position on Earth's surface measured from the equator northward or southward through 90 degrees.

light water—a fire fighting liquid chemical compound designed to form a surface film to smother fires.

line of position (LOP)—a locus of points along which a position must be located.

longitude—the angular distance of a position on Earth's surface measured from the prime meridian eastward or westward through 180 degrees.

loran—an electronic navigation system in which the time difference in the reception of pulse signals originated at a master and one or more secondary radio stations is used to obtain lines of position; the intersection of two such lines forms a fix.

magnetic signature—the magnetic field associated with a metal ship.

main battery—the largest or most powerful armament of a ship or aircraft.

mainmast—the second mast of a ship with two or more masts, except when the first is taller.

maneuvering board—a printed sheet used in solving relative motion problems.

marlinspike seamanship—skill with rope, line, and other deck gear.

mean time—time based on the relationship of the mean Sun with Earth, that is, a make-believe Sun that travels around Earth at the equator at a constant speed of 15 degrees per hour.

mine barrage—a field of mines sowed in a water area to discourage the passage of shipping through the area.

mine countermeasures (MCM)—the branch of naval warfare that includes all methods, procedures, and techniques for preventing or reducing damage to ships from mines.

naval surface gunfire support—gunfire from ships in support of a land operation.

navigation—the art and science of directing a ship or aircraft from one position to another.

officers country—the living quarters of officers aboard ship.

parallel ruler—a hinged two-part pair of straightedges designed to permit transfer of a parallel line from one place to another on a plot.

piloting—navigation near land using landmarks, aids to navigation, and depth soundings.

point defense—the defense of a portion of a perimeter surrounding a ship or outpost by a weapon system capable of interdicting any threat that might materialize at that location.

port—seagoing term for left; an observation window on a vessel.

pursuit curve—a curved path followed by a missile that homes in on and eventually overtakes and intercepts a target.

pyrotechnics—ammunition, flares, or fireworks used for signaling, illuminating, or marking targets, or for setting them on fire.

radioactive fallout—dustlike radioactive windborne particles, produced by the explosion of a nuclear device or weapon.

range of guns—the distance a projectile from a gun can be fired.

range of tide—the vertical distance between high and low tide levels in a body of water.

RAP—rocket-assisted projectile; the incorporation of a rocket motor in the base of a gun projectile to extend its range.

relative wind—direction and speed at which a wind is blowing relative to a vessel.

repair party—a group of specialists organized to control damage and make repairs throughout a ship during battle.

rifled gun—a gun with grooves inside the barrel that cause an exiting projectile to spin in order to provide stability during its flight.

rifling—spiral grooves cut inside a gun bore to impart spin to a projectile being fired.

RIM—a military designation for a ship-launched air-intercept guided missile.

rotary winged aircraft—aircraft that have two or more rotor blades that serve to lift the aircraft into the air.

rules of the road—the nautical rules by which ships maneuver to avoid collisions while under way; traffic rules for vehicles on land.

running rigging—adjustable rigging for handling sails, masts, booms, and the like.

scope of chain—the length of an anchor chain, usually divided into 15-fathom segments called shots.

seamanship—skill in handling a boat or ship, or in doing those things related to the job of a seaman.

shoring—process of placing props, usually wooden, against structures or cargo in a ship to prevent breaking, sagging, or movement in a seaway, or to hold a ship upright in dry dock.

short stay—position of an anchor cable straight up and down, or nearly so, with the anchor barely holding the bottom.

shot (of anchor chain)—a 15-fathom section of anchor chain, joined to the next shot by a detachable link.

shrapnel—shell fragments from a high-explosive shell.

smart bomb—a non–self-propelled air-dropped precision munition that can be guided to impact with a target.

solar time—time based on the relationship of the Sun to Earth.

soundings—depth of water.

special weapons—unconventional CBR weapons of any type, especially nuclear weapons.

stadimeter—an optical device used to determine the distance to an object of known height.

standard time—a 15-degree-wide sector or zone of the Earth in which the same time is kept by all in it; uses as a basis the relationship of the mean Sun with the central meridian of the zone.

standing rigging—heavy metal or wire supports for spars, masts, or booms permanently installed.

stand-on vessel—a vessel obliged to maintain course and speed during an approach situation with another vessel while under way; See also give-way vessel.

starboard—seagoing term for right.

star shell—a projectile that detonates in the air and releases an illuminating parachute flare.

stateroom—an officer's berthing quarters on board ship.

stokes stretcher—a contoured stretcher designed to aid in transporting injured victims up and down stairs and ladders.

sweep—a mine-clearing operation on land or sea; a series of military strikes through an area to rid it of enemy forces.

topographic map—a map of terrain showing water, elevations, and landmarks.

train (of a gun)—horizontal rotation of a gun or gun mount.

trajectory—the path of a projectile, missile, or bomb in flight.

true bearing—a bearing using true north as the reference.

true wind—direction and speed at which a wind is blowing relative to Earth's surface.

unmanned aerial vehicle (UAV)—a remotely controlled unmanned aircraft.

variable time fuse—a fuse that is actuated by the reflection of self-generated radar emissions from the target as a projectile passes near it.

vertical launch system (VLS)—missile launch tubes mounted vertically within a ship's hull.

warhead—forward section of a torpedo or missile that carries the explosive charge; the nose cone.

waterline—the line on a vessel's hull to which it sinks in the water.

watertight integrity—the ability of a compartment on a vessel to withstand flooding.

water washdown system—a system of external piping on a ship, often temporary, that allows topside external surfaces to be continually wetted with spray to minimize adhesion of chemical and biological agents and nuclear fallout.

weapons of mass destruction (WMD)—CBR weapons that can inflict massive destruction over a large area, or mass casualties among a population.

zone time—time reckoned according to the relationship of the mean Sun with the central meridian of each 15-degree-wide time zone.

BIBLIOGRAPHY

NAVAL KNOWLEDGE

Books

Brittin, Burdick H., and Liselotte B. Watson. *International Law for Seagoing Officers*. 5th ed. Annapolis: Naval Institute Press, 1986.

Collins, John A. *Grand Strategy: Principles and Practices*. Annapolis: Naval Institute Press, 1973.

Davidson, Michael J. *A Guide to Military Criminal Law*. Annapolis: Naval Institute Press, 1999.

Filbert, Brent G., and Alan G. Kaufman. *Naval Law*. Annapolis: Naval Institute Press, 1997.

Frieden, David, ed. *Principles of Naval Weapons Systems*. Annapolis: Naval Institute Press, 1985.

Grove, Eric. *The Future of Sea Power*. Annapolis: Naval Institute Press, 1990.

Hobbs, Richard R. *Naval Science 1*. 4th ed. Annapolis: Naval Institute Press, 1996.

———. *Naval Science 2*. 4th ed. Annapolis: Naval Institute Press, 1997.

———. *Naval Science 3*. 4th ed. Annapolis: Naval Institute Press, 1998.

Hughes, Wayne P., Jr. *Fleet Tactics and Coastal Combat*. 2d ed. Annapolis: Naval Institute Press, 1992.

Manual for Courts-Martial, United States 2008. Washington, D.C.: Government Printing Office, 2008.

Strategic Assessment 1996: Elements of U.S. Power. Washington, D.C.: National Defense University, 1996.

United States Navy Regulations, 1990. Washington, D.C.: Government Printing Office, 1990.

Booklets and Pamphlets

Naval Doctrine Command. *Naval Doctrine Publication 1: Naval Warfare*. Washington, D.C.: Department of the Navy, 1994.

———. *Naval Doctrine Publication 2: Naval Intelligence*. Washington, D.C.: Department of the Navy, 1994.

———. *Naval Doctrine Publication 4: Naval Logistics*. Washington, D.C.: Department of the Navy, 2001.

———. *Naval Doctrine Publication 5: Naval Planning*. Washington, D.C.: Department of the Navy, 1996.

———. *Naval Doctrine Publication 6: Naval Command and Control*. Washington, D.C.: Department of the Navy, 1996.

U.S. Delegation Report, Resumed Seventh Session of the Third United Nations Conference on Law of the Sea. New York, 21 August–15 September 1978.

Articles

Fisher, Rand H., and Kent B. Pelot. "The Navy Has a Stake in Space." U.S. Naval Institute *Proceedings*, October 2001.

Friedman, Norman. "The Real Purpose of Strategy." U.S. Naval Institute *Proceedings*, December 2007.

Jacobs, Jan C. "U.S. Naval Aviation and Weapons Development in Review." U.S. Naval Institute *Proceedings*, May 2008.

Johnson, J. Lee. "Looking Beyond Iraq: Developing a Future Strategy." U.S. Naval Institute *Proceedings*, May 2008.

Journal on Defense, Intelligence, and Diplomacy. National Youth Leadership Forum, 2001.

Kumar, Shashi. "U.S. Merchant Marine and World Maritime Review." U.S. Naval Institute *Proceedings*, May 2008.

Mayo, Dick. "From the Sea . . . to Cyberspace." U.S. Naval Institute *Proceedings*, October 2000.

Studeman, Mike. "7 Myths of Intelligence." U.S. Naval Institute *Proceedings*, February 2009.

Talmadge, Eric. "New U.S. Submarines Trade Nukes for SEALs." Associated Press, February 27, 2008.

Truver, Scott C. "U.S. Navy in Review." U.S. Naval Institute *Proceedings*, May 2008.

Zelibor, Thomas E. "FORCEnet Is Navy's Future." *Armed Forces Journal*, December 2003.

Papers

"A Cooperative Strategy for 21st Century Seapower." Navy, Marine Corps, and Coast Guard White Paper, 2007.

"CNO Guidance for 2006—Meeting the Challenge of a New Era." Adm. M. G. Mullen, USN, 2006.

"Forward—From the Sea." Navy and Marine Corps White Paper, 1994.

"From the Sea—Preparing the Naval Service for the Twenty-first Century." Navy and Marine Corps White Paper, 1992.

"Operating Forward . . . from the Sea." Navy and Marine Corps White Paper, 1997.

"Vision . . . Presence . . . Power." 2000 Program Guide to the U.S. Navy.

Internet

Currie, Duncan: archive.greenpeace.org. "Table of Contents to the UN Law of the Sea Convention."

DARPA: darpa.mil. "A Compendium of DARPA Programs."

De Boer, Bart: ShipParade.com. "Ship Alphabet."

Federal Bureau of Investigation: fbi.gov.

Maritime Administration: marad.dot.gov.

Military Sealift Command: msc.navy.mil.

North Atlantic Treaty Organization: nato.int.

Sempa, Francis P: geocities.com. "MacKinder's World."

LEADERSHIP

Books

Chalker, Edsel O. *Leadership Education 1*. Air Force Junior ROTC Text. Maxwell Air Force Base, Ala: Air Training Command/Air University, 1979.

Department of Leadership and Law, U.S. Naval Academy. *Fundamentals of Naval Leadership*. Annapolis: Naval Institute Press, 1984.

Hobbs, Richard R. *Naval Science 3*, 4th ed. Annapolis: Naval Institute Press, 1998.

Johnson, Brad W. and Gregory P. Harper. *Becoming a Leader the Annapolis Way*. New York: McGraw Hill, 2005.

Naval Education and Training Support Command, Pensacola. *A Manual for Navy Instructors*. NAVEDTRA 107. San Diego: Naval Instructional Technology Development Center, 1974.

Montor, Karel, et al. *Naval Leadership: Voices of Experience*. Annapolis: Naval Institute Press, 1998.

Articles

McDermott, Padraic. "Leading Surface Warfare Officers Straight-to-the Fleet." Naval Institute *Proceedings*, January 2009.

Van Tol, J. M. "Worse Than a Crime—A Mistake." U.S. Naval Institute *Proceedings*, May 2008.

NAVAL SKILLS

Books

Burgess, Richard R., ed. *The Naval Aviation Guide*. 5th ed. Annapolis: Naval Institute Press, 1996.

Crenshaw, Capt. R. S., Jr., USN (Ret.). *Naval Shiphandling*. Annapolis: Naval Institute Press, 1975.

Cutler, Thomas J. *The Bluejacket's Manual*. 23d ed. Annapolis: Naval Institute Press, 2000.

Day, Cyrus L. Rev. by Ray O. Beard Jr. and M. Lee Hoffman Jr. *The Art of Knotting and Splicing*. 4th ed. Annapolis: Naval Institute Press, 1986.

Dodge, David O., and S. E. Kyriss. *Seamanship*. 2d ed. Annapolis: Naval Institute Press, 1981.

Frieden, David, ed. *Principles of Naval Weapons Systems*. Annapolis: Naval Institute Press, 1985.

Hobbs, Richard R. *Marine Navigation: Piloting and Celestial and Electronic Navigation*. 4th ed. Annapolis: Naval Institute Press, 1998.

——. *Naval Science 1*. 4th ed. Annapolis: Naval Institute Press, 1996.

——. *Naval Science 2*. 4th ed. Annapolis: Naval Institute Press, 1997.

——. *Naval Science 3*. 4th ed. Annapolis: Naval Institute Press, 1998.

Llana, Christopher B., and George P Wisneskey. *Handbook of the Nautical Rules of the Road*. 2d ed. Naval Institute Press, 1991.

Mack, Vice Adm. William P., USN (Ret.), and Lt. Cdr. Royal Connell, USN. *Naval Ceremonies, Customs, and Traditions*. Annapolis: Naval Institute Press, 1980.

Martin, Donald, Paul Anderson, and Lucy Bautamiun. *Communication Satellites*, 5th ed. Reston, Va.: American Institute of Aeronautics and Astronautics, Inc., 2007.

Naval Ships' Technical Manual. Washington, D.C.: Naval Sea Systems Command, 2008.

Noel, Capt. John V., Jr., USN (Ret.). *Knights Modern Seamanship*. 17th ed. New York: Van Nostrand Reinhold, 1984.

Shufeldt, Capt. H. H., USNR (Ret.), and G. D. Dunlap. Rev. by Bruce Allan Bauer. *Piloting and Dead Reckoning*. 4th ed. Annapolis: Naval Institute Press, 1999.

Tate, William H. *A Mariner's Guide to the Rules of the Road*. 2d ed. Annapolis: Naval Institute Press, 1982.

Winters, David D. *The Boat Officers Handbook*. 2d ed. Annapolis: Naval Institute Press, 1991.

Articles

Koch, Andrew. "U.S. Navy's DDG-51 Destroyers to Be Modernized." *Jane's Defense Weekly*, July 14, 2004.

Molenda, Patrick A. "Don't Forget Dedicated Mine Countermeasures." U.S. Naval Institute *Proceedings,* October 2001.

Papers

"Agents of Bioterrorism: Biological Toxins." American College of Surgeons, October 2003.

Internet

American Geophysical Union: agu.org. "Problem with the Magnetic Pole Locations on Global Charts."

Directory of U.S. Military Rockets and Missiles: designation-systems.net. "Raytheon RIM-161 *Standard* SM-3."

Raytheon: raytheon.com. "Standard Missile-2."

U.S. Coast Guard: uscg.mil. "Lighthouses, Lightships & Aids to Navigation."

U.S. Navy: chinfo.navy.mil. "AGM-65 Maverick Guided Missile."

——. "AGM-88 HARM Missile System."

——. "AGM-154 Joint Standoff Weapon."

——. "AGM-114B/K/M Hellfire Missile."

——. "AIM-9 Sidewinder Missile."

——. "AIM-120 Advanced Medium-Range, Air-to-Air Missile."

——. "Joint Direct Attack Munition (JDAM)."

——. "Penguin Anti-Ship Missile."

——. "RIM-116A Rolling Airframe Missile (RAM)."

——. "Sea Sparrow Missile (RIM-7)."

——. "SLAM ER Missile Systems."

——. "Standard Missile."

——. "Vertical Launch ASROC (VLA) Missile."

INDEX

INDEX, LEADERSHIP

INDEX, NAVAL SKILLS

ABOUT THE AUTHOR

CDR. RICHARD HOBBS has been involved with the Navy's NJROTC program for more than thirty years as a writer/editor of many of its instructional textbooks and other materials. A 1966 graduate of the U.S. Naval Academy, Commander Hobbs had thirty-plus years of service as a former Sailor and surface line officer in the Regular and Reserve Navy. He has also worked in industry as a ceramics engineer and production manager, in publishing as an editor on the staff of the Naval Institute Press, and in education as a Naval Academy and community college instructor and high school AP and general physics teacher.

In addition to instructional materials for the NJROTC program, Commander Hobbs has also written the widely acclaimed *Marine Navigation: Piloting, Celestial and Electronic*, a standard text and reference book in the field for the last thirty-five years, and is a contributor of several articles on marine navigation and other related topics to *World Book Encyclopedia*. A certified tennis instructor, he recently retired after twenty years of teaching physics and coaching tennis at a local high school near Annapolis. An avid sailor, after many years living aboard their motorsailor *R n R*, he and his family reside in Maryland and in Florida.